D1665353

Jorina Brysbaert and Karen Lahousse (Eds.)
On the Role of Contrast in Information Structure

Trends in Linguistics Studies and Monographs

Volume 382

On the Role of Contrast in Information Structure

Edited by
Jorina Brysbaert and Karen Lahousse

DE GRUYTER
MOUTON

ISBN 978-3-11-099789-7
e-ISBN (PDF) 978-3-11-098659-4
e-ISBN (EPUB) 978-3-11-098661-7
ISSN 1861-4302

Library of Congress Control Number: 2024930563

Bibliographic information published by the Deutsche Nationalbibliothek
The Deutsche Nationalbibliothek lists this publication in the Deutsche Nationalbibliografie;
detailed bibliographic data are available on the internet at http://dnb.dnb.de.

© 2024 Walter de Gruyter GmbH, Berlin/Boston
Typesetting: Integra Software Services Pvt. Ltd.
Printing and binding: CPI books GmbH, Leck

www.degruyter.com

Contents

Part III: **Analyzing contrast using the Question Under Discussion model**

Jorina Brysbaert and Karen Lahousse

1 The complex nature of contrast

Abstract: This chapter highlights some key elements in current research on the intricate concept of contrast. We explore its multifaceted nature and the challenges in defining it, by discussing parameters such as the size of the set of alternatives, the explicit or implicit mention of alternatives, and the specific discourse relations involved. This discussion shows that contrast is not a unified notion but rather a term encompassing various degrees and types of contrastivity, which is empirically demonstrated by the chapters in Part II of this volume, and analyzed from a more methodological (annotation) point of view by the chapters in Part III. Furthermore, we briefly discuss different linguistic marking strategies for contrast, highlighting in particular its interaction with syntax and prosody, and we present the relation between contrast, topic and focus in accounts of information structure, which is at the center of the papers in Part I of the volume.

1 The notion of contrast

Although all language users have implicit knowledge of which sentences (and discourse segments more in general) are contrastive, the notion of *contrast* – to which this volume is dedicated – is not easy to define and is often used as a term for multiple realities. In the last decades, it has become clear that contrast is not a unitary notion but rather a cover term for different degrees and types of contrastivity, which can be defined with respect to several parameters relative to the alternatives involved in the oppositive relation, mainly (i) the size of the set of alternatives, (ii) the explicit or implicit mention of the alternatives, and (iii) the specific discourse relations the alternatives are involved in (e.g. absence or presence of correction, i.e. rejection of alternatives). The complexity of this phenomenon is reinforced by the fact that these aspects of contrastivity interact with different domains of language, and by the fact that contrast can apply to both *topic* and *focus* in accounts of information structure (see Repp 2016 and Cruschina 2021a for detailed overviews of the literature).

The purpose of this introduction is not to provide an exhaustive review of the literature on contrast, but to highlight some key elements in the research on contrast (sections 1.1–1.4), before presenting the contributions in this volume (section 2).

https://doi.org/10.1515/9783110986594-001

1.1 Contrast and alternatives

According to Repp (2016: 270) (see also Umbach 2004), contrastivity refers to dissimilarities between alternatives. Hence, in (1), *Pete* and *Marc* are opposing alternatives, just as *Rome* and *London*, in the two similar events "person x went to place y".

(1) *Pete **went to** Rome but Marc **went to** London.*
     (Repp 2016: 271)

The alternatives can be more or less explicitly given in the discourse context, and pertain to an open or closed set. In the case of an explicit closed set (3), i.e. a limited set of alternatives which are overtly expressed, the contrast is generally perceived as "stronger" and tends to be more overtly marked across languages. The number and explicitness of the alternatives thus has an influence on the degree of contrastivity (see section 1.4). This explains why the cleft structure in the discourse context in (3) seems to be "more contrastive" than in (2), where the specific set of potential alternatives to John is not mentioned explicitly.

(2) – *Which one of your friends came to visit you?*
     – *It's John who came.*

(3) – *Which one of your friends came to visit you, Peter, John or Mary?*
     – *It's John who came.*

In the linguistic literature, it has often been claimed that a contrastive interpretation only emerges if the number of alternatives is limited. Chafe (1976: 34) takes this stand: "(. . .) the speaker assumes that a limited number of candidates is available in the addressee's mind (whether or not the addressee could in fact list all of them). Often the number is one, often it is larger, but when it is unlimited the sentence fails to be contrastive". Lombardi Vallauri (2000: 229) also argues that a constituent can only receive a contrastive interpretation when "the focused element is a closed system item (in Halliday's (1967: 206–207) sense, i.e. it belongs to a closed paradigm of words in the language)" or when "the context dramatically restricts the list of the referents that could occur in place of one that is focused".

1.2 The linguistic marking of contrast

Most researchers study the interaction of contrast with other domains of language, in particular syntax (e.g. Repp 2009; Lahousse, Laenzlinger, and Soare 2014; Cruschina and Remberger 2017; Cruschina 2021a) and prosody (e.g. Brunetti, D'Imperio, and Cangemi 2010; Brunetti, Avanzi, and Gendrot 2012; Repp and Drenhaus 2015; Riester, Schröer, and Baumann 2020; Seeliger and Repp 2020). For instance, contrast has been shown to be encoded by different linguistic means, such as contrastive adverbials (e.g. Csűry 2001; Altenberg 2006; Lenker 2010; Dupont 2021; Brysbaert and Lahousse 2022), clefts (e.g. Hedberg 1990; Davidse 2000; Scappini 2013; Destruel and Velleman 2014; Lahousse and Borremans 2014; Lahousse, Laenzlinger, and Soare 2014; Bourgoin 2017), left dislocation (e.g. Barnes 1985; Calvé 1985; Ashby 1988; Geluykens 1992; Anagnostopoulou 1997; Grohmann 2000; Lambrecht 2001; Arregi 2003; Ott 2014; Samek-Lodovici 2015; Horváth 2018), topicalization markers (e.g. on French: Choi-Jonin 2003; Fløttum 2003; Anscombre 2006; Lagae 2007; Velghe and Lahousse 2015; Velghe 2015), focus fronting (Bianchi, Bocci, and Cruschina 2015, 2016, see overview in Cruschina 2021a), etc.

In authentic data, the contrastive nature of a sentence is often simultaneously marked at several levels of language (lexicon, morphology, syntax, discourse, prosody, . . .), which adds to the gradability of the notion of contrast. For instance, in (1), there is a contrast between *Pete* and *Marc* and between *Rome* and *London*, which is further reinforced by the presence of *but* and prosodic marking in spoken language. An alternative way to express (1) would be (4), where a cleft structure, with the typical cleft prosody, would render more or less the same contrastive interpretation.

(1)   *Pete* **went to** *Rome* but *Marc* **went to** *London.*
      (Repp 2016: 271)

(4)   *Pete went to Rome but it was Marc who went to London.*

Since contrast can be marked by various prosodic, syntactic and lexical means, the identification and annotation of contrast in corpora of spontaneous speech is not straightforward (Ritz, Dipper, and Götze 2008; Cook and Bildhauer 2011, 2013). Although a few initiatives have recently been taken to develop annotation guidelines for information structure (Götze et al. 2007; Brunetti, De Kuthy, and Riester 2016; De Kuthy, Reiter, and Riester 2018; Riester, Brunetti, and De Kuthy 2018), there is no consensus on the "best practice".

1.3 The relation between contrast, topic and focus

In the literature on information structure, much attention has gone to the notions of *topic* and *focus*. The topic (underlined in (5)) can be defined as "the entity that a speaker identifies about which then information [. . .] is given", whereas the focus (in bold face) "indicates the presence of alternatives that are relevant for the interpretation of linguistic expressions" (Krifka 2008: 18, 40):

(5) A: *When did Aristotle Onassis marry Jacqueline Kennedy?*
B: <u>*He married her*</u> **in 1968.**
(Krifka 2008: 42)

Linguists generally agree that the notion of *contrast* is involved in information structure as well, but there is still discussion as to how it is related to the other notions and how it can be integrated in the framework. Contrast has sometimes been equated with focus in general, particularly within Alternative Semantics (Rooth 1992), where it has been argued that focus always conveys a kind of contrast. Other researchers have pointed out that focus need not always be contrastive (Lambrecht 1994, see also Cruschina 2021a for an overview), and that contrast should be seen as a notion that is compatible with both focus and topic, creating the subtypes *contrastive focus* and *contrastive topic* (e.g. Krifka 2008; Repp 2010; Büring 2016; Cruschina 2021b).

According to Krifka (2008: 23–24, 33), contrastive focus (in bold face in (6)) is mainly used in corrections and implies that alternatives are explicitly mentioned:

(6) A: *Mary stole the cookie.*
B: *(No,)* **Peter** *stole the cookie.*
(Krifka 2008: 24)

Contrastive topics (in capital letters in (7)) are topics that contain a focused element (in bold face), in addition to the other focus in the clause (underlined) (Krifka 2008: 44–45, 47, see also Erteschik-Shir 2007 on "subordinate f-structures" in topical constituents):

(7) A: *What do your siblings do?*
B: *MY* **SISTER** <u>*studies medicine*</u>, *and MY* **BROTHER** *is* <u>*working on a freight ship*</u>.
(Krifka 2008: 44)

Still other researchers consider contrast to be an autonomous information-structural category existing next to topic and focus, instead of being a feature creating a subtype of topic and focus (e.g. Vallduví and Vilkuna 1998; Molnár 2002; Molnár and Winkler 2010; Repp 2010, 2016). For instance, although Molnár (2002) and Molnár and Winkler (2010) admit that the concept of contrast is relevant to the definition of focus and topic, they believe that contrast can also be considered as a notion in its own right. Unlike Krifka (2008), Molnár (2002: 157) clearly emphasizes that "contrastiveness is not only a feature of topicality and focusing". However, Molnár (2002: 157) and Molnár and Winkler (2010: 1393) also pinpoint a certain "overlap" between the notion of contrast and the notions of focus and topicality. More specifically, some functions of contrast are comparable to those of focus and topic: contrast is a "highlighting device" and therefore serves to emphasize certain words or parts of sentences, just like focus, but it is also a "coherence-creating device", ensuring "discourse linking" and "givenness marking", which is the main function of topics (Molnár and Winkler 2010: 1393–1394). According to Molnár and Winkler (2010: 1396), contrast is therefore a complex concept with a "dual character".

Repp (2010, 2016) seems to take a more nuanced position: she does not explicitly state that the term contrast should have the same status as the terms focus and topic, but studies contrast in its own right, not limiting herself to a comparison of contrast with the notions of focus and topic.

1.4 Types of discourse relations and degrees of contrast

The notion of contrast has also been discussed in the literature on discourse structure and discourse relations: contrast is seen as a frequent type of rhetorical relation (e.g. Asher and Lascarides 2003; Umbach 2004, 2005; Spedaner and Lobanova 2009; Webber et al. 2019; see also overview in Repp 2016: 275–279). Quite some attention has been given to the semantic identification and classification of oppositional relations. In general, a tripartite distinction is made between contrastive (8), concessive (9) and corrective (10) relations, but other terms are used as well (e.g. opposition, adversative, replacive, etc.) and the exact meaning of the different terms may vary from study to study.

(8) *I've read sixty pages, whereas she's read only twenty.*
     (Izutsu 2008: 648)

(9) *Although John is poor, he is happy.*
     (Izutsu 2008: 649)

(10) *John is not American but British.*
     (Izutsu 2008: 649)

Repp (2010: 1335, 2016: 271–279) highlights that the concept of contrast does not necessarily function in the same way in all types of discourse relations: in her view, different types of oppositional relations come with different degrees of contrast.

For example, the relation established in (11), a correction, would be "more contrastive" than the oppositional relation expressed in example (1) above:

(11)   *Miller was hired, not Smith.*
        (Repp 2016: 276)

The idea that corrections display the highest degree of contrast is also central to Cruschina (2021a), who builds on Molnár's (2002: 149) hierarchy of necessary conditions for contrast (12):

(12)   highlighting (i.e. prosodic highlighting of focus) > dominant contrast (i.e. exclusion of certain possibilities) > membership in a set > limited set of candidates > explicit mentioning of alternatives
        (Molnár 2002: 149)

Cruschina (2021a: 4) refers to Vallduví and Vilkuna (1998: 83), who argue that contrast turns out to be "a cover term for several operator-like interpretations of focus that one finds in the literature", "including exhaustive focus (Szabolcsi 1981), identificational focus (Horvath 1986; É. Kiss 1998), and contrastive focus (Rizzi 1997)". He demonstrates that the crosslinguistic data on focus fronting, which is associated with different interpretations and types of focus, can be accounted for if the binary distinction between contrastive and non-contrastive (new information) focus is replaced by a *scale* of focus subtypes with different degrees of contrast: information focus (involving a "contextually open set" of alternatives, which is "only pragmatically delimited" (Cruschina 2021a: 5), exhaustive focus, mirative focus (contrast against expectations which can be implicit, cf. Bianchi, Bocci, and Cruschina 2015, 2016) and corrective focus. Among these, corrective focus, which involves a rejection of explicit alternatives, has the highest degree of contrast:

(13)   *information focus > exhaustive focus > mirative focus > corrective focus*
        lowest degree of contrast   highest degree of contrast
        (Cruschina 2021a: 2)

2 Structure of this volume and contributions

The volume consists of three parts: "Contrast versus topic and focus" (Part I, see section 2.1), "Different types of contrast" (Part II, see section 2.2) and "Analyzing contrast using the Question Under Discussion model" (Part III, see section 2.3). In

Part I, the notion of contrast is examined with respect to the two main concepts in information structure, i.e. focus (Chapters 2 and 3) and topic (Chapter 4). Part II tackles the distinction between several subtypes of contrast, based on prosodic evidence in Spanish (Chapter 5), word order data in German (Chapter 6), and a comparison between spoken and signed French (Chapter 7). The chapters in Part III show how different types of contrast can be annotated and analyzed using the Question Under Discussion model (Chapters 8 and 9).

2.1 Contrast versus topic and focus

Chapter 2 "Experimental testing of focus fronting in British English", by **Samek-Lodovici and Dwyer**, reports on a large-scale experiment testing the relation between focus and contrast in British English. Building on the assumption that, in Italian, focused constituents can be fronted under a contrastive reading but not under a non-contrastive reading (e.g. Rizzi 1997, 2004; Belletti 2001, 2004), the authors experimentally investigate the grammaticality of focus fronting in British English, across corrective, open question (e.g. *Who did John hit?*) and closed question (e.g. *Who did John hit, Tom or Bill?*) exchanges. The experiment reveals that speakers of British English assess fronted foci as less natural than in-situ foci in all three exchange types, supporting the idea that contrastive focalization can be interpreted in-situ (Rooth 1992, 2016; Wagner 2020). Interestingly, however, fronting in response to closed questions is assessed as more grammatical than fronting in response to open questions. This result is in line with Neeleman and Vermeulen's (2012) definition of contrast, according to which contrast is licensed by closed questions, and with Skopeteas and Fanselow (2011), who demonstrate that speakers may or may not convey a contrastive interpretation when replying to an open question. Unexpectedly, the experiment also shows that fronting in response to open questions is considered more grammatical than fronting in corrective exchanges. The authors hypothesize that this effect is due to the adverse impact of processing on grammaticality assessments: the processing load of corrections is heavier than that of (closed and open) questions, which may cause the former to be judged less grammatical overall.

The role of focus and contrast is further explored through a corpus study of Italian left dislocations in Chapter 3 "Contrast and left dislocations: Contrastive discourse relations beyond contrastive topics", by **Cimmino**. While left dislocations have typically been approached as topic-signaling devices, allowing for example to mark contrastive topics (for Italian: e.g. Frascarelli 2017; Cruschina 2021b), Cimmino concentrates on the non-dislocated part of these structures and the potential contrastive discourse function(s) associated with it. She analyzes the discourse functions of 200 object left dislocations in Italian, extracted from four diamesically (spoken/written) and diaphasically (formal/informal) different corpora, representing different text types (informative/argumentative). Taking into account syntactic, informational and textual features of the left dislocations in context, following the multilevel method (Cimmino 2017, 2023; Cimmino and Panunzi 2017), 36 out of the 200 instances (< 20%) are identified as contrastive foci left dislocations, i.e. left dislocations performing a contrastive discourse function in their non-dislocated, non-topical part. Cimmino then shows that these left dislocations with contrastive foci can be involved in contrastive, corrective or counter-expectative discourse relations, and that the focus can be of different types: predicate focus (14/36 examples) or narrow focus (22/36 examples, including polarity focus). Importantly, in all examples, the left dislocation structure does not express the semantic discourse relation itself – since the contrast remains present when the dislocation is substituted with SVO order – but it plays a crucial role in the organization of the text, by signaling textual prominences. Cimmino therefore argues that Italian left dislocations highlight the already semantically expressed contrast. Furthermore, with respect to the function performed by contrastive foci left dislocations, her analysis reveals that there is no diamesic or diaphasic variation. However, she hypothesizes that this type of left dislocations is typical of polemical stretches of text, containing disputatious writing or speech.

In Chapter 4 "Contrast and topics: An enquiry into Hindi Particle *-to*", **Bhalla** provides evidence for the distinctiveness of contrast and topic as information-structural categories, based on an analysis of the Hindi enclitic particle *-to*. According to previous accounts (Kidwai 2000, 2004), this particle is a morphological topic marker, conveying either a thematic (i.e. aboutness topic) or contrastive topic interpretation. Bhalla provides counter-examples to this hypothesis, showing that in Hindi, (i) topical constituents may be morphologically unmarked, i.e. topic marking by *-to* is optional, and (ii) the particle *-to* can also mark non-topical constituents. She therefore argues that *-to* is not a topic marker *per se*, and that there is no direct correspondence between the particle *-to* and the information-structural notion of topic. A more thorough examination of the non-topical *to*-marked constituents then reveals that these always receive a contrastive interpretation, which arises from uncertainty and scalar implicatures evoked by the *to*-particle. In other words, *to*-marking of a non-topical constituent is possible if and only if the marked entity is in a contrastive discourse relation with some alternative in the common ground. From this, Bhalla concludes that the particle *-to* can mark "pure contrast", and that contrast and topic should be seen as two independent informational-structural categories.

2.2 Different types of contrast

Part II starts with the Chapter "Mirativity, obviousness, and reversal as instances of contrast on different levels of meaning: Evidence from Spanish intonation" by **Fliessbach**. This paper deals with the intonational marking of contrastive focus in Spanish. In the linguistic literature on (Castilian) Spanish, three different intonational contours have been associated with contrastive focus: an early rise-fall (L+H* L%), a late rise-fall (L* HL%), and higher H tone scaling on early rise-falls (L+¡H* L%) (e.g. Face 2001a,b, 2002; Gabriel 2007; Prieto & Roseano 2009–2013; Hualde & Prieto 2015). Through a production experiment, in which 18 speakers of Spanish are asked to participate in made-up conversations, Fliessbach shows that these three contours are actually markers of different types of contrastive focus, arising out of different discourse configurations related to (un)expectedness and (dis)agreement. More specifically, he distinguishes between three instances of contrast on different levels of meaning: (i) mirativity, i.e. contrast or mismatch between expectations and an assertion, associated with L+¡H* L%, (ii) obviousness, i.e. contrast between the presumption of relevance of an assertion and the expectability of a response to it, strongly associated with L* HL%, and (iii) reversal, i.e. contrast between two assertions. Comparative observations are provided in languages with morphological encoding of (dis)agreement and (un)expectedness, i.e. German, Romanian, Kogi, Kurtöp and Turkish. Based on these cross-linguistic data, and in line with Cruschina (2021a), Fliessbach argues that contrast is not a binary feature: there is no binary distinction between contrastive and non-contrastive focus, but different "types" of contrastive focus. However, unlike Cruschina (2021a) and Repp (2016), he does not propose a scale of contrastiveness, but claims that (dis)agreement and (un)expectedness are independent parameters that can be combined to create complex contrasts. A formalization of the results is provided using the dynamic model of meaning in dialogue put forward by Farkas and Bruce (2010).

Zieleke's article "Contrast via information structure: On topic development with German *aber* in post-initial position" focuses on one specific position of the syntactically mobile German contrast marker *aber* 'but': the post-initial position, i.e. the position following a constituent in the prefield. The author first presents accounts of contrastive markers, some of which rely on information-structural alternatives and derive the other uses of contrast (argumentative or denial of expectation) by inference. Other accounts propose a list of contrastive relations without assuming one to be the basic type of contrast. Against this backdrop, her goal is to provide an integrated account for cases in which the prefield-constituent followed by *aber* is a prototypical topic, such as a definite NP, and cases in which this constituent is not typically associated with topicality, such as focus particles. The empirical basis of the article consists of 200 randomly selected examples of post-initial *aber* in the newspaper *Die Zeit*. All examples are analyzed with respect to two factors: topic type (non-topic, potential aboutness-topic, potential frame-setting) and, for the topical prefield-constituents only, the type of topic progression: (explicit or accommodated) contrastive topics or topic promotion. Zieleke shows that potential aboutness-topics and frame-setters are almost equally frequent in the corpus and are double as frequent as the non-topics, which, surprisingly, still make up about a quarter of the corpus examples. She argues that all topical prefield-constituents followed by *aber* can be analyzed as "alternative topics". The non-topical prefield-constituents marked by *aber* are either sentence adverbs or expressions of comparison and simultaneity. Since sentence adverbs indicate alternative worlds, the contrastive interpretation shifts to a denial of expectation. To the extent that expressions of comparison and simultaneity refer to ordered scales, the interpretation shifts to an argumentative contrast.

In Chapter 7 "Definition of contrast in spoken and signed data: An overview", **Lombart** argues against a binary distinction between [+ contrast] and [− contrast] and instead proposes a typology consisting of degrees of contrast, in line with typologies proposed by Umbach (2004), Hartmann and Zimmermann (2009), Kimmelman (2014), and Navarrete-González (2019, 2021). The typology takes into account the way in which the alternatives are exploited, and integrates information structure, discourse structure and formal considerations. The main conceptual stance in her contribution is that there are three types of contrast: discourse opposition (parallel contrast), selection (selective contrast), and correction (corrective contrast). The empirical basis of her article consists of a cross-modal comparison of the expression of contrast in interactional signed and spoken language, specifically in Belgian French. The author provides a detailed analysis of a large series of signed and spoken examples of the three types of contrast and shows that they can be accounted for by the proposed typology of contrast. To the extent that the encoding of contrast is different in signed and spoken languages, this analysis demonstrates that the proposed typology applies independently of the specific way in which contrast is formally marked.

2.3 Analyzing contrast using the Question Under Discussion model

Brunetti's paper "Contrast in a QUD-based information-structure model" is based on a detailed analysis of authentic data in short excerpts of oral and written interviews in French (2630 words) and Italian (1770 words), in which she identifies 121 instances of different types of contrastive relations. She applies to these data the model of information structure annotation proposed by Riester, Brunetti, and De

Kuthy (2018), Riester (2019), and Brunetti, De Kuthy, and Riester (2021), adopting the widespread assumption that every utterance can be considered the answer to an (implicit or explicit) question in the discourse: the "Question under Discussion" or QUD (Roberts [1996] 2012, among many others), which can be reconstructed (see Beaver and Velleman 2016 for an overview). This assumption is however taken a step further: the reconstruction of the QUDs is operationalized through the identification of principles which restrict the potential QUDs that a given utterance may answer in a specific context. Against this backdrop and in line with Umbach (2005), Brunetti argues that contrast is accounted for by the principle "Parallelism", which applies to two or more utterances answering the same QUD: contrastive focus is an instance of "simple parallelism" and contrastive topic of "complex parallelism". This distinction allows her to capture the intuition that contrastive focus involves one contrast set (of alternatives being opposed with respect to the same background), whereas contrastive topic involves two contrast sets (Büring 2003). Interestingly, Brunetti also zooms in on some specific instances in the corpora displaying contrastive relations without Parallelism. She argues that they are (i) instances of a concessive interpretation, (ii) show up in contexts with multiple "crossing" contrastive relations blocking the reconstruction of Parallelism, or (iii) relate to contrast between entities inside a proposition, rather than contrast between propositions.

In Chapter 9 "Contrast, concession, and QUD-trees", **Hesse, Klabunde and Benz** also test the QUD model of information structure annotation proposed by Riester, Brunetti, and De Kuthy (2018), Riester (2019), and Brunetti, De Kuthy, and Riester (2021), on a dataset containing instances of 24 German discourse markers such as *sondern* 'but', *obwohl* 'although', *doch* 'still, after all', *trotzdem* 'however', some of which are unambiguously contrastive or concessive, while others are ambiguous. These examples have been retrieved from the QUDGen corpus (Hesse et al. 2022). This corpus consists of 30 car and motorcycle reviews, of about 720 words each, from the German newspapers *Frankfurter Allgemeine Zeitung* and *Die Welt*, which have been annotated with QUD trees and extensions of the guidelines. Their goal is to verify the hypothesis put forward by the annotation guidelines (and specific analyses of concession and contrast in Büring 2003, Jasinskaja and Zeevat 2008, Jasinskaja 2012, and Brunetti, De Kuthy, and Riester 2021) that a contrastive interpretation corresponds with a coordinating QUD structure (i.e. a coordinating multi-nucleus rhetorical relation, in which the two sub-QUDs of contrastive topics mirror one another), while a concessive interpretation corresponds with a subordinating QUD structure (i.e. with a subordinating rhetorical relation, hence nucleus-satellite, in which a satellite answers a dedicated sub-QUD). The authors show that this hypothesis is borne out by 90% of all the corpus examples of contrastive and concessive discourse markers in German. They elaborate in depth on counter-examples of the "subordinating contrast" type and show that they pertain to "hypotheticals, counterfactuals or at least a contra-expectation, or some form of explicit or implicit topic restriction". With respect to three instances of coordinating concession, they show that these are only apparent counter-examples.

References

Altenberg, Bengt. 2006. The function of adverbial connectors in second initial position in English and Swedish. In Karin Aijmer & Anne-Marie Simon-Vandenbergen (eds.), *Pragmatic Markers in Contrast*, 11–37. Oxford: Elsevier.

Anagnostopoulou, Elena. 1997. Clitic left dislocation and contrastive left dislocation. In Elena Anagnostopoulou, Henk van Riemsdijk & Frans Zwarts (eds.), *Materials on Left Dislocation*, 151–192. Amsterdam: John Benjamins.

Anscombre, Jean-Claude. 2006. Les locutions *quant à, pour ce qui est de, en ce qui concerne* : chronique d'un discours annoncé. *Modèles Linguistiques* 54. 155–169.

Arregi, Karlos. 2003. Clitic left dislocation is contrastive topicalization. *University of Pennsylvania Working Papers in Linguistics* 9(1). 31–44.

Ashby, William J. 1988. The syntax, pragmatics, and sociolinguistics of left- and right-dislocations in French. *Lingua* 75. 203–229.

Asher, Nicholas & Alex Lascarides. 2003. *Logics of Conversation*. Cambridge: Cambridge University Press.

Barnes, Betsy K. 1985. *The Pragmatics of Left Detachment in Spoken Standard French*. Amsterdam/ Philadelphia: John Benjamins.

Belletti, Adriana. 2001. "Inversion" as focalization. In Aafke C.J. Hulk & Jean-Yves Pollock (eds.), *Subject Inversion in Romance and the Theory of Universal Grammar*, 60–90. Oxford: Oxford University Press.

Belletti, Adriana. 2004. Aspects of the low IP area. In Luigi Rizzi (ed.), *The Structure of CP and IP. The Cartography of Syntactic Structures*, 16–51. Oxford: Oxford University Press.

Bianchi, Valentina, Giuliano Bocci & Silvio Cruschina. 2015. Focus fronting and its implicatures. In Enoch O. Aboh, Jeannette Schaeffer & Petra Sleeman (eds.), *Romance Languages and Linguistic Theory: Selected Papers from "Going Romance" Amsterdam 2013*, 3–19. Amsterdam: John Benjamins.

Bianchi, Valentina, Giuliano Bocci & Silvio Cruschina. 2016. Focus fronting, unexpectedness, and evaluative implicatures. *Semantics and Pragmatics* 9. 1–54.

Bourgoin, Charlotte. 2017. The role of the English *it*-cleft and the French *c'est*-cleft in research discourse. *Discours. Revue de linguistique, psycholinguistique et informatique* 21. 1–29. https://doi.org/10.4000/discours.9366

Brunetti, Lisa, Mathieu Avanzi & Cédric Gendrot. 2012. Entre syntaxe, prosodie et discours : les topiques sujet en français parlé. *SHS Web of Conferences* 1. 2041–2054. https://doi.org/10.1051/shsconf/20120100209

Brunetti, Lisa, Kordula De Kuthy & Arndt Riester. 2016. Annotation guidelines for questions under discussion and information structure. Paper presented at the Workshop on information structure and the architecture of grammar, Barcelona, 28 October, 2016.

Brunetti, Lisa, Kordula De Kuthy & Arndt Riester. 2021. The information-structural status of adjuncts: A question-under-discussion-based approach. *Discours. Revue de linguistique, psycholinguistique et informatique* 28. https://doi.org/10.4000/discours.11454

Brunetti, Lisa, Mariapaola D'Imperio & Francesco Cangemi. 2010. On the prosodic marking of contrast in Romance sentence topic: Evidence from Neapolitan Italian. In *Proceedings of the 5th International Conference on Speech Prosody, Chicago, USA, 2010*. http://www.isle.illinois.edu/speechprosody2010/program.php

Brysbaert, Jorina & Karen Lahousse. 2022. Marking contrastive topics in a topic shift context: Contrastive adverbs versus emphatic pronouns. *Discours. Revue de linguistique, psycholinguistique et informatique* 31. https://doi.org/10.4000/discours.12189

Büring, Daniel. 2003. On d-trees, beans, and b-accents. *Linguistics and Philosophy* 26(5). 511–545.

Büring, Daniel. 2016. (Contrastive) topic. In Caroline Féry & Shinichiro Ishihara (eds.), *Handbook of Information Structure*, 64–85. Oxford: Oxford University Press.

Calvé, Pierre. 1985. Dislocation in spoken French. *The Modern Language Journal* 69(3). 230–237.

Chafe, Wallace L. 1976. Givenness, contrastiveness, definiteness, subjects, topics, and point of view. In Charles N. Li (ed.), *Subject and Topic*, 25–55. New York: Academic Press.

Choi-Jonin, Injoo. 2003. Ordre syntaxique et ordre référentiel. Emplois de la locution prépositive *quant à*. In Bernard Combettes, Catherine Schnedecker & Anne Theissen (eds.), *Ordre et distinction dans la langue et le discours*, 133–147. Paris: Honoré Champion.

Cimmino, Doriana. 2017. *La Topicalizzazione in Italiano in Prospettiva Contrastiva con l'Inglese. Il Caso della Scrittura Giornalistica Online*. Basel: Basel University dissertation.

Cimmino, Doriana. 2023. On the topic-marking function of left dislocations and preposings: Variation across spoken and written Italian and English. In Alessandra Barotto & Simone Mattiola (eds.), *Discourse Phenomena in Typological Perspective*, 337–368. Amsterdam/Philadelphia: John Benjamins.

Cimmino, Doriana & Alessandro Panunzi. 2017. La variazione funzionale delle strutture marcate a sinistra in italiano. Uno studio su corpora tra parlato e scritto. *Studi di Grammatica Italiana* 36. 117–179.

Cook, Philippa & Felix Bildhauer. 2011. Annotating information structure: The case of topic. In Stefanie Dipper & Heike Zinsmeister (eds.), *Beyond Semantics: Corpus-based Investigations of Pragmatic and Discourse Phenomena*, 45–56. Bochum: Bochumer Linguistische Arbeitsberichte.

Cook, Philippa & Felix Bildhauer. 2013. Identifying "aboutness topics": Two annotation experiments. *Dialogue & Discourse* 4(2). 118–141.

Cruschina, Silvio. 2021a. The greater the contrast, the greater the potential: On the effects of focus in syntax. *Glossa: A Journal of General Linguistics* 6(1). 1–30. https://doi.org/10.5334/gjgl.1100

Cruschina, Silvio. 2021b. Topicalization in the Romance languages. In Mark Aronoff (ed.), *Oxford Research Encyclopedia of Linguistics*, 1–28. Oxford: Oxford University Press.

Cruschina, Silvio & Eva-Maria Remberger. 2017. Focus fronting. In Andreas Dufter & Elisabeth Stark (eds.), *Manual of Romance Morphosyntax and Syntax*, 502–535. Berlin: De Gruyter.

Csűry, István. 2001. *Le Champ Lexical de mais: Étude Lexico-grammaticale des Termes d'Opposition du Français Contemporain dans un Cadre Textologique*. Debrecen: Kossuth Egyetemi Kiadó.

Davidse, Kristin. 2000. A constructional approach to clefts. *Linguistics* 38(6). 1101–1131.

De Kuthy, Kordula, Nils Reiter & Arndt Riester. 2018. QUD-based annotation of discourse structure and information structure: Tool and evaluation. In Nicoletta Calzolari, Khalid Choukri, Christopher Cieri, Thierry Declerck, Sara Goggi, Koiti Hasida, Hitoshi Isahara, Bente Maegaard, Joseph Mariani, Hélène Mazo, Asuncion Moreno, Jan Odijk, Stelios Piperidis, Takenobu Tokunaga (eds.), *Proceedings of the Eleventh International Conference on Language Resources and Evaluation (LREC 2018)*. https://aclanthology.org/L18-1304

Destruel, Emilie & Leah Velleman. 2014. Refining contrast: Empirical evidence from the English *it*-cleft. In Christopher Piñón (ed.), *Empirical Issues in Syntax and Semantics*, 197–214. Paris: CSSP.

Dupont, Maïté. 2021. *Conjunctive Markers of Contrast in English and French: From Syntax to Lexis and Discourse*. Amsterdam/Philadelphia: John Benjamins.

É. Kiss, Katalin. 1998. Identificational focus versus information focus. *Language* 74(2). 245–273.

Erteschik-Shir, Nomi. 2007. *Information Structure. The Syntax-Discourse Interface*. New York: Oxford University Press.

Face, Timothy L. 2001a. Focus and early peak alignment in Spanish intonation. *Probus. International Journal of Latin and Romance Linguistics* 13. 223–246.

Face, Timothy L. 2001b. *Intonational Marking of Contrastive Focus in Madrid Spanish*. Columbus: The Ohio State University dissertation.

Face, Timothy L. 2002. Local intonational marking of Spanish contrastive focus. *Probus. International Journal of Latin and Romance Linguistics* 14. 71–92.

Farkas, Donka F. & Kim B. Bruce. 2010. On reacting to assertions and polar questions. *Language and Speech* 27(1). 81–118.

Fløttum, Kjersti. 2003. À propos de "quant à" et "en ce qui concerne." In Bernard Combettes, Catherine Schnedecker & Anne Theissen (eds.), *Ordre et Distinction dans la Langue et le Discours*, 185–202. Paris: Honoré Champion.

Frascarelli, Mara. 2017. Dislocations and framings. In Andreas Dufter & Elisabeth Stark (eds.), *Manual of Romance Morphosyntax and Syntax*, 472–501. Berlin: Mouton de Gruyter.

Gabriel, Christoph. 2007. *Fokus im Spannungsfeld von Phonologie und Syntax: Eine Studie zum Spanischen*. Frankfurt am Main: Vervuert.

Geluykens, Ronald. 1992. *From Discourse Process to Grammatical Construction. On Left-dislocation in English*. Amsterdam: John Benjamins.

Götze, Michael, Thomas Weskott, Cornelia Endriss, Ines Fiedler, Stefan Hinterwimmer, Svetlana Petrova, Anne Schwarz, Stavros Skopeteas & Ruben Stoel. 2007. Information structure. In Stefanie Dipper, Michael Götze & Stavros Skopeteas (eds.), *Interdisciplinary Studies on Information Structure*, 147–187. Potsdam: Universitätsverlag Potsdam.

Grohmann, Kleanthes K. 2000. A movement approach to contrastive left dislocation. *Rivista di Grammatica Generativa* 25. 3–66.

Halliday, Michael A.K. 1967. Notes on transitivity and theme in English: Part 1. *Journal of Linguistics* 3(1). 37–81.

Hartmann, Katharina & Malte Zimmermann. 2009. Morphological focus marking in Gùrùntùm (West Chadic). *Lingua* 119(9). 1340–1365.

Hedberg, Nancy. 1990. *Discourse Pragmatics and Cleft Sentences in English*. Minnesota: University of Minnesota dissertation.

Hesse, Christoph, Maurice Langner, Ralf Klabunde & Anton Benz. 2022. Testing focus and non-at-issue frameworks with a question-under-discussion-annotated corpus. In *Proceedings of the Language Resources and Evaluation Conference*, 5212–5219. Marseille: European Language Resources Association. https://aclanthology.org/2022.lrec-1.559

Horvath, Julia. 1986. *Focus in the Theory of Grammar and the Syntax of Hungarian*. Dordrecht: Foris.

Horváth, Márton Gergely. 2018. *Le Français Parlé Informel. Stratégies de Topicalisation*. Berlin/Boston: De Gruyter.

Hualde, José Ignacio & Pilar Prieto. 2015. Intonational variation in Spanish. European and American varieties. In Sónia Frota & Pilar Prieto (eds.), *Intonation in Romance*, 350–391. Oxford: Oxford University Press.

Izutsu, Mitsuko Narita. 2008. Contrast, concessive, and corrective: Toward a comprehensive study of opposition relations. *Journal of Pragmatics* 40. 646–675.

Jasinskaja, Katja. 2012. Correction by adversative and additive markers. *Lingua* 122(15). 1899–1918.

Jasinskaja, Katja & Henk Zeevat. 2008. Explaining additive, adversative, and contrast marking in Russian and English. *Revue de Sémantique et Pragmatique* 24. 65–91.

Kidwai, Ayesha. 2000. *XP-adjunction in Universal Grammar: Scrambling and Binding in Hindi-Urdu*. Oxford: Oxford University Press.

Kidwai, Ayesha. 2004. The topic interpretation in universal grammar. In Veneeta Dayal & Anoop Mahajan (eds.), *Clause Structure in South Asian Languages*, 253–289. Dordrecht: Springer.

Kimmelman, Vadim. 2014. *Information Structure in Russian Sign Language and Sign Language of the Netherlands*. Amsterdam: University of Amsterdam dissertation.

Krifka, Manfred. 2008. Basic notions of information structure. *Acta Linguistica Hungarica* 55(3). 243–276.

Lagae, Véronique. 2007. Détachement, cadrage et reformulation : le cas de la locution *en fait de*. In Nelly Flaux & Dejan Stosic (eds.), *Les Constructions Détachées: Entre Langue et Discours*, 15–40. Arras: Artois Presses Universités.

Lahousse, Karen & Marijke Borremans. 2014. The distribution of functional-pragmatic types of clefts in adverbial clauses. *Linguistics* 52(3). 793–836.

Lahousse, Karen, Christopher Laenzlinger & Gabriela Soare. 2014. Contrast and intervention at the periphery. *Lingua* 143. 56–85.

Lambrecht, Knud. 1994. *Information Structure and Sentence Form: Topic, Focus and the Mental Representations of Discourse Referents*. Cambridge: Cambridge University Press.

Lambrecht, Knud. 2001. Dislocation. In Martin Haspelmath, Ekkehard König, Wulf Oesterreicher & Wolfgang Raible (eds.), *Language Typology and Language Universals: An International Handbook*, 1050–1078. Berlin: De Gruyter.

Lenker, Ursula. 2010. *Argument and Rhetoric. Adverbial Connectors in the History of English*. Berlin/New York: De Gruyter Mouton.

Lombardi Vallauri, Edoardo. 2000. The role of discourse, syntax and the lexicon in determining the nature and extent of focus. *Lingvisticae Investigationes* 23(2). 229–252.

Molnár, Valéria. 2002. Contrast – from a contrastive perspective. In Hilde Hallelgard, Stig Johansson, Bergljot Behrens & Cathrine Fabricius-Hansen (eds.), *Information Structure in a Cross-linguistic Perspective*, 147–161. Amsterdam/New York: Rodopi.

Molnár, Valéria & Susanne Winkler. 2010. Edges and gaps: Contrast at the interfaces. *Lingua* 120(6). 1392–1415.

Navarrete-González, Alexandra. 2019. The notion of focus and its relation to contrast in Catalan Sign Language (LSC). *Sensos-e* 6(1). 18–40.

Navarrete-González, Alexandra. 2021. The expression of contrast in Catalan Sign Language (LSC). *Glossa: A Journal of General Linguistics* 6(1). 1–22.

Neeleman, Ad & Reiko Vermeulen. 2012. The syntactic expression of information structure. In Ad Neeleman & Reiko Vermeulen (eds.), *The Syntax of Topic, Focus, and Contrast: An Interface-based Approach*, 1–38. Berlin/New York: De Gruyter.

Ott, Dennis. 2014. An ellipsis approach to contrastive left-dislocation. *Linguistic Inquiry* 45(2). 269–303.

Prieto, Pilar & Paolo Roseano. 2009–2013. Atlas Interactivo de la Entonación del Español. http://prosodia.upf.edu/atlasentonacion/

Repp, Sophie. 2009. Topics and corrections. In Arndt Riester & Torgrim Solstad (eds.), *Proceedings of Sinn und Bedeutung 13*, 399–414. Stuttgart: University of Stuttgart.

Repp, Sophie. 2010. Defining 'contrast' as an information-structural notion in grammar. *Lingua* 120(6). 1333–1345.

Repp, Sophie. 2016. Contrast: Dissecting an elusive information-structural notion and its role in grammar. In Caroline Féry & Ishishara Shinichiro (eds.), *The Oxford Handbook of Information Structure*, 270–289. Oxford: Oxford University Press.

Repp, Sophie & Heiner Drenhaus. 2015. Intonation influences processing and recall of left-dislocation sentences by indicating topic vs. focus status of dislocated referent. *Language, Cognition and Neuroscience* 30(3). 324–346.

Riester, Arndt. 2019. Constructing QUD trees. In Malte Zimmermann, Klaus von Heusinger & Edgar Onea (eds.), *Questions in Discourse. Vol. 2: Pragmatics*, 163–192. Leiden: Brill.

Riester, Arndt, Lisa Brunetti & Kordula De Kuthy. 2018. Annotation guidelines for questions under discussion and information structure. In Evangelia Adamou, Katharina Haude & Martine Vanhove (eds.), *Information Structure in Lesser-described Languages: Studies in Prosody and Syntax*, 403–443. Amsterdam: John Benjamins.

Riester, Arndt, Tobias Schröer & Stefan Baumann. 2020. On the prosody of contrastive topics in German interviews. In *Proceedings of the 10th International Conference on Speech Prosody, Tokyo, Japan, 2020*, 280–284. doi: 10.21437/SpeechProsody.2020-57

Ritz, Julia, Stefanie Dipper & Michael Götze. 2008. Annotation of information structure: An evaluation across different types of texts. In Nicoletta Calzolari, Khalid Choukri, Bente Maegaard, Joseph Mariani, Jan Odijk, Stelios Piperidis & Daniel Tapias (eds.), *Proceedings of the Sixth International Conference on Language Resources and Evaluation [LREC]*, 2137–2142. Marrakech: European Language Resources Assocation [ELRA].

Rizzi, Luigi. 1997. The fine structure of the left periphery. In Liliane Haegeman (ed.), *Elements of Grammar. Handbook of Generative Syntax*, 281–337. Dordrecht: Kluwer Academic Publishers.

Rizzi, Luigi. 2004. Locality and the left periphery. In Adriana Belletti (ed.), *Structures and Beyond: The Cartography of Syntactic Structures*, 223–251. Oxford/New York: Oxford University Press.

Roberts, Craige. 2012 [1996]. Information structure: Towards an integrated formal theory of pragmatics. *Semantics and Pragmatics* 5(6). 1–69.

Rooth, Mats. 1992. A theory of focus interpretation. *Natural Language Semantics* 1(1). 75–116.

Rooth, Mats. 2016. Alternative semantics. In Shinichiro Ishihara & Caroline Féry (eds.), *The Oxford Handbook of Information Structure*, 19–40. Oxford: Oxford University Press.

Samek-Lodovici, Vieri. 2015. *The Interaction of Focus, Givenness, and Prosody: A Study of Italian Clause Structure*. Oxford: Oxford University Press.

Scappini, Sophie. 2013. Un sous-type de la construction clivée en "c'est. . .qu": La structure d'enchaînement "et c'est pour ça que" . . . et d'autres exemples. *Studia UBB Philologia* 58(4). 81–95.

Seeliger, Heiko & Sophie Repp. 2020. Competing prominence requirements in verb-first exclamatives with contrastive and given information. In *Proceedings of the 10th International Conference on Speech Prosody, Tokyo, Japan, 2020*, 1–5. doi: 10.21437/SpeechProsody.2020-29

Skopeteas, Stavros & Gisbert Fanselow. 2011. Focus and the exclusion of alternatives: On the interaction of syntactic structure with pragmatic inference. *Lingua* 121(11). 1693–1706.

Spedaner, Jennifer & Anna Lobanova. 2009. Reliable discourse markers for contrast relations. In *Proceedings of the 8th International Conference on Computational Semantics, Tilburg, the Netherlands, 2009*, 210–221. https://aclanthology.org/W09-3719.pdf

Szabolcsi, Anna. 1981. Compositionality in focus. *Folia Linguistica* 15(1–2). 141–162.

Umbach, Carla. 2004. On the notion of contrast in information structure and discourse structure. *Journal of Semantics* 21. 155–175.

Umbach, Carla. 2005. Contrast and information structure: A focused-based analysis of *but*. *Linguistics* 43(1). 207–232.

Vallduví, Enric & Maria Vilkuna. 1998. On rhema and kontrast. In Peter Culicover & Louise McNally (eds.), *The Limits of Syntax*, 79–108. New York: Academic Press.

Velghe, Tom. 2015. *Les Marqueurs de Thématisation en Français. Syntaxe, Discours et Prosodie*. Leuven: KU Leuven dissertation.

Velghe, Tom & Karen Lahousse. 2015. Thematic markers in informal written French: *Pour ce qui est de, au niveau (de)* and *en matière de*. *Journal of French Language Studies* 25(3). 423–444.

Velleman, Leah & David Beaver. 2016. Question-based models of information structure. In Caroline Féry & Shinichiro Ishihara (eds.), *The Oxford Handbook of Information Structure*, 86–107. Oxford: Oxford University Press.

Wagner, Michael. 2020. Prosodic focus. In Daniel Gutzmann, Lisa Matthewson, Cecile Meier, Hotze Rullmann & Thomas Zimmermann (eds.), *The Wiley Blackwell Companion to Semantics*, 1–64. Oxford: Wiley-Blackwell.

Webber, Bonnie, Rashmi Prasad, Alan Lee & Joshi Aravind. 2019. *The Penn Discourse Treebank 3.0 Annotation Manual*. Philadelphia: University of Pennsylvania. https://catalog.ldc.upenn.edu/docs/LDC2019T05/PDTB3-Annotation-Manual.pdf

Part I: **Contrast versus topic and focus**

Vieri Samek-Lodovici and Karen Dwyer

2 Experimental testing of focus fronting in British English

Abstract: This paper presents experimental results concerning the grammaticality of focus fronting in British English. The experiment involved 101 participants who were asked to assess spoken stimuli involving in-situ and fronted focalization across open questions, closed questions, and corrective replies to an incorrect statement. The experiment showed that (i) in-situ foci were deemed significantly more natural than fronted foci across all three exchange types, (ii) fronted foci were deemed significantly more natural when used as replies to closed questions than open questions, (iii) fronted foci were assessed as significantly more natural as replies to open questions than as corrective replies. We also provide our interpretation of these results, arguing that they provide empirical support for (a) the in-situ analysis of contrastive focalization (Rooth 1985, 1992), (b) the grammaticality of contrastive replies to open questions (Skopeteas and Fanselow 2011), (c) the definition of contrast proposed in Neeleman and Vermeulen (2012), and (d) the degrading effect of linguistic processing on naturalness judgements.

1 Introduction

This paper presents experimental results concerning the grammaticality of focus fronting affecting DP/PP complements in British English across three types of conversational exchanges: replies to open questions, replies to closed questions, and corrective replies to an incorrect statement. Its distinctive features, described in further detail below, include (i) its size, it involved 101 participants; (ii) the usage of spoken experimental stimuli which allowed for prosodic cues (e.g. stressed foci) that decreased the chances to misinterpret the stimuli through an incorrect assignment of focus and topic features (for example by interpreting fronted foci as topics) as it might happen with written stimuli; (iii) the careful design of the stimuli to prevent effects related to the syntactic properties of the assessed sentences; specifically, we ensured that the assessed sentences varied across four tenses and involved verbs taking animate and inanimate complements, as well as nominal and prepositional complements.

The experiment provided three main results, all statistically significant: (i) in-situ foci were assessed as significantly more natural than fronted foci across all three exchange types, confirming similar experimental results across corrective,

https://doi.org/10.1515/9783110986594-002

mirative, and lexically contrastive exchanges provided for Italian in Bianchi, Bocci, and Cruschina (2015), for Spanish in Cruschina (2019),[1] and for imperative clauses in Italian, Spanish, and English in Frascarelli and Jiménez-Fernández (2021); (ii) fronted foci in response to closed questions were assessed as significantly more natural than fronted foci in response to open questions; (iii) fronted foci in response to open questions were assessed as significantly more natural than fronted foci in corrective responses.

Some of these results, especially (i) and (iii), were unexpected. We provide our interpretation in section 5, discussing how they provide support for (a) the in-situ analysis of contrastive focalization, (b) the availability of contrastive replies to open questions as per Skopeteas and Fanselow (2011) and against widely held assumptions to the contrary, (c) the definition of contrast as involving the denial of focus alternatives as proposed in Neeleman and Vermeulen (2012), and (d) the degrading effect of linguistic processing on naturalness judgements.

Section 2 provides the theoretical context that led us to running this experiment. Section 3 details the experiment's components and overall organization. Section 4 provides the statistical results. Section 5 offers our interpretation of the results, already summarised above.

2 Theoretical context

Ever since Rizzi's (1997, 2004) and Belletti's (2001, 2004) seminal works on the position of contrastive and non-contrastive focus in Italian, focused constituents have been generally assumed to be able to front when involving a contrastive interpretation and unable to front under a non-contrastive, presentational reading. Exactly how contrast should be defined and which discourse contexts elicit its presence, however, has been and still is under debate; see amongst others Rooth (1992, 2016), Büring (1997, 2003), Kiss (1998), Molnár (2002), Kenesei (2006), Zimmerman (2007, 2008), Krifka (2008), Repp (2010, 2016), Horvath (2010), Krifka

---

1 Bianchi, Bocci, and Cruschina (2015) and Cruschina (2019) use the term 'contrastive' for focalized items like *TAXI* in (i) where focus involves contrast against another lexical item but does not involve a corrective interpretation. Since the term *contrast* is very frequently used in the information structure literature for corrective exchanges, we prefer to characterize exchanges like (i) as *lexically contrastive* and keep using the unqualified term *contrastive* for the corrective exchanges examined in this paper.

(i) A: *I am going home.*
  B: *Take a TAXI$_F$ (not the subway).*

and Musan (2012), Neeleman and Vermeulen (2012), Bianchi and Bocci (2012), and Cruschina (2021), as well as the works in Molnár and Winkler (2006), Repp and Cook (2010), and in this volume.

Experimental data revealing which discourse contexts genuinely allow for fronting, and hence under current assumptions also which contexts allow for the presence of contrast, play an important role in advancing this debate, as they provide a clearer picture of the linguistic data that need to be explained, as well as test the divergent predictions made by competing analyses about those data. The experiment reported here tested the availability of focus fronting in corrective, open question, and closed question exchanges with the goal of determining whether close questions involved contrast, as this in turn distinguishes between Krifka's (2008) and Neeleman and Vermeulen's (2012) analyses of contrast, as further explained below.

Corrective exchanges like (1) were included in the experiment with the expectation that they would provide the benchmark case for grammatical sentences containing contrast. Rizzi (1997) and most subsequent literature, including the more articulated investigation in Bianchi and Bocci (2012), Bianchi (2013) and Bianchi, Bocci, and Cruschina (2015) on Italian data, assume that corrective exchanges involve contrast and license focus fronting as its visible, albeit optional, effect. To our surprise, these exchanges were instead assessed as those where fronting is least natural amongst those we tested, showing how important it is to empirically and crosslinguistically test even the most uncontroversial assumptions. In section 5, we interpret this unexpected result as due to the degradation of naturalness assessment brought about by processing load and interpret them as potential evidence for in-situ analyses of contrastive focalization. (The 'F' subscript marks the focused phrase. Main stress is in capitals.)

(1) Contrastive exchanges:
   A: *John hit Bill.*
   B: *TOM$_F$ he hit.*

Similarly, the experiment included open question exchanges like (2) under the widely held assumption that they do not license contrast, and hence could not license fronting either, thus potentially acting as a benchmark for the absence of contrast. Our experimental results challenge this assumption, showing that fronting in open question exchanges is more readily available than in corrective exchanges. In section 5, we follow Skopeteas and Fanselow (2011) in interpreting this result as stemming from the possibility for speakers to provide contrastive replies even in contexts that do not require the presence of contrast.

(2)   Open question exchanges:
      A: *Who did John hit?*
      B: *TOM$_F$, he hit.*

Finally, we included closed questions exchanges, illustrated in (3). These were the cases most pertinent to our original research goal, which aimed at empirically identifying the most successful analysis of contrast amongst the two provided in Neeleman and Vermeulen (2012) and Krifka (2008). Their analyses appeared particularly fit for empirical testing because they make convergent predictions for corrective and open question exchanges, but diverge with respect to closed questions, which are considered to involve contrast (and hence potentially fronting) under Neeleman and Vermeulen (2012: 8–9), whereas they are necessarily non-contrastive under Krifka (2008: 258–59), as explained in more detail below (see also Samek-Lodovici 2018).

(3)   Closed question exchanges:
      A: *Who did John hit, Tom or Bill?*
      B: *TOM$_F$, he hit.*

Neeleman and Vermeulen (2012) define contrast as denying the validity of at least one of the alternative propositions contained in the focus value of a sentence. Intuitively, the focus value of a sentence contains all the propositions formed by replacing the focused constituent with a contextually salient alternative as per Rooth (1985, 1992, 2016). For example, the focus value of (3B) consists of the propositions 'John hit Tom' and 'John hit Bill'. Under Neeleman and Vermeulen's analysis, speaker B may use contrast to deny the alternative 'John hit Bill', thus predicting the grammaticality of contrast-induced focus fronting in (3B).

Under Krifka (2008: 259), instead, focus is contrastive whenever the Common Ground – the shared knowledge formed by all propositions that both interlocutors know to hold and be mutually known to hold – contains at least one proposition that differs from the proposition being asserted but it is also a member of its focus value (i.e. a proposition identical to the asserted proposition but for the focused constituent). For example, in the corrective exchange in (1) above, the proposition 'John hit Tom' asserted by speaker B involves contrast because it differs from the proposition 'John hit Bill' introduced into the Common Ground by speaker A and, crucially, the proposition 'John hit Bill' just mentioned also belongs to the focus value of speaker B's assertion.

Under Krifka's analysis, however, contrast is predicted to be absent in closed question exchanges like (3) because questions are maintained to manage expectations about the future updating of the Common Ground and as such they cannot add propositions to it. Therefore, question (3A) does not add any proposition to the Common Ground, which remains empty. Consequently, (3B) does not involve contrastive focalization, since the asserted proposition – namely 'John hit Tom' – does not contrast with any proposition in the Common Ground. Since contrast is absent, focus fronting is predicted to be unavailable as well.[2]

Our experimental results showed closed question exchanges emerge as the most natural context for focus fronting. This result would appear to support Neeleman and Vermeulen's analysis. The results associated with open question and corrective exchanges, however, do not fit the convergent predictions made by either of Krifka's and Neeleman and Vermeulen's analyses, a point we return to in section 5.

The next two sections describe the experimental setup and presents the experimental results in statistical terms, followed by our interpretation in section 5.

3 Method

3.1 Participants

One hundred and one participants were recruited from University College London, Queen Mary University and York University by advertisement and through the Prolific online recruitment service, which is used widely in academic research. All participants (48 male, 51 female, 2 other) were aged 18–65 and were native British speakers of English. Informed consent was obtained from all participants, who were remunerated at a rate of £9.50 per hour for participation in the study.

3.2 Materials

This study aimed to measure participants' grammaticality judgements of focus fronting across three conversational exchanges: open questions, closed questions, and corrective exchanges.

---

2 More precisely, the prediction follows from Krifka's (2008) characterization of contrast once combined with the assumption that contrast optionally licenses fronting. As pointed out by an anonymous reviewer, this latter assumption is raised only in passing in Krifka (2008: 259) which mentions "[the existence of] evidence for particular marking strategies for contrastive focus like the use of particular syntactic positions [. . .]". Therefore, while the prediction follows from Krifka's analysis, it should not be attributed to Krifka directly.

The task consisted of 96 mini dialogues in the form of adjacency pairs (Schegloff and Sacks 1973; Sacks, Schegloff, and Jefferson 1974). Within Conversation Analysis, adjacency pairs refer to two successive turns in conversation produced by different participants whereby the second utterance is conditionally relevant by its prior turn, for example, question-answer, statement-correction, greeting-greeting, invitation-acceptance, request-acceptance, and so on. All adjacency pairs in the study were of the type questions-answer action or statement-correction action. Each adjacency pair included a single utterance from speaker A setting the discourse context and a single response from speaker B containing the experimental item or a filler item. As further explained below, speaker A's utterance was presented in written form, whereas speaker's B response was presented as audio, i.e. the participants heard a spoken sentence.

The 96 adjacency pairs included 36 fronted target items where focus occurred fronted, 36 corresponding in-situ items where focus remained in-situ, and 24 fillers. In each adjacency pair, the context provided by speaker A was one of three forms: (i) an open question (e.g. *Who did John hit?*); (ii) a closed question with two choices (e.g. *Who did John hit, Tom or Bill?*); or (iii) a statement (e.g. *John hit Bill*).

For the open and closed question contexts, speaker B's response consisted of an answer focalizing the constituent corresponding to the wh-phrase. For the fronted target items, speaker B's response involved focus fronting (e.g. *TOM, he hit*). For each target item there was a corresponding in-situ item where focus remained in-situ (e.g. *he hit TOM*). For corrective exchanges, the context provided by speaker A was a statement that speaker B's response corrected (e.g. A: *John hit Bill.* – B: *TOM, he hit*). Here, too, for each target item there was a corresponding item where focus remained in-situ (e.g. A: *John hit Bill.* – B: *He hit TOM*).

Across all three contexts, speaker B's responses consisted of pre-recorded single sentences. Having single sentences ensured that naturalness judgements were made in regard to the target item and not influenced by linguistic information within additional sentences that could affect the focus, topic, or givenness status of the constituents in the target item. Presenting auditory stimuli provided a more naturalistic presentation of the stress pattern of the fronted element and mitigated against participants attempting to apply their own prosody, which again could potentially determine an incorrect assignment of focalization and topic features to the target sentences that could affect their grammaticality judgements (on this issue, see Frascarelli and Jiménez-Fernández 2017, 2021).

Also, six of the target responses to the closed questions fronted the first alternative mentioned in the question (e.g. A: *Who did John hit, Tom or Bill? –* B: *TOM, he hit*), while the remaining 6 closed question responses fronted the second alternative (A: *What did Jane send, roses or tulips?* – B: *TULIPS, she sent*).[3] This alternation in closed questions was designed to mitigate against participants demonstrating a bias towards selecting items that had occurred in a particular position in the context, or assuming that the task was investigating their judgements of a recency effect. However, to ensure that judgements of fronted sentences could not be attributed to a lexical bias towards specific items or to change in prosody, the same 12 choices (six corresponding to the first alternative and six for the second) were kept invariant across the responses to the 3 fronted contexts (i.e. B's response used *TOM*, rather than Bill, across the related open and closed question items as well as in the related statement-correction item. Similarly for the adjacency pairs involving the second alternative, say *TULIPS*).

Additionally, there were two sets of 12 non-corresponding in-situ fillers, which deviated from the target items more significantly. The first set involved adjacency pairs where speaker A produced the same open and closed questions described above (e.g. A: *Who did John hit?* and A: *Who did John hit, Tom or Bill?*), but speaker B's response was a single word (e.g. B: *Tom.*), while in the second set B's response consisted of a single sentence containing a negative marker negating the presupposition in speaker A's question (e.g. *He didn't hit anyone*). Examples of experimental stimuli are listed in Table 1.

Table 1: Task stimuli for target items and corresponding in-situ items for open and closed questions, corrective exchanges, and non-corresponding filler items.

Exchange type	Speaker A's written context	Speaker B's spoken response	
		Fronted	In-situ
Open questions	Who did John hit?	TOM, he hit.	He hit TOM.
Closed questions (1st alternative)	Who did John hit, Tom or Bill?	TOM, he hit.	He hit TOM.
Closed questions (2nd alternative)	What did Jane send, roses or tulips.	TULIPS, she sent.	She sent TULIPS.
Corrective exchanges	John hit Bill.	TOM, he hit.	He hit TOM.
			Non-corresponding in-situ Fillers
Open questions	Who did John hit?		TOM.
Closed questions	Who did John hit, Tom or Bill?		He didn't hit anyone.

---

3 The speakers' identifiers 'A' and 'B' used in these examples are provided for clarity. They did not appear in the experimental stimuli. See the *Procedures* section below.

Twelve verbs were used across all item sentences and had an equal distribution of either Determiner Phrase (DP) (*N=6*) or Prepositional Phrase (PP) (*N=6*) expressing an animate (*N=6*) or inanimate argument (*N=6*); see Table 2. Prepositional phrases had either '*to*', '*with*', '*about*', and '*for*' as head and were equally distributed across animate and inanimate arguments of the verb. Four tenses were used across the sentences: past tense (either regular or irregular form), present simple, present perfect, or present progressive. Each tense occurred 3 times and these were equally distributed across the DP and PP animate and inanimate argument structures.

Table 2: Verbs and tenses used across speaker A's contexts and speaker B's responses (both experimental items and fillers).

	Determiner Phrase	**Prepositional Phrase**	**Tense**
Animate	*hit*	*speak to*	Past
	see	*worry about*	Present
	meet		Present perfect
		wait for	Present progressive
Inanimate	*send*		Past
		paint with	Present
	have	*travel to*	Present perfect
	buy	*apply to*	Present progressive

The audio stimuli used as target items were recorded by the second author on an Olympus DM-20 dictaphone and edited in Audacity, an open-source digital audio editor, to create separate sound files. Recordings of responses for the adjacency pairs were saved as individual mp3 files and uploaded onto UCL Gorilla. All the stimuli involve main stress on the focused word, e.g. *TOM, he hit*. All audio stimuli are available for inspection online via the UCL Research Data Repository (RDR) at Samek-Lodovici and Dwyer (2022).

3.3 Procedures

The naturalness judgement task was presented online on the Gorilla platform (Anwyl-Irvine et al. 2020). Prior to the administration of the grammaticality judgement task, and following the completion of informed consent and providing of demographic information, working memory function was assessed using the WAIS-III (Wechsler 1997) Reverse Digit Span, which requires verbal working memory and attention, and, additionally, tests cognitive control and executive function. This was administered to determine that potential differences in naturalness judgements were independent of working memory. For this reason, the score on Reverse Digit Span was entered as a covariate in the main analysis.

3.3.1 Working memory

Each trial began with a black fixation point on a white background. This was followed by a sequence of randomised digits, each presented in turn for 2000ms before disappearing from the screen. On the right of the screen was a red number pad with digits from 0 to 9. The participants were asked to repeat the sequence of randomised digits in reverse order by entering them on the keypad. They were instructed to wait until all numbers had been shown before entering their response and to not write the numbers down as a memory strategy. If the participant responds correctly to three sequences of the same length, the next trial presents a longer sequence with one additional digit. The task automatically finishes when the participant responds incorrectly on three occasions under the same span length. The working memory span score represents the longest number of sequential digits that is correctly reported. The responses provided by the participants were scored automatically by the software. Prior to the task, they were given a trial of two sequences in order to familiarise themselves with the format of the task and to ensure they knew how to use the on-screen keypad.

3.3.2 Grammaticality judgements

Participants were informed that they would be presented with contextualised mini dialogues involving two speakers (speaker A and speaker B). Presentation of the dialogues was randomised automatically by the software.

At the start of the judgement task, before all trials, participants were told that speaker A's utterances would be presented in written form on the screen for 3 seconds. They were also asked to read aloud speaker A's statements or questions as they were presented on the screen. Figure 1 shows how the utterance was then presented in each trial.

Once this context disappeared from the screen, the target item (speaker B's spoken response) was presented auditorily while simultaneously showing an empty speech bubble on the screen (Figure 2).

Participants were asked to carry out a grammaticality judgement of speaker B's utterance after they heard each sentence: they were instructed to rate the grammaticality of the target sentences according to a 7 item Likert scale by pressing buttons 1 to 7 on the on-screen keyboard (Figure 3).

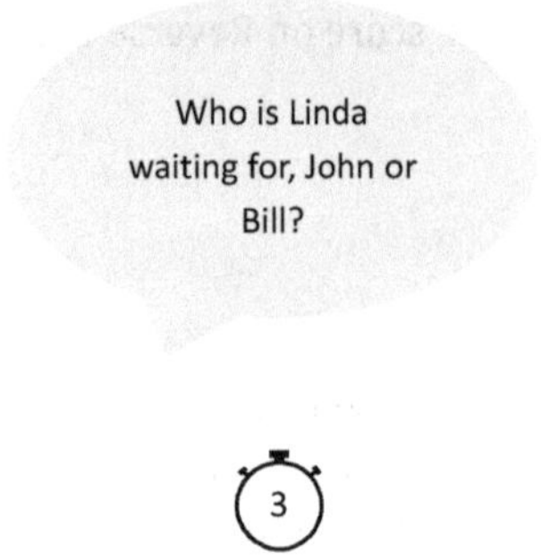

Who is Linda
waiting for, John or
Bill?

Figure 1: Presentation of speaker A's utterance.

Figure 2: Presentation of B's response.
Participants saw this image while listening
to B's response.

unnatural | 1 | 2 | 3 | 4 | 5 | 6 | 7 | natural

Figure 3: Presentation of the Likert scale.

Their responses to each item were recorded automatically by the software. There was no limit to the allowed response time but once the participant had responded by providing a judgement score (i.e. by pressing a button), the task automatically moved to the next trial item. There was no time limit for the entire task duration either. Completion time was on average approximately 15 minutes.

4 Results

The experimental data gathered in this experiment and used for the statistic analysis described in this section are available for inspection at Samek-Lodovici and Dwyer (2022).

The Likert scores for grammaticality judgement responses across the 101 participants were summed to produce 6 total scores: 3 for the target fronted structures and 3 for the corresponding in-situ items, with the following means (M) and standard deviations (std): open questions fronted M=45.87 (std=17.65) vs. open questions in-situ items M=72.5 (std=11.65); closed questions fronted M=47.65 (std=17.35) vs. closed questions in-situ items M=72.35 (std=12.34); corrective exchanges fronted M=38.46 (std=15.62) vs. corrective exchanges in-situ items M=60.1 (std=18.08)). Data were entered into a one-way repeated measures ANCOVA with working memory scores as a covariate and analyzed in IBM SPSS Statistics for Windows, Version 27.0. Mauchly's test indicated that the assumption of sphericity had been violated, $\chi^2(14) = 465.96$, $p < 0.001$. Therefore, degrees of freedom were corrected using Greenhouse-Geisser estimates of sphericity ($\varepsilon = 0.39$).

The repeated measures ANCOVA with a Greenhouse-Geisser correction determined that there was a statistically significant effect of structure type ($F(1.937, 191.802) = 5.524$, $p = 0.005$), there was no effect of working memory ($F(1,99) = 1.338$, $p = 0.25$), and no interaction between structure and working memory ($F(1.937, 191.802) = 2.013$, $p = 0.14$), demonstrating that working memory did not influence judgements.[4]

Post hoc analysis of pairwise comparisons with a Bonferroni adjustment were carried out to compare differences between item types. These revealed that there was a significant difference between each of the 3 contexts for fronted structures and their in-situ counterparts: fronted replies to open questions vs. in-situ replies ($p < 0.001$); fronted replies to closed questions vs. in-situ replies ($p < 0.001$); fronted replies to corrective exchanges vs. corrective exchanges in-situ replies ($p < 0.001$), with participants scoring all 3 fronted structures less natural than their in-situ versions in each case.

The Bonferroni adjusted pairwise comparisons of the fronted items showed that participants rated fronted replies to closed questions significantly more natural than fronted replies to open questions ($p < 0.05$), and fronted replies to open questions significantly more natural than fronted replies to corrective exchanges ($p < 0.001$). Fronted replies to closed questions were also scored as significantly more natural than fronted replies in corrective exchanges ($p < 0.001$).

---

4 The F-value is the ratio of two variances (two mean squares), measuring the dispersal of the data points around the mean. The F-value is calculated as: F-value = variation between sample means / variation within the samples. The further the individual data points are from the mean, the higher the degree of variance. The F-value is large when the variation between the sample means is high relative to the variation within each of the samples. The p-value (probability value) represents the likelihood that the data would have occurred by random chance (i.e. that the null hypothesis is true). It is a value between 0 and 1 – the smaller the p-value, the stronger the evidence that the null hypothesis should be rejected.

The box and whisker chart for the target fronted sentences and corresponding in-situ sentences is provided in Figure 4. From left to right, the figure lists the box and whisker charts for fronted items in open question responses, in-situ items in open question responses, fronted items in closed question responses, in-situ items in closed question responses, fronted items in corrective responses, and in-situ items in corrective responses. Each box and whisker chart shows the median and mean value for each context (respectively marked as the line dividing the 2nd and third quartiles, and as 'X'). To avoid cluttering, these numbers were cut at one decimal place. The two-decimal place averages are 3.82 (OpenQsFronted), 6.04 (OpenQsIn-Situ), 3.97 (CloseQsFronted), 6.03 (ClosedQsInSitu), 3.20 (CorrectExchFronted), and 5.01 (CorrectExchInSitu) respectively.

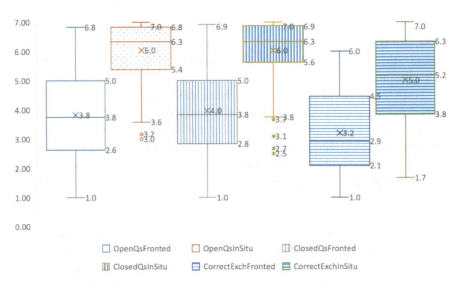

Figure 4: Box and whisker charts for the target fronted sentences and corresponding in-situ sentences.

5 Discussion

When we designed the experiment, we expected fronting to be most natural in corrective exchanges due to the widely assumed presence of contrast under these contexts, and least natural with open questions due to the equally widely assumed absence of contrast in these second set of contexts. The experimental results do not fit with these assumptions, showing that they do not accurately capture the linguistic reality of focus fronting in British English and need to be reconsidered. Below, we offer our interpretation of these results, taking the naturalness judgements provided by the experimental participants as proxy for grammaticality judgements. Note that our experiment only concerned the fronting of focused complements, thus remaining insensitive to any subject/object asymmetries such as those described in Breul (2007) and Skopeteas and Fanselow (2010).

5.1 Fronting vs in-situ focalization

We start with the divergence between in-situ and fronted focalization, where the higher grammaticality of in-situ foci over fronted ones emerged as statistically significant across all three exchange types. This result lends support to claims that contrastive focalization can be interpreted in-situ (Rooth 1992, 2016; Wagner 2020: section 3.16) and, therefore, also to the claim that contrastive focalization per se does not require the existence of a left-peripheral FocusP projection obligatorily attracting all contrastive foci to its specifier (Samek-Lodovici 2015, 2024. See also Brunetti 2004, Costa 2013, Abe 2016, Borise and Polinsky 2018 respectively proposing in-situ focalization in Italian, Spanish, Japanese, Georgian within wider analyses of specific phenomena, as well as Kolliakou 2004, Szendrői 2010, Samek-Lodovici 2010 in relation to focalization within DPs).

An in-situ focalization analysis would still have to explain why foci may front despite fronting being disfavoured relative to in-situ realization. Analyses that allow contrastive focalization to occur in-situ usually view its fronting as licensed by independent optional processes such as, in Italian, the syntactic marking of the rest of the clause as discourse-given through the application of right dislocation (Samek-Lodovici 2015), or, in Dutch, the marking of the focus background in terms of syntactic-sisterhood (Neeleman and van de Koot 2008).

Fronting might remain associated with the presence of contrast, but only as an optional operation constructing a syntactically marked structure that facilitates the conveyance of the intended interpretation, as proposed in Skopeteas and Fanselow's (2011) analysis of contrastive replies to open questions, discussed in greater length in section 5.2 below.

In all these analyses, the additional processing required by the independent processes responsible for fronting could be the factor that determines its experimentally attested lower grammaticality relative to in-situ constructions. Since the additional processes responsible for fronting are all optional, it is sufficient for some speakers to disfavour the additional processing associated with those processes to lower its overall grammaticality, independently of the specific context being tested (see also Breul 2007).

While the analyses supporting focalization in-situ must explain the cases where fronting remains marginally acceptable, the FocusP analyses á la Rizzi (1997) positing a left-peripheral FocusP projection face an even harder task in explaining the high grammaticality of in-situ focalization. These analyses maintain that contrastively focused phrases obligatorily raise to the specifier of FocusP for interpretative reasons, with fronting corresponding to structures where movement is visible (i.e. occurring before spell-out) and in-situ focalization corresponding to structures where movement is covert (i.e. post spell-out), or, as in Bianchi (2019), assuming that fronting precedes spell-out but it is followed by the deletion of the specFocusP copy. Crucially, under all of these analyses, the processing load of the in-situ constructions would appear at best identical and at worst higher than the processing load of their fronted counterparts, thus offering no explanation for why the in-situ option is preferred by native speakers across all contexts.

5.2 Fronting across different exchanges

The experiment shows that fronting under closed questions is significantly more grammatical than under open questions, where, in turn, it is significantly more grammatical than in corrective exchanges. These results raise three questions: (i) why fronting in open question exchanges emerges as grammatical against widely held expectations; (ii) why fronting in corrective exchanges is assessed as marginally grammatical at best and less grammatical than under open questions, again against widely held expectations; (iii) whether the experiment provided sufficient information to empirically test the analyses of contrast in Neeleman and Vermeulen (2012) and Krifka (2008) as originally planned.

Starting with question (i), the assumption that contrast-induced focus fronting should not occur in open question exchanges is rooted in Rizzi's (1997) and Belletti's (2001, 2004) seminal papers on Italian focalization, with Rizzi's examining contrast-induced focus fronting in the left-periphery, and Belletti's analysing non-contrastive focalization located between T and VP. Together, these papers suggested a division of labour with contrastive focus targeting the left-periphery and non-contrastive focus targeting a lower region within TP.

Hard evidence for the unavailability of focus fronting in open question exchanges is hard to come by. On the contrary, there are multiple experimental results that attest the presence of focus fronting under open questions. They include the fronting of non-contrastive object foci in Southern Peninsular Spanish in Jiménez-Fernández (2015a), the higher frequency of focus fronting under open questions when measured against fronting under corrective exchanges in Catalan in Feldhausen and Vanrell Bosch (2014) – a result very similar to those reported in this paper for British English – and, finally, the experimental results reported in Skopeteas and Fanselow

(2011) about the interpretation of fronted object foci in open question exchanges across Hungarian, German, Spanish, and Greek.

The latter study shows that in German, Spanish, and Greek fronted objects can be interpreted contrastively even when occurring in replies to open questions, with contrast interpreted as excluding focus-induced alternatives as in Neeleman and Vermeulen's definition. Skopeteas and Fanselow propose an interesting reason for why fronting might be available in open questions exchanges. Under their analysis, open questions remain associated with non-contrastive focalization. However, speakers may nevertheless reply with a marked structure – namely focus fronting – to signal a marked interpretation, namely a contrastive one. Put differently, open questions do not themselves license contrastive focalization in their replies, but they do not disallow it either. If correct, the relatively high 3.82 average score assigned to fronting under open questions in our experiment would reflect the presence of participants that chose to interpret fronted replies in these exchanges as grammatical because they are potentially licensed by a contrastive interpretation.

Once coupled with Neeleman and Vermeulen's definition of contrast, Skopeteas and Fanselow's (2011) analysis also accounts for the higher average assigned to fronting in closed questions (3.97) relative to open questions (3.82). If closed questions license contrast as proposed by Neeleman and Vermeulen, and contrast licenses fronting, then fronting is necessarily more natural under closed questions, where it is inevitably present, than under open questions, where its presence is dependent on the choice of individual speakers to allow a contrastive interpretation rather than mandated by the discourse context. Since the same cannot be said under Krifka's analysis where closed questions do not license contrast, these experimental results offer some support to Neeleman and Vermeulen's analysis of contrast.

Question (ii), seeking the reason for the marginal grammaticality of fronting in corrective exchanges, is the most difficult. Here, we can only offer two hypotheses that need further research.

The first hypothesis concerns the possible presence of two grammars across speakers of British English, one allowing for focus fronting in corrective exchanges and the other disallowing it (on the availability of micro parametrization in relation to focus fronting, albeit in Spanish varieties, see Jiménez–Fernández 2015b). If this were the case, the participants' judgements for fronting in corrective exchanges should cluster into two groups, with participants that disallow fronting returning relatively low grammaticality values and those allowing for fronting relatively higher values. As shown by the histogram in Figure 5, the average values assigned by the 101 participants across the 12 stimuli involving fronting in corrective exchanges provides some initial support to this hypothesis, as they appear to cluster in two groups, one in the 1.5–3.0 range, assessing fronting as marginally ungrammatical, and the other, less numerous, in the 4.5–5.0 range, assessing fronting as marginally grammatical.

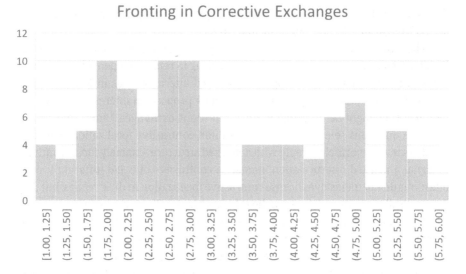

Figure 5: Number of participants with similar mean value for the 12 stimuli involving fronting under corrective exchanges.

As suggested by an anonymous reviewer, the same clusters would also be expected to be absent for the in-situ responses of corrective exchanges, which again would appear to be the case on inspection of the corresponding histogram provided in Figure 6.

The second hypothesis exploits the adverse impact of processing on naturalness assessments discussed in section 5.1 above. Corrective exchanges are the most processing intense amongst those tested because corrections require speakers to withdraw the proposition being corrected from the Common Ground and replace it with a new correct one (van Leusen 2004). If processing effort adversely affects naturalness judgements, then it would affect the judgements for corrective exchanges the most due to their heavier processing load, providing a potential explanation for the observed low grammaticality judgements when compared with the other exchanges. If this effect is real, it should be controlled for during the experiment design phase with the goal of teasing apart the effects of processing from those of grammaticality. Adding stimuli that are certainly ungrammatical while less likely to involve heavy processing would provide a helpful point of comparison.

Finally, let us consider question (iii), concerning the analyses of contrast in Krifka (2008) and Neeleman and Vermeulen (2012). The experimental results appear only partially informative. On the one hand, focus fronting appears most natural in closed question exchanges, a result that taken in isolation supports the definition of contrast in Neeleman and Vermeulen (2012), since only their definition allows for

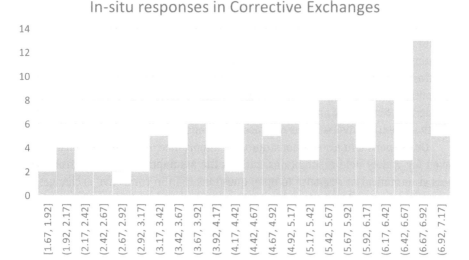

Figure 6: Number of participants with similar mean value for the 12 stimuli involving in-situ responses under corrective exchanges.

contrast – and hence optional fronting – to be licensed in these exchanges for the reason explained in section 2. Furthermore, in the discussion of question (i) above we saw how Neeleman and Vermeulen's analysis can combine with Skopeteas and Fanselow's (2011) insights to provide an account for the occurrence of fronting in open questions exchanges.

However, even Neeleman and Vermeulen's analysis maintains that contrast is present in corrective exchanges, a fact not confirmed by the experimental results. As discussed above in relation to question (ii), only a better understanding of the linguistic factors determining this outcome will determine whether Neeleman and Vermeulen's hypothesis remains valid, or whether it should be partly revised.

6 Conclusion

This paper reports the results of an experiment concerning the grammaticality of focus fronting in corrective and open/closed question exchanges in British English, while controlling for prosody as well as verbal tense and argument type (DP/PP, animate/inanimate).

Collectively, the 101 participants assessed (i) in-situ focalization as more natural than fronting across all exchanges, (ii) fronting in response to closed questions as more natural than under open questions, and (iii) fronting in response to open questions as more natural than in corrective statements. As explained in section 5, there are reasons to interpret these results as potential evidence for (i) an in-situ analysis of contrastive focalization, (ii) the availability of contrast-induced fronting even in response to open questions whenever speakers wish to convey a contrastive interpretation as per Skopeteas and Fanselow (2011), (iii) the definition of contrast proposed by Neeleman and Vermeulen (2012) where contrast conveys the denial of one of the alternative propositions evoked by focalization, and, finally, (iv) the potential adverse effect of processing loads on grammaticality assessments.

Our experiment also demonstrates the importance of running empirical tests even for widely held assumptions, such as the assumption that focus fronting is less grammatical in response to open questions than in corrective exchanges, an assumption refuted by our results.

References

Abe, Jun. 2016. Make short answers shorter: Support for the in situ approach. *Syntax* 19(3). 223–255.

Anwyl-Irvine, Alexander, Jessica Massonnié, Adam Flitton, Natasha Kirkham & Jo Evershed. 2020. Gorilla in our midst: An online behavioral experiment builder. *Behavior Research Methods* 52(1). 388–407.

Audacity Team. 2014. Audacity (Version 2.0.6.) [computer program]. https://www.audacityteam.org/

Belletti, Adriana. 2001. 'Inversion' as focalization. In Aafke Hulk & Jean Yves Pollock (eds.), *Subject Inversion in Romance and the Theory of Universal Grammar*, 60–90. Oxford: Oxford University Press.

Belletti, Adriana. 2004. Aspects of the low IP area. In Luigi Rizzi (ed.), *The Structure of CP and IP. The Cartography of Syntactic Structures*, Vol. 2, 16–51. Oxford: Oxford University Press.

Bianchi, Valentina. 2013. On 'focus movement' in Italian. In Maria Victoria Camacho, Ángel Jiménez-Fernández, Javier Martín-González & Mariano Reyes-Tejedor (eds.), *Information Structure and Agreement*, 193–216. Amsterdam/Philadelphia: John Benjamins.

Bianchi, Valentina & Giuliano Bocci. 2012. Should I stay or should I go? Optional focus movement in Italian. In Christopher Piñón (ed.), *Empirical Issues in Syntax and Semantics* 9. 1–18. http://www.cssp.cnrs.fr/eiss9/

Bianchi, Valentina, Giuliano Bocci & Silvio Cruschina. 2015. Focus fronting and its implicatures. In Enoch Aboh, Amy Schaffer & Petra Sleeman (eds.), *Romance Languages and Linguistic Theory 2013: Selected papers from 'Going Romance' Amsterdam 2013*, Vol. 8, 1–20. Amsterdam: John Benjamins.

Bianchi, Valentina. 2019. Spelling out focus-fronting chains and wh-chains: The case of Italian. *Syntax* 22(2–3). 146–161.

Borise, Lena & Maria Polinsky. 2018. Focus without movement: Syntax-prosody interface in Georgian. *Proceedings of North2015-East Linguistic Society (NELS)* 48. https://lingbuzz.net/lingbuzz/004026

Breul, Carsten. 2007. Focus structure, movement to spec-foc and syntactic processing. In Kerstin Schwabe & Susanne Winkler (eds.), *On Information Structure, Meaning and Form: Generalizations across Languages*, 255–274. Amsterdam: Benjamins.

Brunetti, Lisa. 2004. *A Unification of Focus*. Padova: Unipress.

Büring, Daniel. 1997. *The Meaning of Topic and Focus*. London: Routledge.

Büring, Daniel. 2003. On d-trees, beans, and b-accents. *Linguistics and Philosophy* 26(5).
511–545.

Costa, João. 2013. Focus in situ: Evidence from Portuguese. In *From Syntax to Cognition. From Phonology to Text*, Vol. 1, 621–662. Berlin: Mouton De Gruyter.

Cruschina, Silvio. 2019. Focus fronting in Spanish: Mirative implicature and information structure. *Probus* 31(1). 119–146.

Cruschina, Silvio. 2021. The greater the contrast, the greater the potential: On the effects of focus in syntax. *Glossa: A Journal of General Linguistics* 6(1). 1–30.

Feldhausen, Ingo & Maria Del Mar Vanrell Bosch. 2014. Prosody, focus and word order in Catalan and Spanish: An optimality theoretic approach. In Susanne Fuchs, Martine Grice, Anne Hermes & Doris Mücke (eds.), *Proceedings of the 10th International Seminar on Speech Production (ISSP)*, 122–125. Köln: Universität Köln.

Frascarelli, Mara & Ángel Jiménez-Fernández. 2017. Subextraction at the discourse grammar interface: A featural approach to island effects. In Olga Fernández-Sorian, Elena Castroviejo & Isabel Pérez-Jiménez (eds.), *Boundaries, Phases, and Interfaces. Case Studies in Honor of Violeta Demonte*, 224–254. Amsterdam/Philadelphia: John Benjamins.

Frascarelli, Mara & Ángel Jiménez-Fernández. 2021. How much room for discourse in imperative? The lens of interface on English, Italian and Spanish. *Studia Linguistica* 75(3). 375–434.

Horvath, Julia. 2010. 'Discourse features', syntactic displacement and the status of contrast. *Lingua* 120(6). 1346–1369.

IBM Corp. 2020. IBM SPSS Statistics for Windows (Version 27.0). Armonk, New York: IBM Corp.

Jiménez-Fernández, Ángel. 2015a. When focus goes wild: An empirical study of two syntactic positions for information focus. *Linguistics: Beyond and Within (http://Lingbaw.Com)* 1. 119–133.

Jiménez-Fernández, Ángel. 2015b. Towards a typology of focus: Subject position and microvariation at the discourse-syntax interface. *Ampersand: An International Journal of General and Applied Linguistics* 2. 49–60.

Kenesei, István. 2006. Focus as identification. In Valéria Molnár & Susanne Winkler (eds.), *The Architecture of Focus*, 137–168. Berlin: Mouton de Gruyter.

Kiss, Katalin É. 1998. Identificational focus versus information focus. *Language* 74(2). 245–273.

Kolliakou, Dimitra. 2004. Monadic definites and polydefinites: Their form, meaning and use. *Journal of Linguistics* 40(2). 263–323.

Krifka, Manfred. 2008. Basic notions of information structure. *Acta Linguistica Hungarica* 55(3). 243–276.

Krifka, Manfred & Renate Musan. 2012. Information structure: Overview and linguistic issues. In Manfred Krifka & Renate Musan (eds.), *The Expression of Information Structure*, 1–44. (The Expression of Cognitive Categories 5). Berlin/Boston: De Gruyter Mouton.

Molnár, Valéria. 2002. Contrast – from a contrastive perspective. In Hilde Hasselgård, Stig Johansson, Bergljot Behrens & Cathrine Fabricius-Hansen (eds.), *Information Structure in a Crosslinguistic Perspective*, 147–161. Amsterdam: Rodopi.

Molnár, Valéria & Susanne Winkler (eds.). 2006. *The Architecture of Focus*. Berlin: Mouton de Gruyter.

Neeleman, Ad & Hans van de Koot. 2008. Dutch scrambling and the nature of discourse templates. *The Journal of Comparative Germanic Linguistics* 11(2). 137–189.

Neeleman, Ad & Reiko Vermeulen. 2012. The syntactic expression of information structure. In Ad Neeleman & Reiko Vermeulen (eds.), *The Syntax of Topic, Focus, and Contrast: An Interface-based Approach*, 1–38. Berlin/New York: Mouton de Gruyter.

Repp, Sophie. 2010. Defining 'contrast' as an information-structural notion in grammar. *Lingua* 120(6). 1333–1345.

Repp, Sophie. 2016. Contrast. In Caroline Féry & Ishihara Shinichiro (eds.), *The Oxford Handbook of Information Structure*, 270–289. Oxford: Oxford University Press.

Repp, Sophie & Philippa Cook (eds.). 2010. Contrast as an Information-Structural Notion in Grammar. [Special issue]. *Lingua* 120(6).

Rizzi, Luigi. 1997. The fine structure of the left periphery. In Liliane Haegeman (ed.), *Elements of Grammar: Handbook in Generative Syntax*, 281–337. Dordrecht: Kluwer.

Rizzi, Luigi. 2004. Locality and the left periphery. In Adriana Belletti (ed.), *Structures and Beyond: The Cartography of Syntactic Structures*, Vol. 3, 223–251. Oxford: Oxford University Press.

Rooth, Mats. 1985. *Association with Focus*. Amherst: University of Massachusetts at Amherst dissertation.

Rooth, Mats. 1992. A theory of focus interpretation. *Natural Language Semantics* 1(1). 75–116.

Rooth, Mats. 2016. Alternative Semantics. In Caroline Féry & Ishihara Shinichiro (eds.), *The Oxford Handbook of Information Structure*, 19–40. Oxford: Oxford University Press.

Sacks, Harvey, Emanuel A. Schegloff & Gail Jefferson. 1974. A simplest systematics for the organization of turn-taking for conversation. *Language* 50(4). 696–735.

Samek-Lodovici, Vieri. 2010. Final and non-final focus in Italian DPs. *Lingua* 120(4). 802–818.

Samek-Lodovici, Vieri. 2015. *The Interaction of Focus, Givenness, and Prosody. A Study of Italian Clause Structure*. Oxford: Oxford University Press.

Samek-Lodovici, Vieri. 2018. Contrast, contrastive focus, and focus fronting. In Ruoying Zhao & Yan Zhang (eds.), *UCL Working Papers in Linguistics 30*, 57–77. London: University College London.

Samek-Lodovici, Vieri. 2024. Focalization in-situ vs focus projection focused topics, focused questions, focused heads, and other challenges. In Dennis Ott & Ángel Gallego (eds.), *Cartography and Explanatory Adequacy*. Oxford: Oxford University Press.

Samek-Lodovici, Vieri & Karen Dwyer. 2022. *Experimental Testing of Focus Fronting in British English – Experimental Results and Audio Stimuli* [dataset]. London: University College London.

Schegloff, Emanuel A. & Harvey Sacks. 1973. Opening up closings. *Semiotica* 8(4). 289–327.

Skopeteas, Stavros & Gisbert Fanselow. 2010. Focus types and argument asymmetries. In Carsten Breul & Edward Göbbel (eds.), *Comparative and Contrastive Studies of Information Structure*, 169–198. Amsterdam: Benjamins.

Skopeteas, Stavros & Gisbert Fanselow. 2011. Focus and the exclusion of alternatives: On the interaction of syntactic structure with pragmatic inference. *Lingua* 121(11). 1693–1706.

Szendrői, Kriszta. 2010. A flexible approach to discourse-related word order variations in the DP. *Lingua* 120(4). 864–878.

van Leusen, Noor. 2004. Incompatibility in context: A diagnosis of correction. *Journal of Semantics* 21(4). 415–441.

Wagner, Michael. 2020. Prosodic focus. In Daniel Gutzmann, Lisa Matthewson, Cecile Meier, Hotze Rullmann & Thomas Zimmermann (eds.), *The Wiley Blackwell Companion to Semantics*, 1–64. Oxford: Wiley–Blackwell.

Wechsler, David. 1997 [1955]. *Wechsler Adult Intelligence Scale*, 3rd edn. San Antonio: The Psychological Corporation.

Zimmermann, Malte. 2007. Contrastive focus. In Gisbert Fanselow, Caroline Féry & Manfred Krifka (eds.), *The Notions of Information Structure*, Vol. 6, 147–160. Potsdam: Universitätverlag Potsdam.

Zimmermann, Malte. 2008. Contrastive focus and emphasis. *Acta Linguistica Hungarica* 55(3). 347–360.

Doriana Cimmino

3 Contrast and left dislocations: Contrastive discourse relations beyond contrastive topics

Abstract: Left Dislocations (LDs), described as topic-marking syntactic devices, are generally associated with contrastive topics. Less attention has been paid to contrast associated with their foci. The present chapter investigates the use(s) of LDs contrastive foci in actual texts, that is, LDs conveying contrast through non-topical linguistic material. The study is based on 200 LDs extracted from four diamesically and diaphasically varied corpora, namely DB-IPIC, KIPARLA, ICOCP, and NUNC, which are representative of different text types. In these corpora, LDs performing a contrastive discourse function are retrieved and described. The description of LDs discourse functions follows a multilevel analysis, based on a functional and textual approach. The features considered for analysis are the extension and type of foci, and the semantic and pragmatic effects produced in the text they occur in. Moreover, the exploitations of LDs contrastive function is observed in relation to the different text types represented in the corpora, to investigate their relationship with the context. The multilevel analysis reveals that LDs with contrastive foci are characterized by a predicate or a narrow focus and can be involved in contrastive, corrective or counter-expectative discourse relations, but also in simple contrast(s) between alternative referents, and between predicates or their polarity. The expression of contrast does not depend on LDs syntactic and informational traits, but on the semantic and pragmatic cues in the context. Indeed, LDs do not have the function to convey contrast, but to organize the text structure to highlight contrast. Finally, the analysis of text types reveals that diamesic and diaphasic variation does not impact the use of LDs with contrastive foci. The hypothesis is made that LDs with contrastive foci are typical of argumentative polemic stretches of text.

1 Introduction

Left Dislocations (henceforth LDs) are generally described as topic-marking constructions. This label refers both to their information structure, and to their discourse function. Their information structure is described as bipartite topic-comment pairs, in which the left dislocated constituent bears a topical information

https://doi.org/10.1515/9783110986594-003

function, while the rest of the structure bears a comment informational function (see, among others, Halliday 1967; Reinhart 1981; Lambrecht 1994, 2001).[1,2]

(1)   *The cake you baked* /*TOPIC* *I ate it* /*COMMENT*

At the discourse level, the topic-comment information partition can be exploited to introduce new topics or to shift the topic of conversation. See the classic example of topic shifting from Lambrecht (2001: 1074). Here the referent "veal" is presented as a new topic:

(2)   Husband and wife at the dinner table; H. looks at the food on his plate:
      H: *It has no taste, this chicken.*
      W: *Veal, it is worse.*
      (Lambrecht 2001: 1074)

In LDs, contrast can be associated with both topic and comment information units (even in the same utterance). It is well understood that, for example, the left dislocated constituents carrying the information function of topic can contrast with alternative topics in the discourse. Consider the authentic example in (3), in which the LD of an indirect object creates a contrast between the referent *a lei* 'to her' and another person the text refers to in the previous co-text.

(3)   *Invece **a lei** non **l'ha presa** come speaker.*
      'On the contrary, **her he didn't choose her** to be the speaker.'
      (Frascarelli and Hinterhölz 2007: 94)

The occurrence in (3) is an example of a contrastive topic, which can be defined as "an element that induces alternatives which have no impact on the focus value and creates oppositional pairs" to other topics (Frascarelli and Hinterhölz 2007: 87).[3]

Contrast in LDs can also be associated with the non-topical part of the structure, thus having an impact on the interpretation of the proposition and the prag-

---

1 The definition of categories such as topic-comment/topic-focus/theme-rheme is a highly debated issue in the literature. Here I do not delve into these distinctions; the definitions adopted in this paper will be clarified in the methods section (§ 2.2.1).
2 In all the examples, the phenomena under scrutiny are italicized, while bold may be used to highlight further linguistic material relevant to the analysis of the example. Superscripts report the information structure annotation.
3 For a functional approach to the description of Italian contrastive topics see Cresti (2000) and Ferrari (2003).

matic exploitation of the contrastive focus in context. The association between LDs foci and contrast is understudied in the literature, at least in Romance languages (Cimmino and Panunzi 2017, for Italian; Garassino and Jacob 2018, for Romance languages; also Huddleston and Pullum 2002 for English).[4]

Cimmino and Panunzi (2017) point out that LDs can highlight contrastive discourse relations both in speech and writing. In the following example, extracted from a daily newspaper, they show that the LD *italiano non lo è diventato* 'Italian he did not become one' packages the information[5] to highlight the opposition discourse relation between Mohamed's aspiration to acquire Italian citizenship (*I bambini nati in Italia hanno l'aspirazione di essere italiani* 'Children born in Italy aspire to be Italian') and the fact that, in reality, he did not become Italian.

(4) *"I bambini nati in Italia hanno l'aspirazione di essere italiani", ha detto il president Napolitano. Mohamed Hosny Abou Warda era uno di loro e* **italiano** $/^{TOP}$ **non lo è diventato** $/^{COM}$
"'Children born in Italy aspire to be Italian", said the president Napolitano. Mohamed Hosny Abou Warda was one of them and **Italian** $/^{TOP}$ **he did not become one** $/^{COM,6}$
(Cimmino and Panunzi 2017: 168)

What emerges from Cimmino and Panunzi's (2017) study is that, in given contexts, LDs can contrast their non-topical portion with the previous or following co-texts. Hence, they can fulfill a contrastive discourse function without playing a key role in the topical organization of the text of occurrence, but in the logical relations and coherence of the text.[7] In their data, the contrastive function is found to be typical of spoken texts and rarely exploited in written (journalistic, in the study) prose.

Garassino and Jacob (2018) investigate how polarity focus is used in Romance languages, mainly based on formal spoken language (*Direct Europarl*, collecting

---

4 Please note that, even though they do not directly speak about contrast in LDs, some scholars acknowledge the repercussions of left dislocated constituent displacement on the focal part of the structure. Benincà, Salvi, and Frison (1988: 134) observe that "The dislocation of the direct object is favored when the verb itself constitutes the information focus, [. . .]". In the same direction, Ferrari et al. (2008: 214) highlight that LDs can be exploited in texts to shift the left dislocated constituent from its default position at the end of the utterance "possibly leaving it free for a different constituent.".
5 With the expression 'information packaging' I refer to Chafe (1976).
6 The translations provided in English are literal and mimic the Italian syntax to show the linear syntactic order of LDs constituents.
7 To my knowledge, this is the first analysis dedicated to this aspect in Italian LDs. However, see already Simone (1997) and Andorno and Crocco (2018) on polarity contrast in right dislocations.

speeches held by members of the European Parliament, Cartoni and Meyer 2012).[8] They claim that clitic LDs, in given contexts, can bring about a polarity focus interpretation. In particular, "in contexts presenting a given or inferable antecedent proposition" LDs realize a "focalization of the predicate" (Garassino and Jacob 2018: 237, note 13). As shown in (5), the predicate and its direct object *troviamo una soluzione* 'we find a solution' are already given in the text due to the preceding proposition *dobbiamo trovare una soluzione* 'we must find a solution'. This allows for a focalization of the polarity of the verb, assessing the truth of the proposition.

(5) A: *No, niente, eh, dobbiamo trovare una soluzione.*
     'Nothing, well, we must find a solution.'
     B: *Ah va be', **la soluzione gliela troviamo.***
     'Ah well, **the solution, we're going to find it**.'
     (LIP corpus, in Garassino and Jacob 2018: 228)

Garassino and Jacob (2018) note that at the discourse level the polarity reading codified by LDs may be exploited to cancel implied or expressed expectations in the text. According to the study, the connection between LDs and the encoding of a polarity focus lies in the framing function performed by the structure.

In the present chapter, I further investigate the contrastive discourse function of Italian LDs associated with their foci. Exclusively considering the non-topical portion of the structure allows the observation of contrastive discourse functions performed by LDs beyond the widely studied contrastive topics. I use data extracted from a diamesically and diaphasically varied data basis, to describe the extension and type of foci associated with Italian LDs expressing contrast in their non-topical part (henceforth contrastive foci LDs). Data show that Italian LDs can convey different types of contrast, which directly depend on the context and not on LD inherent syntactic, informational or functional features (contra Garassino and Jacob 2018). I show that in the data observed, there is a weak association between contrast and LDs overall and no direct association with diamesic or diaphasic variation (contra Cimmino and Panunzi 2017). I finally claim that contrastive foci LDs which perform a contrastive discourse function are often associated with polemic stretches of text.

The remainder of the chapter is structured as follows. Section 2 is concerned with the empirical and theoretical tools used in the study. The approach used for the description of LDs discourse function, and, in particular, the definition of LD used for

---

8 Their definition of polarity focus is the following: "The term polarity focus [. . .] covers a range of linguistic phenomena of prosodic, lexical and syntactic nature which convey an emphasis on the positive polarity of a proposition." (Garassino and Jacob 2018: 228).

the corpus search are clarified in §2.1; the definition of contrastive discourse function in relation to LDs, along with other preliminary concepts necessary for the data analysis, are provided in §§ 2.2 and 2.3. In Section 3, the corpora selected, and the data used for the study are presented. The data analysis is reported and discussed in §§ 4 and 5. Section 4 focuses on the general phenomenology of contrastive foci LDs, providing a description of the extension and type of foci, and a discussion of the association of contrast with LDs. Section 5 describes the variation throughout the different corpora, showing that the diamesic and diaphasic variation does not impact the use of contrastive foci LDs. I make the hypothesis that contrastive foci LDs are associated with polemic stretches of text. Section 6 summarizes the main results of the study.

2 Methods

2.1 Empirical tools

In Italian literature, the label *dislocazione a sinistra* 'left dislocation (LD)' has been used as a cover term for various kinds of marked structures. For example, among other traits, the issue is discussed whether to include the presence of the resumptive pronoun in the definition (Benincà, Salvi, and Frison 1988; Rizzi 1997; Ferrari 2003; Ferrari et al. 2008). The very definition of the phenomenon is significantly affected by the theoretical perspective assumed for its description, mainly whether syntactic or functional (see, e.g., Antinucci and Cinque 1977; Berruto 1985; Berretta 2002; Frascarelli 2003).[9]

In this chapter, the theoretical perspective assumed is functional, with particular attention to the dimension of the text; however, and precisely because of this, the definition adopted only takes into account syntactic traits (although with no reference to Generative theories). A functional definition would bias the informational and textual analysis.

The definition used for the corpus search is the following:

> LDs are syntactic structures in which a canonically post-verbal constituent appears in a pre-verbal position and is reduplicated by a clitic co-referential pronoun.

The corpus search was conducted semiautomatically on corpora of spoken and written Italian (described in §3). The corpora were automatically searched for the clitic pronouns *ne, ci, la, lo, le, li, gli, mi, ti/te, vi*, and their elided forms *c', l', m', t', v'*.

---

9 For an overview of the definitory issues of Italian LDs, also compared to English LDs, see Cimmino (2017).

The occurrences retrieved were then manually checked. This kind of query allows the collection of LDs characterized by dislocated constituents carrying different syntactic forms, namely Noun Phrase (6), Prepositional Phrase (7), Adjective Phrase (8), and Clause (9), in the different functions of argumental constituents, that is Direct or Indirect Objects.

(6) NP: *La torta l'ho mangiata.*
    'The cake I ate it.'

(7) PP: *A Maria, le ho regalato dei fiori.*
    'To Maria, I gave flowers to her.'

(8) AdjP: *Bello non lo è.*
    'Beautiful, he is not it.'

(9) C: *Che è sempre saggio lo sappiamo tutti.*
    'That he is always wise we all know it.'

The query based on clitic pronouns does not identify Subject LDs, since the pronoun system of Italian does not have subject clitic pronouns for their resumption.[10] In Italian literature, subject LDs are identified through resumptive tonic pronouns, and/or the presence of linguistic material between the dislocated constituent and the rest of the clause (Benincà, Salvi, and Frison 1988), like the constituents in bold in (10) and (11) respectively. Prosodic breaks between the dislocated constituent and the rest of the clause can also be reliable hints of dislocated subjects (for an overview of the defining features of subject dislocation, see De Cesare 2014).

(10) *Maria, lei non è mai d'accordo con Carlo.*
     'Maria, **she** never agrees with Carlo.'

(11) *Giuseppe, la verdura, la mangia di rado.*
     'Giuseppe, **vegetables**, he eats them rarely.'

Other scholars (Duranti and Ochs 1979; Berruto 1986; Simone 1997) maintain that, having a different resumptive strategy, Italian subject LD cannot be directly compared with object LD. For this paper, I chose to follow the latter line of thinking.

---

10 This is true for the standard variety of Italian, while several dialects do have a clitic resumption for the subject (Rohlfs 1968).

2.2 Theoretical tools

The occurrences collected were analyzed following a multilevel method for the analysis of LDs discourse functions. The method was first developed for the analysis of two Italian and English Left Marked Structures (LMSs) in written texts, namely, LDs and Preposings (Cimmino 2017), and subsequently fine-tuned for the analysis of LMSs in both written and spoken Italian (Cimmino and Panunzi 2017) and in a cross-linguistic perspective (Cimmino 2023).[11] Following this method, the discourse functions of the collected LDs are described looking at possible interactions of their syntactic, informational, and textual features in context. A crucial tenet of the method is indeed that discourse functions must be investigated taking into account not only the syntactic and informational features of the occurrences, but above all their interactions with the text of occurrence. LDs discourse functions are conceived as acting beyond the utterance, and in particular on the organization of the text.[12] Thus, if the utterance is defined as "the counterpart of the accomplishment of a single speech act" (Cresti 2020: 185), LDs not only concern the utterance, but also the discourse as a whole. Another main assumption is that the syntactic, informational, and textual features must be investigated separately, to guarantee a rigorous description of their mutual interaction and of their preferential associations in the context of occurrence. Here, I exclusively touch upon aspects relevant to the description of LDs contrastive discourse function. The reader is referred to the aforementioned studies for further details.

2.2.1 LD topic-comment information partition

As clarified in the introduction, here I focus exclusively on the contrastive functions of LDs looking at the non-topical portion of the structures. In what follows, I provide details on their information partition. LDs may – but, crucially, also may not – show a topic-comment information partition at the utterance level, as in the following example (12):

---

[11] The approach is inspired by two corpus-driven and bottom-up theoretical frameworks for the segmentation of spoken and written discourse, namely the Language into Act Theory (L-ACT) (Cresti 2000; Cresti and Moneglia 2010) and the Basel Model for the segmentation of written discourse (Ferrari et al. 2008; Ferrari 2014). These theoretical models have been firstly conceived for the description of Italian, then applied to European languages and beyond.

[12] For the concept of organization of the text, I refer to the Basel Model for the segmentation of discourse (Ferrari et al. 2008), as a multilayered architecture governed by semantico-pragmatic principles.

(12) *nella società/*[TOP] *ci sto per conquistare la gente* alla battaglia per il social-ismo/[COM]

'in the society/[TOP] (I)'m there to win people over to the battle for socialism/[COM]'

(modified from DB-IPIC, ipubcv01, 126)

The left dislocated constituent *nella società* 'in the society' constitutes the topic information unit of the utterance, while the resumptive clitic pronoun *ci* 'there' and the rest of the structure fill the comment information unit. In this study, I adopt a pragmatic definition of topic (Hockett 1958; Cresti 2000). The 'pragmatic topic' (henceforth TOP, as in Cresti 2000) is the optional information unit that defines the illocutionary and/or textual relevance domain of the comment. When present, TOP provides sufficient information to the interpretation of the illocutionary act; as such, it allows a displacement from the immediate context of utterance (Cresti and Moneglia 2018). Indeed, the comment could be interpreted in isolation from the context, following the guidance provided by the TOP, without explicit reference to referents or events external to the immediate context and co-text of the utterance.

The comment is the necessary and sufficient information unit realizing a speech act; therefore, utterances could be constituted of the sole comment unit (henceforth COM). COMs carry the illocutionary force of the utterance, which can be identified and classified based on prosodic cues (Cresti 2020). The classification of the illocutionary classes' main types is based on the affective disposition of the speaker towards the addressee and on the resulting relationship with him/her. Differently from previous approaches, illocution is not conceived of as the attitude of the speaker towards his/her own utterance (Bally 1950), and it is not translatable in a locative act characterized by a performative verb (Searle 1969). The identification and classification of illocution are based on the observation of large corpora of spoken language, primarily Italian, and then confronted cross-linguistically (Cresti 2005, 2017, 2018). For the sake of brevity, I do not provide the details of the classification, referring the reader to the aforementioned literature. However, for the purposes of the present study, it is worth defining the illocutionary act of contrast. In the L-AcT classification, contrast at the illocutionary level is conceived as a specific expression of the speaker's beliefs. It is not the result of reasoning but of a moral "disagreement with the interlocutor" combined with "a manifestation of annoyance and disappointment" (Cresti 2005: 10).

I follow the Language into Act Theory for the definition of Focus as well. According to L-AcT, focus coincides with the pragmatic domain of the COM, more precisely, it constitutes its semantic apex within the boundaries of its pragmatic domain. Prosodically, the focus signals a prominence through a "perceptually relevant F0 movement" or a "lengthening of the syllables" (Cresti 2011: 72). The syntactic form of the prototypical focus is a verb form; however, as I will show in § 4.2, in LDs the focus of the structure often coincides with a noun, which may carry the syntactic function of subject. Above all, differently from other functional definitions of focus (see e.g. Krifka 2007), in this study focus is not conceived of as a Common Ground management device or as the content answering a question under discussion in the given context. Focus as conceived here is considered within the functional domain of the illocutionary force of the utterance, not in the management of the co-text. Indeed, the completion of an action has "its origin in the speakers' thoughts and in the affective dynamics among speakers" (Cresti 2011: 67) and not in the coherence of the text. Consistently, the description of the contrastive discourse function is carried out keeping the semantic, informational, and textual levels of analysis distinct.

2.2.2 LD contrastive discourse function

I assume contrast to be a semantic relationship of opposition standing between items of the same type.[13] The opposition can involve referents, as well as predicates or their specific semantic traits; also, it can involve pragmatic units, such as TOPs and COMs, that is the domain and carrier of the illocutionary force of the utterance, respectively (§ 2.2.1 above). In simpler terms, I will describe all the occurrences of contrastive foci LDs involved in the expression of a semantic relationship of opposition. This semantic relationship involves the necessity to correct, restrict, or (partially) deny previous linguistic material (following a.o. Halliday 1967; Chafe 1976). The contrasted linguistic material occurring in the left co-text may not be explicitly encoded, but implicitly conveyed; in particular, the latter would be the case of the "denying of an assumption" (Lang 2000), conveying a counter-expectative relation.

A crucial aspect of the description of LDs functions is the textual perspective. As already clarified above (§2.2), the analysis of LDs discourse functions is carried out looking not only at their syntactic and informational traits but also at their impact on the organization of the text. To determine what function LDs perform, I look at the relation between LD linguistic material (for this study, the linguistic material filling the COM) and the left and right co-texts in its text of occurrence. In contrastive foci LDs, the linguistic material filling the COM corrects, restricts, or partially denies previous or ensuing linguistic material in the text. The analysis of contrastive foci LD function(s) is by no means linked to a priori defined prosodic, syntactic, or informational traits.

---

13 I follow the most widespread view that contrast is an "orthogonal notion of information structure that can be associated with foci and topics" (see Cruschina 2021: 3 and references cited therein). For a reflection on the units to be considered in contrastive relations see Dimroth (2002).

The same approach is taken to reconstruct the superset of alternatives of contrastive foci in LDs. The alternatives are reconstructed starting from the semantic and pragmatic cues provided by the focus and the text. This allows it to transparently reflect the reconstruction of alternatives by the hearer, instead of presupposing a question under discussion in the text (contra Krifka 2007).

3 Corpora and data

3.1 Corpora variation

The study is based on 200 LDs extracted from four corpora, namely DB-IPIC, KIPARLA, ICOCP, and NUNC (described below in detail §§ 3.1.1, 3.1.2). This corpora selection allows for a diamesic (spoken/written) and diaphasic (formal/informal) variation, represented by different text types (informative/argumentative). In particular, the degree of formality and the text type analyses are based both on an overall evaluation of the communicative contexts and settings, and on the examination of every single occurrence. A thorough description of each occurrence is necessary, since, for example, formal occurrences could be found in informal stretches of texts (see on this point §3.1.2), as well as argumentative passages in informative texts (see §5).

The three parameters of variation considered allow for a systematic investigation of LDs discourse functions. Indeed, Italian LDs can be used both in spoken and written language (Berruto 1985), with significant differences between the discourse functions exploited in the two media (Ferrari 2003; Cimmino and Panunzi 2017). Moreover, the quantitative results provided by Garassino and Jacob (2018) show that LDs marking a contrast on polarity are rare in formal spoken language, while Cimmino and Panunzi (2017) show that LDs highlighting contrastive illocutionary acts are often found in informal spoken language. Hence, these insights from the literature indicate that the diamesic variation may be crucial for the observation of contrastive foci LDs as well, and that discrepancies may also lie in the diaphasic variation.

3.1.1 Spoken corpora

Both corpora of spoken Italian used for the analysis are representative of spontaneous speech, as they are collections of spontaneous conversations not guided by interviewers or specific activities. The communicative contexts are both private and public, monologic and dialogic. Some examples of communicative settings are narratives of holidays, friends making a cake, friends talking about private life (for informal communicative events), political speeches, university lessons, and discussions during office hours (for the formal ones). Both corpora thus allow for a rich diaphasic variation.

DB-IPIC (DataBase for Information Patterning Interlinguistic Comparison, Panunzi and Gregori 2012) is a multilingual online resource for spontaneous spoken language, including Italian, Brazilian Portuguese, and Castilian Spanish. For the present study, the Italian corpus, amounting to 124'735 words, was considered. All the occurrences of LD found in the corpus have been used for the analysis. Also, the pragmatic annotation by information categories following the Language into Act Theory (Cresti 2000) was used for the analysis.

KIParla (Mauri et al. 2019) is an online corpus for spontaneous spoken Italian and is representative of different regional and societal varieties, amounting to approximately one million tokens. The query interface allows for fine-grained research of communicative contexts. I selected public formal conversations, including, for example, university exams, lessons, and office conversations. The selection of this specific diamesic variety was motivated by the necessity to enlarge the data basis for formal spontaneous speech of DB-IPIC. I only considered the first 19 LD occurrences retrieved in the corpus search; that is, a sufficient number of examples to balance the base of spoken data for the analysis. I annotated the data by information categories following L-AcT.

3.1.2 Written corpora

The written section of the data basis considered portrays a standard formal and informal variety of Italian. ICOCP-QOL is representative of the journalistic prose of online newspapers, while NUNC represents the informal side of the online language.

ICOCP-QOL consists of texts extracted from Italian daily online newspapers, with a total amount of 260'000 words, taken from a comparable corpus of written online news (Cimmino 2017; De Cesare et al. 2016)[14] which also includes German, French, and Spanish sub-corpora. The journalistic articles collected in the ICOCP-QOL were published on the official websites of the most circulated national newspapers and were extracted from various thematic sections, such as the national and international news, business, politics, sports, society, and culture sections of *repubblica.it*,

---

[14] An updated and searchable version of the ICOCP-QOL corpus is available at contrast-it.philhist. unibas.ch (De Cesare 2019).

corriere.it, and *lastampa.it*. I considered all the occurrences found with the corpus query described in §2.1. The language represented is considered formal standard Italian, both when it occurs in the news or in reported speech and interviews contained in the news. In agreement with McLaughlin (2011: 210), I consider reported speech in the news a "representation" of the spoken word in writing, that is a form of oral language adapted to the standard written variety of newspapers.

NUNC (*Newsgroup UseNet Corpora*, Barbera 2013) is a huge collection of newsgroups written texts drawn from public web forums, amounting to 600 million words and representative of the genre in Italian, English, French, German and Spanish. I only considered a limited subsection of Italian texts amounting to 100'000 words. The language represented by this kind of texts is an informal standard (but also often substandard) variety. The communicative context is characterized by short monologues or (often) asynchronous conversations by the users, arguing about several different topics (informatics, cinema, music, etc.).

3.2 Data used for the analysis

The data used for the analysis were extracted from the corpora selected based on the definition and the query words detailed in §2.1. The absolute number of occurrences retrieved, and the parameters of variation considered are summarized in Table 1.[15]

Table 1: Number of LDs and their parameters of variation.

variation	spoken	written
formal	49 (public)	54 (newspapers)
informal	51 (private)	46 (web groups)
total	100	100

4 Contrastive discourse function in Italian LDs

Based on the method outlined in 2.2, I identified 36 occurrences of contrastive foci LDs performing a contrastive discourse function. Out of 200 LDs retrieved in the data extracted from the corpora selected, less than 20% convey a semantic relation-

---

15 The data considered in the present chapter partially overlap with those used in Cimmino and Panunzi (2017). More precisely here I use data from the DB-IPIC and ICOCP corpora.

ship of opposition, correcting, restricting, or (partially) denying previous linguistic material in their COM portion. Overall, there is a weak association between contrast and LD foci.

Cimmino and Panunzi (2017: 161–162) claim that in their spoken data, contrastive LDs often fulfill the function of "highlighting a counter-assertive illocutionary act". This would be typical of LDs expressing contrast in the COM information unit, which partake in the construction of the logical connections of the text of occurrence. For example, in the dialogue in (13), speakers *PAO and *ROS are discussing what strategy is better to convince migrants to become members of their party.

(13) *PAO: *gli vado a leggere un versetto della Bibbia* /^{COM} *a un immigrato* ?
       'Do I read a biblical verse/ ^{COM} to a migrant?'
       *ROS: < ***a un immigrato*** > /^{TOP} ***gli dico quello che penso*** /^{COM} Paola //
       '**to a migrant** /^{TOP} **I will say him what I think** /^{COM} Paola //'
       (DB-IPIC, ipubcv01, 279–280, taken from Cimmino and Panunzi 2017: 162)

*PAO asks *ROS if the best option is to read them a biblical verse. The question is ironic since the political association they both adhere to is a quasi-extremist left-wing party. *ROS argues that he would be sincere; so he does not appreciate the irony of his interlocutor, shifting to a completely different approach. It is precisely through an illocutionary act of contrast,[16] packaged in the form of an LD, that the shifting to the new approach is codified. The LD is thus textually exploited to highlight the contrastive relation between the illocutionary acts produced by the two speakers. More precisely, the left dislocated constituent *a un immigrato* 'to a migrant', codified in the TOP information unit, acts as a cohesive device, signaling the relevant turn with which the contrast is established. Moreover, it leaves the focal part of the utterance free for the contrastive part of the utterance. The focal part of the utterance, *gli dico quello che penso* 'I will say him what I think', is uttered in direct opposition to the COM unit of the preceding dialogic turn *gli vado a leggere un versetto della Bibbia?* 'do I read a biblical verse to (a migrant)?'. The contrast produced is hence expressed at the logical level, while the TOP of the text remains constant.

I completely agree with Cimmino and Panunzi (2017) when they claim that these kinds of LDs highlight the contrast produced in the text, playing a role in its logical dimension. However, from the analysis of the data I used for this study it emerges that not all the LDs conveying contrast on the focal part of the utterance

---

16 Cimmino and Panunzi (2017) follow Cresti (2020) for the classification of illocutionary types. See here §2.2.1 for a brief description of the model of classification.

are characterized by a predicate focus.[17] In some cases, the contrast is produced towards a narrower portion of the COM, such as a referent occurring in the final position, or in the sole predicate of the structure (see §§ 4.1 and 4.2). A different extension of the focus produces different pragmatic effects in the text, causing the kind of LDs under examination not to play a role in the logical dimension of the text. It is thus worth keeping the two aspects distinct; first investigating the extension of the focus in the LD, that is, the linguistic material involved in the contrastive relation, and then the type of focus, like the pragmatic effects produced in the text of occurrence. As for the extension of focus, in the data I analyzed, the information partition prosodically encoded by LDs rules out a broad focus guiding the listener toward a predicate (14 occurrences out of 36) or a narrow focus (22 occurrences). That is to say that with Italian LDs with a topic-comment partition[18] the extension of the focal part is generally to be interpreted either in the verb, or in the post-verbal focal position, or the verb and the post-verbal position.[19] I will now show the case of LDs conveying predicate foci.

4.1 Contrastive foci LDs with predicate focus: Reconstructing discourse relations

Let us again consider (13) above, where the contrastive foci LD conveys a predicate focus. The presence of a predicate focus is proven by the fact that the pitch accent is on a constituent in an unmarked position and all the linguistic material filling the COM information unit is new in the text.[20] The nature of contrast conveyed by the structure in context is determined by the open set created in the text. The option *gli dico quello che penso* 'I will say him what I think' contrasts with the alternative antecedent *gli vado a leggere un versetto della Bibbia [. . .]?* 'Do I read him a biblical verse [. . .]?' and both are included in the set 'action to be taken to muster followers'. Based on the cues contained in the co-text, a contrastive discourse relation of

---

17 Here I adopt the label 'predicate focus' (as in Cruschina 2022: 5) to designate focus also involving the predicate and broad focus to signal the entire sentence.
18 It is not always the case that LDs have a topic-comment partition (on the issue cf. for Italian LDs Cresti 2000; Ferrari 2003; Cimmino 2023).
19 For an overview of the relationship between syntactic structures and focus in Romance Languages, see Cruschina (2022: 15).
20 Here I follow Lombardi Vallauri (2001: 229) in considering that a formal hint to analyze the extension of the focus in Italian is its position, whether marked or unmarked. Moreover, an informational hint is the givenness/newness of the linguistic material, which can determine what portion of the utterance is relevant in the interpretation of the focus with respect to the left co-text.

the corrective type can be reconstructed.[21] Indeed the two COM units are not just in simple opposition, as the speaker uttering the contrastive foci LDs argues for a cancellation of the content asserted by the interlocutor.

It is worth noticing that the expression and the reconstruction of the contrastive discourse relation are completely independent from the presence of the LD. Consider the manipulated version in (13'), where the LD is substituted with an SVO order of the constituents and the clitic resumption has been eliminated:

(13')   *PAO: *gli vado a leggere un versetto della Bibbia* $/^{COM}$ *a un immigrato* ?
        'Do I read a biblical verse/ ^{COM} to a migrant?'
        *ROS: **dico quello che penso a un immigrato** $/^{COM}$ **Paola //**
        '**I will say what I think to a migrant** $/^{COM}$ Paola //'

From a semantic point of view, a contrastive-corrective relation between the two predicates can still be reconstructed. However, from an informational point of view, the utterance appears unnatural, since the given information *a un immigrato* 'to a migrant' follows the new information expressed by the predicate (for the communicative dynamism of the utterance, Firbas 1971). For the same reason, a natural realization of the utterance would at least require a prosodic prominence on the contrasted predicate (dico quello che penso/ ^{COM} a un immigrato/ Paola//) producing an information partition after the predicate. Yet, the reason for this phenomenon is not to be found on the prosodic and information level, but on the impact an LD can have on the organization of the text. The key difference between (13) and (13') is indeed that the LD is able to signal textual prominences.[22] The two COM units in contrast include linguistic elements that need to be singled out from the rest of the utterance and the discourse since the discourse relation they convey is the most relevant at that given moment in the text. Due to the presence of an LD, the linguistic material in the COM units is isolated through the information partition and the predicate is displaced in a focal position. In other words, the LD produces a textual organization consistent with the relevance of the semantic discourse relation expressed by the text. The reorganization of linguistic material according to the semantico-pragmatic architecture of the text is precisely what I claim to be the general function of LDs.[23]

Going back to the type of discourse relations conveyed by contrastive foci LDs with a predicate focus, I found occurrences expressing not only corrective but

---

21 On the reconstruction of the discourse relations and the alternatives of the focus, see § 2.2.2.
22 For the definition of prominence, I refer to von Heusinger and Schumacher (2019).
23 For the impact of LDs on the organization of texts, cf. Cimmino 2023, §5.3.

also counter-expectative discourse relations, in the dataset analyzed. Consider the following passage extracted from the NUNC corpus of online informal prose (14). This text was produced in an online discussion on whether to go to a concert, or not. In the discussion, some web users argued against going, given the high price of the concert ticket and the low quality of the nightclub. The user that produced the LD under scrutiny is building a counterargument first acknowledging these standpoints, then affirming that he does not intend to forfeit the concert. The counter-argumentative sequence is constructed paratactically, due to its logico-grammatical complexity: in the concessive move, an argument in favor of the negative standpoints is produced, then a counter-expectative discourse marker introduces the speaker's personal view.[24]

(14) *Ti do pienamente ragione sugli apprezzamenti al locale, infatti è un pezzo che il Maffia è, diciamo, boicottato. Però* **questo concerto** /^{TOP} **non me lo perderei per nulla al mondo** /^{COM}.
'I fully agree with you about the comments on the nightclub, indeed it's been some time since the Maffia is, let's say, boycotted. But **this concert** /^{TOP} **I wouldn't miss it for anything in the world** /^{COM}.'
(NUNC)

The LD participates in this complex counter-argumentative discourse dynamic, highlighting the counter-expectative move. The LD produces a topic-comment partition separating the TOP *questo concerto* 'this concert' from the COM *non me lo perderei per nulla al mondo* 'I wouldn't miss it for anything in the world'. The information partition, similarly to the occurrence in (13), does not fulfill a topic-marking discourse function (§ 1), in fact the referent in TOP is used to anchor the COM to the ongoing discourse. The focal portion of the utterance is thus left free for the predicate, which is characterized by negative polarity, and for the adverbial phrase, which strengthens the negation. The focalization of the negative polarity and the reinforcing adverbial phrase highlight the counter-expectative contrastive relation overtly codified by *però* 'however'. The COM information unit including part of the LD is thus in contrast with a concessive dialogic move in a particularly complex counter-argumentative sequence. Again, as for the occurrence in (13), the LD exclusively plays a role in the organization of the text and not in the expression of the contrastive relation itself.

---

24 For a thorough description of Italian counter-argumentative sequences from a textual and grammatical point of view, see Calaresu (2022: 70) and the rich bibliography therein cited.

4.2 Contrastive foci LDs with a narrow focus and its alternatives

As mentioned in § 4 above, in the majority of the contrastive foci occurrences analyzed, LDs convey a narrow focus. These structures leave the rightmost position available for linguistic material which is contrasted with possible alternatives in the context of occurrence. In Italian, the constituents which potentially occupy the rightmost position in LDs are often the verb or the subject. Consider the canonical and non-canonical order examples below:

(15)   **(S)VO** *(Io) ho mangiato la torta di Maria.*
       'I ate Maria's cake'

(15a) **O(S)clV** *La torta di Maria l'ho mangiata.*
       'Maria's cake (I) ate it'

(15b) **OclVS** *La torta di Maria l'ho mangiata io.*
       'Maria's cake (I) ate it I'

In the O(S)clV version (15a), the verb constitutes the information focus (Benincà, Salvi, and Frison 1988: 134), while in the OclVS the focus is on the subject. Occasionally, even non-argumental constituents can occupy the rightmost position. In the data considered, the most frequent option is the narrow focus on a verb or part of the verb (11 occ. out of 22), while the subject (5 out 22) and the non-argumental constituents (6 out 22) occupy the narrow focus less frequently. Let us see how the contrastive relation is established with alternatives in the co-text, in all the syntactic configurations described above. Consider the example in (16), with the indirect locative object *in altri luoghi* 'in other places' contrasted with *al cinema* 'at the cinema'.

(16)   *Ripeto "donne per un mistero" ha (sic) me è risultato un film inopportuno, perché **il teatro lo si fa in altri luoghi** e non <u>al cinema</u>.*
       'I repeat "women for a mystery" to me turned out to be an inappropriate film, because **the theater it is done in other places** and not <u>at the cinema</u>.'
       (NUNC)

The narrow focus is exploited to build a corrective-contrastive relation between the two referents. The alternative that occupies the LD focus is the one chosen by the author of the text, while the alternative in the text is explicitly discarded through the negation adverb *non* 'not'. The discarded alternative is explicitly mentioned in the right co-text.

Similarly, in the following example, the narrow focus is exploited to contrast subject referents: *il pm* 'the prosecutor' and *noi* 'we'.

(17)   VL: *Embè, e che vantaggio ha il pm a riaprire le indagini, scusa?*
'And so, what advantage does the prosecutor have in reopening the investigation, sorry?'
GT: *No, **il vantaggio ce l'abbiamo noi** [. . .]*
'No, **the advantage we have it** [. . .]'
(ICOCP-QOL)

The contrastive relation is corrective, and the discarded alternative is explicit; however, differently from the example in (16), the discarded alternative is codified in the left co-text and then subsequently corrected by the focus of the LD. In both cases, the LD plays a role in the reconstruction of the contrastive relation. In (17) the left dislocated constituent *il vantaggio* 'the advantage' creates an anaphoric reference to the portion of text where the discarded alternative is explicitly codified. On the contrary, in (16) the left dislocated constituent *il teatro* 'the theatre' anchors the contrastive relation to the rest of the text. Therefore, in (16), the cohesive function of the LD does not directly partake in the reconstruction of the contrastive relation, which is instead explicitly signaled through the negation.

As seen in the invented example in (15a), narrow foci can also be codified on the verb. Consider the authentic example in (18) extracted from the public conversation section of the IPIC corpus. Teachers *GEB, *GEC and *MAA are discussing the composition of the next class committee. *GEB doubts that the president in charge at the time is willing to confirm his role. Specifically, he is insinuating that this will never happen. *GEC replies affirming that the president is willing to confirm his role, as he was answering a polar question, therefore, he does not recognize *GEB's argumentative attitude. On the contrary, *MAA apperceives the polemic nuance of *GEB's words and strongly rebuts his doubt, with a contrastive illocutionary act packaged in an informationally partitioned LD.

(18)   *GEB: *se il rappresentante tutt'ora in carica/ è [/1] è disposto a confermare l' incarico hhh / oppure < no > //*
'if the class president still in office/ is [/1] willing to confirm his role hhh / or < not > //'
*GEC: *[<] < sì > //*
'[<] < yes > //'
*GEC: *fino a marzo . . . /*
'until March. . . /'

*MAA: *la disponibilità* /^{TOP} *la dà* //^{COM}
'his willingness /^{TOP} he ensures it //^{COM}'
(DB-IPIC, ipubcv02, 36–39)

The example shows that when the narrow focus has scope over the verb the contrast may be played on the polarity of the assertion. The content of the LD uttered by the speaker *MAA has already been mentioned in speaker *GEB's previous dialogic turn; therefore, it would be under informative to repeat the same content. What *MAA is in fact conveying is that, contrary to *GEB's expectations, he commits to that content. In other words, while *GEB assumes that the class president in office is not willing to confirm his role, *MAA is convinced of the opposite. In complete agreement with Garassino and Jacob (2018), I analyze these occurrences as instances of LDs conveying a polarity focus.[25] As example (18) shows, at the discourse level, LDs conveying polarity foci can cancel or attenuate assumptions given in the text. Indeed, the focus of the structure corrects, restricts, or (partially) denies previous assertions. As the two authors clarify (Garassino and Jacob 2018: 238, note 13), this does not mean that LDs are structural means for expressing polarity focus. What they claim is that LDs "convey PF [polarity focus] by virtue of specific pragmatic and contextual properties, departing from their most typical functions" (Garassino and Jacob 2018: 235). The specific pragmatic and contextual properties allowing LDs to convey a polarity focus and their very existence are aspects worth discussing.[26]

Garassino and Jacob (2018: 230) claim that "the propositional content of a sentence containing PF [polarity focus] should be discourse given or inferable". Therefore, the LDs that convey a polarity focus will be entirely given or inferable, except for the polarity of the verb, which constitutes the (narrow) focus of the structure.[27] In the data analyzed for the present study, it is not always possible to reconstruct the preceding proposition which would allow the linguistic material of the LD to be at least inferable. The process of reconstruction does not only include explicit or implicit meaning conveyed by the text, but also the participants' background knowledge and their expectations, which are usually not codified in the text. Consider example (19), where a professor, *PRO, and a student, *STU, are meeting during office hours. The student reminds the professor that they need to agree upon what

---

25 Please note that in their work, Garassino and Jacob (2018) consider both informative and contrastive polarity focus, while I only consider contrastive cases.
26 For the sake of brevity, I will not be concerned here with the second claim about LD typical functions. As I argued in §4.1 above, I think that the general function of LDs is to signal textual prominences.
27 For an analysis of polarity focus as a narrow focus see Féry (2007).

book she needs to study for a future exam since she already sat a similar exam in the past. In an apparently incoherent dialogic move, the professor replies that the student must pass a written examination, packaging the information in an LD, with a contrastive illocutionary act.

(19) *STU: *io dovrei anche concordare con lei eh un libro alternativo perche' ho gia'
    fatto il master Itals*
    'I should also agree with you eh an alternative book because I have already
    done the master Itals'
    *STU: *e a Venezia Ca' Foscari*
    'and in Venice Ca' Foscari University'
    *PRO: *mh mh*
    'mh mh'
    *STU: *quindi avevo gia' parlato con lei due secondi e alla fine della lezione e mi
    aveva detto che*
    'so I had already spoken with you for two seconds and at the end of the lesson
    and you told me that'
    *STU: *qualora avessi gia'*
    'if I already had'
    *PRO: *allora **lei lo scritto** /^{TOP} **lo fa comunque** /^{COM} [. . .]*
    'so **the written part** /^{TOP} **you do that anyway** /^{COM} [. . .]'
    (KIParla)

Based on the actual text, it is impossible to reconstruct an implicit antecedent assertion, in which the student said something like *I do not want to do the written part of the exam*. Therefore, the contrastive illocutionary act and the polarity focus on the predicate conveyed by the LD can be explained only by accommodating[28] that the speaker (the professor in the example) anticipated a possible request from the interlocutor, exclusively based on her intuition. In a nutshell, the data retrieved in the corpora under examination in this study do not corroborate Garassino and Jacob's (2018) hypothesis of the inferrability of the antecedent and warn against the overgeneralization of this tendency.[29]

---

28 For brevity's sake, I do not further discuss this aspect, but by using the term 'accomodating' I do mean that polarity focus triggers the presupposition of an antecedent proposition relevant to its interpretation.

29 This is evident in spontaneous speech, in which the cohesion and coherence of texts profoundly differ from the overt signals of writing (see, among many others, de Beaugrande and Dressler 1981; Halliday 1985; Sornicola 1981).

Garassino and Jacob (2018) highlight a second property of LD that should be considered crucial for the conveyance of polarity focus. In their words, "the connection between LD and PF [polarity focus] lies in LD framing function, where the dislocated element states a condition for p [the proposition containing the polarity focus] to be true" (Garassino and Jacob 2018: 249).[30] Again, as for the givenness or inferrability of the preceding proposition, this claim risks overgeneralizing a tendency. In the data I analyzed, the left dislocated constituent is often codified as the TOP of the structure. In these cases, the left dislocated constituent indicates the domain for the illocutionary act expressed by the utterance. Therefore, I certainly agree with the claim that the left dislocated constituent can set the semantico-pragmatic coordinates for the interpretation of the utterance and the proposition. However, not all occurrences of LDs conveying polarity focus show a topic-comment partition. In the next example, drawn from the monologic familiar section of the IPIC corpus, the LD contains an occurrence of polarity focus on the VP *ce l'hanno* 'they do have them'. The TOP information unit is not filled by the left dislocated constituent, but by the discourse markers *ma in realtà* 'but actually' explicitly signaling a contrastive relation with the previous utterance.

(20) *CLA: *dico / guarda / io posso / posso vedere di / da piglia' qualche soldo / dice / ma in realtà /*[TOP] **i soldi ce l' hanno** /*[COM] **loro** //*[31]
      'I said / look / I can / I can try to / to take some money / he said / but actually/[TOP] **the money (they) do have them** /[COM] **they** //'
      (DB-IPIC, ifammn03,3)

In this case (and other occurrences found in the corpora analyzed in this study), the left dislocated constituent simply acts as a cohesive device, anchoring the contrasting COM part of the LD to the previous co-text. It does not provide a new frame of interpretation for the speech act because it is shared with the previous contrasting utterance. Yet, in other cases, the polarity focus refers to a frame of interpretation external to the referents or events mentioned in the text; therefore, the left dislocated constituent is uttered as a TOP and anchors the focal part of the structure allowing a displacement from the immediate context and co-text of the utterance.[32]

---

30 In another place of the paper, they also suggest that "the dislocated item conveys topic continuity" (Garassino and Jacob 2018: 243).

31 The informational annotation of the examples extracted from the IPIC corpus is extremely simplified. For the complete annotation, I refer the reader to the online database quoted in the references.

32 This is precisely the definition of topic used in this study, cf. § 2.2.1.

In conclusion, the discussion of examples (19) and (20) shows that there is no specific pragmatic and contextual property allowing LDs to convey polarity foci. Even without inferable or framing left dislocated constituent the contrast on the polarity of the verb may rise. I am thus inclined to think that the very redundancy of the affirmation of truth is a sufficient cue for the reconstruction of a contrast on the polarity of the verb by the hearer and may be interpreted accordingly if judged relevant in the context of utterance (for a similar interpretation concerning right dislocations, see Simone 1997: 53).

5 Contrastive foci LDs through language varieties and text types

In this last section, I provide further quantitative and qualitative data in support of the claim that there is no direct relation between specific textual conditions and the contrastive function performed by LDs. The diamesic and diaphasic variation of the corpora selected for this study show that the spoken vs written, and the formal vs informal parameter do not influence the quantity or quality of contrastive foci LDs. In the data retrieved, there is no clear tendency for a positive association with any of these parameters. In Table 2, the absolute frequencies and the percentages relative to the total number of contrastive foci LDs are provided.

Table 2: Distribution of contrastive foci LDs through language varieties.

Contrastive foci LDs	spoken	written
formal	10 (28%)	7 (19%)
informal	7 (19%)	12 (34%)

The figures show that written informal texts have the highest percentage of contrastive foci LDs. However, the parameters *written* and *informal* considered in association with the parameters *formal* and *spoken* do not show a consistent tendency. Moreover, the association between the features *spoken* and *formal* also shows an increase in the number of contrastive foci LDs. Given these quantitative results, I cannot confirm Cimmino and Panunzi's (2017: 168) observation that contrastive foci LDs are typical of spoken informal texts.

On the contrary, the data seems to confirm Garassino and Jacob's (2018) finding that formal written language is characterized by a low frequency of contrastive foci LDs. However, as mentioned previously, the diaphasic trait seems to go in the opposite direction when associated with spoken language. In the data analyzed, spoken formal Italian is second only to written formal text types. Based on the data retrieved in the corpora examined, I maintain that there is no association between the variation parameters considered and the use of contrastive foci LDs.

More interesting is the qualitative observation of the data. Both Cimmino and Panunzi (2017) and Garassino and Jacob (2018) associate contrastive foci LDs with argumentative texts. In particular, the former study considers the dialogicality of the text in which the contrastive foci LDs are found, while the latter hypothesizes that persuasive texts, such as the political speeches analyzed, would frequently exploit polarity foci. In line with their observations, I hypothesize that contrastive foci LDs are preferentially associated with polemical stretches of texts. I first clarify why I talk about stretches of texts and not text types, then I will clarify what I mean by 'polemical'.

Even though, when speaking about text types, it is possible to assign each of them to more or less argumentative communicative aims, it must be clear that "argumentativity constitutes an inherent feature of discourse" (Amossy 2009: 254). Labinaz and Sbisà (2018) convincingly demonstrate that argumentation can contribute to the organization of discourse even in text types not entirely devoted to argumentation. Therefore, if "argumentation is a dimension of discourse" (Labinaz and Sbisà 2018: 625), the presence of stretches of text with the final goal of arguing in favor of a certain point of view is irrespective of the text type to which they belong. This is also the case with the data analyzed here. In the ICOCP-QOL corpus of online news, it is possible to retrieve occurrences of contrastive foci LDs in the text, notwithstanding the primary informative aim of the genre. Consider for example the occurrence in (21), in which the journalist is reporting the words of a politician. Paraphrasing the colorful metaphors used by the speaker, in the reported speech, the politician is contrasting two points of view. The first is attributed to his opponents, who are allegedly rushing the Prime Minister to take important decisions. The second is the speaker's point of view, accusing his opponents of laziness.

(21) *«Leggo di gente che dice che ora bisogna fare presto, fare presto. Gente che non dà a Monti neanche una settimana di tempo, quando **gli ultimi tre anni li ha passati in un sonno totale** e non ha messo mai la sveglia. . . .»*
'«I read about people who say that now we must hurry up, hurry up. People who do not give Monti even a week, when **the last three years he has spent them in a deep sleep** and has never set the alarm clock. . . .»'
(ICOCP QOL)

The newspaper article reporting the contrastive foci LD is an interview with the politician, therefore it is not an argumentative text itself; nonetheless, it contains a contrastive passage because in the interview the politician is contrasting his point of view to his opponents'. This is not the only textual dynamic that may cause a contrastive passage to occur in text types with a different communicative goal. For this reason, it is important to consider single stretches of text rather than the whole text, when describing the usual context of contrastive foci LDs.

To describe the usual context of occurrence of contrastive foci LDs, another clarification may be useful. In the data analyzed, LDs are not highlighting generally argumentative passages but passages that specifically contrast two stances, to reinforce the speaker's point of view. What is specific to these contrastive dialogic moves is that they do not provide data or reasoning in support of their claim, therefore they cannot strictly be defined as argumentative.[33] Instead, the claim to which the speakers commit themselves appears self-validated by the strength with which the undesired option is rejected. A quick rhetorical overturn is created that is sufficient to discard the undesired option. In other words, the textual highlighting provided by the LD is sufficient to make the contrast relevant, even though a coherent argument is missing. This is evident in all the actual occurrences I analyzed (see here examples (16) to (21)). I suggest labeling these kinds of contrastive passages polemical instead of argumentative since they are preferably associated with disputatious writing or speech.

6 Conclusion

Summarizing the results of the analysis, the data used in this study reveal that Italian contrastive foci LDs fulfilling a contrastive discourse function are characterized by a predicate or a narrow focus. In the data analyzed, the narrow focus is the most common option – 22 occurrences versus 14 out of 36 contrastive cases of LDs. With a predicate focus, LDs encode a contrast between illocutionary nuclear units and the left co-text. Contrastive discourse relations are activated with corrective and counter-expectative semantic readings and with different levels of complexity in their logico-grammatical realization. With a narrow focus, contrastive foci LDs can encode contrast between different categories of linguistic material. More precisely, the contrast contextually expressed by contrastive foci LDs can concern referents, (part of) the verb, and the polarity of the verb. The contrast is established between actual or accommodated alternatives in the text.

From these analyses, two interesting aspects emerged, which are interwoven. LDs do not codify contrastive relations in the text. Contrast in LDs is not encoded

---

33 A classic understanding of argumentation is precisely to furnish data to support one's claim, clarifying their relationship to the interlocutors in the form of "if data, then claim" (Toulmin 2003: 91).

in prosody, syntax, or information structure but is reconstructed a posteriori in textual terms. What LDs do is create a textual organization useful for highlighting contrastive relations (as well as other discourse relations which have not been described here, see §1). There is thus no need to investigate the pragmatic and textual conditions explaining a supposed affinity between LDs and contrast, be it expressed through polarity focus or other codifying strategies. The supposed direct affinity between contrast and LDs is in fact mediated from their general function to creating textual prominences. Further quantitative and qualitative data in support of the claim that there is no direct relation between specific textual conditions and the contrastive function performed by Italian LDs are provided from the analysis of language varieties and text types. Neither diamesic nor diaphasic variation of texts are relevant features to predict the presence of contrastive foci LDs. Based on the data used for this study, I hypothesize that Italian contrastive foci LDs may be associated with polemical stretches of texts, that is stretches of texts containing disputatious writing or speech, in which the textual organization is used to highlight the already semantically codified contrast. This hypothesis is worth verifying more broadly in further text types and in future cross-linguistic research.

References

Amossy, Ruth. 2009. Argumentation in discourse: A socio-discursive approach to arguments. *Informal Logic* 29(3). 252–267.

Andorno, Cecilia & Claudia Crocco. 2018. In search for polarity contrast marking in Italian. A contribution from echo replies. In Christine Dimroth & Stefan Sudhoff (eds.), *The Grammatical Realization of Polarity Contrast: Theoretical, Empirical, and Typological Approaches*, 256–287. Amsterdam: John Benjamins.

Antinucci, Francesco & Guglielmo Cinque. 1977. Sull'ordine delle parole in italiano: L'emarginazione. *Studi di Grammatica Italiana* 6. 121–146.

Bally, Charles. 1950. *Linguistique Générale et Linguistique Française*. Bern: Francke Verlag.

Barbera, Manuel. 2013. Una introduzione ai NUNC: Storia della creazione di un corpus. In Manuel Barbera (ed.), *Molti occhi sono meglio di uno: Saggi di linguistica generale 2008–2012*, 97–114. Milano: Qu. A. S. A. R.

Benincà, Paola, Giampaolo Salvi & Lorenza Frison. 1988. L'ordine degli elementi della frase e le costruzioni marcate. In Lorenzo Renzi (ed.), *Grande Grammatica Italiana di Consultazione*, Vol. 1, 129–239. Bologna: Il Mulino.

Berretta, Monica. 2002. Ordini marcati dei costituenti maggiori di frase: Una rassegna. In Silvia Dal Negro & Bice Mortara Garavelli (eds.), *Monica Berretta, Temi e Percorsi della Linguistica. Scritti Scelti*, 149–199. Vercelli: Mercurio.

Berruto, Gaetano. 1985. 'Dislocazioni a sinistra' e 'grammatica' dell'italiano parlato. In Annalisa Franchi De Bellis & Leonardo Maria Savoia (eds.), *Sintassi e Morfologia della Lingua Italiana D'uso. Teorie e Applicazioni Descrittive*, 59–82. Roma: Bulzoni.

Berruto, Gaetano. 1986. Dislocazioni a destra in italiano. In Harro Stammerjohann (ed.), *Tema-Rema in Italiano*, 55–69. Tübingen: Narr.

Calaresu, Emilia Maria. 2022. *La Dialogicità nei Testi Scritti. Tracce e Segnali dell'Interazione tra Autore e Lettore*. Pisa: Pacini Editore.

Cartoni, Bruno & Thomas Meyer. 2012. Extracting directional and comparable corpora from a multilingual corpus for translation studies. In Nicoletta Calzolari, Khalid Choukri, Thierry Declerck, Mehmet Uğur Doğan, Bente Maegaard, Joseph Mariani, Asuncion Moreno, Jan Odijk & Stelios Piperidis (eds), *Proceedings of the Eighth International Conference on Language Resources and Evaluation (LREC)*, 2132–2137. Paris: European Language Resources Association.

Chafe, Wallace. 1976. Givenness, contrastiveness, definiteness, subjects, topics and point of view. In Charles N. Li (ed.), *Subject and Topic*, 25–56. New York: Academic Press.

Cimmino, Doriana. 2017. *La Topicalizzazione in Italiano in Prospettiva Contrastiva con l'Inglese. Il Caso della Scrittura Giornalistica Online*. Basel: Basel University dissertation.

Cimmino, Doriana & Alessandro Panunzi. 2017. La variazione funzionale delle strutture marcate a sinistra in italiano. Uno studio su corpora tra parlato e scritto. *Studi di Grammatica Italiana* 36. 117–179.

Cimmino, Doriana. 2023. On the topic-marking function of left dislocations and preposings. Variation across spoken and written Italian and English. In Alessandra Barotto & Simone Mattiola (eds.), *Discourse Phenomena in Typological Perspective*, 337–368. Amsterdam/Philadephia: John Benjamins.

Cresti, Emanuela. 2000. *Corpus di Italiano Parlato*. Firenze: Accademia della Crusca.

Cresti, Emanuela. 2005. Per una nuova classificazione dell'illocuzione a partire da un corpus di parlato (LABLITA). In Elizabeth Burr (ed.), *Tradizione e Innovazione. Atti del VI Convegno Internazionale della SILFI, 28 giugno – 2 luglio 2000*, 233–246. Firenze: Franco Cesati Editore.

Cresti, Emanuela. 2011. The definition of focus in the framework of the Language into Act Theory (L-AcT). In Alessandro Panunzi, Tommaso Raso & Heliana Mello (eds.), *Pragmatics and Prosody. Illocution, Modality, Attitude, Information Patterning and Speech Annotation*, 39–82. Firenze: Firenze University Press.

Cresti, Emanuela. 2017. The empirical foundation of illocutionary classification. In Anna De Meo & Francesca Maria Dovetto (eds.), *Atti del Convegno, la Comunicazione Parlata, Napoli, SLI – GSCP International Conference Napoli 2016*, 243–264. Napoli: Aracne.

Cresti, Emanuela. 2018. Per una classificazione empirica dell'illocuzione. Lo stato dell'arte. In Marco Biffi, Francesca Cialdini & Raffaella Setti (eds.), *"Acciò che'l nostro dire sia ben chiaro". Scritti per Nicoletta Maraschio*, 261–279. Firenze: Accademia della Crusca.

Cresti, Emanuela. 2020. The pragmatic analysis of speech and its illocutionary classification according to Language into Act Theory. In Shlomo Izre'el, Heliana Mello, Alessandro Panunzi & Tommaso Raso (eds.), *In Search for the Reference Unit of Spoken Language: A Corpus Driven Approach*, 181–220. Amsterdam: Benjamins.

Cresti, Emanuela & Massimo Moneglia. 2010. *Informational Patterning Theory and the Corpus Based Description of Spoken Language*. Firenze: Firenze University Press.

Cresti, Emanuela & Massimo Moneglia. 2018. The definition of the TOPIC within Language into Act Theory and its identification in spontaneous speech corpora. *Revue Romane* 53 (1). 30–62.

Cruschina, Silvio. 2021. Topicalization in the Romance languages. In Mark Aronoff (ed.), *Oxford Research Encyclopedia of Linguistics*. Oxford: Oxford University Press. https://doi.org/10.1093/acrefore/9780199384655.013.650

Cruschina, Silvio. 2022. Focus and focus structures in the Romance Languages. In Mark Aronoff (ed.), *Oxford Research Encyclopedias of Linguistics*. Oxford: Oxford University Press. https://doi.org/10.1093/acrefore/9780199384655.013.649

De Beaugrande, Robert-Alain & Wolfgang Dressler. 1981. *Introduction to Text Linguistics*. London/New York: Longman.

De Cesare, Anna-Maria. 2014. Subject dislocations in Italian and in a contrastive perspective with French. In Iørn Korzen, Angela Ferrari & Anna-Maria De Cesare (eds.), *Tra Romanistica e Germanistica: Lingua, Testo, Cognizione e Cultura / Between Romance and Germanic: Language, Text, Cognition and Culture*, 35–54. Bern: Lang.

De Cesare, Anna-Maria, Davide Garassino, Rocío Agar Marco, Ana Albom & Doriana Cimmino. 2016. *Sintassi Marcata dell'Italiano dell'Uso Medio in Prospettiva Contrastiva con il Francese, lo Spagnolo, il Tedesco e l'Inglese. Uno Studio Basato sulla Scrittura dei Quotidiani Online*. Frankfurt am Main: Lang.

De Cesare, Anna-Maria. 2019. CONTRAST-IT e COMPARE-IT. Due nuovi corpora per l'italiano contemporaneo. *CHIMERA. Romance Corpora and Linguistic Studies* 6. 43–74.

Dimroth, Christine. 2002. Topics, assertions and additive words: How L2 learners get from information structure to target language syntax. *Linguistics* 40. 891–923.

Duranti, Alessandro & Elinor Ochs. 1979. Left dislocation in Italian conversation. In Talmy Givón (ed.), *Discourse and Syntax*, 377–418. New York: Academic Press.

Ferrari, Angela. 2003. *Le Ragioni del Testo. Aspetti Sintattici e Interpuntivi dell'Italiano Contemporaneo*. Firenze: Accademia della Crusca.

Ferrari, Angela. 2014. The Basel model for paragraph segmentation: The construction units, their relationships and linguistic indication. In Salvador Pons Bordería (ed.), *Discourse Segmentation in Romance Languages*, 23–54. Amsterdam: John Benjamins.

Ferrari, Angela, Luca Cignetti, Anna-Maria De Cesare, Letizia Lala, Magda Mandelli, Claudia Ricci & Enrico Roggia. 2008. *L'Interfaccia Lingua-Testo. Natura e Funzioni dell'Articolazione Informativa dell'Enunciato*. Alessandria: Edizioni dell'Orso.

Féry, Caroline. (2007). Information structural notions and the fallacy of invariant correlates. In Caroline Féry, Gisbert Fanselow & Manfred Krifka (eds.), *The Notions of Information Structure*, 161–184. Potsdam: Universitätsverlag Potsdam.

Firbas, Jan. 1971. On the concept of communicative dynamism in the theory of functional sentence perspective. *Sborník prací Filozofické Fakulty Brněnské Univerzity A* 19. 135–144.

Frascarelli, Mara. 2003. Topicalizzazione e ripresa clitica. Analisi sincronica, confronto diacronico e considerazioni tipologiche. In Nicoletta Maraschio & Teresa Poggi Salani (eds.), *Italia Linguistica Anno Mille. Italia Linguistica Anno Duemila*, 547–562. Roma: Bulzoni.

Frascarelli, Mara. 2017. Dislocations and framings. In Andreas Dufter & Elizabeth Stark (eds), *Manual of Romance Morphosyntax and Syntax*, 472–501. Berlin: Mouton De Gruyter.

Frascarelli, Mara & Roland Hinterhölzl. 2007. Types of topics in German and Italian. In Susanne Winkler & Kerstin Schwabe (eds.), *On Information Structure, Meaning and Form*, 87–116. Amsterdam/Philadelphia: Benjamins.

Garassino, Davide & Daniel Jacob. 2018. Polarity focus and non-canonical syntax in Italian, French and Spanish: Clitic left dislocation and *sì che / sí que*-constructions. In Christine Dimroth & Stefan Sudhoff (eds), *The Grammatical Realization of Polarity Contrasts: Theoretical, Empirical, and Typological Approaches*, 227–254. Amsterdam: John Benjamins Publishing.

Halliday, Michael A.K. 1967. Notes on transitivity and theme in English: Part 2. *Journal of Linguistics* 3(2). 199–244.

Halliday, Michael A. K. 1985. *Spoken and Written Language*. Victoria: Deakin University Press.

von Heusinger, Klaus & Petra B. Schumacher 2019. Discourse prominence: definition and application. *Journal of Pragmatics* 154. 117–127.

Hockett, Charles F. 1958. *A Course in Modern Linguistics*. New York: The Macmillan Company.

Huddleston, Rodney & Geoffrey K. Pullum. 2002. *The Cambridge Grammar of the English Language*. Cambridge: Cambridge University Press.

Krifka, Manfred. 2007. Basic notions of information structure. In Caroline Féry, Gisbert Fanselow & Manfred Krifka (eds.), *The Notions of Information Structure*, 13–55. Potsdam: Universitätsverlag Potsdam.

Labinaz, Paolo & Marina Sbisà. 2018. Argumentation as a dimension of discourse. The case of news articles. *Pragmatics & Cognition* 25(3). 602–630.

Lambrecht, Knud. 1994. *Information Structure and Sentence Form. Topic, Focus and the Mental Representation of Discourse Referents*. Cambridge: Cambridge University Press.

Lambrecht, Knud. 2001. Dislocation. In Martin Haspelmath, Ekkehard König, Wulf Oesterreicher & Wolfgang Raible (eds.), *Language Typology and Language Universals: An International Handbook*, Vol. 2, 1050–1078. Berlin/New York: De Gruyter.

Lang, Ewald. 2000. Adversative connectors on distinct levels of discourse: A re-examination of Eve Sweetser's three-level approach. In Elizabeth Couper-Kuhlen & Bernd Kortmann (eds.), *Cause – Condition – Concession – Contrast*, 235–256. Berlin/New York: Mouton De Gruyter.

Lombardi Vallauri, Edoardo. 2001. The role of discourse, syntax and the lexicon in determining the nature and extent of focus. *Lingvisticæ Investigationes* 23(2). 229–252.

Mauri, Caterina, Silvia Ballarè, Eugenio Goria, Massimo Cerruti & Francesco Suriano. 2019. KIParla corpus: A new resource for spoken Italian. In Raffaella Bernardi, Roberto Navigli & Giovanni Semeraro (eds.), *Proceedings of the 6th Italian Conference on Computational Linguistics CLiC-it*. https://ceur-ws.org/Vol-2481/

Panunzi, Alessandro & Lorenzo Gregori. 2012. DB-IPIC. An XML database for the representation of information structure in spoken language. In Heliana Mello, Alessandro Panunzi & Tommaso Raso (eds.), *Pragmatics and Prosody, Illocution, Modality, Attitude, Information Patterning and Speech Annotation*, 133–150. Firenze: Firenze University Press.

Reinhart, Tanya. 1981. Pragmatics and linguistics: An analysis of sentence topic. *Philosophica* 27. 53–94.

Rizzi, Luigi. 1997. The fine structure of the left periphery. In Liliane Haegeman (ed.), *Elements of Grammar. Handbook of Generative Syntax*, 281–337. Dordrecht: Kluwer.

Rohlfs, Gerhard. 1968. *Grammatica Storica della Lingua Italiana e dei Suoi Dialetti. Morfologia*. Torino: Einaudi.

Searle, John R. 1969. *Speech Acts: An Essay in the Philosophy of Language*. Cambridge: Cambridge University Press.

Simone, Raffaele. 1997. Une interprétation diachronique de la « dislocation à droite » dans les langues romanes. *Langue Française* 115. 48–61.

Sornicola, Rosanna. 1981. *Sul Parlato*. Bologna: Il Mulino.

Toulmin, Stephen. 2003. *The Uses of Argument. Updated Edition*. Cambridge: Cambridge University Press.

Corpora

DB-IPIC – http://www.lablita.it/app/dbipic/ (Panunzi and Gregori 2012)

KIPARLA – http://kiparla.it/ (Mauri et al. 2019)

ICOCP – https://contrast-it.philhist.unibas.ch/en/corpora/contrast-it-corpus/ (De Cesare 2019)

NUNC – http://www.bmanuel.org/projects/ng-HOME.html (Barbera 2013)

Ojaswee Bhalla

4 Contrast and topics: An enquiry into Hindi particle *-to*

Abstract: This paper provides evidence from Hindi (Indo-Aryan; SOV base order) to argue for 'topic' and 'contrast' being independent Information Structure (IS) categories with a distinct ontological status in the packaging of information in the language. Topic is a pragmatic discourse *role* that an entity can take up whereas contrast is a discourse *relation* that an entity or a unit of information enters into with some other contextually available alternative to it in the discourse. That contrast requires an independent categorical status is argued for on the basis of the evidence provided by the Hindi particle *-to*. This paper argues that the phrasal enclitic particle *-to* is not a morphological topic marker *per se*, contrary to the standard assumption in the literature (Kidwai 2000, 2004). Empirical evidence is provided in the form of firstly, non-topical constituents (like attributive adjectives) that can be marked by this particle and secondly, by its marking of nominal constituents that do not occur in sentence initial position and hence, are not biased for a topic interpretation in the language. This is claimed on the basis of the *Tell me about X* diagnostic test (Neeleman et al. 2009) employed to ascertain the topical constituent in a sentence. This motivates a dissociation of the IS notion of topic and this particle and consequently, it is argued that this particle cannot be assumed to be a grammatical reflex of the linguistic category of topics (cf. Matić and Wedgwood 2013). This paper shows that in the non-topical cases (like the in-situ object nominal), a sentence with a *to*-marked entity can evoke a scalar implicature and an uncertainty implicature that then instantiate the contrastive discourse relation (similar to Kim's 2013 proposal for Korean *-nun*). Since these contrast-inducing implicatures are not conventionally linked to the particle *-to* and are contingent on certain syntactic and pragmatic factors, this further provides evidence for proposing an indirect and not a direct mapping between the at-issue IS notions and the morphological particle *-to* in Hindi.

1 Introduction

Within the literature on Information Structure (IS) as a domain that interfaces with the strictly linguistic modules of syntax, morphology, phonology etc. on the one hand and the broader cognitive modules dealing with information update via pragmatic reasoning and inference mechanism on the other hand (Zimmermann

https://doi.org/10.1515/9783110986594-004

and Féry 2009; Féry and Ishihara 2016), there are certain notions that are considered to be the basic building blocks of IS that structure the information contained in an utterance as per the communicative requirements of the interlocutors at the utterance time. These notions are 'topic' versus 'comment', 'focus' versus 'background', 'given' versus 'new'. One definition of the topic-comment pair is that the topic is what the sentence is 'about' and the comment part is the rest of the sentence that conveys information about the topical constituent (Reinhart 1981). Informally, focus is that information that is relatively new in a sentence, the rest of the material is background in that sentence; given material is discourse-old and is both hearer and speaker known whereas new information is not known to the addressee prior to that utterance of a sentence (Hinterwimmer 2011).[1] By these definitions, these IS notions are not mutually exclusive and can coincide on a particular constituent for its interpretation.[2] In comparison to these, 'contrast' as a relevant linguistic category has been relatively recently added to the inventory of basic IS notions (see Molnár 2002, 2006; Repp 2010; Neeleman and Vermeulen 2012); that signals the availability of relevant alternatives and their juxtaposition in discourse.

Focusing on topic and contrast, the frameworks that have formalized the notion of topic have been broadly of three types: topic-as-an-entity (Reinhart 1981; Krifka 2008), topic-as-a-frame (Chafe 1976; Jacobs 2001), topic-as-a-salient-question-under-discussion (von Fintel 1994). While Reinhart's (1981) definition proposes topic to be the entity that a sentence is in a pragmatic relation of 'being about' with, Krifka (2008) outlines topic to be the entity or the set of entities about which information is expressed in the comment and which is added to the Common Ground content.[3] The frame-based conception of topics views sentence topics to be "the frame within which the sentence holds" (Chafe 1979: 51) or "a domain of possible reality to which proposition expressed by Y is restricted" (Jacobs 2001: 656). This

---

1 Topic as an IS notion is discussed in this paper. For a formal treatment of focus see Rooth (1992), Selkirk (1984); for a formal treatment of givenness see Schwarzschild (1999), Rochemont (2019).

2 For example, in the following discourse unit, for Speaker B's response 'John' is the topic, the given material as well as the backgrounded material whereas 'killed Jack' is focal, the comment part as well as the new material in Speaker B's reply.

Speaker A: Tell me something about John.

Speaker B: John killed Jack.

3 Common Ground (CG) is the shared set of mutual acceptances (propositions) and the discourse referents between the interlocutors of a speech event in a discourse (see Stalnaker 1974, 2002). For Krifka, information is stored in the CG and this CG is continuously modified by every utterance move during the course of a conversation.

includes spatio-temporal adverbs or scene-setting adverbs (like *healthwise*). Within the Question Under Discussion (QUD) analyses, discourse is organized as a hierarchically structured set of questions and an utterance move answers an implicit or explicit salient question under discussion – the topic – at that point. Contrast, on the other hand, has been associated with a set of alternatives, which may be implicit or explicit, and whose set membership may be priorly known and restricted or it could be contextually inferable (see Kiss 1998; Vallduví and Vilkuna 1998; etc.). The common factor across these different perspectives on contrast is that for a contrastive interpretation of some unit of information in a sentence, there has to be a contextually available alternative to it and the discourse status of the two alternatives should be different.

Against this backdrop of topic and contrast, this paper brings in data from Hindi, an Indo-Aryan language, and discusses the case of the enclitic particle *-to* which has been conventionally analysed as a morphological topic marker of the language (Kidwai 2000, 2004). This analysis claimed that the constituents marked by *-to* receive either a thematic topic or a contrastive topic interpretation, which are an interpretive effect of the fulfilment of a specific semantic property of *-to* as a topic marker. This paper argues against such a subsumed status of contrast that is contingent on the topic interpretation of a constituent (for languages like Hindi that can have the same morphological marking on their thematic topic and contrastive topic constituents) and provides evidence to claim a distinct ontological status for contrast as an IS notion.

Section 1.1 discusses the empirical distribution of the particle under investigation. Section 1.2 reviews the traditional treatment of this particle as a morphological topic marker for Hindi and highlights the predictions that such an analysis makes. Section 2 problematizes the topic marker analysis of particle *-to* by providing evidence of this particle marking constituents of categories not appropriate to receive a topic interpretation. By employing a diagnostic text to ascertain the topical constituent in a sentence in section 2.1, it is argued in section 2.2 that particle *-to* can mark constituents that have appropriate topic-type categorical status but are not the topic of a sentence. This weakens the topic marker analysis for particle *-to* and pushes for a dissociation between this linguistic item and topicality as a notion. Section 3.1 analyses the topic-type but non-topical constituents that are marked by particle *-to* in Hindi and shows that a third interpretation of pure contrast (that is not contingent on topicality) is also permissible for certain *to*-marked constituents. This contrast is shown to be indicated via licensing of certain implicatures. After providing an overview of implicatures in section 3.2, the Hindi data and the evoked implicatures are analysed in sections 3.3 and 3.4. Section 4 concludes the paper and raises further cross-linguistic questions drawn from the insights of this analysis.

1.1 Empirical distribution of the Hindi particle *-to*

The Hindi lexicon has a phrasal enclitic particle *-to* (see (1), where the particle *-to* marks the subject nominal 'Ram') and a homonymous free word *to* (see (2) and (3)).[4] While no lexical meaning has been attributed to the enclitic particle *-to* in the literature (although Montaut (2015) has traced an etymological link of it back to the Sanskrit third person pronoun *ta-*), the free word *to* is traditionally treated as an adverbial which is equivalent to the English 'then' and can function to introduce the apodosis of a conditional statement (2) or can stand alone as a complete question (with a rising intonation) in a narrative context (3).[5]

(1) Context: There was an office party held one day. The next day, in a conversation about listing who all attended and who all did not attend that party, someone says (Ram being one of the employees in that office):
ram=to   aja
ram=TO   come.PFV.3MS
'Ram came'

(2) əgər   ram   aega   to   mɛ   parʈi   mẽ   dʒaũga
     if   ram   come.FUT.3MS   then I   party   LOC   go.FUT.1MS
     'If Ram will come, then I will go to the party'

(3) Context: A mother scolds her teenage son that his room is extremely messy and dirty. To this, the son retorts:
to
'so ?'/'then ?' (with rising intonation)

Distributionally, the occurrence of the enclitic particle *-to* is limited to once per clause. Marking of more than one constituent with this particle, as in the case of (4) where both the subject and the object nominal are *to*-marked, leads to ungrammaticality.

---

4 Glossing abbreviations followed throughout the text:
TO – particle *-to*; ERG – ergative case, LOC – locative case; DAT – dative case; GEN – genitive case; COM – comitative case; PFV – perfective aspect; PRS – present tense; FUT – future tense; AUX – auxiliary; IMP – imperative; PQP – polar question particle; 1 – 1st person; 2 – 2nd person; 3 – 3rd person; M – masculine; F – feminine; S – singular; P – plural.
5 This paper only focuses on the enclitic *-to* and discusses the interpretative import available for the *to*-marked constituents vis-à-vis the notions of topic and contrast. Henceforth, the free word *to* (which gets an adverbial 'then' interpretation, see (2) and (3)) will not be discussed in the paper.

(4)   Context: Two friends are discussing which fruits they saw their common friend
      'Ram' eat at a picnic and one person says:
      *   *ram=ne=to*   *kela=to*   *kʰaja*
           ram=ERG=TO   banana=TO   eat.PFV.3MS
           'Ram ate the banana'

Besides marking a nominal ('boys' in (5a)), this particle can mark a range of lexical
categories depending on the discourse context specification of the sentence – like
adjectives ('tall' in (5b)), numerals ('two' in (5c)), postpositions ('under' in (5d)),
lexical verbs ('stand' in (5e)) and adverbs ('today' in (5f)). A possible discourse continuation for (5b) is 'but two short ones are standing near the house door'; the sentence in (5c) can be continued with 'and three are standing near the building'; the
sentence in (5d) can be continued with 'and not climbed above the tree'; (5f) can
be continued with 'unlike yesterday when no one came'. The pattern that appears
to be common across all the discourse configurations that facilitate *to*-marking of
different lexical categories is that the *to*-marked lexical item is relevant for the
given utterance and possibly taken up or juxtaposed in the succeeding utterance.
Thus, felicitous *to*-marking of a lexical item in a sentence is contingent on the dis-
course-pragmatic factors within which that utterance is anchored.

(5)   Context: A person is being stalked by a few suspicious people in his locality.
      That person can often see from his window that some people stand near a tree
      outside his home. He reports the scenario one day to a concerned friend and
      says:

a. *adʒ*	*do*	*ləmbe*	**ləɽke=to**	*peɽ=ke*	*nitʃe*	*kʰəɽe*	*hɛ̃*
b. *adʒ*	*do*	**ləmbe=to**	*ləɽke*	*peɽ=ke*	*nitʃe*	*kʰəɽe*	*hɛ̃*
c. *adʒ*	**do=to**	*ləmbe*	*ləɽke*	*peɽ=ke*	*nitʃe*	*kʰəɽe*	*hɛ̃*
d. *adʒ*	*do*	*ləmbe*	*ləɽke*	*peɽ=ke*	**nitʃe=to**	*kʰəɽe*	*hɛ̃*
e. *adʒ*	*do*	*ləmbe*	*ləɽke*	*peɽ=ke*	*nitʃe*	**kʰəɽe=to**	*hɛ̃*
f. **adʒ=to**	*do*	*ləmbe*	*ləɽke*	*peɽ=ke*	*nitʃe*	*kʰəɽe*	*hɛ̃*
today	two	tall	boys	tree=GEN	under	stand.3MP	be.AUX.PRS

'Today two tall boys are standing under the tree'

The empirical distribution of this particle is not restricted to declarative clause
(like the sentences in (5a)–(5f)) since it can mark a constituent in an imperative
clause (6) and also an interrogative clause. For the interrogative cases, this particle
cannot occur in an information-seeking, constituent question (7) or a polar question containing the Hindi polar question particle *kyaa* 'what' (8). It can only occur
in confirmational questions (9) that have a declarative syntax but a prosodic profile
of interrogatives i.e., clause final rising intonation. Such *to*-marked questions are

associated with a positive speaker bias – the speaker asks the addressee to confirm their belief regarding the content of the proposition.

(6) Context: A person has come back home after office and says to his/her partner (who was at home):
    ek   gɪlas   pani=to   dena
    one   glass   water=TO   give.IMP.2s
    'Give (me) one glass of water'

(7) Context: An organisation had invited all the people in their office to a party. The next day, a person who couldn't attend the party asks a colleague (who attended the party):
    * parţɪ=mẽ   kɔn=to   aja
      party=LOC   who=TO   come.PFV.3MS
      'Who came to the party?' (intended)

(8) Context: An organisation had invited all of their employees to a party but the event was overlapping with the cricket world cup match. The next day, a person who did not attend the party asks a colleague (whom he assumed would have gone to the party):
    * kja   parţi=to   hʊɪ
      PQP   party=TO   happen.PFV.3FS
      'Did the party happen?' (intended)

(9) Context: Two friends are discussing who all attended the office party last night. The one who couldn't attend assumes that their common friend Ram would have definitely gone to the party. He asks the other person (who had attended the party):
    parţɪ=mẽ   ram=to   aja
    party=LOC   Ram=TO   come.PFV.3MS
    'Ram came to the party, right?' (intended)

This section has introduced the enclitic particle -to in Hindi and covered its empirical distribution in the language. To summarize, it can mark a range of lexical categories in a sentence and can occur in declarative, imperative and (restricted) interrogative clauses. It can occur in confirmational questions but not in information-seeking, wh-constituent questions or polar questions. Across the board, the distribution of this particle is limited to once per clause.

The next section discusses the existing formal treatment of this particle as the morphological topic particle for the language and then proceeds to raise issues with this analysis.

1.2 Particle -*to* as a topic marker: Kidwai (2000)

Kidwai (2000) proposes that the enclitic particle -*to* is the morphological topic marker for Hindi, similar to Japanese -*wa* and Korean -*(n)un* topic particles. She adopts Reinhart's (1981) notion of sentential topics being the entities 'about' which the sentence provides information and assumes the label of thematic topics for such aboutness topics. In her analysis, contrastive topics are also aboutness-based topics but along with an additional stipulation of there being a relevant set of alternatives for the topical constituent in the discourse. She claims Hindi particle -*to* to be a topic marker parallel to the Japanese -*wa* particle based on the evidence of similar IS interpretations available for the marked constituents in these languages. A thematic topic interpretation and a contrastive topic interpretation is available for the *to*-marked constituents in Hindi (examples (10) to (12) cited from Kidwai 2000: 45), parallel to the traditional interpretations available for the Japanese data containing topic marker -*wa* (examples (13) to (15) cited from Miyagawa 1987: 186).[6] While the generic nominals 'dogs' and 'whales' receive a thematic topic interpretation in (10) and (13) respectively, this interpretation is also ascribed to the specific referential nominal 'John' in (11) and (14). In examples (12) and (15), the nominal 'rain' receives a contrastive topic interpretation and is juxtaposed with a discourse-explicit alternative 'hailstones' in (12) and 'snow' in (15) respectively.

(10) *kutte-to   wəfadar   hote   hẽ*
      dogs-TOP   faithful   be-HAB   are
      'Dogs are faithful' (thematic)

(11) *dʒɔn-to   kɪtab   pəɽta   hɛ*
      John-TOP   book   reads   is
      'As for John, he reads books' (thematic)

---

6 The interlinear glosses and the translations for the cited data are reproduced in original. The glossing abbreviations followed by Miyagawa (1987) and Kidwai (2000) are: TOP – topic, HAB – habitual, PROG – progressive; TP – topic particle; COP – copula; DO – direct object.

(12) *barɪʃ-to   ho   rəhɪ   hɛ, pər   ole   nəhɪ pəɾ rəhe   hɛ̃*
     rain-TOP   be   PROG   is   but   hailstones   not   fall   PROG   is
     'It's raining, but there's no hail' (contrastive)

(13) *kudʒira   wa   hoŋju-dobutsu   desu*
     whales   TP   mammals   COP
     'Whales are mammals' (thematic)

(14) *dʒon   wa   hon   o   jonda*
     John   TP   book   DO   read
     'As for John, he reads a book' (thematic)

(15) *ame   wa   futeimasu   ga,   juki   wa   futeimasen*
     rain   TP   falling   but   snow   not-falling
     'It's raining, but it isn't snowing' (contrastive)

Proposing *-to* to be a bonafide topic marker, Kidwai (2000) locates the source of such thematic and contrastive topic interpretation for the Hindi data in (10)–(13) in a semantic property ascribed to the class of topic particles by Miyagawa (1987) – the set anaphoricity property. This property stipulates that the topic particles have to make reference to an identifiable set of individuals or entities (that has to be present in the immediate context of discourse). The interlocutors in a discourse must share the knowledge of this set of individuals/entities.[7] Topic particles have an anaphoric relation with the set as a whole and therefore, every member of the set must be exhaustively represented in a statement containing that topic particle. The licensing of a thematic topic interpretation requires all members of the set being referentially picked out by the topic marker. In examples (10) and (13), the Hindi *-to* and the Japanese *-wa* pick all members of the set of 'dogs' and 'whales' respectively, thereby resulting in exhaustive representation of the whole set in the sentences containing these particles. The relevant identifiable set in (11) and (14) is the singleton set {John}. The sole member of this set is referentially picked out by the language-specific topic particles in these sentences. This results in a thematic topic interpretation of the marked nominal.

A contrastive topic interpretation is made available when the topic marker picks out only some members of the identifiable set in the discourse context. These

---

7 Note that this stipulation of set anaphoricity as a property can also be understood in the more widespread IS terms – that the relevant, identifiable set of individuals or entities be 'given' and discourse-old for both interlocutors.

selected set members enter into an 'IN CONTRAST TO' relation to the remaining members of the set. This results in the requisite exhaustive representation of the set as a whole.[8] In sentences (12) and (15), the relevant, contextually available, identified set of entities is {rain, hailstones} and {rain, snow} respectively. Particle -*to* picks out {rain} in (12), which then gains an 'in contrast to' relation with the remaining section of the set – {hailstones}. This leads to an exhaustive representation of the complete set in a sentence containing particle -*to* (as required by its set-anaphoricity property) and a contrastive topic interpretation for the *to*-marked 'rain' in the sentence.

In this analysis, the difference between a thematic and a contrastive topic interpretation depends on how the set anaphoric property of the topic particle is satisfied – whether all members of the set are picked out by the particle or only some – and how exhaustive representation is achieved in either case. Within this account, the 'contrast' in contrastive topic interpretation is contingent on the assumption of particle -*to* being a topic particle itself. This assumption theoretically implies that a *to*-marked entity has to obligatorily receive a topic interpretation – either thematic or contrastive. It also implies that the contrastive interpretation for a *to*-marked entity is contingent on the particle -*to* being analyzed as a topic marker in the language. This can be extended to predict that there cannot be a non-topical, pure contrastive interpretation for a *to*-marked entity in Hindi.

The next section first introduces the working definitions of topic and contrast assumed for this paper and then proceeds to provide counter-evidence to the predictions made by Kidwai's proposal. It presents empirical data in conjunction with a diagnostic test to argue against a direct correspondence between the IS notion of topic and the enclitic particle -*to*, as would have been the case if this particle was indeed the topic particle itself.

---

8 This requirement of exhaustive representation of the identifiable set of individuals/entities with some members being represented by virtue of being in an 'in contrast to' relation with the marked member in the sentence implies that for the proponents of set anaphoricity property (i.e. Miyagawa and Kidwai), the contrastive topic interpretation comes with an implicit exhaustive reading – that the rest of the alternatives do not satisfy the property specified in the utterance and hence are exhausted. This inference, however, is not explicitly mentioned or commented upon or defended by Kidwai in her analysis. In the IS literature, contrastive topic interpretations are usually not assumed to be accompanied by such exhaustive readings (see Lee 2000; Büring 2003; Wagner 2012). I thank an anonymous reviewer for pointing this out.

2 Problem with a topic marker analysis of particle *-to*

For the analysis developed in this paper for Hindi, I assume an entity-type definition of topics out of the three conceptions of topics mentioned in the introduction of this paper (topic-as-an-entity; topic-as-a-frame; topic-as-a-question under discussion).[9] This choice is made on the basis of the following factors: the literature that posits particle *-to* to be the Hindi topic marker assumes Reinhart's topics-as-an-entity perspective since this particle marks entities in the discourse (similar to Portner and Yabushita's (1998) rationale for the analysis of Japanese topic constituents involving particle *-wa*) and therefore it is this understanding of the IS notion of topics that I assume at the outset. Secondly, the diagnostic test (introduced and operationalized in the next section) to demarcate the topical constituents from the non-topical constituents in a sentence is formulated for entity-type topics and not the other two non-entity type topics.

Empirical investigation highlights a distributional restriction on the type of entity particle *-to* can mark. In example (16), uttered in an out-of-the-blue context (i.e., a context with no prior CG), the referent of the specific indefinite subject nominal 'a friend of mine' is not known to the hearer. The comparison of the minimal pair (16a) and (16b), that vary only in terms of the *to*-marking of this subject nominal, shows that the unmarked nominal is grammatical in (16a) whereas marking of this discourse-new entity by particle *-to* in (16b) leads to ungrammaticality.

(16)   Context: A person starts a conversation with a stranger about a famous personality called 'Ram' (who is known by everyone) and begins by saying:
   a.   *merɪ   ek   dost=ne   ram=se   ʃadɪ   kɪ*
   b.   * *merɪ   ek   dost=ne=to   ram=se   ʃadɪ   kɪ*
         my   one friend=ERG=TO Ram=COM marriage do.PFV.3FS
         'A friend of mine got married to Ram'

Thus, the Hindi particle *-to* can only mark those entities whose referent is a part of the Common Ground between the speaker and the addressee at the utterance time.

---

9 Taking a topic to be either an entity in the discourse or a spatio-temporal frame of predication does not affect the two core insights drawn from the Hindi data and its discussion in the paper – that the sentence topic (whether it be an entity or a frame) may be morphologically unmarked in Hindi and that the particle *-to* does not always mark sentence topics (and is therefore not a topic marker *per se* in Hindi but can optionally mark topical constituents). Therefore, in my understanding, the proposal being developed here would remain unaffected if both the topic-as-an-entity and the topic-as-a-frame were together taken to be the working definitions of topics.

Since *to*-marking of an entity is contingent on the availability of that entity in CG, I adopt Krifka's definition of topic that incorporates the communicative model of CG and articulates the distinction between entities that are hearer known versus those that are not for analysing the Hindi data – "topical constituents identify the entity or set of entities under which the information expressed in the comment constituent should be stored in the C(common) G(round) content" (Krifka 2008: 265). Thus, only discourse-given topical constituents can be marked by particle -*to* in Hindi.[10]

As for contrast, I adopt Kim's (2013) definition of contrast as the working definition for it in this paper. Kim (2013) posits that "contrast is a relation between discourse referents that are partitioned with respect to some semantic property P such that it is established (either via assertion or implicature) that the value 'true' results when P is applied to one part of the set and 'false' or 'unknown' when applied to the other" (Kim 2013: 50). The merit of assuming this definition for this paper is that it specifies the exact linguistic status of what contrast is – a discourse relation – and how the juxtaposition of the alternatives, that are essential for contrast (see Repp 2010), is conveyed either as part of the assertion or as an implicature as a different semantic value vis-a-vis the sentence predicate. I extend Kim's definition by proposing that contrast can be viewed as discourse relation between discourse referents or entities as well as between properties or predicates associated with these discourse referents or entities in a proposition. The applicability of extending this definition will become apparent in section 2.2.

Maintaining an independent status for the notion of contrast has two advantages: firstly, any designata in a sentence can receive a contrastive interpretation (provided that there is an alternative to this designata available in the context and that the discourse status of this alternative be different from the contrast-marked designata). Secondly, an interpretative system can then be postulated wherein a Contrastive Topic (CT) is a combinatorial sum of two interpretive effects: a topic discourse role that a sentential constituent takes up and this constituent entering into a contrastive discourse relation with some contextually-available alternative.

Having made explicit the definitions of topic and contrast being assumed for this paper, consider now the Hindi data discussed in example (5) in sub-section 1.1 in light of the conventionally assumed topic marker analysis for particle -*to* (specified in the previous sub-section). If this particle is the morphological topic marker for Hindi, then this logically entails that it should only mark topical constituents in a sentence. However, example (5) presents data where this enclitic particle can

---

10 Note that this does not exclude the option of there being discourse-new topics in Hindi but it is claimed that particle -*to*, if it is indeed the topic marker (which I eventually argue that it is not), cannot mark such discourse-new and hearer-unknown entities.

potentially mark a range of lexical categories in a sentence – a nominal, an adjective, a numeral, an adverb, a postposition or a verb. Out of all these, a topic-as-an-entity definition can apply to nominal categories and a topic-as-a-frame definition can apply to the adverbs. The remaining categories (i.e. an adjective, a numeral, a postposition or a verb) do not have the appropriate categorical type to which any of these topic definitions can be applied. Therefore, they are not the right candidates to receive a topic interpretation and thus, *to*-marking of such non-topic-type constituents provides the first counter-evidence for a topic marker analysis of particle *-to*.

The next research task is to analyze whether, provided that there is more than one candidate of the appropriate categorical type to receive the topic interpretation, the particle *-to* always marks the topical candidate? The first step towards unpacking this question is to identify which is the topical constituent in a sentence and which is not. The next sub-section 2.1 introduces and operationalizes a diagnostic test to identify the topical constituent in an unmarked Hindi sentence. The findings are then employed in sub-section 2.2 to evaluate whether particle *-to* can mark both the topical and the non-topical constituents or not.

2.1 Diagnostic test for topichood

I use the label Aboutness Topic (AT) constituent to refer to the Krifka or Reinhart style entity-denoting constituent about which a sentence provides information. Contrastive Topic (CT) constituent is an AT topic that is in a contrastive discourse relation with some contextually available and relevant alternative.

Neeleman et al. (2009) proposed a *Tell me about X* test that pre-designates the topical constituent of a sentence by incorporating it in the test template as X and asking the addressee to provide information about it. The succeeding sentence is pragmatically felicitous if the addressee also structures their response positing X to be the topical constituent (AT). The other felicitous possibility is where the addressee provides information not about X but about Y, which is another contextually relevant alternative to X. In this case, Y receives the CT interpretation. In the English example (17a), 'John' is the AT constituent that is pre-designated as the topical constituent using the template in Speaker A's utterance and made the appropriate AT in Speaker B's response. In (17b), information is provided about the contextually available alternative to 'John' – 'I' – that gets the CT interpretation in speaker B's response. Invoking Kim's definition of contrast, the assertion of (17b) directly conveys that the discourse status of the alternative 'John' is unknown to the speaker and different from the discourse status of the alternative 'I'.

(17) Context: After a dinner party, two friends meet up and start discussing who liked what from the buffet table at the party:
  a. Speaker A: *Tell me about John. What did he like?*
     Speaker B: *[John]$_{AT}$ liked the chicken pasta.*
  b. Speaker A: *Tell me about John. What did he like?*
     Speaker B: *I don't know about John but [I]$_{CT}$ liked the chicken pasta.*

The felicity of the question-answer pair is contingent on the pre-designated topical constituent in the speaker A's utterance being given the topic discourse role in speaker B's utterance. Thus, this test can be employed to demarcate the topical constituent (AT/CT) of a sentence. This diagnostic test is next applied to the Hindi data.

From the perspective of the typological bifurcation of the world's languages as being either topic-prominent or subject-prominent (Li and Thompson 1976), Indo-Aryan (and hence, Hindi) has been categorized as a subject-prominent language. Following this, Kidwai (2004) postulated that the subject Noun Phrases (NPs) receive a default topic interpretation in a Hindi sentence and gave a syntactic, feature-based derivational mechanism for this.[11] Employing the topichood diagnostic test to check this claim, example (18) illustrates that this correspondence of subjects being the default topics seems to hold true *prima facie*. The subject NP 'Rahul' is the topic of the sentence (pre-designated by the diagnostic template) and this topic congruence leads to pragmatic felicity of speaker B's utterance in discourse.

(18) Speaker A: *mʊdʒʰe*   *rahʊl=ke*   *bare=mẽ* *bətao*
                  I.DAT   Rahul=GEN   about   tell.IMP.2SG
                  'Tell me about Rahul'
     Speaker B: *[rahʊl=ne]$_{TOPIC}$*   *seb*   *kʰaja*
                  Rahul=ERG   apple   eat.PFV.3MSG
                  'Rahul ate the apple'

However, example (19) shows that it is not the subjects that receive the default topic interpretation in Hindi but it is the sentence initial position that is biased to receive the default topic interpretation. Since Hindi is an SOV language, in the base word order constructions, subjects are in the sentence initial position and

---

11 She had reformulated the syntactic EPP (Extended Projection Principle) feature as the checking requirement for each sentence to have a topic (and not a subject as previously assumed, cf. Chomsky's P&P approach). In her analysis, the EPP requires the topical constituent to occupy [spec,TP] position and this accords a topic interpretation to subjects in Hindi. I refer the reader to Kidwai (2004) to understand the syntactic derivation proposed in full (and to Bhalla (2021) for arguments against this proposal).

are prime candidates to receive topic interpretation. Example (19) is a case where speaker A marks the object nominal as the pre-designated topical constituent for the addressee's response. Speaker B's and speaker C's utterances vary only in terms of the subject versus the object nominal occupying the sentence initial position, respectively. Speaker B's infelicitous response has the subject 'Rahul' and not the pre-designated topic constituent 'apple' in the sentence-initial position. In comparison, speaker C's felicitous response has the pre-designated topic constituent (the object nominal) in the sentence initial position.

(19) Speaker A: *mʊdʒʰe   seb=ke   bare=mẽ bətao*
                 I.DAT   apple=GEN about   tell.IMP.2SG
                 'Tell me about the apple'
     Speaker B: # *[rahʊl=ne]*$_{TOPIC}$ *seb*   *kʰaja*
                 Rahul=ERG   apple eat.PFV.3MSG
                 'Rahul ate the apple'
     Speaker C: *[seb]*$_{TOPIC}$ *rahʊl=ne*   *kʰaja*
                 apple   Rahul=ERG eat.PFV.3MSG
                 'The apple, Rahul ate'

From this minimal pair, it can be argued that it is the sentence initial position and not the subject NP that is biased to receive a topic interpretation in Hindi. This section focused on the topic status of constituents in an unmarked sentence in Hindi. The next section shifts the focus to sentences with *to*-marked constituents and checks their topical status vis-à-vis the methodology established here.

2.2 Testing *to*-marked XPs in Hindi

Examples (20) and (21) are uncontroversial vis-à-vis the previous literature since they re-affirm that the Hindi particle *-to* can mark AT and CT sentential constituents. Using the methodology of the *Tell me about X* test as part of the discourse contexts in (20) and (21), 'Ravi' and 'children' are pre-designated to be the topical constituent of the speaker B's utterances in these two examples, respectively. In (20), *to*-marked 'Ravi' is the AT about which information is provided and the CG content between the interlocutors is updated. In (21), the set of alternatives made available by the context is {Neha, Ravi}. The *to*-marked 'Ravi' receives the CT interpretation in this case as information is provided about it (hence, the topic role accorded to it) and it is in a contrastive relation with the contextually relevant alternative 'Neha', whose discourse status is unspecified and hence, different from that of the marked member of the alternatives set.

(20) Context: Two friends A and B have met up after a long time. A asks B about
      B's son Ravi and says, "Tell me about Ravi. What class is he in now?". To this,
      B responds:
      rəvɪ=to   əb   barvĩ=mẽ   hɛ
      Ravi=TO   now   12ᵗʰ=LOC   be.AUX.3SM
      '[Ravi]ₐₜ is in the 12ᵗʰ (class) now'

(21) Context: Two friends A and B have met up after a long time. B has two children:
      Neha and Ravi. A enquires about B's children and says, "Tell me about your
      children. What classes are they in now?". To this, B responds:
      rəvɪ=to   əb   barvĩ=mẽ   hɛ
      Ravi=TO   now   12ᵗʰ=LOC   be.AUX.3SM
      '[Ravi]꜀ₜ is in the 12ᵗʰ (class) now'

From this data, it follows that the topic marking by particle -*to* is optional in Hindi
since there can be unmarked topics (18)–(19) or *to*-marked topics (20)–(21) in a
sentence. Section 2.1 has established that sentence initial position is the topic bias
position in Hindi. Since Hindi has the base word order SOV, the ideal (for testing)
topic-type but non-topical candidate is the non-sentence-initial, in-situ object NP. In
example (22), particle -*to* marks the in-situ object NP 'banana'. This is not the sentential topic since the discourse context employs the diagnostic template to pre-des-
ignate 'Ravi' as the topical constituent. The *to*-marked object nominal is not the
topic since the utterance in (22) would be an infelicitous response to a preceding
contextual question of 'Tell me about the banana'. Therefore, this data is problematic for a topic marker analysis of particle -*to* as it is not marking the topical constituent in this sentence.

(22) Context: Ravi's mother gave an orange and a banana to him to eat. Her
      husband knows this information. After some time she sees the banana peel
      and not the orange peel in the dustbin. When her husband asks her, "Tell me
      about Ravi. What did he eat?", she tells him that:
      rəvɪ=ne   kela=to   kʰa   lija
      Ravi=ERG   banana=TO   eat   take.PFV.3MS
      'Ravi has eaten the banana'

To bring back the discussion of *to*-marking non-topical lexical categories (see
example (5)), example (23) is a case where an attributive adjective 'big' is being

marked by this particle in a particular discourse context.[12] This evidence, that adjectives do not have the appropriate categorical status to receive a topic interpretation and can yet be marked by particle *-to* in Hindi, strengthens the argument against a topic marker analysis of particle *-to*.

(23) Context: Ravi's mother gave a small sized banana and a big sized banana to him to eat. Her husband knows this information. After some time she sees the bigger banana peel and not the smaller banana peel in the dustbin. When her husband asks her, "Tell me about Ravi. What did he eat?", she tells him that:
ravɪ=ne   baɽa=to   kela   kʰa   lija
Ravi=ERG   big=TO   banana   eat   take.PFV.3MS
'Ravi has eaten the big banana'

To summarize this section, topical constituents may or may not be marked by enclitic particle *-to* in Hindi. In addition to topical entities, this particle can mark non-topical entities as well as non-topic-type categories in the language. On the basis of these observations, I propose that topicality (as an inherent property) should be dissociated from particle *-to*. I argue that particle *-to* is only indirectly related to the IS notion of topic and this interpretative effect is contingent on a syntactic configuration (sentence initial position) and a categorical restriction on the constituent being marked by *-to* (that it must be an entity or a discourse referent whose denotation is available in the CG). The discussion has thus far looked at the (indirect) mapping between this particle and the concept of topicality. The next section analyzes the interpretative import of this particle in cases where no topic interpretation is accorded to the marked constituent and argues for an independent contrastive interpretation as being possible for these *to*-marked constituents in Hindi.

3 Particle *-to* and contrast

This section looks closely at the non-topical constituents that get marked by the particle *-to* in Hindi and analyzes their interpretative import for a sentence (and the nature of the contribution of particle *-to* in this interpretation). Section 3.1

---

12 Note that this marking is felicitous only if there is an alternative to the property described by the attributive adjective (as associated with a discourse referent) in the CG. For the discourse context of (23), the CG has two bananas that vary in terms of the size property. Because of this type of Hindi data, I had proposed to extend the domain of Kim's definition of contrast to include properties of entities and not just entities or discourse referents in a context.

establishes contrast to be the independent interpretative effect available in these configurations and sections 3.3 to 3.4 analyze the mechanism by virtue of which this contrastive interpretation gets manifested in the *to*-marked Hindi data.

3.1 Interpretation of non-topical *to*-marked object nominal

A closer investigation of examples (22) and (23) highlights that the Hindi particle *-to* can mark a non-topical lexical item if and only if there is a relevant alternative to the marked designata in the CG.[13] In example (24), which is a modified version of example (22), the discourse context of the pragmatically felicitous (22) is changed such that it only contains one entity {banana} in the revised CG. Marking of the object NP 'banana' with particle *-to* leads to infelicity in this configuration in (24). The same pragmatic licensing requirement (for obligatory presence of a relevant type of alternative) was indicated in footnote 12 for example (23) in the case of a *to*-marked non-topical adjective.

(24) Context: Ravi's mother gave a banana to him to eat. Her husband knows this information. After some time she sees the banana peel in the dustbin. When her husband asks her, "Tell me about Ravi. Did he eat the banana?", she tells him that:

rəvɪ=ne   kela=(#to)   kʰa   lija
Ravi=ERG   banana=TO   eat   take.PFV.3MS
'Ravi has eaten the banana'

Besides this difference in terms of their licensing requirement, non-topical *to*-marked constituents also have an added reading to contribute to the sentence's interpretation that gives them a distinct status. In the utterance of the *to*-marked object nominal in example (22), repeated here as (25), certain inferences are also evoked besides the bare assertion of the proposition. These inferences are crucially absent in the unmarked counterpart of the sentence at issue. Because of this differ-

---

13 Note that this requirement on felicitous *to*-marking is not applicable when this particle marks a sentence-initial topical constituent. Depending on the number of relevant entities in the CG, the marked subject nominal 'Ravi' in the following example can receive either an AT (if there is only one referent in the CG) or a CT (in case of more than one relevant referent in the CG) interpretation:

rəvɪ=ne=to   kela   kʰa   lija
Ravi=ERG=TO banana   eat   take.PFV.3MS
'Ravi has eaten the banana'

ence, these inferences can then be traced back to the presence of particle *-to* within the larger meaning of the sentence. Some of these inferences are specified in (26).[14]

(25) Context: Ravi's mother gave an orange and a banana to him to eat. Her husband knows this information. After some time she sees the banana peel and not the orange peel in the dustbin. When her husband asks her, "Tell me about Ravi. What did he eat?", she tells him that:

rəvɪ=ne   kela=to   kʰa   lija
Ravi=ERG   banana=TO   eat   take.PFV.3MS
'Ravi has eaten the banana'

(26) Assertion: Ravi ate the banana.
Inference 1: The speaker does not know whether Ravi ate the orange.
Inference 2: The speaker knows that Ravi did not eat the orange.

Thus, *to*-marking of the in-situ object NP requires the alternatives to be available in the context and adds inferences, besides the bare assertion, to the speaker meaning conveyed by uttering that proposition. Assuming Kim's definition of contrast (outlined in section 2), I claim that *to*-marking of a non-topical constituent in a sentence evokes *inferences* that signal the marked entity being in a contrastive discourse relation with some alternative in the CG. This definition of contrast requires that the truth value of the predicate when applied to the alternative be either 'unknown' or 'false', in juxtaposition to the truth value of the asserted entity satisfying the predicate as 'true'. Applying this to example (25), it can be seen that for the assertion and inferences outlined in (26) – inference 1 indicates the 'unknown' truth value and inference 2 indicates the 'false' truth value for the application of the property P ('being eaten by Ravi') on the remaining member {orange} of the alternatives set while the assertion indicates that the application of this property on {banana} returns a true truth value.[15]

---

14 There can be inferences other than the two specified in (26) for the sentence given in example (25). For example: the speaker may know that Ravi had also eaten the orange but the speaker does not want to tell the addressee about the discourse status of this remaining alternative entity. This could be out of a fear of a possible scolding from Ravi's father in case he had eaten both fruits. Or this could be out of politeness concerns since the speaker may assume that the addressee is only interested in the discourse status of one entity and highlights only that information.
15 Similar inferences are evoked in the case of *to*-marking of a non-topical, attributive adjective, like in example (23) – that the speaker does not know whether Ravi ate the smaller banana or that the speaker knows that Ravi did not eat the smaller banana.

Assertion: Eat (Ravi, banana) = true
Inference 1: Eat (Ravi, orange) = unknown
Inference 2: Eat (Ravi, orange) = false

Based on this, I argue that particle *-to* marked constituents can also receive a pure contrastive interpretation (besides an AT and a CT interpretation) and this contrast is independent of the requirement of the marked constituent being a sentence topic (as stipulated by the topic marker analysis of particle *-to*). Since the working definition of contrast adopted for this paper employs the technical notion of 'implicature' (and not the general term 'inference' as used in this section) in its implementation of contrastive discourse relation, the next section provides an overview of the notion of implicatures, which is subsequently utilized in section 3.3 to analyze the inferences mentioned in this section as being implicatures that satisfy Kim's definition of contrast. Section 3.4 discusses the association between Hindi particle *-to* and these contrastive implicatures as being conversational and not conventional in nature.

3.2 Background on implicatures

An implicature is a type of inference that is considered to be a part of the total meaning conveyed by a speaker when uttering a sentence in a particular discourse context.[16] The literature on implicatures can be traced back to the influential work by Grice (1975, 1978) who proposed that discourse participants follow certain mutually known norms of conversation that govern permissible conversational moves in a discourse. These norms are called maxims of conversations and a version of them is listed in (27).

(27)   Maxim of Quality: Try to make your contribution one that is true
       Maxim of Quantity: Make your contribution as informative as is required
       Maxim of Relation: Be relevant
       Maxim of Manner: Be perspicuous

These norms are condensed into a pragmatic principle called the Cooperative Principle – "make a conversational contribution such as is required, at the stage at which it occurs, by the accepted purpose or direction of talk exchange in which one

---

16 The other two generally assumed inference types being entailments and presuppositions. These are not discussed here but interested readers can see, a.o., Chierchia and McConnel-Ginet (1990).

is engaged" (Simons 2012: 2). Implicatures arise because of a shared presumption of the speakers of a language that all discourse participants are cooperative and they adhere to the maxims of conversation. Adherence to or violation of a maxim in uttering a sentence in a context can lead to the evocation of an implicature.

The two types of implicatures that are relevant for the Hindi data discussed in this paper are an uncertainty implicature and a scalar implicature. An uncertainty implicature conveys that the speaker is indicating their certainty regarding only the content encoded in the assertion but implying their uncertainty regarding the discourse status of some contextually relevant but not asserted entities in the discourse. A scalar implicature, on the other hand, is an implicature that arises because of the adherence to or violation of the maxim of quantity. It is triggered by "the use of an informationally weaker term in an implicational scale" (Blome-Till-man 2013: 12). An implicational scale can be defined as "a set of lexical items that form a linear ordering according to their informational or logical strength" (Horn 1972). The strength involved in ranking a semantic scale is based on a logical entailment relation where a statement containing a more informative/stronger item asymmetrically entails a statement containing a less informative/weaker item.[17] For example, the English quantifiers 'all' and 'some' can be ranked on a semantic implicational scale where 'some' is logically weaker than 'all', i.e. 'some' < 'all.' Therefore, 'Some students came to school' implicates the negation of the logically stronger proposition i.e. 'Not all students came to school.'

A standard 'recipe' deriving a scalar implicature from the meaning of an utterance in a context in interaction with the cooperative principle has been formulated in Tomioka (2020: 24), which is cited in (28). Here, φ and ψ are variables that stand for propositions.

(28) a. The speaker S says φ.
   b. S could have made a stronger and/or more informative claim by saying ψ.
   c. The reason for S's not saying ψ may well be that S fails to believe that ψ is true.
   d. Assuming S is knowledgeable or has a strong opinion about the truth/falsity of ψ, one can conclude that S believes that ψ is false.

The next section 3.3 employs the terms introduced in this section to discuss the contrastive inferences that were seen to be evoked in section 3.1.

---

17 There is another type of implicational scale – a pragmatic implicational scale – that is based on a context-specific ranking of lexical items (like a prestige-based ranking) and is not calculated based on the logical entailment relation. For example, a person may ascribe different prestige levels to signatures of different members of the Beatles group, thereby ranking them on a pragmatic scale.

3.3 The Hindi contrastive implicatures

Returning to the non-topical, *to*-marked Hindi data under discussion in (25)–(26), repeated here as (29)–(30), it can be seen that the inferences 1 and 2 listed in (26) are actually an uncertainty implicature and a scalar implicature as specified in (30). For the given discourse context in (29), the relevant set of entities is {banana, orange}. By uttering (29), the speaker is asserting with certainty the discourse status of the *to*-marked entity and since the speaker is cooperative, simultaneously implying his/her uncertainty regarding the discourse status of the contextually relevant, left out entity 'orange'. This speaker uncertainty is expressed as the uncertainty implicature in (30).

(29) Context: Ravi's mother gave an orange and a banana to him to eat. Her husband knows this information. After some time she sees the banana peel and not the orange peel in the dustbin. When her husband asks her, "Tell me about Ravi. What did he eat?", she tells him that:
    rəvɪ=ne   kela=to   kʰa lija
    Ravi=ERG   banana-TO   eat   take.PFV.3MS
    'Ravi has eaten the banana'

(30) Assertion: Ravi ate the banana.
    Uncertainty Implicature: The speaker does not know whether Ravi ate the orange.
    Scalar Implicature: The speaker knows that Ravi did not eat the orange.

The inference 2 listed in (26) is a scalar implicature as specified in (30) because it is triggered by the use of an informationally weaker item in the sentence in (29). Since this example contains two non-related, discrete units in the context, the implicational scale based on informativeness cannot be a linear scale here. The relevant implicational scale here is one that is based on a partially ordered set (POSET) relation between the atomic sub-units 'banana' and 'orange' and their composite sum 'banana AND orange'. In this scale, the atomic sub-units are ranked equal for their informative strength and they both are informationally weaker than their composite sum. This is shown in (31).

(31) Implicational Scale: {banana},{orange} <{banana AND orange}

The logical reasoning underlying the proposition in (29) – 'Ravi ate the banana' implicating the negation of the informationally stronger proposition 'Ravi ate both the banana and the orange' and the subsequent deduction of the implicature that

'Ravi did not eat the orange' is listed as steps from (32a)–(32d). The scalar implicature in (30) can thus be calculated by adopting Tomioka's standard recipe as listed in (28) in conjunction with the poset relation-based implicational scale established out of the relevant entities in the discourse.

(32) a. Let proposition P: Ravi ate the banana.
          proposition Q: Ravi ate the orange.
          proposition R: Ravi ate both the banana and the orange.
      b. R entails P
          R entails Q
          P does not entail R
          Q does not entail R
      c. => On a scale, R is informationally stronger than P and Q
          => implicational scale: banana, orange < banana AND orange
      d. P implicates that it is not the case that R is true
          ~ 'Ravi ate the banana' implicates that 'It is not the case that Ravi ate the banana AND the orange'[18]
          ~ 'Ravi ate the banana' implicates that 'It is not the case that Ravi ate the banana OR It is not the case that Ravi ate the orange'[19]
          ~'Ravi ate the banana' implicates that 'It is not the case that Ravi ate the orange'

To conclude, the specific interpretative import of *to*-marked, non-topical, in-situ object NPs in a sentence is of evoking an uncertainty and a scalar implicature that then instantiate the contrastive discourse relation in the context. These implicatures have also been attested for the Japanese -*wa* (see Hara 2006a, 2006b; Tomioka 2010a, 2010b) and the Korean -*nun* particle (see Lee 2000, 2006, 2007; Kim 2013, 2018, 2019). However, these analyses associate such implicatures to a contrastive topic marking of a constituent by -*wa* or -*nun*. This paper differs from such analyses by proposing that it is 'contrast' itself and not a 'contrastive topic' marking that is the sufficient criterion for licensing such implicatures. The uncertainty and scalar implicatures (as contrastive implicatures) can be evoked when the marked constit-

---

18 This step involves application of standard De Morgan's Law: ¬ [x & y] = ¬ [x] V ¬ [y]
(here ¬, &, V stand for logical negation operator, conjunction operator and disjunction operator).
19 At this step, one of the disjuncts is in contradiction with the assertion. Because of this, the other disjunct gets valued true.

uent receives a contrastive interpretation and the topicality of that constituent is not a controlling factor in this interpretation.[20]

3.4 Diagnosing conventional v/s conversational status of the implicatures

Since the implicatures discussed in the preceding section are available only when particle -*to* marks the non-topical constituent, one research question that is pertinent is whether these implicatures are conventionally tied to this particle or whether they are conservational implicatures typologically. Before we diagnose the status of the Hindi contrastive implicatures under discussion (see (29)–(30)), conversational and conventional implicatures are introduced and differentiated below.

Conversational implicatures have been defined as "an implicature, the supposition of which is necessary for maintaining the assumption that the speaker is co-operative" (Grice 1975). These implicatures arise due to the interaction of the semantic content of the proposition uttered by a speaker within a context and the co-operative principle. Example (33) shows a conversational implicature licensed by the meaning of speaker B's sentence (the speaker slept while watching the movie) in the given discourse context and speaker A's assumption that speaker B is a cooperative interlocutor whose utterance move will be relevant to the topic of conversation (whether the movie was interesting or not).

(33) Context: Two friends, A and B, are talking about a movie that B had gone to see last night.
      Speaker A: *How was the movie? Was it good?*
      Speaker B: *I slept within the first half an hour.*
                Assertion: The speaker slept within 30 minutes of the movie's start.
                Implicature: The movie was boring.

---

20 It should be noted that the *to*-marked in-situ, object NP in Hindi is not obligatorily associated with a fall-rise prosodic contour or a B-accent (that is standardly assumed to accompany CT topics) and hence, this diagnostic is not applicable for motivating a distinct lexical status for a CT marker -*to*, parallel to the analyses proposing a CT -*wa* or -*nun* marker (see references in text). This judgement regarding the optional status of a fall-rise prosodic contour has been corroborated from 8 native Hindi linguists who participated in a formal syntax-semantics summer school in 2017 (LIS-SIM, Theme: Workshop on Information Structure; Instructor: Prof. Patrick Grosz) in Solang, India.

In contrast, conventional implicatures are a type of implicature that arise due to the conventional meaning associated with a particular lexical item in a sentence. In example (34), the conventional implicature is evoked because of the meaning associated with the lexical connective 'but' that conveys the unexpectedness of the situation described by the second clause in juxtaposition to the situation described by the first clause.

(34)   *He is from a village but he speaks English fluently.*
        Assertion: He is from a village. He is fluent in English.
        Implicature: A person from a village is not expected to speak English fluently.

Grice (1972) proposed a set of diagnostic characteristics (35) that conversational implicatures typically exhibit. This section employs this set of diagnostic properties to determine the type of contrastive implicatures that are evoked in the Hindi data under observation.

(35)   a.   Calculability: The addressee must be able to follow the series of inferences that derives the implicature.
       b.   Detachability: Conversational implicatures are not tied to particular linguistic expressions. If a sentence generates an implicature ψ, then φ', a sentence that is distinct from φ but expresses the same meaning as φ, gives rise to the same implicature ψ.
       c.   Indeterminacy: In a given situation, there may be more than one way to explain why the speaker made an utterance in a way that she did. Thus, there may be a disjunction of multiple possible implicatures associated with such an utterance.
       d.   Cancellability: Conversational implicatures can be negated without causing a logical contradiction.

Out of the four characteristics mentioned above, Hindi *to*-marked sentences cannot be evaluated for 'detachability' because there is no equivalent linguistic paraphrase for a sentence containing particle *-to* that conveys the same meaning. Calculability has been exhibited in the preceding section where the standard recipe of scalar implicatures was implemented to outline the steps of inferences that derive the contrastive scalar implicature in Hindi. Indeterminacy of the scalar implicature can be adduced by observing that a sentence containing a *to*-marked object NP can generate epistemic (speaker knowledge-oriented) implicatures like the uncertainty or the scalar implicature or it could also implicate other possible, non-epistemic inference (see footnote 14). Thus, multiple possible implicatures could be associated with a *to*-marked sentence in Hindi.

Cancellability requires that the implicature be negated without generating a logical contradiction in the given discourse context. Keeping the Hindi test sentence constant (as in example (29)), the sequence in (36) proves that the implicature 'B' generated by the test sentence 'A' can be cancelled and the form 'A and not B' does not cause any logical contradiction.

(36) Sentence A: *rəvɪ=ne kela=to kʰaja*
            'Ravi ate the banana'
      Sentence B: *rəvɪ=ne seb nəhɪ kʰaja*
            'Ravi did not eat the apple'
      Not B: It is not the case that Ravi did not eat the apple.
            ≈ Ravi ate the apple.
      A and not B: *rəvɪ=ne kela=to kʰaja. us=ne seb bʰɪ kʰa lɪja*
            'Ravi ate the banana, he also ate the apple'

From these diagnostic characteristics it can be concluded that the Hindi scalar implicature is calculable, indeterminate and cancellable. Based on these factors, I claim that the contrastive implicatures discussed here are not conventional implicatures that are lexically tied to the particle -*to* but are conversational implicatures that are triggered because of the total semantic content of the utterance in the given discourse context (including the meaning contribution of particle -*to*) and the assumption of the cooperative principle.

4 Conclusion

This paper has shown that contrast and topic are two discursive interpretations that are associated with enclitic particle -*to* in Hindi. However, unlike the previous treatment of this particle where topicality was the primary notion linked to this particle and contrast was a subsumed notion under the notion of topic (since contrast was contingent on how the set-anaphoric property of -*to* as a topic particle is satisfied), this paper has argued that contrast and topic require an independent ontological status and are only indirectly associated with this particle, contingent on certain syntactic and pragmatic factors.

Matić and Wedgwood (2013), and subsequently Kim (2013, 2015) critique directly linking an IS category with some grammatical reflex in language (and thereby giving it a 'universal' status), without adequately accounting for the full range of effects exhibited by that linguistic phenomenon. According to them, "if a unifying theoretical entity such as a cross-linguistic category is to be explanatory (or even useful), it should participate in a chain of causal reasoning from the existence of this entity, through any processes it triggers or participates in, and through its interactions with any relevant external factors, to the different effects we see in the data" (Matić and Wedgwood 2013: 137). Similar to their approach, the direction of enquiry in this paper has raised an issue with the one-to-one correspondence implied by a topic marker analysis of the Hindi particle *-to* and the IS notion of topic. This paper has claimed, contrary to the conventional understanding, that this particle is not a topic marker *per se*. It has shown that this particle can mark topical constituents, contrastive topic constituents and pure contrast marked constituents without one of these interpretations being an obligatory reflex of this particle. I conclude the paper here but the Hindi data and the discussion herein open up further domains of enquiry questioning the common core of particle *-to,* and cross-linguistically other such alleged topic particles, such that it can motivate a topic and a contrastive discursive effect, depending on the interaction of this particle with other syntactic-pragmatic factors. One approach (that I have developed and argued for in Bhalla (2021)) employs the notion of discourse prominence or salience (see a.o. Chiarcos 2011; Chiarcos, Claus, and Grabski 2011; Falk 2014) and claims that Hindi particle *-to* is a prominence lending cue (cf. von Heusinger and Schumacher 2019) that increases the salience of the marked sentential unit of information.[21] The common thread connecting the aboutness topic, contrastive topic and pure contrast interpretation of a constituent is the increase in discourse prominence status of them (similar to Mulkern 2007), which the speaker then employs to flag to the hearer that the marked unit of information is relevant for the current utterance and possibly for the upcoming discourse too.[22]

This paper is relevant because it motivates a re-investigation of the primary assumptions that link a linguistic notion with a grammatical reflex in any formal treatment of a grammatical phenomenon.

---

[21] Discourse salience is defined as "the degree of relative prominence of a unit of information, at a specific point in time, in comparison to the other units of information" (Chiarcos, Claus, and Grabski 2011: 2).

[22] I refer the reader to Bhalla (2021) to see the details of the idea linking salience, topic and contrast sketched here. I thank the anonymous reviewer who pointed out the work on informational prominence by Matthiessen (1992) and whose intuitions resonate with my own on this topic.

References

Bhalla, Ojaswee. 2021. *'To'-marked XPs in Hindi*. New Delhi: Jawaharlal Nehru University PhD dissertation.

Blome-Tillmann, Michael. 2013. Conversational implicatures (and how to spot them). *Philosophy Compass* 8(2). 170–185.

Chafe, Wallace. 1976. Givenness, contrastiveness, definiteness, subjects, topics and point of view. In Charles N. Li (ed.), *Subject and Topic*, 25–56. New York: Academic Press.

Chiarcos, Christian. 2011. On the dimensions of discourse salience. *Bochumer Linguistische Arbeitsberichte* 3. 31–44.

Chiarcos, Christian, Berry Claus & Michael Grabski (eds.). 2011. *Salience: Multidisciplinary Perspectives on its Function in Discourse*. Berlin/Boston: De Gruyter Mouton.

Chierchia, Gennaro & Sally McConnell-Ginet. 1990. *Meaning and Grammar: An Introduction to Semantics*. Cambridge: MIT Press.

Falk, Simone. 2014. On the notion of salience in spoken discourse-prominence cues shaping discourse structure and comprehension. *TIPA. Travaux Interdisciplinaires sur la Parole et le Langage* 30. http://journals.openedition.org/tipa/1303

Féry, Caroline & Shinichiro Ishihara (eds.). 2016. *The Oxford Handbook of Information Structure*. Oxford: Oxford University Press.

Grice, Herbert Paul. 1975. Logic and conversation. In Peter Cole & Jerry L. Morgan (eds.), *Syntax and Semantics 3: Speech Acts*, 41–58. New York: Academic Press.

Grice, Herbert Paul. 1978. Further notes on logic and conversation. In Peter Cole (ed.), *Pragmatics*, 113–127. (Syntax and Semantics 9). Leiden: Brill.

Hara, Yurie. 2006a. *Grammar of Knowledge Representation: Japanese Discourse Items at Interfaces*. Delaware: University of Delaware dissertation.

Hara, Yurie. 2006b. Implicature unsuspendable: Japanese contrastive wa. *Proceedings of Texas Linguistics Society* 8. 35–45.

Hinterwimmer, Stefan. 2011. Information structure and truth-conditional semantics. In Klaus von Heusinger, Claudia Maienborn & Paul Portner (eds.), *Semantics: An International Handbook of Natural Language Meaning*, Vol. 2, 1875–1908. Berlin/Boston: De Gruyter Mouton.

Horn, Laurence Robert. 1972. *On the Semantic Properties of Logical Operators in English*. Los Angeles: University of California dissertation.

Jacobs, Joachim. 2001. The dimensions of topic-comment. *Linguistics* 39(4). 641–682.

Kidwai, Ayesha. 2000. *XP-Adjunction in Universal Grammar: Scrambling and Binding in Hindi Urdu*. Oxford: Oxford University Press.

Kidwai, Ayesha. 2004. The topic interpretation in Universal Grammar. In Veneeta Dayal & Anoop Mahajan (eds.), *Clause Structure in South Asian Languages*, 253–289. Dordrecht: Kluwer.

Kim, Ilkyu. 2013. *Korean -(n)un, Salience, and Information Structure*. New Haven: Yale University dissertation.

Kim, Ilkyu. 2015. Is Korean -(n)un a topic marker? On the nature of -(n)un and its relation to information structure. *Lingua* 154. 87–109.

Kim, Ilkyu. 2016. Can Korean -(n)un mark (contrastive) focus? *Language Sciences* 56. 105–117.

Kim, Ilkyu. 2018. Is contrastive implicature induced by Korean CT-marking (n)un conventional or conversational? *Korean Journal of Linguistics* 43(2). 223–247.

Kiss, Katalin É. 1998. Identificational focus versus information focus. *Language* 74(2). 245–273.

Krifka, Manfred. 2008. Basic notions of information structure. *Acta Linguistica Hungarica* 55(3–4). 243–276.

Lambrecht, Knud. 1994. *Information Structure and Sentence Form*. Cambridge: Cambridge University Press.

Lee, Chungmin. 2000. Contrastive predicates and conventional scales. In Arika Okrent & John Boyle (eds.), *Papers from the 36th Annual Meeting of the Chicago Linguistic Society*, 243–257. http://clee.pe.hu/papers/CT-CLSrev.pdf

Lee, Chungmin. 2006. Contrastive topic/focus and polarity in discourse. In Klaus von Heusinger & Ken Turner (eds.), *Where Semantics meets Pragmatics*, 381–420. Leiden: Brill.

Li, Charles N. & Sandra A. Thompson. 1976. Subject and topic: A new typology of language. In Charles N. Li (ed.), *Subject and Topic*, 457–489. New York: Academic Press.

Matić, Dejan & Daniel Wedgwood. 2013. The meanings of focus: The significance of an interpretation-based category in cross-linguistic analysis. *Journal of Linguistics* 49(1). 127–163.

Matthiessen, Christian M. I. M. 1992. Interpreting the textual metafunction. In Martin Davies & Louise Ravelli (eds.), *Advances in Systemic Linguistics: Recent Theory and Practice*, 37–82. London: Pinter.

Miyagawa, Shigeru. 1987. Wa and the WH phrase. In John Hinds, Shoichi Iwasaki & Senko K. Maynard (eds.), *Perspectives on Topicalization: The Case of the Japanese wa*, 185–220. Amsterdam: John Benjamins.

Molnár, Valéria. 2002. Contrast – from a contrastive perspective. In Hilde Hasselgård, Stig Johansson, Bergljot Behrens & Cathrine Fabricius-Hansen (eds.), *Information Structure in a Crosslinguistic Perspective*, 147–161. Amsterdam: Rodopi.

Molnár, Valéria. 2006. On different kinds of contrast. In Valéria Molnár & Susanne Winkler (eds.), *The Architecture of Focus*, 197–234. Berlin: Mouton de Gruyter.

Montaut, Annie. 2015. The discourse particle to and word ordering in Hindi: From grammar to discourse. In M. M. Jocelyne Fernandez-Vest & Robert D. Van Valin (eds.), *Information Structuring of Spoken Language from a Cross-linguistic Perspective*, 263–284. Berlin: Mouton de Gruyter.

Mulkern, Ann E. 2007. Knowing who's important: Relative discourse salience and Irish pronominal forms. In Nancy Hedberg & Ron Zacharski (eds.), *The Grammar-Pragmatics Interface: Essays in honor of Jeanette K. Gundel*, 113–142. Amsterdam: John Benjamins.

Neeleman, Ad, Elena Titov, Hans van de Koot & Reiko Vermeulen. 2009. A syntactic typology of topic, focus and contrast. In Jeroen van Craenenbroeck (ed.), *Alternatives to Cartography*, 15–52. Berlin/Boston: De Gruyter Mouton.

Neeleman, Ad & Reiko Vermeulen (eds.). 2012. *The Syntax of Topic, Focus, and Contrast: An Interface-based Approach*. Berlin/Boston: De Gruyter Mouton.

Portner, Paul & Katsuhiko Yabushita. 1998. The semantics and pragmatics of topic phrases. *Linguistics and Philosophy* 21(2). 117–157.

Reinhart, Tanya. 1981. Pragmatics and linguistics: An analysis of sentence topics in pragmatics and philosophy. *Philosophica* 27(1). 53–94.

Repp, Sophie. 2010. Defining 'contrast' as an information-structural notion in grammar. *Lingua* 120(6). 1333–1345.

Rochemont, Michael. 2019. Topics and givenness. In Valéria Molnár, Verner Egerland & Susanne Winkler (eds.), *Architecture of Topic*, 47–66. Boston/Berlin: De Gruyter.

Rooth, Mats. 1992. A theory of focus interpretation. *Natural Language Semantics* 1(1). 75–116.

Schwarzschild, Roger. 1999. Givenness, AvoidF and other constraints on the placement of accent. *Natural Language Semantics* 7(2). 141–177.

Selkirk, Elisabeth O. 1984. *Phonology and Syntax*. Cambridge: MIT Press.

Stalnaker, Robert. 1974. Pragmatic presupposition. In Milton Karl Munitz & Peter K. Unger (eds.), *Semantics and Philosophy*, 197–214. New York: New York University Press.

Stalnaker, Robert. 2002. Common ground. *Linguistics and Philosophy* 25(5–6). 701–721.

Tomioka, Satoshi. 2010. Contrastive topics operate on speech acts. In Malte Zimmermann & Caroline Féry (eds.), *Information Structure: Theoretical, Typological, and Experimental Perspectives*, 115–138. Oxford: Oxford University Press.

Tomioka, Satoshi. 2020. Conversational implicature. In Wesley M. Jacobsen & Yukinori Takubo (eds.), *Handbook of Japanese Semantics and Pragmatics*, 773–798. Boston/Berlin: De Gruyter Mouton.

Vallduví, Enric & Maria Vilkuna. 1998. On rheme and kontrast. *The Limits of Syntax* 29. 79–108.

von Fintel, Kai. 1994. *Restrictions on Quantifier Domains*. Amherst: University of Massachusetts at Amherst dissertation.

von Heusinger, Klaus & Petra B. Schumacher. 2019. Discourse prominence: Definition and application. *Journal of Pragmatics* 154. 117–127.

Wagner, Michael. 2012. Contrastive topics decomposed. *Semantics and Pragmatics* 5. 1–54.

Zimmermann, Malte & Caroline Féry (eds.). 2009. *Information Structure: Theoretical, Typological, and Experimental Perspectives*. Oxford: Oxford University Press.

Part II: **Different types of contrast**

Jan Fliessbach

5 Mirativity, obviousness, and reversal as instances of contrast on different levels of meaning: Evidence from Spanish intonation

Abstract: Three intonational contours have been identified as markers of contrastive focus in the literature on Castilian Spanish: an early rise-fall (L+H* L%), a late rise-fall (L* HL%), and higher H tone scaling on early rise-falls (L+¡H* L%). This contribution argues that this abundance of contours for contrastive focus is due to a conflation of different kinds of contrast, which arise out of specific discourse configurations. We explore three axes of pragmatic variation that can give rise to such configurations: 1) whether a turn is a provocation or a response, i.e. the first or second part of an adjacency pair, 2) relative polarity, i.e. whether responses reverse or confirm a previous provocation, and 3) non-at-issue meanings such as mirativity or obviousness. We propose to treat mirativity, obviousness, and reversal as instances of contrast on different levels of meaning: a contrast between two assertions (reversal), a contrast between an assertion and expectations (mirativity), or a contrast between the presumption of relevance of a provocation and the expectability of its response (obviousness). Comparative observations about the interaction of polarity particles with suffixes for (un)expectedness in Kogi, Kurtöp, and Turkish are combined with evidence from a production experiment on Spanish intonation to show that (dis)agreement and (un)expectedness are two dimensions of dialogue meaning that can create contrasts, both individually and in combination. We therefore conclude that intonation research needs a notion of contrast that includes what it is that contrasts and that allows for simple and complex contrasts. Such a perspective will acknowledge that the Spanish L+¡H* L% and L* HL% contours are not primarily markers of contradiction, but rather of mirativity and obviousness, respectively.

Acknowledgements: This article has benefited from the helpful comments of two anonymous reviewers. I also want to thank Uli Reich, Timo Buchholz, Paolo Roseano, Lisa Brunetti, and Clara Huttenlauch for fruitful discussions at various stages of the project. The empirical observations would not have been possible without the support by María Sancho Pascual and the PRESEEA Madrid group, as well as the study participants.

https://doi.org/10.1515/9783110986594-005

1 Introduction: The problem of contrastive intonation in Spanish

There is abundant research on the intonation of contrastive focus in Spanish, in particular in the Castilian Spanish variety. Yet the results of these studies are in part inconsistent among each other. Face (2001b,a, 2002) proposes several different markers of contrastive focus, with an early rise-fall nuclear configuration L+H* L% as the main intonational marker. According to Face (2002), higher scaling of the H target on early rise-falls is an additional phonetic marker of contrastive focus.[1] Gabriel (2007) does not include scaling, but restricts contrastive focus marking to L+H* L%. Prieto & Roseano (2009–2013) and Hualde & Prieto (2015), on the other hand, take a late rise-fall L* HL% to be a more emphatic marker of contrastive focus than L+H* L%. Hualde & Prieto (2015: 369) state that "although the overall shape of the contour is essentially the same (rise-fall), there is an important different alignment of the H with respect to the tonic, resulting in perceptually quite different contours. [. . .] Where both nuclear contours are found, L* HL% carries a greater emphatic, contradictory force". This difference is reflected in the fact that Prieto & Roseano (2009–2013) took L+H* L% to be a free variant of the low falling L* L% intonation in neutral or broad focus statements, with L* HL% presented as the marker of contrastive focus. Finally, Prieto & Roseano (2009–2013) and Hualde & Prieto (2015) attribute upstepped H targets in early rise-falls (L+¡H* L%) to exclamatives, but leave open the question how this configuration relates to the scaling differences observed in Face (2002).

All in all, it is clear that the state of the art on contrastive focus intonation in Spanish is inconsistent in these regards. This begs the question whether the problem is rooted in the description of phonological forms or in the pragmatic notions associated with them. This paper discusses evidence for the latter to be the case, and interprets the inconsistent results on Spanish intonation as due to a conflation of different kinds of contrast under the notion of 'contrastive focus'. It thereby tackles a problem already noted in Repp (2016: 7): "languages may differ as to how contrastive discourses must be before certain marking strategies are applied [and] many studies (e.g. in the Romance prosody literature [. . .]) ignore this potentially important aspect". The present article differs from Repp (2016) in that it does not require a contrastiveness scale. Such a scale is presupposed by the idea that discourse configurations must overcome a contrastiveness threshold to license certain forms of

---

[1] It is unclear how his proposal relates to the phonological idea of upstepped (or categorically higher) L+¡H* L%.

contrast marking. Cruschina (2021: 2) explicitly spells out a contrastiveness scale in the form: information focus < exhaustive focus < mirative focus < corrective focus.[2]

Instead of ranking correction and mirativity, we will understand them as arising from independent parameters of meaning in dialogue that can combine to create complex contrasts. This means, for example, that combinations of correction and mirativity are possible, but also combinations of correction and obviousness. The first parameter we will discuss describes whether a turn is a provocation or a response, i.e. the first or second part of an adjacency pair (Sacks et al. 1974, Schegloff & Sacks 1973).[3] The second parameter is dependent on the first one: the discourse update of a responding move can contrast with its provocation (i.e. a biased question or an assertion) in terms of disagreement (also called reversal or denial; Farkas & Bruce 2010), a contrastive relation that is not possible for a provocation in our simplified model of dialogue.[4] The third parameter we will discuss arises from expectations based on shared assumptions that can match or conflict with the at-issue discourse update associated with a turn in dialogue, with both a match (obviousness) and a mismatch (mirativity) creating different kinds of contrast: a contrast between expected and accepted content in the case of miratives, and a contrast between the expectability of a response and the presumption of relevance underlying its provocation in the case of statements of the obvious (Sperber & Wilson 1995: 270). This perspective allows not only for mirative or obvious (dis)agreement, but also for (dis)agreement without any expectational evaluation and for mirative/obvious provocations that neither accept nor reject any proffered content. It might still be possible to rank these configurations according to a contrastiveness scale. The important point here is that their inherent differences would license differences in marking even if such a scale would not apply.

The present proposal is inspired by the insight that contrast is a "multi-faceted phenomenon" that requires "fine-grained comparisons of alternative types and/or discourse relations" (Repp 2016: 289). Cruschina (2021: 2) states that "the binary distinction between contrastive and non-contrastive focus, which is tra-

---

2 Note that this proposal is similar, though not identical, to the hierarchy of common ground revision strength in Verhoeven & Skopeteas (2015: 24), which goes "confirmation < selection < completion < correction". Note also that we use greater-than signs here for comparability, while Cruschina (2021: 2) uses > as arrows pointing up the scale.

3 With the renewed interest in representing discourse structure in the form of Question Under Discussion trees (Hesse et al. 2020, Riester 2019, among others), the idea of connecting or pairing utterances that raise and settle issues has regained popularity in the linguistic literature. We still think that specific notions for the parts of such pairs are needed and will refer to them as provocations and responses.

4 But see Beyssade & Marandin (2007) for the idea that French provocations can prosodically mark the anticipation that they will disagree with responses.

ditionally advocated to explain the syntactic distribution of focus, must be abandoned in favour of the identification of different 'degrees' or 'types' of contrastive focus." While Cruschina discusses degrees of contrast, this article explores types of contrast.[5]

Section 2 introduces the kinds of discourse meanings involved in the creation of the aforementioned contrasts via examples from languages with morphological marking for them. Section 3 then discusses further evidence for their independence from a production study on different kinds of contrast as marked by Spanish intonation. Section 4 formalizes the observed discourse configurations within an extended version of the Farkas & Bruce model. Section 5 concludes with the general implications for the notion of contrast, with a comparison of our observations with some relevant parts of the literature on intonational meaning, and with some open questions.

2 Morphological encoding of (dis)agreement and (un)expectedness

Given the relative evasiveness of intonational forms, languages with morphological means to express (dis)agreement and (un)expectedness lend themselves as a starting point for the argument made here. After laying out the distinction between (dis)agreement (also called *relative polarity*, Farkas & Bruce 2010) and *absolute polarity* with examples from German and Romanian in Subsection 2.1, Subsections 2.2 and 2.3 will introduce *mirativity* (unexpectedness marking) and *obviousness* (expectedness marking) with examples from Turkish, Kogi, and Kurtöp. We will also discuss examples that shed light on the relation between markers of (un)expectedness and relative polarity. Section 3 will subsequently return to the question of Spanish "contrastive" intonation.

2.1 (Dis)agreement

German *nein* 'no' is ambiguous between agreement and reversal in responses to negative provocations (1). Speakers have to use the particle *doch* 'yes[REVERSE]' if they want to convey a reverse response unambiguously without further explanation .

---

5 See Fliessbach (2023) for more background and an extension of this proposal to Spanish discourse particles.

(1)   (German)
    a.   **A:** Anna ist nicht gegangen.   [−]
        'Anna hasn't left.'
    b.   **B:** Nein.   [?]
        'No.'
    c.   **B:** Nein, du hast recht, sie ist nicht gegangen.   [SAME,−]
        'No, you're right, she hasn't left.'
    d.   **B:** Nein, du hast unrecht, sie ist gegangen.   [REVERSE,+]
        'No, you're wrong, she has left.'
    e.   **B:** Doch.   [REVERSE,+]
        'Yes[REVERSE].' (she has)

A second case in point to illustrate morphological marking of reversal is Romanian (Farkas & Bruce 2010: 112). Romanian has three polarity particles: *nu* 'not/no', *da* 'yes', and *ba* '[REVERSE]'. Their distribution is restricted in provocations, with only the absence (2a), (3a) or presence (4a), (5a) of *nu* 'not' distinguishing between positive and negative absolute polarity. Responses have additional options: *da* 'yes' marks agreement or confirmation of a positively biased provocation. *Nu* also occurs in responses, but does not suffice to mark disagreement with a biased provocation. This is marked with *ba* '[REVERSE]' (2b), (4b), (5b).

(2)   (Romanian)
    a.   **A:** Ana a plecat.   [+]
        'Ana has left.'
    b.   **B:** Ba nu, n-a plecat. / # Nu, n-a plecat.   [REVERSE,−]
        'No, she hasn't left.'

(3)   a.   **A:** Ana a plecat?
        'Has Ana left?'
    b.   **B:** Nu. / Nu, n-a plecat. / # Ba nu. / # Ba nu, n-a plecat.   [−]
        'No, she hasn't.'

(4)   a.   **A:** Ana nu a plecat.   [−]
        'Ana hasn't left.'
    b.   **B:** Ba da. / Ba da, a plecat. / Ba a plecat.   [REVERSE,+]
        'You're wrong, she has left.'

(5)   a.   **A:** Ana nu a plecat?   [−]
        'Hasn't Ana left?'

b. **B:** Ba da. / Ba da, a plecat. / Ba a plecat. [REVERSE,+]
   '*Yes, she has.*'

(Farkas & Bruce 2010: 112)

In the following, we will refer to the relative polarity axis of discourse meaning as (dis)agreement. We should bear in mind that we only see responses as specified for (dis)agreement, a restriction that does not apply to (un)expectedness.

2.2 Mirativity

As mentioned above, disagreement can be seen as a case of contrastive focus (Gabriel 2007: 39, 54). Yet many more contrastive relations have been brought up in the literature. Among them are the selection between salient alternatives (Lee 2017: 10), but also mirativity. The inclusion of expectations in the definition of focus is not new. Zimmermann (2008: 354) defines contrastive focus marking as an expression of "the speaker's assumption that the hearer will not consider the content of [the marked constituent] or the speech act containing [the marked constituent] likely to be(come) common ground". What distinguishes Zimmermann's definition of contrastive marking from disagreement is the understanding that, even in the absence of open disagreement, speakers calculate the likelihood of proffered content to become common ground. In cooperative dialogue, this calculation can be seen as based on the prior common ground, from which possible worlds are accessed (Fliessbach 2023).[6] The speaker will consider proffered content unlikely to become common ground if there are few or no possible worlds accessible from the common ground in which the proffered content is true.[7] And while "few" is a relative notion that need not lead to any form of contrast, a speech act proffering content that is not accessible at all from the prior common ground would require overt marking to be felicitous (Reich 2018). This can be seen in the grammatical marking of surprise, or mirativity (DeLancey 1997, 2012, Hengeveld & Olbertz 2012, Rett 2011, Rett & Sturman 2020), which can be understood as the marking of a mismatch between expected and asserted content (Fliessbach 2023).

The first question that arises is whether a specific language will mark such a contrast differently than cases of disagreement. This can be seen most easily in languages with morphological marking of mirativity, as opposed to non-morphological

---

6 And possibly ranked according to epistemic, bouletic, or deontic ordering sources. In a deviation from Kratzer (2012) and Bianchi et al. (2016), we do not consider a stereotypical ordering source to be a distinct kind of modality, but rather a different temporal perspective on modality.

7 Or if those that are accessible are ranked low.

mirative strategies such as focus fronting (Brunetti 2009, Bianchi et al. 2016, Cruschina 2019, 2021) and mirative intonation (Rett & Sturman 2020).[8]

Turkish is an example for a language in which evidential morphology is routinely extended to mirative uses. Past tense expressions referring to completed events receive either -di / -du for 'direct experience' or -miş / -muş for 'indirect experience/hearsay'. These suffixes change their meaning when attached "to a stative or existential expression or to verb complexes conveying iterative, habitual, or durative notions" (Aksu Koç & Slobin 1986: 161). (6) is a Turkish provocation used as a compliment after hearing someone play the piano (Aksu Koç & Slobin 1986: 162).

(6)   (Turkish)

Kız-	ınız	çok	iyi	piyano	çal-ıyor-muş
daughter	2PL.POSS	very	good	piano	play-PRES-MIR

'Your daughter plays the piano very well!'

                                                     (Aksu Koç & Slobin 1986: 162)

In such an example, an inference or hearsay interpretation of -muş is not available due to the first hand knowledge of the speaker. Instead, it conveys that the speaker was not prepared for the experience and can be paraphrased as "No matter how high my expectations might have been, what I have just heard exceeded them" (DeLancey 1997: 38). According to native speaker judgements, -miş / -muş is not only felicitous in provocations such as (6), but also responses such as (7b, c).[9]

(7)   (Turkish)

Context: A and B are listening to A's son play the piano.

a. **A:**
Oğl-	um	çok	iyi	piyano	çal-m-ıyor
son	my	very	good	piano	play-NEG-PRES

'My son does not play the piano very well.'

b. **B:**
Evet	oğl-	unuz	çok	iyi	piyano	çal-m-ıyor-muş
yes	son	your	very	good	piano	play-NEG-PRES-MIR

'Indeed, your son does not play- miş the piano well!'

c. **B:**
Hayir	oğl-	unuz	çok	iyi	piyano	çal-ıyor-muş
no	son	your	very	good	piano	play-PRES-MIR

'No, your son does play- miş the piano very well!'

---

8 The evasiveness of intonational or syntactic marking has even led some researchers to only consider morphological marking as "grammatical" (Aikhenvald 2004, 2012).

9 Note that *evet* 'yes' and *hayir* 'no' alone are again ambiguous in responses to negative provocations. I thank Deniz Özyıldız and Kardelen Günaydin for their help, while all possible errors of course remain my own.

(7c) shows that disagreement and mirativity can be marked in a response and create a context update with two contrasts: an at-issue contrast between two discourse commitments ('*No, he does . . .*'), and a non-at-issue contrast between the interlocutors' expectations and the asserted content (-*muş* '*Wow!*'). The disagreement wouldn't be stronger or weaker if mirativity wasn't marked.[10] Rather, no mismatch between expectations and the assertion would be marked, leaving only the contrastive relation between the two commitments. Similarly, the contrast between the expectations and the confirmed content in (7b) is not lessened by the fact that there is no disagreement about the at-issue content.[11]

2.3 Obviousness

A sometimes overlooked aspect of mirativity is the fact that it can stand in paradigmatic relationship not only with its own absence, but also with statements of the obvious (assertion of information that follows from shared knowledge, Reich 2018: 116). This can be seen in Kogi (also written Cogui), an Arhuacic language from the Chibchan family (Hammarström et al. 2022), and in Kurtöp (also written Kurtokha), a Bumthangic language from the East Bodish branch of the Sino-Tibetan family (Hammarström et al. 2022).

Kogi can mark complex epistemic perspectives via four prefixes that attach to the finite auxiliary verb. We can compare their effect to a sentence without such a prefix that conveys a statement on the internal state of the addressee (8). Adding the prefix *ni-* signals "something that the speaker assumes to be obvious to the addressee (i.e., the state of being/getting tired)" (9), (10) (Bergqvist 2016: 18). The use of *na-*, on the other hand, alerts the addressee to something he has failed to notice (11), (12).[12]

---

10 In terms of Destruel et al. (2019: 3), it has the same degree of *contrariness*, because the "degree of commitment that an addressee is established to have to a contrary focal alternative" is the same.
11 It would be interesting, though, to test whether -*miş* / -*muş* in (7b) would score higher in acceptability ratings if (7a) contained -*miş* / -*muş* as well, thereby creating a case of overt alignment between A and B both in terms of at-issue commitments and non-at-issue evaluations.
12 There are also two corresponding forms *shi-* and *sha-*, which encode the same expectability distinction. They have been seen as the interrogative counterparts of *ni-* and *na-*, but actually invite "the addressee to challenge or amend the expectations and assumptions of the speaker" (Bergqvist 2016: 28). A fifth prefix -*ska* marks uncertainty or conjecture.

(8) (Kogi)

    uba   ma-Ø-kwí -hĭ
    eye   2o-3s-have-PRTC
    '*You are tired(?)*' (lit., the eyes have you)

(9)   uba   na-kwĭ   ni-Ø-gua-tăw
    eye   1o-have.PRTC   SPKR.SYM-3s-do-PROG
    '*I'm getting tired*' (said yawning)

(10) uba   ma-kwĭ   ni-Ø-gua-tăw
    eye   2o-have.PRTC   SPKR.SYM-3s-do-PROG
    '*You're getting tired*' (suggesting the addressee should go to bed)

(11) uba   na-kwĭ   na-Ø-gua-tăw
    eye   1o-have.PRTC   SPKR.ASYM-3s-do-PROG
    '*I'm getting tired*' (said as a reason for wanting to go to bed)

(12) uba   ma-kwĭ   na-Ø-gua-tăw
    eye   2o-have.PRTC   SPKR.ASYM-3s-do-PROG
    '*What you are is tired*' (said to alert the addressee)

(Bergqvist 2016: 18)

Assuming that (9) and (10) are provocations, the use of *ni-* acknowledges the redundancy of the assertion and thereby allows for the perlocutionary effects of excuse or suggestion indicated by Bergqvist. Unfortunately, we do not know whether these sentences would be possible as responses, and if so, to which kind of provocations they would respond.

The grammar of Kurtöp by Hyslop (2011) offers another glimpse into the possibilities of combining markers of (dis)agreement with markers of (un)expectedness. Kurtöp has two mirative suffixes, *-na* and *-ta* (Hyslop 2011: 592–594, 601–602, 618, 622, 625).[13] They contrast with *-pala*, which marks information as not-unexpected and not based on evidence to which the speaker has exclusive access. According to Hyslop (2011: 588), all affirmative statements and questions require one marker of evidentiality or "related categories", whereas these categories "are not encoded in negative statements or imperatives". There are however exceptions to this rule, which show that the incompatibility between negative statements and markers of

---

13 As well as a mirative copula *nâ* and the egophoric suffix *-shang*. *-ta* can combine with the particle *=sa* to mark mirative perfective aspect or unexpected outcome.

expectedness is not categorical. The suffix -ta combines with the negator *min* 'no/ not' in (13): "A typical example [for minta] is when someone self-corrects" (Hyslop 2011: 618).

(13) (Kurtöp)

net	zon	minta	net	sum	Pema	Drakpa	net
1.PL	two	COP.EQ.NEG.MIR	1.PL.ABS	three	Pema	Drakpa	1.PL.ABS
sum							
three							

'*Not the two of us. . . three of us, (with) Pema Drakpa (there were) three of us*'
(Hyslop 2011: 618)

Hyslop (2011: 597) also gives the example (14), where -*pala* combines with the negative absolute polarity prefix *ma*- in an agreement. It seems that positive relative polarity licenses -*pala* in a sentence with negative absolute polarity. This again shows that the notion of a "negative statement" is insufficient to rule out markers of (un)expectedness. A response with a negation can agree with a negative provocation, and marking such an agreeing response as expected can add a sense of shared assumptions and mutual understanding.

(14) (Kurtöp)

Context: This example is part of a two-person narrative about how life used to be in the village in Kurtö. The interlocutor has just stated that she did not suffer, and the response in the example serves to "immediately agree" (Hyslop 2011: 597) with that statement.

wit-ya	ma-chut-pala
2.ABS-also	NEG-cut-PFV

'*You didn't suffer, either*' (Hyslop 2011: 597)

Examples (13) and (14) show two things that are important for our general argument: 1) much as in Turkish, relative polarity in Kurtöp is in principle independent from the dimension of expectability, and 2) the confirmation of an assertion by the interlocutor or the self-correction by the speaker, when based on previously held assumptions, can make additional markers of expectability available in contexts where sentence-internal negation would otherwise block them.

2.4 Taking stock

In section 2, we have reviewed the literature on morphologically encoded mirativity and linked it to literature on morphologically encoded obviousness. We see this as an important step to prove the grammatical validity of the notion of (un)expectedness. Moreover, we have shown that (dis)agreement marking can be independent from the encoding of (un)expectedness, notwithstanding the possibility for portmanteau morphs to express both. These insights will be important building blocks for our goal of understanding 'contrastive focus intonation' in Spanish. The following section 3 will present the results of an experiment, reported with additional methodological background in Fliessbach (2023), that was designed to test the degree to which it is possible to elicit intonational variability in Spanish sentences by controlling the aforementioned parameters. In the present article, we will reflect on the results in terms of their implications for the notion of contrast.

3 (Dis)agreement and (un)expectedness in Spanish intonation

Evidence from languages genealogically unrelated to Spanish can only serve as an indication of the space of possible discourse configurations, but does not tell us if and how Spanish intonation cues them. While Spanish lacks the morphological marking found in languages such as Turkish, Kogi, or Kurtöp, intonation can be employed as an alternative strategy to mark (dis)agreement and (un)expectedness in responding turns in dialogue. A brief review of the results of an experiment first reported in Fliessbach (2023: 187–227) shows the impact of both relative polarity and expectability on Spanish intonation, and thereby helps us understand the puzzle of incongruent results presented in section 1.

3.1 Experimental method and procedure

The experiment recapitulated in this section, reported in more detail in Fliessbach (2023), tested the hypothesis that both (un)expectedness and (dis)agreement would have an impact on the prosodic form of Spanish sentences. Here, we will discuss it with a special emphasis on the notion of contrast. Accepting the aforementioned hypothesis would support the idea that the two parameters of meaning can interact to create complex contrasts, not only via morphological means (as illustrated in section 2), but also prosodically. The experimental design was an adaptation of the Discourse Completion paradigm. The participants were shown context descriptions and dialogues between two speakers (A and B) that contained between two and five turns, with a target turn by B towards the end of the sequence. The participants were told that they would play B's role. The turns by A were pre-recorded by a native speaker to keep their prosodic form constant. The participants had to read and memorize the context and the entire dialogue before they would interact with the pre-recorded voice. The playback of A's turns was controlled manually by an experimenter to approximate the timing and fluidity of an oral conversation.

The context descriptions systematically changed the degree of expectability of the context update brought about by the target turn. A neutral interrogative context with a declarative target response (neutral assertion) served as a baseline for prosodic comparison with an unexpected response (mirative assertion) and an expected response (obvious assertion). Prosodic variability induced by (dis)agreement was tested on the obvious level of the expectability scale, leading to obvious confirmations (agreement + obviousness) and obvious reversals (disagreement + obviousness). Five out of six target sentences had declarative syntax.[14] Moreover, the experiment included one *wh*-exclamative condition to check if marked prosody follows from marked syntactic form. The final word of the target sentences remained the same across the six conditions. (15) shows a stimulus for a neutral declarative sentence. (16) shows a stimulus for a mirative declarative sentence. (17) shows a stimulus for a sentence with *wh*-exclamative syntax. (18) shows a stimulus for an obvious assertion. (19) shows a stimulus for an obvious confirmation. (20) shows a stimulus for an obvious reversal. Six such blocks were recorded, each with a different target word: *limonada* 'lemonade', *gobierno* 'government', *alemana* 'German$_{FEMININE}$', *mandarina/mandarino* 'tangerine/tangerine tree', *Bilbao* 'Bilbao', *vegana* 'vegan$_{FEMININE}$'. The pre-recorded stimuli by speaker A are accessible via hyperlinks behind the adjacent 🔊 symbols. For the purpose of illustration, two *'typical'* target recordings per condition are also linked.[15]

---

14 Being mainly concerned with Spanish prosody, the experiment did not test the relation between mirativity and fronting (Cruschina 2019), or between insubordination and obviousness (Elvira-García 2016, Schwenter 2016) in Spanish. These syntactic strategies would be alternative ways of marking some of the contrasts discussed here. See Fliessbach (2023) for general background and naturalistic data from dialogue corpora.

15 We thank a reviewer for the suggestion to include these. Note, however, that the audios for speaker B were not part of the original materials, but are part of the results and are presented together with the materials for reasons of space. They are only *'typical'* in the sense of positive statistical association discussed below.

(15)   (Spanish)

Con una amiga estas resolviendo un crucigrama. Te pregunta de dónde viene Adidas.
'You're solving a crossword puzzle with a friend. She asks you where Adidas is from.'

A: ¿Oye, de dónde es Adidas? 🔊
'Listen, where is Adidas from?'

B: Adidas es una empresa alemana. 🔊 🔊
'Adidas is a German company.'

(16)   Con una amiga estas resolviendo un crucigrama. Buscáis una empresa alemana de automóviles con cuatro letras. Queréis poner Audi, pero no entra con el resto del crucigrama. Buscas en línea y te das cuenta de que Seat forma parte del grupo Volkswagen. Esto no te lo esperabas.
'You're solving a crossword puzzle with a friend. You're looking for a German automotive company with four letters. You want to write down Audi, but it doesn't fit with the rest of the puzzle. You search online and become aware that Seat is part of the Volkswagen Group. You didn't expect that.'

A: Audi no entra. Y Seat no puede ser. 🔊
'Audi doesn't fit. And it can't be Seat.'

B: Espera, lo busco en internet.
'Wait, I'll check online.'

A: Vale. 🔊
'OK.'

B: ¡Seat es una empresa alemana! 🔊 🔊
'Seat is a German company!'

(17)   Con una amiga quieres ir a Múnich para el Oktoberfest. Cuando queréis ir al aeropuerto, ella llega vestida de trajes típicos bávaros, con sombrero y todo.
'With a friend, you want to go to Munich for the Oktoberfest. When you want to go to the airport, she arrives dressed in typically Bavarian clothes, with a hat and all.'

A: ¿Te gusto así? 🔊
'Do I look good to you like this?'

B: ¡Qué buena alemana! 🔊 🔊
'What a great German!'

(18) Sale en las noticias que viene Merkel a Madrid. Una amiga tuya siempre se cree la más lista de todos y se comporta como un verdadero sabelotodo. Te pregunta si es de Inglaterra o de Alemania, aunque todo el mundo lo sabe. Dile de dónde es y hazle sentir que debería saberlo.
'It's in the news that Merkel is coming to Madrid. A friend of yours always thinks she's the smartest of all and behaves like a real know-it-all. She asks if Merkel's from England or Germany, even though everbody knows that. Tell her where she's from and let her feel that she should know that.'

A: Oye,¿Merkel es inglesa o alemana? ◀ᵈ⫯
'Listen, is Merkel English or German?'

B: Merkel es alemana. ◀ᵈ⫯ ◀ᵈ⫯
'Merkel is German.'

(19) Sale en las noticias que viene Merkel a Madrid. Una amiga tuya siempre se cree la más lista de todos y se comporta como un verdadero sabelotodo. Cuando quiere asegurarse de que Merkel es alemana, le haces sentir que debería saberlo.
'It's in the news that Merkel is coming to Madrid. A friend of yours always thinks she's the smartest of all and behaves like a real know-it-all. When she wants to make sure that she's German, you let her feel that she should know that.'

A: Oye, Merkel es alemana, ¿verdad? ◀ᵈ⫯
'Listen, Merkel is German, right?'

B: Merkel es alemana. ◀ᵈ⫯ ◀ᵈ⫯
'Merkel is German.'

(20) Sale en las noticias que viene Merkel a Madrid. Una amiga tuya siempre se cree la más lista de todos y se comporta como un verdadero sabelotodo. Tu amiga piensa que Merkel es del Reino Unido, aunque todo el mundo sabe que es alemana. Hazle sentir que debería saberlo.
'It's in the news that Merkel is coming to Madrid. A friend of yours always thinks she's the smartest of all and behaves like a real know-it-all. Your friend thinks that Merkel is from Great Britain, even though everybody knows she's German. Give her the feeling that she should know that.'

A: Merkel es inglesa, ¿sabes? ◀ᵈ⫯
'Merkel is English, you know?'

B: Merkel es alemana. ◀ᵈ⫯ ◀ᵈ⫯
'Merkel is German.'

The recordings of 18 participants were analyzed after having discarded 7 teenage participants (who were found to be too intimidated by the setup in an isolation booth) and one participant who was under the influence of alcohol. 648 target turns were annotated in Praat (Boersma & Weenink 2017). Sp_ToBI annotation (Beckman et al. 2002, Estebas-Vilaplana & Prieto 2008, Hualde & Prieto 2015) was done manually and automatically. Automatic annotation was done using a modified version of Eti_ToBI (Elvira-García et al. 2016). There was 72.4% agreement between automatic and manual annotation for entire nuclear configurations (pitch accent + boundary tone), which gives a Cohen's Kappa of .679 (z = 45.5). Agreement was higher for pitch accents (86.1%; Kappa = .777; z = 27.5) than for boundary tones (81%; Kappa = .695; z = 27.8). This was partly due to the settings chosen in Eti_ToBI, which allowed for the maximal amount of boundary tones, including H!H%, L!H% and !H%. These differ from HL%, LH% and H% only in terms of scaling of the final stretch of detectable pitch, which lead to the decision to collapse them into one for subsequent analysis (Fliessbach 2023: 203).

Similarly, inclusion of the H+L* pitch accent in the set of possible annotations introduced additional variability in cases where a low pitch accent was preceded high phrase accent (H–) that did not align with the boundary between two prosodic words, but continued into the final prosodic word as in Figure 1. By comparing many such examples, we came to the conclusion that most of these cases were not actually H+L* pitch accents. Therefore, all cases with H+L* were grouped together irrespective of the subsequent boundary tone and should be seen as annotation errors. They make up only 2,3% of manual annotations and 4.6% of automatic annotations, so the other results should still hold. The rare nuclear configurations L+H* L!II% ($N_{man.}$=15, $N_{aut.}$=9), L+¡H* L!H% ($N_{man.}$–4, $N_{aut.}$=3), and H* L% ($N_{mut.}$=3, $N_{aut.}$=11) were grouped as *other*.[16]

---

16 L+H* L!H% has been proposed as another obviousness marker (Hualde & Prieto 2015: 369–370). This seems to be supported by our data, but with comparatively low frequencies even in the three obvious conditions. A perception experiment that directly compares it to L* HL% is needed.

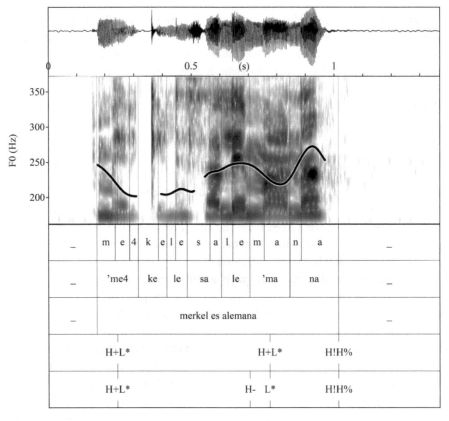

Figure 1: Two possible annotations for H before L* in (18). 🔊

3.2 Results and discussion

Table 1 shows the distribution of the collapsed nuclear configurations according to the experimental conditions together with indications of significant positive or negative deviation from the expected values for each field based on the adjusted standardized residuals of two χ^2-tests (Fliessbach 2023: 206), one for the automatic and one for the manual annotation.[17] The most general finding is that L+H* L%, L* L%, and L+H* HL% are much more frequent than other contours. The fact that L+H* L% occurs quite generally and is positively associated with all non-ob-

---

[17] Calculated with the CrossTable() command from the gmodels package (Warnes et al. 2018) as described in Field et al. (2012: 812-828).

Table 1: Number of nuclear configurations by condition. Positive (+) or negative (−) deviation from expected value according to adjusted standardized residuals of χ^2 test. Brackets (*) for $n_{row}<30$.

nuc. config.	annotation	neut. decl.	mir. decl.	wh-excl.	obv. decl.	obv. confir.	obv. rev.	sum
L* H%	auto	7	2^{-*}	2^{-*}	6	16^{+***}	8	41
	manual	8	0^{-**}	2^{-*}	7	13^{+**}	9	39
H+L* X%	auto	4	0^{-*}	3	8	9^{+*}	6	30
	manual	2	0	2	2	$6^{(+*)}$	3	15
L* HL%	auto	3	2^{-*}	2^{-*}	18^{+***}	10	7	42
	manual	3^{-***}	0^{-***}	3^{-***}	42^{+***}	18	16	82
L* L%	auto	29	7^{-***}	37^{+**}	21	26	30	150
	manual	33^{+*}	4^{-***}	37^{+***}	19	25	26	144
L+H* H%	auto	15	12	9	6	12	8	62
	manual	8	9	4	4	6	2	33
L+H* HL%	auto	18	33^{+***}	16	25	14^{-*}	23	129
	manual	9^{-*}	22	5^{-**}	17	17	26^{+***}	96
L+¡H* L%	auto	7	28^{+***}	14	4^{-*}	5	3^{-**}	61
	manual	5^{-*}	37^{+***}	13	1^{-***}	5^{-*}	2^{-**}	63
L+H* L%	auto	19	23	24	14	14	16	110
	manual	35^{+*}	36^{+*}	42^{+***}	11^{-***}	13^{-**}	17^{-*}	154
other	auto	6	1	1	6	2	7	23
	manual	5	$0^{(-*)}$	$0^{(-*)}$	5	5	7	22
sum	auto	108	108	108	108	108	108	648
	manual	108	108	108	108	108	108	648

vious conditions (at least in the manual annotation) indicates that it is relatively unmarked. Nevertheless, the findings do not fully support the view that L+H* L% is a free variant of L* L% (proposed for example in Prieto et al. 2010–2014, Estebas Vilaplana & Prieto 2010, Hualde & Prieto 2015, Gabriel 2007), because the latter is negatively associated with mirative contexts, whereas L+H* L% is positively associated with mirative contexts (only in the manual annotation). The fact that L* L% is positively associated with *wh*-exclamatives indicates that *wh*-exclamative syntax alone does not trigger mirative intonation.[18] The idea that "L* HL% carries a greater emphatic, contradictory force" (Hualde & Prieto 2015: 369) than L+H* L% is not supported by the results. Rather, the late rise-fall seems associated

---

18 See Fliessbach (2023: 40–52) for a discussion of the relation between *wh*-exclamative syntax and mirative prosody.

with obviousness, an intuition already expressed by Estebas-Vilaplana & Prieto (2008: 277–279) and Torreira & Grice (2018).[19] Obvious confirmations show less clear-cut results. While positively associated with L* H%, they also often bear L* L% intonation.[20] Nevertheless, (dis)agreement clearly induces variability within the obvious level of the expectedness variable. The manual annotation data indicates a positive association between the obvious reversal condition and L+H* HL%. If we follow the overviews in Estebas Vilaplana & Prieto (2010), Prieto et al. (2010–2014) and Hualde & Prieto (2015: 386), L+H* HL% marks insistence in contradiction statements. Obviousness is either a secondary meaning associated with this contour (or perhaps even the late fall HL% alone), or the experimental design triggered an additional insistence interpretation.[21] The infrequent nuclear configurations L+H* L!H%, L+¡H* L!H%, and H* L% seem to occur mostly in obvious contexts, which would corroborate observations made in Hualde & Prieto (2015: 369) (and the references cited there). Their low frequency does however not allow for inferential statistical analysis.

All in all, these results lead us to accept the hypothesis that both (un)expectedness and (dis)agreement have an impact on the prosodic form of Spanish sentences and can interact to create complex contrasts. The following section 4 is an attempt to formally capture this complexity in a dynamic model of meaning in dialogue. This will be followed by the concluding section 5, in which we also provide a brief outlook on points of convergence and divergence with similar commitment-based proposals.

4 At-issue (dis)agreement, non-at-issue (un)expectedness

To give a more precise representation of the proposal and the examples above, we can capture them within the model of dialogue put forward by Farkas & Bruce (2010) and extend it in a way discussed (but not adopted) in Rett (2021).

---

19 See section 4 for a discussion of possible reasons for Prieto & Hualde's intuition.
20 We do not know if these are simply cases without marking or cases in which prenuclear intonation or other acoustic features are used to indicate obviousness.
21 *Insistence* on a rejection differs from the *expectability* of a rejection in that the former requires an overtly expressed denial in preceding turns.

4.1 The Farkas and Bruce model

Farkas & Bruce (2010) formalize the similarities and differences between assertions and polar questions so as to account for the systematic partial overlap in reactions to them. To achieve this, the model distinguishes between the sets of public *discourse commitments* (DC) of the interlocutors A and B and the common ground (CG), which contains the intersection of the interlocutor's DCs. It also distinguishes between salient items under discussion (Roberts 2012), which are placed by the interlocutors onto a stack called the *Table* (T), and a component called the *projected set* (ps) that projects the CG after the next context update. The model follows Krifka (2001) in assuming a declarative operator D and a polar question operator PQ, which are defined over indicative and interrogative sentences respectively, and over a speaker a and an input context K_i. They both restrict an output context K_o by pushing an item on the Table, but differ in that the indicative sentence introduces a singleton set and therefore projects just one future CG (21), whereas the interrogative sentence introduces a non-singleton set and therefore projects more than one future CG (22). This means that tacit agreement can happen with a declarative provocation, but not with a polar question.

(21) *Declarative* **D** $(S[D], a, K_i) = K_o$ such that
    a. $DC_{a,o} = DC_{a,i} \cup \{p\}$
    b. $T_o = push(\langle S[D]; \{p\}\rangle, T_i)$
    c. $ps_o = ps_i \bar{\cup} \{p\}$

(22) *Polar Question* **PQ** $(S[I], K_i) - K_o$ such that
    a. $To = push(\langle S[I]; \{p, \neg p\}\rangle, T_i)$
    b. $ps_o = ps_i \bar{\cup} \{p, \neg p\}$

An important innovation of the model is to formally incorporate the particularity of responses.[22] Assertion confirmation (AC) and total denial (TD) are formalized as in (23) and (24) respectively, and share the requirement that input context conditions have to be met. They differ in the polarity of the commitment they add to the respondent's DC, and in whether they either push a new issue onto the Table (24) or else empty it by making the projected set at K_i the CG at K_o (23).

---

22 As opposed to what we call provocations (also Fliessbach 2023: 27) as a shorthand for a formalized perspective on 'adjacency pair first parts' (Sacks et al. 1974, Schegloff & Sacks 1973).

(23)   *Assertion Confirmation* **AC**
    a. *Input context conditions*:
        i. $top(T_i) = \langle S[D]; \{p\}\rangle$
        ii. p in $DC_{a,i}$
    b. *Change*:
        AC$(b, K_i) = K_o$ where $DC_{b,o} = DC_{b,i} \cup \{p\}$

(24)   *Total Denial* **TD**
    a. *Input context conditions*:
        i. $top(T_i) = \langle S[D]; \{p\}\rangle$
        ii. p in $DC_{a,i}$
    b. *Change*:
        i. **TD**$(b, K_i) = K_o$ where $DC_{b,o} = DC_{b,i} \cup \{\neg p\}$
        ii. $T_o = push(\langle S'[D]; \{\neg p\}\rangle, T_i)$

4.2 Extending the model

Rett (2021) modifies this model by differentiating between at-issue and non-at-issue content (NAI), with the latter being inaccessible to denial or confirmation. Rather, non-at-issue content is added directly to CG_o.[23]

(25)   **D**, for sentences $S[D]$ with at-issue content p and non-at-issue content q: $(S[D]$, a, $K_i) = K_o$ such that
    a. $DC_{a,o} = DC_{a,i} \cup \{p\}$
    b. $T_o = push(\langle S; \{p\}\rangle, T_i)$
    c. $ps_o = ps_i \bar{\cup} \{p\}$
    d. $CG_o = CG_i \cup \{q\}$

Following proposals by Wu (2008), Reich (2018) and Fliessbach (2023: 81–98), we can formalize mirativity / obviousness as non-at-issue commitments to the impossibility / necessity of the proffered content from the perspective of the input common ground CG_i. A neutral declarative such as (26a) would be formalized as in (27), a declarative with a modal verb (26b) would be formalized as in (28), a statement of the obvious (26c) as in (29), and a mirative statement (26d) as in (30).

---

23 She further argues for a distinction between "emotive markers" and other markers of non-at-issue content, a distinction we will not adopt due to reasons put forward in Fliessbach (2023).

(26)   (Spanish)

    A: ¿Y qué pasa con Juan?
                L* H%
    'And what about John?'

a. **B:** Ha venido.
          L* L%
    'He has come.'

b. **B:** Tiene que haber venido.
                 L* L%
    'He must have come.'

c. **B:** ¡Ha venido!
          L* HL%
    'He has come!'

d. **B:** ¡No ha venido!
          L+¡H* L%
    'He hasn't come!'

(27) **D**, for sentences $S[D]$ with at-issue content $\{p\}$:
    $(S[D], a, K_i) = K_o$ such that
    a. $DC_{a,o} = DC_{a,i} \cup \{p\}$
    b. $T_o = push(\langle S[D]; \{p\}\rangle, T_i)$
    c. $ps_o = ps_i \bar{\cup} \{p\}$

(28) **D**, for sentences $S[D]$ with at-issue content $\{\Box p\}$:
    $(S[D], a, K_i) = K_o$ such that
    a. $DC_{a,o} = DC_{a,i} \cup \{\Box p\}$
    b. $T_o = push(\langle S[D]; \{\Box p\}\rangle, T_i)$
    c. $ps_o = ps_i \bar{\cup} \{\Box p\}$

(29) **D**, for sentences $S[D]$ with at-issue content $\{p\}$ and non-at-issue content $\{\Box p\}$:
    $(S[D], a, K_i) = K_o$ such that
    a. $DC_{a,o} = DC_{a,i} \cup \{p\}$
    b. $T_o = push(\langle S[D]; \{p\}\rangle, T_i)$
    c. $ps_o = ps_i \bar{\cup} \{p\}$
    d. $CG_o = CG_i \cup \{\Box p\}$

(30) **D**, for sentences $S[D]$ with at-issue content $\{\neg p\}$ and non-at-issue content $\{\Box p\}$:
  $(S[D], a, K_i) = K_o$ such that

    a. $DC_{a,o} = DC_{a,i} \cup \{\neg p\}$

    b. $T_o = push(\langle S[D]; \{\neg p\}\rangle, T_i)$

    c. $ps_o = ps_i \bar{\cup} \{\neg p\}$

    d. $CG_o = CG_i \cup \{\Box p\}$

The intended meaning of $\Box$ is necessity. This deviates from the definition of mirative import in Bianchi et al. (2016: 13), according to which "the proposition expressed by the clause is less likely than at least one distinct alternative proposition with respect to a contextually relevant modal base and stereotypical ordering source". A definition in terms of one more likely alternative runs the risk of over-generating contexts in which mirative marking is appropriate. Consider (31) and (32). If only one more likely alternative was necessary to license mirative intonation, it would be possible in b in both examples without any further justification. This seems to hold for (31). The fact that parents are not allowed to name their child Lucifer allows A to accommodate the direct CG update '*Whatever his name is going to be, it will not be Lucifer*' $CG_o = CG_i \cup \{\Box\neg p\}$. Yet we argue that a mirative interpretation in (32) would need to be justified by adding additional expectations to the context. (32) would require A to either accommodate that there were reasons at the input CG to believe '*Whatever his name is going to be, it will not be Eric*' or request an explanation of the non-at-issue content conveyed prosodically in b. It also seems likely that (32d) would be relatively infelicitous compared to (32e), which can serve as another diagnostic for the strength of the mirative import.

> Context: James is a common male name. Eric is less frequent. Naming a child Lucifer is forbidden by law. A and B check an attendance chart.

(31) a. **A:** What's this boy's name?

      b. **B:** Let me check. . . His name is Lucifer!

(32) a. **A:** What's this boy's name?

      b. **B:** Let me check. . . His name is Eric!

      c. **A:** Why would that be surprising?

      d. **B:** # Well, James would be more common.

      e. **B':** Well, I thought no boy attending our event would ever be called Eric. The name has become so unpopular.

A definition of mirativity in terms of expected impossibility of the at-issue content at CG_i (as proposed here), and the corresponding definition of obviousness in terms of expected necessity of the at-issue content, runs the risk of undergenerating acceptable contexts. An empirical comparison is still pending, and could well show further differences in formal marking and interpretation.[24]

Turning back to our proposal for Spanish intonation, the comparison between (26b) and (26c) intends to show that obvious intonation differs from the use of a modal verb by expressing necessity of the prejacent relative to a directly updated *CG*, as opposed to proffered necessity relative to a projected *CG* in ps_o. With a modal matrix-verb (26b), the interlocutor can challenge it. If he does, it becomes the question under discussion. If he doesn't, it enters the CG via agreement. This means that tacit agreement is still less direct than a CG update triggered by non-at-issue content since tacit agreement completes in the subsequent context update. The comparison between (26c) and (26d) shows that mirative intonation can have the same direct CG update as obvious intonation if it targets the negation of the at-issue content. Moreover, the comparison between (26a) and (26d) shows that a response to an unbiased provocation can still be contrastive in the sense that it marks the asserted proposition as unexpected. While this does not lead to a conversational crisis in the sense of Farkas & Bruce (2010) because of inconsistent discourse commitments, it still leads to an inconsistency between a commitment and the expectations based on the CG. After asserting ¬p and NAI-marking that $\Box p$ relative to CG_i, the resulting inconsistency forces the interlocutors to search for ways of reconciling the CG with ¬p.

While the contrastiveness of mirativity is therefore quite straightforward, obviousness does not seem contrastive at first glance. Nevertheless, the intuition that "L* HL% carries a greater emphatic, contradictory force" (Hualde & Prieto 2015: 369) than L+H* L% can still be motivated if we consider not only the context-update potential of a statement of the obvious, but also the possible conversational implicatures it can trigger. According to Sperber & Wilson (2012: 38), the communicative principle of relevance is that "every act of ostensive communication communicates a presumption of its own relevance". And according to Sperber & Wilson (1995: 270), this requires a two-fold presumption of optimal relevance: "(a) The ostensive stimulus is relevant enough for it to be worth the addressee's effort to process it. (b) The ostensive stimulus is the most relevant one compatible with the communicator's abilities and preferences". Obviousness marking on a responding move might trigger the conversational implicature that the provocation was not entitled to this presumption. Depending on the kind of provocation (assertion,

---

24 A full exploration of the strength of necessity at CG_i would require a debate similar to the one about strong vs. weak *must* (Mandelkern 2019, von Fintel & Gillies 2010, 2021, Lassiter 2016, Goodhue 2017). This is beyond the scope of this article.

question, imperative, etc.), this means different things. In the case of a question provocation, the default assumptions accompanying question acts apply (speaker ignorance, addressee competence, addressee compliance, issue resolution goal, Farkas 2022: 297, also Dayal 2016: 4). Speaker ignorance and addressee competence construct an epistemic gradient between the interlocutors (Heritage 2012: 32). By marking the response to a question as obvious, the person that has asked the question is framed as having had access to the answer already, which in turn undermines the ignorant stance. This in turn could be part of the emphatic effect Hualde and Prieto noticed.

More generally, obvious responses to imperatives might be more polite than obvious responses to questions and assertions. Answering *Of course I will serve you another cup of tee* to the request *Please pour me another cup of tee* seems more polite than the answer *The square root of 100 is obviously 10* to the question *What is the square root of 100*. Imperatives do not have speaker ignorance as part of their felicity conditions, so an obvious response to an imperative does not create a similar pragmatic contrast to the one that arises from an obvious response to a question or an assertion.

5 Conclusions and outlook

This article took the incongruent results on contrastive focus intonation in Castilian Spanish as a point of departure for reflecting on parameters of discourse meaning that can give rise to contrastive discourse configurations, both simple and complex. Instead of a scale of contrastiveness, it proposed that (dis)agreement and (un)expectedness can be marked independently, either morphologically (Section 2) or prosodically (Section 3). The results reported in section 3 support the view that languages can have more than one "contrastive" intonational contour because contrast is not a binary feature.

L* HL%, seen by Prieto & Roseano (2009–2013) and Hualde & Prieto (2015) as a more emphatic marker of contrastive focus than L+H* L%, turned out to be strongly associated with obviousness. Yet these seemingly contradictory findings can actually help us understand contrastivity. If a speaker marks her response as self-evident, this can contrast with the presumption of relevance underlying the provocation. Moreover, the function of Spanish L+¡H* L% can also be seen as a kind of contrast. A speaker of Castilian Spanish can accept a proffered proposition and still use L+¡H* L% to mark it as contrasting with the expectations she would have previously assumed to share with her interlocutor. Example (32) also illustrated that a formalization in terms of necessity/impossibility can explain restrictions on the use of (un)expectedness marking that are not as easily captured by a definition in terms of marking the existence of one more/less likely alternative.

The present proposal is far from being the first attempt at capturing the meaning of intonational forms in a dynamic, interpersonal model. Portes & Reyle (2014) and Beyssade & Marandin (2007) are proposals for analyses of French intonation that share several insights with our approach, and the account for English intonation by Steedman (2007) is also comparable due to its focus on speaker-addressee relations. Steedman (2007) and Beyssade & Marandin (2007) understand the intonational contours they discuss as ways for the speaker to attribute a commitment (Steedman 2007) or a disposition for uptake/acceptance (Beyssade & Marandin 2007) to the hearer. The direct CG update we argued for in section 4 can also be understood as an attribution, but not of a commitment to a proposition. Rather, it attributes (shared) expectations towards the at-issue content. When the speaker uses intonation to mark the (un)expectedness of the at-issue content and the hearer wants to show that he does not share the expectation, he will need to use some form of a '*Hey wait a minute!*' challenge (Tonhauser et al. 2013: 81), as illustrated in (32c).

Our proposal is therefore closer to Beyssade & Marandin (2007) than to Steedman (2007), but it still makes different predictions. According to Beyssade & Marandin (2007), a falling contour in French indicates that the speaker anticipates that the proffered content will be taken up unchallenged by the hearer, a rising contour means the proffered content will probably be challenged by the hearer and then lead to a conversational crisis because the speaker anticipates already that she will not be willing to revise her stance, and a rising-falling contour means the proffered content will probably be challenged but not lead to a conversational crisis, because the speaker is willing to revise her stance if challenged to do so. Note that this model includes calculations on the part of the speaker over two future context updates, first by the hearer, then again by the speaker. If such a calculation was behind the Spanish configurations discussed here, the experiment in section 3 would probably not have led to the results we observed. Expectationally neutral assertions, statements of the obvious, and obvious confirmations would be indistinguishable, because neither of these cases means that the speaker assumes her statement to be contentious.

As a final point of comparison, we can state that the proposal for an analysis of the French implication rise-fall (IRF) by Portes & Reyle (2014) also bears some resemblance to our account of Spanish intonation, but ultimately makes different predictions. They argue that the IRF triggers the presupposition of an underspecified contrast that becomes specified by occurring in different types of situations.[25] If Spanish contours such as L* HL% or L+¡H* L% were similarly underspecified, we would not be able to explain the fact that they pattern with different expectational conditions as in section 3.

It remains to be seen whether it will be possible to reach a model of meaning in dialogue capable of capturing the functions of intonational configurations crosslinguistically. What we have shown is that models developed for French or English can inspire an account of Castilian Spanish contours, but require substantial modification to cover the variability we observe empirically. Beyond the discussion about the pragmasemantics of intonation, there are important next steps in the empirical investigation of the contours we found. The perceptual validity of the differences between L+¡H* L%, L+H* HL%, L* H%, and L* HL% still needs to be tested. A more detailed account of prenuclear intonation also seems important, particularly in light of the findings by Face (2007) that indicate their importance for the distinction between speech acts.

Finally, the range of phenomena that fall under the notion of contrastive discourse relations are yet to be determined. If future evidence continues to support the independence of (un)expectedness from (dis)agreement, it would be interesting to test whether semantically more complex discourse updates are perceived as more contrastive, which would be evidence in favour of a contrastiveness scale, or simply as different but unordered. We can state for now that, despite the abundant use of the notion of contrast in research on information structure, the quest to establish a full inventory of contrastive discourse relations is still ongoing. The fact that they are expressed by forms that span from affixes over particles and syntactic movement to intonation makes it one of particular interest.

6 Audio supplement links

Example 15
   A: https://osf.io/f6m5g
   B: https://osf.io/vguwn
   B: https://osf.io/z6s89

Example 16
   A: https://osf.io/nxywh
   A: https://osf.io/bgezq
   B: https://osf.io/wjscm
   B: https://osf.io/h83ka

---

25 They name twelve situation types, four of which would fall under our notion of disagreement. Incredulity and obviousness are also among them, but not formally defined.

Example 17
    A: https://osf.io/ghxn2
    B: https://osf.io/ykfwp
    B: https://osf.io/58rxj
Example 18
    A: https://osf.io/bx2hw
    B: https://osf.io/r7mpu
    B: https://osf.io/uxsre

Example 19
    A: https://osf.io/juzy8
    B: https://osf.io/wkzmv
    B: https://osf.io/zb8ra
Example 20
    A: https://osf.io/ctxg3
    B: https://osf.io/mqj6u
    B: https://osf.io/br7mt
Figure 1
    https://osf.io/94zvh

References

Aikhenvald, Alexandra Y. 2004. *Evidentiality* ([Oxford linguistics]). Oxford, New York: Oxford University Press.

Aikhenvald, Alexandra Y. 2012. Review of "Gabriele Diewald, Elena Smirnova (eds.). 2010. Linguistic realization of evidentiality in European languages". *Studies in Language* 36(2). 431–439. https://doi.org/10.1075/sl.36.2.07aik.

Aksu Koç, Ayhan & Dan I. Slobin. 1986. A psychological account of the development and use of evidentials in Turkish. In Wallace L. Chafe & Johanna Nichols (eds.), Evidentiality (Advances in Discourse Processes 20), 159–167. Norwood & N.J: Ablex publishing corporation.

Beckman, Mary E. & Manuel Díaz-Campos & Julia Tevis McGory & Terrell A. Morgan. 2002. Intonation across Spanish, in the Tones and Break Indices framework. *Probus. International Journal of Latin and Romance Linguistics* 14(1). 9–36.

Bergqvist, Henrik. 2016. Complex Epistemic Perspective in Kogi (Arwako). *International Journal of American Linguistics* 82(1). 1–34. https://doi.org/10.1086/684422.

Beyssade, Claire & Jean-Marie Marandin. 2007. French intonation and attitude attribution. In *The Proceedings of the 2004 Texas Linguistic Society Conference: Issues at the Semantics-Pragmatics Interface*, 1–12.

Bianchi, Valentina & Giuliano Bocci & Silvio Cruschina. 2016. Focus fronting, unexpectedness, and evaluative implicatures. *Semantics and Pragmatics* 9(3). 1–54.

Boersma, Paul & David Weenink. 2017. *Praat: Doing phonetics by computer [Computer program]*. Version 6.0.30. http://www.praat.org/ (27 November, 2023).

Brunetti, Lisa. 2009. Discourse functions of fronted foci in Italian and Spanish. In Andreas Dufter & Daniel Jacob (eds.), *Focus and background in Romance languages* (Studies in Language Companion Series 112), 43–82. Amsterdam: Benjamins.

Cruschina, Silvio. 2019. Focus Fronting in Spanish: Mirative implicature and information structure. *Probus* 31(1). 119–146. https://doi.org/10.1515/probus 2018 0008.

Cruschina, Silvio. 2021. The greater the contrast, the greater the potential: on the effects of focus in syntax. *Glossa: a journal of general linguistics* 6(1). https://doi.org/10.5334/gjgl.1100.

Dayal, Veneeta. 2016. *Questions*. First edition (Oxford Surveys in Semantics and Pragmatics 4). Oxford, United Kingdom: Oxford University Press.

DeLancey, Scott. 1997. Mirativity: the grammatical marking of unexpected information. *Linguistic Typology* 1(1). https://doi.org/10.1515/lity.1997.1.1.33.

DeLancey, Scott. 2012. Still mirative after all these years. *Linguistic Typology* 16(3). 529–564.

Destruel, Emilie & David I. Beaver & Elizabeth Coppock. 2019. It's Not What You Expected! The Surprising Nature of Cleft Alternatives in French and English. *Frontiers in Psychology* 10. 1400. https://doi.org/10.3389/fpsyg.2019.01400.

Elvira-García, Wendy. 2016. *La prosodia de las construcciones insubordinadas conectivo-argumentativas del español*. Barcelona: Universitat de Barcelona dissertation. https://www.tesisenred.net/handle/10803/400949 (last consulted on 13 February 2024).

Elvira-García, Wendy & Paolo Roseano & Ana María Fernández-Planas & Eugenio Martínez-Celdrán. 2016. A tool for automatic transcription of intonation: Eti_ToBI a ToBI transcriber for Spanish and Catalan. *Language Resources and Evaluation [LANG RESOUR EVAL]* 50(4). 767–792. https://doi.org/10.1007/s10579-015-9320-9.

Estebas Vilaplana, Eva & Pilar Prieto. 2010. Castilian Spanish intonation. In Pilar Prieto & Paolo Roseano (eds.), *Transcription of intonation of the Spanish language* (LINCOM Studies in Phonetics 6), 17–48. München.

Estebas-Vilaplana, Eva & Pilar Prieto. 2008. La notación prosódica del español: una revisión del Sp_ToBI. *Estudios de fonética experimental* 17. 263–283.

Face, Timothy L. 2001a. Focus and early peak alignment in Spanish intonation. *Probus. International Journal of Latin and Romance Linguistics* 13. 223–246.

Face, Timothy L. 2001b. *Intonational marking of contrastive focus in Madrid Spanish: PhD thesis.* Columbus: The Ohio State University.

Face, Timothy L. 2002. Local intonational marking of Spanish contrastive focus. *Probus. International Journal of Latin and Romance Linguistics* 14. 71–92.

Face, Timothy L. 2007. The role of intonational cues in the perception of declaratives and absolute interrogatives in Castilian Spanish. *Estudios de Fonética Experimental* 16. 185–225.

Farkas, Donka F. 2022. Non-Intrusive Questions as a Special Type of Non-Canonical Questions. *Journal of Semantics* 39(2). 295–337. https://doi.org/10.1093/jos/ffac001.

Farkas, Donka F. & Kim B. Bruce. 2010. On Reacting to Assertions and Polar Questions. *Language and Speech* 27(1). 81–118. https://doi.org/10.1093/jos/ffp010.

Field, Andy P. & Jeremy Miles & Zoë Field. 2012. *Discovering statistics using R.* London & Thousand Oaks: Sage.

von Fintel, Kai & Anthony S. Gillies. 2010. Must . . . stay . . . strong! *Natural Language Semantics* 18(4). 351–383. https://doi.org/10.1007/s11050-010-9058-2.

von Fintel, Kai & Anthony S. Gillies. 2021. Still going strong. *Natural Language Semantics* 29(1). 91–113. https://doi.org/10.1007/s11050-020-09171-x.

Fliessbach, Jan. 2023. *The intonation of expectations in Spanish: On marked declaratives, exclamatives, and discourse particles* (Open Romance Linguistics 3). Berlin: Language Science Press. https://doi.org/10.5281/zenodo.7929375.

Gabriel, Christoph. 2007. *Fokus im Spannungsfeld von Phonologie und Syntax: Eine Studie zum Spanischen.* Frankfurt am Main: Vervuert.

Goodhue, Daniel. 2017. Must φ is felicitous only if φ is not known. *Semantics and Pragmatics* 10(14). https://doi.org/10.3765/sp.10.14.

Hammarström, Harald & Robert Forkel & Martin Haspelmath & Sebastian Bank (eds.). 2022. *Glottolog 4.6*. Jena: Max Planck Institute for the Science of Human History. https://glottolog.org/ (last consulted on 13 February 2024).

Hengeveld, Kees & Hella Olbertz. 2012. Didn't you know? Mirativity does exist! *Linguistic Typology* 16(3). 487–503. https://doi.org/10.1515/lity-2012-0018.

Heritage, John. 2012. The Epistemic Engine: Sequence Organization and Territories of Knowledge. *Research on Language & Social Interaction* 45(1). 30–52. https://doi.org/10.1080/0835 1813.2012.646685.

Hesse, Christoph & Anton Benz & Maurice Langner & Felix Theodor & Ralf Klabunde. 2020. Annotating QUDs for generating pragmatically rich texts. In *Proceedings of the workshop on discourse theories for text planning*, 10–16. Dublin, Ireland: Association for Computational Linguistics. https://aclanthology.org/2020.dt4tp-1.3 (last consulted on 13 February 2024).

Hualde, José Ignacio & Pilar Prieto. 2015. Intonational variation in Spanish. European and American varieties. In Sónia Frota & Pilar Prieto (eds.), *Intonation in Romance*, 350–391. Oxford: Oxford University Press.

Hyslop, Gwendolyn. 2011. *A Grammar of Kurtöp*. Eugene, Oregon: UO Libraries. https://www.proquest.com/docview/868530580 (last consulted on 13 February 2024).

Kratzer, Angelika. 2012. *Modals and conditionals* (Oxford Studies in Theoretical Linguistics 36). Oxford: Oxford Univ. Press.

Krifka, Manfred. 2001. Quantifying into Question Acts. *Natural Language Semantics* 9. 1–40. https://doi.org/10.1023/A:1017903702063.

Lassiter, Daniel. 2016. Must, knowledge, and (in)directness. *Natural Language Semantics* 24(2). 117–163. https://doi.org/10.1007/s11050-016-9121-8.

Lee, Chungmin. 2017. Contrastive topic, contrastive focus, alternatives, and scalar implicatures. In Chungmin Lee & Ferenc Kiefer & Manfred Krifka (eds.), *Contrastiveness in Information Structure, Alternatives and Scalar Implicatures* (Studies in Natural Language and Linguistic Theory 91), 3–21. Cham: Springer International Publishing. https://doi.org/10.1007/978-3-319-10106-4.

Mandelkern, Matthew. 2019. What 'must' adds. *Linguistics and Philosophy* 42(3). 225–266. https://doi.org/10.1007/s10988-018-9246-y.

Portes, Cristel & Uwe Reyle. 2014. The meaning of French "implication" contour in conversation. In Nick Campbell & Dafydd Gibbon & Daniel Hirst (eds.), *Speech prosody 2014*, 413–417. Dublin, Ireland.

Prieto, Pilar & Joan Borràs-Comes & Paolo Roseano. 2010–2014. *Interactive Atlas of Romance Intonation*. http://prosodia.upf.edu/iari/ (27 November, 2023).

Prieto, Pilar & Paolo Roseano. 2009–2013. *Atlas interactivo de la entonación del español.* http://prosodia.upf.edu/atlasentonacion/ (last consulted on 13 February 2024).

Reich, Uli. 2018. Presupposed modality. In Marco García García & Melanie Uth (eds.), *Focus Realization in Romance and Beyond* (Studies in Language Companion Series [SLCS]), 203–227. Amsterdam & Philadelphia: John Benjamins Publishing Company.

Repp, Sophie. 2016. Contrast: Dissecting an Elusive Information-structural Notion and its role in Grammar. In Caroline Féry & Shinichiro Ishihara (eds.), *The Oxford Handbook of Information Structure* (Oxford handbooks in linguistics), 1–33. Oxford & New York: Oxford University Press.

Rett, Jessica. 2011. Exclamatives, degrees and speech acts. *Linguistics and Philosophy* 34(5). 411–442. https://doi.org/10.1007/s10988-011-9103-8.

Rett, Jessica. 2021. The Semantics of Emotive Markers and Other Illocutionary Content. *Journal of Semantics* 38(2). 305–340. https://doi.org/10.1093/jos/ffab005.

Rett, Jessica & Beth Sturman. 2020. Prosodically marked mirativity. In *Proceedings of the west coast conference on formal linguistics (wccfl)*, vol. 37. Vancouver, B.C.: University of British Columbia. https://doi.org/10.14288/1.0389873.

Riester, Arndt. 2019. Constructing QUD trees. In Malte Zimmermann & Klaus von Heusinger & Edgar Onea Gáspár (eds.), *Questions in discourse* (Current research in the semantics/pragmatics interface), 164–192. Leiden & Boston: Brill.

Roberts, Craige. 2012. Information structure in discourse: Towards an integrated formal theory of pragmatics. *Semantics and Pragmatics* 5(6). 1–69. https://doi.org/10.3765/sp.5.6.

Sacks, Harvey & Emanuel A. Schegloff & Gail Jefferson. 1974. A simplest systematics for the organization of turn-taking for conversation. *Language* 50(4). 696–735. https://doi.org/10.1353/lan.1974.0010.

Schegloff, Emanuel A. & Harvey Sacks. 1973. Opening up closings. *Semiotica* 8(4). 289–327. https://doi.org/10.1515/semi.1973.8.4.289.

Schwenter, Scott A. 2016. Meaning and interaction in Spanish independent si-clauses. *Language Sciences* 58. 22–34. https://doi.org/10.1016/j.langsci.2016.04.007.

Sperber, Dan & Deirdre Wilson. 1995. *Relevance: Communication and cognition*. 2nd ed. repr. Malden: Blackwell Publishing.

Sperber, Dan & Deirdre Wilson. 2012. The mapping between the mental and the public lexicon. In Deirdre Wilson & Dan Sperber (eds.), *Meaning and relevance*, 31–46. Cambridge: Cambridge University Press.

Steedman, Mark. 2007. Information-Structural Semantics for English Intonation. In Chungmin Lee & Matthew Gordon & Daniel Büring (eds.), *Topic and Focus: Cross-Linguistic Perspectives on Meaning and Intonation*, 245–264. Dordrecht: Springer Netherlands.

Tonhauser, Judith & David I. Beaver & Craige Roberts & Mandy Simons. 2013. Toward a Taxonomy of Projective Content. *Language* 89(1). 66–109.

Torreira, Francisco & Martine Grice. 2018. Melodic constructions in Spanish: Metrical structure determines the association properties of intonational tones. *Journal of the International Phonetic Association* 48(01). 9–32. https://doi.org/10.1017/S0025100317000603.

Verhoeven, Elisabeth & Stavros Skopeteas. 2015. Licensing Focus Constructions in Yucatec Maya. *International Journal of American Linguistics* 81(1). 1–40. https://doi.org/10.1086/679041.

Warnes, Gregory R. & Ben Bolker & Thomas Lumley & Randall C. Johnson. 2018. *gmodels: Various R Programming Tools for Model Fitting*. R package version 2.18.1. https://CRAN.R-project.org/package=gmodels (last consulted on 13 February 2024).

Wu, Jiun-Shiung. 2008. Antonyms? Presuppositions? On the Semantics of Two Evaluative Modals Jingran and Guoran in Mandarin. *Journal of Chinese Language and Computing* 18(4). 161–173.

Zimmermann, Malte. 2008. Contrastive focus and emphasis. *Acta Linguistica Hungarica* 55(3–4). 347–360. https://doi.org/10.1556/ALing.55.2008.3-4.9.

Regina Zieleke

6 Contrast via information structure: On topic development with German *aber* in post-initial position

Abstract: In order to distinguish different relations of contrast, research on German *aber* 'but' also takes into account its syntactic position. In post-initial position, i.e. between prefield-constituent and finite verb ('Forefield particle' in Sæbø 2003) which is generally associated with signaling a topic shift (cf. Breindl 2011), *aber* is said to express one of the contrastive relations defined via information structural properties (cf. e.g. Sæbø 2003). As corpus data reveal, however, post-initial *aber* may also 'formally isolate' non-topical constituents such as comparative constructions (e.g. *noch weniger* 'even less') and even sentence adverbials such as *tatsächlich* 'indeed/in reality'. Interestingly, such divergences from potential topicality also involve different contrastive relations commonly analyzed in terms of inferences instead of information structural properties. In this paper, we investigate how topic development, i.e. the topic potential of the prefield constituent, as well as the topic progression between the conjuncts, can be employed as a formal means to distinguish different kinds of contrast in corpus data: a Structural Contrast relying on specific patterns of topic development and a Non-Structural Contrast where topicality is not the primary level of contrast, but other formal means may be indicative.

1 Introduction

Much work on contrastive markers (i.e. 'proto-typical contrastive connectives' such as English *but*, German *aber*, French *mais*) is dedicated to identifying and describing different contrastive relations (e.g. Lakoff 1971; Blakemore 1989; Rudolph 2012). For example, Jasinskaja (2012) suggests three contrastive relations: "formal contrast or semantic opposition uses, illustrated in (1), highlighting the similarities and differences between two propositions; argumentative uses, as in (2), giving an argument and a counterargument for the same claim or suggestion (e.g. that we should buy the ring, in this case); and concessive, or denial of expectation uses in (3), where the second conjunct denies an inference suggested by the first" (Jasinskaja 2012: 1899, examples (1–3)):

https://doi.org/10.1515/9783110986594-006

(1) *This ring is beautiful,* **but** *that one isn't.*   (formal contrast/opposition)

(2) *This ring is beautiful,* **but** *expensive.*   (argumentative contrast)

(3) *This ring is beautiful,* **but** *we won't buy it.*   (denial of expectation)

As the quote by Jasinskaja (2012) shows, researchers employ different properties and aspects of language for the description of different relations. Information structural properties of the contrasted conjuncts have been widely discussed for 'formal contrast/opposition' uses in terms of parallel topic-comment- or topic-focus-structure (e.g. Sæbø 2003; Umbach 2005; Breindl, Volodina, and Waßner 2014). For the other kinds of contrast, however, information structure becomes a secondary factor, since they are generally analyzed in terms of inferences (of a differentially weighted relevance of properties in (2) and an underlying expectation in (3), see e.g. Winterstein (2012) and König (1991), respectively).

In this article, I will investigate the potential of information structural aspects as a means to distinguish different contrastive relations, more specifically the topic development from first to second conjunct of a contrastive connection. The point of departure for this investigation is contrast with the underspecified German *aber* in post-initial position, i.e. the position between the prefield-constituent and finite verb. This position is not only frequent in written data, it is also ascribed with the very specific function to formally isolate the prefield constituent and mark it as a 'shifted' sentence topic (Breindl 2011).

While the notion of topicality is a complex one with different values as to what counts as topical, there are certain linguistic expressions that are not typically considered as topics, such as sentence adverbials and focus particles. Yet, we find data where post-initial *aber* formally isolates such expressions that do not comply with the topic-marking function suggested in the literature. Interestingly, this divergence from potential topicality also involves different kinds of contrast, compare (4) and (5): in (4), the prefield constituent *der andere* 'the other one' is a natural candidate for an aboutness topic; the contrast here resembles Jasinskaja's 'formal contrast'-example in (1) above. In (5), on the other hand, *aber* isolates the constituent *vor allem* 'above all' which cannot be considered as topical; the contrastive relation here resembles Jasinskaja's 'argumentative contrast' example in (2), instead.

(4) *Dieser Ring ist schön, der andere* **aber** *(ist es) nicht.*
    'This ring is beautiful, but the other one is not.'

(5) *Dieser Ring ist schön, vor allem* **aber** *ist er teuer.*
    'This ring is beautiful, but above all it is expensive.'

The goal of this article is to integrate such cases into one account of contrast: post-initial *aber* formally isolates the prefield constituent and marks it as an *alternative*. The interpretation as different contrastive relations depends on the topic-status of this constituent.

Section 3 will take a closer look at the topic-isolating function of German adverb connectives and contrastive *aber* in particular suggested by Breindl (2011) as well as the notion of topicality. In order to apply this notion to corpus data, I suggest to tease apart the topic potential of an expression, i.e. whether a constituent provides the features typically associated with aboutness- or frame-setting topics, and the relative topic status, i.e. the topic progression from one conjunct to the other. This distinction provides annotation criteria for corpus data with post-initial *aber* presented in section 4. The study reveals that topicality is indeed the relevant level of alternatives for the majority of contrast with post-initial *aber*, but not for all of the data. In fact, a surprisingly high number of constituents formally isolated by *aber* are not topical. As the discussion in section 5 shows, however, there are other formal means such as verb mode and simultaneity that indicate different kinds of contrast, leading to a proposal of Structural versus Non-Structural Contrast as identified via the analysis of topic development with German *aber* in post-initial position. In order to be able to incorporate these findings into the discussion of different kinds of contrast with *aber* as defined by information structural aspects, section 2 will start with a discussion of different relevant approaches to this topic.

2 Information structure and contrast with *aber*

In this section, I will (selectively) discuss approaches to contrastive relations defined in information structural terms. There are substantial differences between such approaches subject to, on the one hand, the (language-)specific contrastive marker analyzed and the variety of contrastive relations they can express[1] and, on the other hand, the status of information structure within the description of contrast. What all approaches share is that contrast, in general, is defined in terms of *alternatives*: contrastive markers conjoin something positive and something negative (cf. e.g. Sanders,

---

1 For example, both English *but* and French *mais* have a corrective use as in *Peter didn't go to Paris, but to Rome*, whereas German and Spanish, for example, use a different contrastive marker specified for the corrective relation (*sondern* and *sino*, respectively). In Russian, in turn, the marker for correction *a* 'and/but' is also used for 'formal contrast / opposition' as in (1), whereas *no* 'but' is reserved for the other contrastive relations (see e.g. Malchukov 2004; Jasinskaja 2012). Moreover, the contrastive markers behave differently in terms of their syntactic integrability – as will become relevant for German *aber*, cf. section 3.1 below.

Spooren, and Noordman 1992) relative to a specific feature, depending on the contrastive relation described.

In terms of information structure, alternatives adhere to the notions of focus and contrastive topics. This section will therefore gather approaches that analyze contrast in terms of contrastive topics, foci, or both (Sæbø 2003 for the former with German *aber*, Umbach 2005 for the latter with English *but*, and Jasinskaja 2010, 2012 for a 'Question under Discussion' account). Subsequently, the status of information structure within the description of contrast will be addressed (for the afore-mentioned 'formal approaches', information structural aspects of the conjuncts are central to all contrastive relations, whereas neutral approaches such as Breindl, Volodina, and Waßner (2014) consider them as one set of features among many).

Sæbø (2003) analyzes German *aber* as a topic particle and ascribes contrast to contrastive topics. He argues that contrast is the result of *aber's* presupposition involving topic alternatives and negation: "The context entails the negation of the result of replacing the topic of the sentence by an alternative" (definition of 'Semantic Opposition (Contrast)', Sæbø 2003: 262). In his example shown in (6), the alternative topic *(für) mittlere* 'for intermediate-size (companies)' replaces *(für) kleine Betriebe* 'for small companies' "in the sense that if we substitute the latter for the former, a contradiction arises" (Sæbø 2003: 261).

(6) *[Für kleine Betriebe]*$_{T1}$ *hält sich der Schaden noch in Grenzen;*
     [für mittlere]$_{T2}$ *wird er* **aber** *allmählich ruinös.*
     'For small companies, the harm is yet limited; for intermediate-size companies, however, it is becoming ruinous.'

According to the author, such an "alternativeness relation between the topic and the alternative" is given when the two alternative expressions denote "individuals, places, times, worlds, or sets of sets of such entities" or "are ordered along some scale" (Sæbø 2003: 268). In cases where the alternativeness is not given a priori, the use of the contrastive marker triggers the accommodation of 'implicit topics', i.e. the hearer has to identify a relevant parallel triggering an implicature of 'Concession' or 'Denial of Expectation' (Sæbø 2003: 266). Sæbø shows this with the example in (7), where *steil* 'steep' and *kurz* 'short' have to be identified as alternatives (2003: 266, example (29a)).

(7) *Die Waldwege sind steil,* **aber** *kurz.*
     'The forest paths are steep, but short.'

Such a parallel interpretation, the author underlines, entirely "depends on what is relevant in the utterance situation and essentially on world knowledge" (Sæbø 2003: 267).

Alternativeness of the elements contrasted in conjunctions with *but* or *aber* is also central for Umbach's (2005) focus-based analysis of English *but*. Drawing attention to the similarity between *aber/but* and focus-sensitive particles such as German *auch* 'too' or English *only*, the author argues that the particularity about the contrastive markers is that they require a (semantic or pragmatic) negation. She calls this characteristic, which also separates *but* from additive *and*, the "confirm+deny condition": two sentences conjoined by *but* respond to a common *quaestio* as in (8) with "yes . . .but no . . ." (Umbach 2005: 7–8, example (12a)).

(8) *Did John clean up his room and wash the dishes?*
  [YES]John cleaned up his ROOM, **but** *[NO] he didn't wash the DISHES.*

The alternatives presented in the confirmation and in the denial are analyzed in terms of information focus, as indicated by the accent on *room* and *dishes* in (8), respectively. Umbach (2005) further points out that *but*-conjunctions may contain more than one pair of alternatives and distinguishes 'simple contrast' from 'double contrast'. Cases of 'simple contrast' as in (8), involve one pair of alternatives to be contrasted, expressed by the (contrastive) sentence foci, i.e. *to clean up the room* and *to wash the dishes*. Cases of 'double contrast' as in (9), in turn, involve two pairs of alternatives, contrastive topics ('theme foci') such as *John* and *Bill* and contrastive foci ('rheme foci') (Umbach 2005: 11, example (19)).

(9) *John cleaned up the ROOM,* **but** *Bill did the DISHES.*

The author points out that the alternatives do not have to be presented in a parallel manner, but "may also be "crossed", one of them relating to a contrastive topic and the other one to a rheme focus" (Umbach 2005: 10).[2] Like Sæbø (2003), Umbach (2005) ascribes other uses of *but* or *aber* to an implicature: since "any *but*-sentence involves a negation [. . .], just like simple negated sentences, *but*-sentences trigger the expectation that the corresponding affirmative holds" (Umbach 2005: 14). The

---

2 She illustrates such 'crossed' versions, which according to her "are perfectly natural and occur frequently" in German but "seem to occur rarely" in English (cf. endnote 12, Umbach 2005: 22), with the English example in (i) and its German equivalent in (ii):

(i) *John cleaned up the ROOM,* **but** *the dishes were washed by BILL.*
(ii) *John hat AUFGERÄUMT,* **aber** *abgewaschen hat BILL.*

interpretation of 'concession', then, is the result of a "causal over-interpretation" that is also available in conjunctions with *and* (Umbach 2005: 14).

The correlation between information structure and the quaestio, or 'Question under Discussion' (QuD, cf. Roberts 1998), has led to a variety of analyses of information structure in general (e.g. Riester et al. 2018). It is also central to Jasinskaja's (2010) comparative account of contrast. Among the five different contrastive relations postulated by the author, two rely on formal aspects of the conjuncts (which is why, in Jasinskaja 2012, she summarizes these two relations under the term 'formal contrast'): contrastive comparison as in (10) and opposition as in (11).

(10) *John likes basketball,* **but** *Mary likes tennis.*

(11) *John likes football,* **but** *Bill doesn't.*

In both cases, the author points out, "the conjoined propositions differ along two dimensions at least" (Jasinskaja 2010: 437). In the case of contrastive comparison, this dimension involves "two (or more) constituents, e.g. the subject and the object of liking in [(10)], leading to a contrastive topic-focus structure" (Jasinskaja 2010: 436). In the case of opposition, the values of one of the two dimensions do not only have to be different, but polar. The polarity may be semantic, i.e. in form of lexical antonyms or positive and negative sentence polarity, or pragmatic in nature, i.e. "one conjunct confirm[ing] and the other den[ying] a contextually salient proposition", as in (12) (Jasinskaja 2010: 437, example (9)).

(12) A: *John and Peter both live in Amsterdam, don't they?*
      B: *No. John lives in Amsterdam,* **but** *Peter lives in Rotterdam.*

The contrastive topic-focus structure is mirrored in the QuD that is central for Jasinskaja's analysis of contrast (building on Jasinskaja and Zeevat 2008). In this approach, contrastive conjunctions are answers to complex QuDs, different in number and type of question variables. Contrastive comparison cases answer a "multiple wh-question" (Jasinskaja 2010: 442), i.e. *Who likes what?* in the case of (10). Opposition cases, in turn, answer a "wh-yes/no-question" (Jasinskaja 2010: 443), i.e. *Who does and doesn't like football?* in the case of (11). Both variables in the question identify the information structural entities in the conjunct, the first corresponding to contrastive topics, the second to contrastive foci.

Other uses of contrastive markers, the author argues, are the result of specific manifestations of the question variables. The argumentative contrast in (2), above, for example, answers a "why-yes/no-question", i.e. *Why should or shouldn't we buy the ring?*.

For the three approaches to contrast discussed so far, contrast relies on the notion of information structural alternatives as expressed by contrastive topics, foci or both. This formal contrast is taken as the basic function, whereas other uses of contrastive markers such as argumentation or denial of expectation "are treated as special cases under additional assumptions" (Jasinskaja 2012: 1900). With this, they are to be distinguished from what Jasinskaja (2012) calls 'inferential approaches to contrast'. The latter "appeal to world knowledge and deep inferential processing" and "take the denial of expectation [. . .] or the argumentative function [. . .] as basic deriving formal contrast as a special case" (Jasinskaja 2012: 1900). Proponents of these approaches are e.g. Blakemore (1989) or Anscombre and Ducrot (1977).[3]

Finally, there are approaches that do not consider one of the different contrastive relations expressed by underspecified contrastive markers to be the base for enrichment for the other types of contrast. One such example is Breindl, Volodina, and Waßner (2014) who describe five different uses of German *aber* as co-existing variants, 'contrastive comparison', 'concessive', 'restrictive', 'argumentative', and 'weak contrast'. The 'concessive' use, for example, simply co-exists with the 'contrastive evaluation' use of *aber*. Among those five contrastive relations, two are defined via information structural properties: 'contrastive comparison (or: semantic opposition)' *aber* as in (13) and 'weak contrast' *aber* as in (14) (Breindl, Volodina, and Waßner 2014: 524–532, examples (18) and (44), respectively).

(13)   *Ihren Ruf verspielte die UNO in den Augen der Malaysier, als sie Kuwait geholfen, die Moslems in Bosnien **aber** im Stich gelassen habe.*
'The UN forfeited their reputation in the eyes of the Malaysians when they helped Kuwait, but deserted the Muslims in Bosnia.'

---

3 Building on the latter, Winterstein (2012), for example, ascribes an argumentative function to all *but*-conjunctions. His approach is based on the concepts of the argumentative force of a proposition and their respective argumentative goals: the second conjunct containing the contrastive marker possesses a higher argumentative force for its goal (Winterstein 2012: 1870). In (2) above, for example, the first conjunct argues for the goal H *we will buy the ring*, while the second conjunct argues for ¬H *we won't buy the ring*. Based on the presented order of the two conjuncts, ¬H receives a stronger argumentative force, making it most likely that the ring won't be bought. Winterstein argues that information structural properties of the conjuncts, i.e. a parallel topic-focus-structure, directly influence the make-up of the argumentative goals H and ¬H, leading to the 'mechanical goals' H_{unique} (goals "that convey that the focus is the only one of its kind") or H_{other} (goals "that convey that the focus is not the only one of its kind, i.e. that there is at least one alternative to the focus that shares the property of the focus" in the first conjunct, cf. Winterstein 2012: 1877). B's answer in (12) above, for example, can be analyzed in terms of H_{other}.

(14) *Damit verließ er uns. Wir **aber** schauten ihm nach und beneideten ihn.*
'With this, he left us. We, in turn, followed him with our eyes and envied him.'

According to the authors, in its 'contrastive comparison (or semantic opposition)' use, *aber* relates conjuncts with a parallel topic-comment-structure: the topics are contrastive (*Kuwait* 'Kuwait' in the first conjunct and *die Moslems* 'the Muslims' in the second conjunct in (13)), i.e. they can be regarded as parts of a superordinate topic (e.g. 'groups of people the UN might have helped'). The respective comments to these topics can be regarded as antonyms or contradictive in the given context (i.e. *helfen* 'to help them' and *im Stich lassen* 'to turn their back on them' in (13)). The authors point out that the comments do not necessarily have to be lexical oppositions or contrastive foci but are often marked by a similar prosodic contour (Breindl, Volodina, and Waßner 2014: 522–523). They also observe that, in this use, the contrastive marker can be omitted, since the comparative interpretation relies on the parallel topic-comment-structure.

'Weak contrast' as in (14) involves a topic shift not otherwise specified 'without a concomitant contrast of the predicates in the comments' (Breindl, Volodina, and Waßner 2014: 532).[4] In (14), the topic of the second conjunct *wir* 'we' shifts from *er* 'he' in the first. What is striking in this use is that the topic of the second conjunct, in contrast to the topic in (13), is given in the comment of the previous conjunct (*uns* 'us') and is not necessarily interpreted as contrastive to *er* (neither are the comments).[5]

With a lack of contrastive alternatives as pivotal for this use of *aber*, 'weak contrast' seems to be the odd one out. Yet, this use of *aber* also relies on specific information structural properties of the conjuncts, i.e. a specific type of topic progression. If we want to maintain an alternative based account of (information structurally defined) contrast, we may argue that here, too, alternatives are at play – albeit on a more abstract, structural level. The unspecified topic shift may yield an interpretation of the two conjuncts as alternatives regarding the topical progression in a discourse, the second conjunct displaying an alternative choice of topic.

From this short discussion of some representative analyses of information structural aspects of contrast with the underspecified contrastive markers *but* and *aber* we can retain the following observations: First, central to such approaches to

---

4 Original quote in German: „ohne dass damit eine Kontrastierung der Prädikate verbunden ist" („schwacher Kontrast", Breindl, Volodina, and Waßner 2014: 532).
5 Interestingly, the authors attest 'weak contrast' with a topological preference of *aber* for the post-initial position between prefield constituent and finite verb as in (14). For the four other contrastive relations they describe, *aber's* position is only marginally relevant. The topological positions possible with *aber* will be introduced in section 3.1.

contrast is the notion of alternatives. This relates to contrastive topics or contrastive foci or both, and may even extend to an abstract structural level in terms of alternative topic choice in discourse. Second, information structure is most, if not only, relevant for the description of *some* uses of the contrastive markers. Even in what Jasinskaja (2012) called 'formal approaches' that take information structural properties of the conjuncts as a starting point for the description of contrast, they become secondary for other uses of *but* and *aber*. For Sæbø (2003), the identification of 'implicit topics' relies on relevance implicatures and world knowledge; for Jasinskaja (2010), the QuD changes from *wh*-questions to the causal *why*. Umbach's (2005) analysis is more robust in this regard, considering that 'all-rheme sentences' such as in (15) still provide two focus alternatives, albeit less straight forward and with recourse to inferential enrichment and 'causal over-interpretation' (Umbach 2005: 10, example (18a)).

(15)   *[It is RAINING]$_F$,* **but** *[we are not going to stay at HOME]$_F$*

A final observation to be drawn from the discussion in this section is that the interplay of contrast, information structure, and the position of German *aber* might prove insightful for the discussion of contrastive relations and their characteristics.

3 Post-initial *aber* and topicality

The previous section has shown the central role of information structural alternatives for contrast with *but* and *aber*. The proto-typical German and English markers of contrast were treated as equal throughout the discussion with greater attention paid to whether contrastive topics or foci (or both) are taken as fundamental for the relation(s) of contrast. But the two markers differ not only in the number of relations they can express (cf. footnote 1), but also in their syntactic behavior. In contrast to English *but*, which as a conjunction is restricted to the Coord-position outside the sentence frame, *aber* is what Breindl, Volodina, and Waßner (2014) call 'conjunct-integrable', i.e. it can occupy different syntactic positions within the German sentence frame with different effects on the interpretation. The post-initial position, i.e. the position between the prefield constituent and the finite verb as in (14) above, is particularly interesting for the discussion of information structural alternatives and contrast. Section 3.1 will class post-initial *aber* among the marker's possible topological positions and describe Breindl's (2011) approach that associates this position with topicality. In section 3.2, I will discuss theoretical implications for the distinction of different contrastive relations and how to integrate them into the general discussion of topicality in the literature.

3.1 German *aber* in post-initial position

As an adverb connective, German *aber* is positionally mobile in that it can occur in different syntactic positions in the German sentence structure. Sæbø (2003: 261) discusses three positions for *aber*, "a particle left adjoined to the Middle Field, a particle right adjoined to the Forefield, [and] a conjunction (left of the Forefield)". This goes in hand with Breindl, Volodina, and Waßner (2014) who categorize not only the meaning but also the syntactic positions of German connectives. In their terminology, *aber* is eligible for 'middlefield position' ("Mittelfeld", cf. (16d)), 'post-initial position' ("Nacherst", cf. (16c)), and 'zero position' ("Nullstelle"[6], cf. (16a)), respectively. The only positional restriction concerns the 'prefield position' ("Vorfeld"), where *aber* is ungrammatical as the only element preceding the finite verb, cf. (16b) (Breindl, Volodina, and Waßner 2014: 1173).

(16) *Sie ging hinaus in die Welt,*
     a.   **aber** *er blieb daheim.*
     b.   ****aber** *blieb er daheim.*
     c.   *er* **aber** *blieb daheim.*
     d.   *er blieb* **aber** *daheim.*
     'She went out into the world, but he stayed at home.'

Breindl, Volodina, and Waßner (2014) observe that *aber* shows different syntactic preferences along the different contrastive relations. Post-initial position, for example, is felicitous for 'contrastive comparison' and 'weak contrast', but is infelicitous for 'concessive' or 'contrastive evaluation' uses of *aber* (cf. Breindl, Volodina, and Waßner 2014: 526–533). However, the syntactic positions do not correlate with *aber*'s different uses in the sense that a certain position is indicative of a certain use.

---

6 Note that, the term 'zero position' comprises two syntactic positions, the Coord-position typical for conjunctions as in (a) and a syntactically and prosodically disintegrated position between the two conjuncts. The latter is usually marked by separating intonation or punctuation such as a comma or a colon: (i) *Ich möchte gern spazieren gehen.* **Aber**: *Heute regnet es leider.* 'I would like to go for a walk. But: Unfortunately, it will be raining today'. This position is infelicitous in (16). Many researchers ascribe a shift in scope to this disintegrated position; Imo (2017), for example, argues that connectives in this position scope over speech acts and are thus to be analyzed as discourse markers (cf. Imo 2017: 50, see also Blühdorn 2017).

Both, 'concessive' and 'contrastive evaluation', for example, are equally felicitous with zero and middlefield positions.

Similarly, Sæbø (2003) deliberates that, in most cases, the syntactic position of *aber* would not make a difference but it may in some: "in particular, the Fore-field particle *aber* [= post-initial position as in (16c), RZ] seems to unambiguously identify the Forefield constituent as one for which the context should provide an alternative and contradict the result of substituting it" (2003: 261). This can also be observed in (16): the interpretations of (16a) and (16d) do not seem to differ, in both cases the predicates *hinaus in die Welt gehen* 'going out into the world' and *daheim bleiben* 'staying at home' are most relevant. In (16c), however, the contrast between *sie* 'she' and *er* 'he' is marked as more relevant for the comparison.[7]

And indeed, the post-initial position is quite special in that regard. Breindl (2011) discusses in detail that German adverb connectives in post-initial position, in general, have two functions: a) to signal their encoded semantic relation, i.e. contrast in the case of *aber*, and b) to formally isolate the (initial) prefield constituent as the topic, thereby signaling a topic shift (Breindl 2011: 17). An example with two instances of adverb connectives in post-initial position is provided by Breindl (2011: 2, example (2)) shown in (17):

(17) *Wir ließen den Stadtochsen vorsichtig wieder hinunter und wollten beim näch-sten Versuch auch die Weiber zu Hilfe holen. [Zu diesem Versuch]* **aber** *kam es nicht. [Unser Stadtochse]* **nämlich** *– war tot!*
'We carefully let the town ox down again and wanted to get help from the women for the next attempt. This attempt, however, did not happen. Our town ox, namely, – was dead!'

Here, both *aber* and *nämlich* 'namely/viz' isolate their preceding constituents, *zu diesem Versuch* 'to this attempt' and *unser Stadtochse* 'our town ox' and mark them as the sentence topics, respectively. Simultaneously, *aber* contributes its contrastive and *nämlich* its causal meaning to the conjunctions. Focal content, on the other hand, is not compatible with post-initial adverb connectives (cf. Breindl 2011: 26).

As mentioned above, Sæbø (2003: 261) postulates that *aber* marks the 'isolated' topic constituent as contrastive. This goes in hand with other claims for contras-tive markers in post-initial position, e.g. Lang and Adamíková (2007) who state that "*aber* and other 'adversative' connectors, if occurring in this position, overtly mark

---

7 With matching intonation patterns, these preferences may be altered. As post-initial *aber* pri-marily relates to written German and this work will mainly be concerned with written corpus data, I will exclude this discussion from this paper.

the preceding constituent as contrastive topic" (Lang and Adamíková 2007: 206). Breindl's (2011) view on the kind of topic that is formally isolated by post-initial adverb connectives, however, is more differentiated. Based on the four dimensions of topic-comment suggested by Jacobs (2001) (i.e. informational separation, predication, addressation, and frame-setting), Breindl (2011) distinguishes four types of topic: 'Familiarity (or 'Continuous') Topics', 'Shifting Topics', 'Contrastive Topics' in Büring's (1997) sense, and 'Frame-setting Topics'. In combination with adverb connectives in post-initial position, 'Familiarity Topics' are infelicitous, as shown in (18) (cf. Breindl 2011: 19; example is my own).

(18) *[Maria]$_{T1}$ ist arm,* * *[sie]$_{T2=T1}$ **aber/nämlich** ist glücklich.*
'Mary is poor, she however/namely is happy.'

The other three types of topics ('Shifting', 'Contrastive', and 'Frame-setting'), in turn, are all attested for adverb connectives in post-initial position. 'Shifting Topic' as in (19) is defined in reference to Givón (1983) as "newly introduced, newly changed or newly returned to" (Givón 1983: 8, cited by Breindl 2011: 20). As Breindl (2011: 20) points out, such topics are either newly established topics in the sense of Daneš's (1970) linear progression, i.e. the topic of the second conjunct takes up (a part of) the comment in the first conjunct, as with *uns* 'us' – *wir* 'we' in (14) above, or 're-established' after a sequence of discontinuity with other topics ("Rethematisierung", Breindl 2011: 20), as in my introspective example in (19). As in Breindl, Volodina, and Waßner (2014), Breindl (2011) points out that the comments do not have to be contrastive or interpreted as such – none of the preceding sentences provides a contrastive alternative to leaving Mary's brother alone in the line to buy popcorn.

(19) *[Maria]$_{T1}$ geht mit ihrem kleinen Bruder ins Kino, um den neuen Spider-Man zu sehen. [Die Schlange vor den Kassen]$_{T2}$ ist sehr lang, denn [alle]$_{T3}$ freuen sich auf den Film. [Er]$_{T4=F3}$ hat sehr gute Kritiken bekommen und verspricht aufwendige Spezialeffekte und viel Action. [Maria]$_{T5=T1}$ **aber** lässt ihren Bruder allein in der Schlange, um schon mal das Popcorn zu kaufen.*
'Mary is going to the cinema with her little brother to watch the new Spider Man. The checkout-queue is very long, because everyone is looking forward to the movie. It got great reviews and promises elaborate special effects and a lot of action. Mary, in turn, leaves her brother alone in the queue to get some popcorn.'

'Contrastive Topics' are defined in Büring's (2006) sense as non-exhaustive alternatives in reference to a(n overt or covert) pertinent question that is "not resolved by the answer" (Büring 2006: 7).[8],[9] This function of "contrastive topics to indicate a strategy of incremental answering" of an overt or covert QuD (Krifka 2008: 268) can also be applied to (20) with *aber* in post-initial position, assuming a covert question along the lines of *Who wants to see the new Spider-Man?*, where the foci, while not alternatives in the classic, i.e. semantic sense, are also interpreted as contrastive.

(20) *[Alle]$_{CT1}$ wollen den neuen Spider-Man sehen. [Maria]$_{CT2}$* **aber** *interessiert sich nicht für Superheldenfilme.*
‘Everyone wants to see the new Spider-Man. Mary, in contrast, doesn't care for super hero movies.’

Finally, Breindl (2011) discusses 'Frame-setting Topics' as possible candidates for the formally isolated constituent with post-initial adverb connectives. As the author points out, 'Frame-setting Topics' represent a category supplementary to the other topic types: the formally isolated frame may represent 'Contrastive Topics' as in (21) (cf. Breindl 2011: 24; example (26) is mine) or a 'Shifting Topic' as in her example in (22), where the local adverbial *dort* 'there' takes up the local description *an den Schildsee* 'to the Schildsee [proper name of a lake]'.

(21) *[Draußen]$_{F1}$ scheint die Sonne. [Im Kino]$_{F2}$* **aber** *ist es angenehm kühl.*
‘Outside, the sun is shining. In the cinema, in turn, it is pleasantly cool.’

(22) *Der Meister Dudel sollte am nächsten Morgen durch Schilda ziehen, mit seiner Flöte die Ratten und Mäuse an sich locken und sie danach [an den Schildsee]$_{F1}$ hinausführen. [Dort]$_{T2=F1}$* **aber** *werde ein Boot bereitstehen [. . .].*
‘The next morning, Master Dudel was supposed to wander through Schilda, allure the rats and mice with his flute, and then bring them to the Schildsee. There, in turn, a boat was to wait for him [. . .].’

In all of the above cases, the topic status of the prefield constituent is independent of the adverb connective isolating it. *Aber* and other adverb connectives in post-in-

---

8 Note that Büring, too, uses the term 'shifting topic' addressing phenomena as in (i): (i) *(Where did Fritz buy this book? –) Bertie$_{CT}$ bought it at Hartlieb$_F$'s.* (example (15b) in Büring 2006: 7). This is a very different notion of 'shift', as the 'shifted' topic is not informationally given, but shifts from one of the contrastive alternatives (Fritz, in this case) to another (i.e. Bertie).
9 A frequently used example for contrastive topics is (ii) A: *What do your siblings do? – B: [My [SISter]$_{Focus}$]$_{Topic}$ [studies MEDicine]$_{Focus}$, and [my [BROther]$_{Focus}$]$_{Topic}$ is [working on a FREIGHTship]$_{Focus}$,* as discussed e.g. by Krifka (2008: 268). For him, the alternativeness results from focus marking within the (aboutness-)topics. Cf. also discussion of double contrast in section 2 above, e.g. example (9).

itial position thus mark what is already there in terms of a pragmatic marker that facilitates processing.

3.2 Topic potential and contrastive relation

From Breindl's (2011) discussion we can retain the following observations: German adverb connectives in post-initial position require a topic shift – and I mean this here in the most basic sense of the term, i.e. the topic of the second conjunct is not identical to the topic of the first. This shift comes about in one out of two ways: a) the new topic (the one immediately preceding the post-initial connective) is a non-exhaustive alternative to an element in the previous conjunct, or b) it is (re-) established from given previous context. Since I find Breindl's (2011) use of the term 'Shifting Topic' for the latter not quite befitting (after all, both involve a topic 'shift'), I suggest to use the term *Topic Promotion* here. For the first kind of topic progression, I will continue to use the fitting and well-established term *Contrastive Topics*. Now, in both kinds of topic progression, the constituent formally isolated by the post-initial adverb connective may either be referential, i.e. what research-ers usually refer to as 'aboutness'-topics (cf. Krifka (2008: 265) who states that the topic is the "entity or set of entities under which the information expressed in the comment constituent should be stored in the CG content"), *or* frame-setting adver-bials, i.e. frame-setting topics.

The necessity to distinguish type of topic progression (Contrastive Topics vs. Topic Promotion), on the one hand, and topic type (aboutness vs. frame-setting), on the other, becomes particularly pertinent for the contrastive *aber*. Recall that Breindl, Volodina, and Waßner (2014) distinguish two kinds of contrast based on these two different topic progressions: 'contrastive comparison' with Contrastive Topics and 'weak contrast' with Topic Promotion (cf. section 2 above).

The status of frame-setting adverbials as sentence topics is, however, not un-controversial. The main argument for Breindl (2011) to consider them as potential topics in correlation with post-initial adverb connectives is based on her observa-tions regarding German: the German prefield position is argued to be the proto-typical topic-position and, besides the sentence subject, frame-setting adverbials are the most frequent type of constituent in the German prefield (Breindl 2011: 24). Other researchers (considering other languages) such as Krifka (2008), on the other hand, restrict the notion of topic to referential aboutness-topics, cf. also Kiss (2002) for whom "[a] topic constituent must be [+referential] and [+specific]" (Kiss 2002: 11). Frame-setting adverbials, in turn, are not referential in the same sense, nor need they be specific.

Krifka (2008) points out that frames are associated with alternativeness since "[t]hey choose one out of a set of frames and state that the proposition holds within this frame" (Krifka 2008: 269).[10] This conceptualization by itself is similar to Jacobs' (2001) definition of frame-setting according to which frames choose "a domain of (possible) reality to which the proposition expressed [. . .] is restricted" (Jacobs 2001: 656), only that for him, frame-setting and aboutness are two possible manifestations of topicality. Jacobs (2001) underlines the similarities between frames and his other dimensions of topicality e.g. by instancing morphological topic-marking in Korean with *-nùn* which is possible on frame-setting adverbials (cf. Jacobs 2001: 655) and by observations concerning patterns of syntactic topic-constructions in German with frame-setters, such as left-dislocation.

For Krifka (2008), the correlation between frames and alternatives brings about similarities between frame-setters and *contrastive* topics:

> What contrastive topics and frame setters have in common is that they express that, for the communicative needs at the current point of discourse, the present contribution only gives a limited or incomplete answer. In the case of contrastive topics, the current CG management contains the expectation that information about a more comprehensive, or a distinct, entity is given; contrastive topic indicates that the topic of the sentence diverges from this expectation. With frame setters, the current CG management contains the expectation that information of a different, e.g., more comprehensive, type is given, and the frame setter indicates that the information actually provided is restricted to the particular dimension specified. (Krifka 2008: 270)

Krifka (2008) subsumes the common alternative-based function of contrastive topics and frames under the concept of *delimitation*. The idea that such a delimitating function can be associated with typically topical and non-topical elements alike goes in hand with Büring's (1997, 2016) discussion of contrastive topics (CT). He observes that CT-marking, which involves prosodic marking in terms of a hat contour, also applies to cases such as (23), where the negation particle *nicht* 'not' – which is usually not regarded as a topical element – is CT-marked (example (23) in Büring 2016: 10).

(23) *Ich habe NICHT$_{CT}$ getrunken, weil ich TRAURIG$_F$ bin.*
      'I didn't drink because I'm sad.'

---

10 In the often-quoted example *(i) A: How is John? – B: {Healthwise/As for his health}, he is [FINE]$_{Focus}$* ((Krifka 2008: 269, example (47)), John being fine can only be said regarding his health – financially, for example, John may not be fine at all.

Büring's (2016) conclusion from examples such as this and his discussion of contrastive topics in general is that "the notion of 'topic' (without 'contrastive') should be used with great caution" or, in fact, not at all (Büring 2016: 25).[11]

This struggle also applies to the very narrow phenomenon of German *aber* in post-initial position. Even if we follow a broad notion of topic as a 'point of departure' in Jacobs' (2001) or Chafe's (1976) sense and determine that "the topic sets *a spatial, temporal, or individual framework* within which the main predication holds" (Chafe 1976: 50), we find examples where the prefield constituent formally isolated by post-initial *aber* is neither. For example, Büring's (2016) example in (23) above can quite uncontroversially be altered to include post-initial *aber* as in (24):

(24) *Ich trinke, weil ich Durst habe, NICHT **aber**, weil ich traurig bin.*
       'I drink because I'm thirsty, but not because I'm sad.'

One could argue, in line with Sæbø (2003: 262, footnote 6), that the ellipsis typical for *aber*-conjunctions blurs the lines between the syntactic positions in that *aber* might not actually be in post-initial position in (24). However, we also find corpus examples such as the following where *aber* is unambiguously post-initial, but the prefield constituents *tatsächlich* 'indeed' in (25) and *vor allem* 'above all' in (26) are neither temporal, spatial, or individual frame, nor likely to be analyzed as topical at all:

(25) *"Girl-Power" sollte ein konsumierbarer Feminismus sein, der endlich gut aussieht und niemandem zu nahe tritt. [. . .] Tatsächlich **aber** bremste die "Girl-Power" die Gleichberechtigung.*
       '"Girl power" was meant to be a consumable form of feminism that, finally, looks attractive and doesn't offend anyone. [. . .] Indeed/In reality CONN, "girl power" curbed equality.'
       DeReKo; Z14/JAN.00188 Die Zeit (Online-Ausgabe), 09.01.2014, "1994"

(26) *Weil die Datenträger mechanisch rotieren, sind sie anfällig für mechanische Fehler [. . .]. Vor allem **aber** verbrauchen sie viel Energie.*
       'Since the data storage devices rotate mechanically, they are susceptible to mechanical defects [. . .]. Above all CONN, they spend a lot of energy.'
       Z14/APR.00389 Die Zeit (Online-Ausgabe), 17.04.2014, „Von Stanford nach Halle"

---

11 The general frustration with the notion of topicality is also described by Molnár, Egerland, and Winkler (2019) who ascribe definitional difficulties to the fact that "a satisfactory theoretical and empirical analysis of topichood presupposes that both the interplay of discourse and grammar and the relation between universal topic features and cross-linguistic variation are taken into consideration" (Molnár, Egerland, and Winkler 2019: 31).

What is most interesting about these examples, is that their interpretation seems to change to other types of contrast altogether. In (25), the contrast is of the Denial of Expectation kind: the violation of the expectation that the concept of "girl power" would become an accessible form of feminism is even encoded in the modal *sollte* 'should have/was meant to be'. In (26), the comparison of two disadvantages of vinyl as a data storage device prompts an interpretation as Argumentative Contrast. While approaches such as Winterstein's (2012, cf. footnote 3 above) assume all instances of contrast to be argumentative, the contrastive evaluation is much more accessible in (26) than in e.g. (20) or (21) above. This may be due to *vor allem* 'above all' already encoding an evaluation, just as the modal *sollte* in (25) already encodes a violated expectation. However, it may also be that the non-topicality of the constituents isolated by *aber* already indicates a change in type of contrast.

The discussion of post-initial *aber* and topicality in this section raises interesting theoretical questions. Is formal contrast defined by certain types of topic development? How do cases with constituents formally isolated by post-initial *aber* that fall outside of any notion of topicality fit into the theory? Can we use the topic potential of post-initial *aber*'s prefield constituents as a means to formally distinguish different uses of *aber*? In the next section, I will discuss a corpus study that addresses these questions.

4 Topic progression with *aber* in post-initial position

The discussion in the previous section has shown that contrast, post-initial *aber*, and topicality are linked in an interesting interplay. Section 2 has shown that contrast is defined in terms of alternatives that information structurally manifest themselves as contrastive topics, foci, or both. Section 3 has shown that post-initial *aber* is prone to mark the formally isolated prefield constituent as a shifted topic (or 'delimitator' in Krifka's (2008) terminology). This topic discontinuity may involve Contrastive Topics or Topic Promotion. Crucially, however, the topic status of the isolated constituent is a point of discussion: next to expressions denoting (sets of) entities that may form aboutness topics, frame-setting adverbials frequently occur in this position and may be analyzed as frame-setting topics. Moreover, the prefield constituent may be an expression not usually analyzed as potential sentence topics, such as sentence adverbials. At first sight, the difference between potentially topical (aboutness expressions and frame-setting adverbials) and non-topical expressions that are formally isolated by post-initial *aber* may indicate different types of contrast altogether.

The goal of this section is to provide corpus data with post-initial *aber* in order to find out whether we can use the topic potential of post-initial *aber*'s prefield constituents as a means to formally distinguish different uses of *aber*. For this, 200 cases of post-initial *aber* are annotated for the prefield constituent's topic potential and the type of topic progression if applicable.

4.1 Corpus data

The data consist of 200 occurrences with post-initial *aber* randomly extracted from the tagged DeReKo newspaper sub-corpus *Die Zeit*. The search request was formulated such that *aber* is followed by a finite verb. In order to exclude elliptical sentences without a prefield constituent while also allowing for prefield constituents of varying size and complexity, *aber* had to be preceded by a minimum of one and a maximum of five words counted from the beginning of the sentence.[12]

Since the conjuncts linked by adverb connectives such as *aber* do not have to be juxtaposed (cf. e.g. Miltsakaki et al. 2004; Asher and Vieu 2005) and may vary in size (cf. e.g. Fetzer 2012; Breindl, Volodina, and Waßner 2014), the extracted preceding context contained at least five sentences. The external conjunct was identified among this preceding context following the criteria by Miltsakaki et al. (2004). Incomprehensible or incomplete conjuncts (e.g. due to ellipsis), as well as those that comprised more than one sentence were excluded from analysis such that 200 occurrences remained.

4.2 Annotation of topic status and progression

As discussed in section 3, the analysis of topicality in association with post-initial *aber* requires the distinction between the potential type of topic (aboutness, frame-setting or non-topic) from the type of topic progression (Contrastive Topics vs. Topic Promotion).

The constituent preceding post-initial *aber* is thus first annotated for topic potential. This is done in accordance with the characteristics for the different notions of topic discussed above: a potential aboutness topic is a constituent denoting (sets of) entities, morpho-syntactically in keeping with DPs such as proper names and pronouns or (referential) PPs. Unlike e.g. Kiss (2002) mentioned above,

---

12 The full search request entered in the web-based application COSMAS II (archive *tagged-T2*, corpus *die Zeit*) reads as follows: "<sa> /+w1:5 aber MORPH(VRB fin)".

however, I also consider kind-denoting and non-referential expressions such as the generic *Gold* 'gold' in (27) or indefinite pronouns such as *einige* 'some' or *andere* 'others' as potential aboutness topics. Potential frame-setting topics are adverbs or adverbial PPs that indicate a spatial or temporal frame or domain[13] (in line with e.g. Chafe 1976 cited above), such as the temporal *im Winter* 'in/during winter' in (28).

(27) *Papiergeld wurde schon öfter in der Geschichte wertlos. [Gold]_{AT}* **aber** *kann man immer gegen irgendwas eintauschen.*
'Throughout history, banknotes have become worthless from time to time. Gold CONN is always exchangeable for something.'
Z14/MAR.00266 Die Zeit (Online-Ausgabe), 20.03.2014; Es geht wild hin und her

(28) *Im Sommer geht es geografisch noch gerecht zu: [. . .]. [Im Winter]_{FT}* **aber** *herrscht ein Ungleichgewicht: [. . .].*
'In summer, things are equitable geografically [. . .]. In winter CONN there is an imbalance: [. . .].'
Z14/FEB.00133 Die Zeit (Online-Ausgabe), 13.02.2014; Olympiateilnehmer

Temporal adverbs that do not denote temporal frames in the strict sense such as *zugleich* or *zeitgleich* 'at the same time' form an exception, as will be discussed in section 5. Finally, the topic status of the prefield constituent preceding post-initial *aber* may be a non-topic. This category corresponds to a 'none of the above'-category and comprises sentence adverbials as in (25) above and infinitival constructions, but also focal constituents marked by focus particles such as *nur* 'only' or *auch* 'too' (cf. Molnár's (1998) concept of focus restriction, see also Molnár, Egerland, and Winkler (2019)).

(i) **Annotation of topic status**
   A) Potential aboutness topics (DPs/PPs denoting (sets of) entities) [AT]
   B) Potential frame-setting topics (adverbs/adverbial PPs denoting space, time, domain) [FT]
   C) Non-topics (sentence adverbials, infinitival constructions, focal constituents) [NT]

The second annotation criterion for the prefield constituent isolated by post-initial *aber* is the type of topic progression. Naturally, this is only applicable if the constituent is annotated as potential aboutness or frame-setting topic in the first place.

---

13 I use the term 'domain' here to include e.g. concessive, final or modal adverbials.

As discussed in the previous section, I distinguish two types of topic progression with post-initial *aber*: Contrastive Topics and Topic Promotion. Contrastive Topics are defined in Büring's (1996, 2016) sense in that the topic forms a non-exhaustive set of alternatives with the topic of the external conjunct. In (27) above, the potential aboutness topic *Gold* 'gold' is a non-exhaustive alternative to the topic of the external conjunct *Papiergeld* 'banknotes', whereas in (28) the potential frame-setting topic *im Winter* 'in/during winter' is an alternative to *im Sommer* 'in/during summer'. The non-exhaustive alternative is not restricted to a certain information structural status in the external conjunct; cf. Umbach's (2005) 'crossed alternatives' or discussion in Breindl, Volodina, and Waßner (2014: 524) mentioned above. For the potential frame-setting topic *neuerdings* 'recently' in (29), for example, the non-exhaustive alternative is not the potential local frame topic *in der Türkei* 'in Turkey', but the temporal adverbial *lange Zeit* 'for a long time' which is part of the external conjunct's comment.

(29) *In der Türkei verfolgte der Staat lange Zeit rachsüchtig nur die eigenen Bürger.*
      *Neuerdings **aber** verfolgt der Staat auch sich selbst.*
      'In Turkey, the state has vindictively persecuted its own citizens for a long time. Recently CONN, the state also persecutes itself.'
      Z14/JAN.00104 Die Zeit (Online-Ausgabe), 02.01.2014; Die Dämonen, die er rief

Because of this latitude as to the information structural status of the explicit alternative, it is not strictly necessary to analyze the potential topic constituent of the external conjunct. Added to that, we find instances where the non-exhaustive alternative is not mentioned explicitly at all. Following Erteschik-Shir (1997, 1999, cited by Lahousse 2007), Lahousse (2007: 1) argues that "spatio-temporal topics, or *stage topics*, can also be implicit". From this it follows that a potentially topical constituent may be analyzed as contrastive via accommodation of a covert, i.e. implicit, non-exhaustive alternative in the preceding conjunct. Lahousse (2007: 4–5) observes that such implicit frames are more likely to be temporal, since the assumption of "a covert stage topic amounts to saying that [the] clause is linked to the previous context" as formally expressed in verbal tense-marking. This applies to cases such as in (30), where the attempts at academic reformation are marked as past, which contrasts with the present tense and the temporal adverb *jetzt* 'now' in the second conjunct. In this study, however, I consider the possibility to accommodate implicit contrastive alternatives to the potential topic isolated by post-initial *aber* more broadly. For the isolated frame *am Arbeitsplatz* 'at work' in (31), for example, we can accommodate the generic alternative 'everywhere else'.

(30) *Unzählige akademische Reformversuche [. . .] haben die hierarchische Struktur der Universität nicht aufbrechen können. [Jetzt]$_{FT}$ **aber** gibt es Anzeichen, dass sich das ändern könnte.*
'Myriads of attempts at academic reformation could not breach the hierarchical structure of universities. Now CONN there are signs of change.'
Z14/MAR.00205 Die Zeit (Online-Ausgabe), 13.03.2014; Forschung aus fairer Produktion

(31) *Die Pflanze braucht Wasser und Luft und vielleicht etwas Liebe. [Am Arbeits-platz]$_{FT}$ **aber** gibt es tausend wichtigere Dinge als Wasser und Luft und vor allem Liebe.*
'The plant needs water and air and maybe some love. At work CONN there are a thousand things more important than water and air and, particularly, love.'
Z14/APR.00149 Die Zeit (Online-Ausgabe), 10.04.2014, Zucht und Ordner

The third and final type of topic progression annotated is Topic Promotion, i.e. 'Shifting Topics' in Breindl's (2011) terminology or 'linear progression' in Daneš's (1970), as shown in (32). As mentioned above, the two conjuncts do not have to be juxtaposed; therefore, cases where a referent was re-introduced after one or more intermediate sentences also counts as Topic Promotion.[14]

(32) *Die Staatsanwältin wirft dem Verteidiger$_i$ einen Schauprozess vor. [Der$_i$]$_{AT}$ **aber** bekommt Szenenapplaus von den Zuschauerbänken.*
'The attorney accuses the defending lawyer$_i$ of a show trial. He$_i$ CONN receives acclamations from the spectator bench.'
Z14/MAI.00418 Die Zeit (Online-Ausgabe), 22.05.2014; Beifall für den Angeklagten

(ii) **Annotation of topic progression**
  (i)   Contrastive Topics (explicit alternative)
  (ii) Accommodated Contrastive Topics (implicit alternative)
  (iii) Topic Promotion
  (iv) Non-topics (therefore not applicable)

---

14 Cf. example (17) above, where the constituent *der Stadtochse* isolated by causal *nämlich* is introduced not in the conjunct immediately preceding, but in the one before that, and example (19).

4.3 Results

Figure 1 shows the results of the annotation of the constituent isolated by post-initial *aber* for topic status and topic progression. The height of the bars indicates the absolute frequency of the different potential topic types. With 81 instances (40.5%) potential aboutness topics are most frequent, followed by 73 cases of potential frame-setting topics (36.5%). Constituents that do not fall under the category of topicality make up 46 occurrences (23%). The grayscale filling of the bars indicates the annotation of topic progression for the two potential types of topic. Non-topical constituents were not applicable for annotation of topic progression. Overall, (explicit) Contrastive Topics (shown in white) is the type of topic progression annotated most frequently with 79 instances (51.2% of the cases where topic progression was annotated, i.e. excluding the non-topical instances). 31 cases were annotated as Accommodated Contrastive Topics (20.1%, shown in light grey). Finally, Topic Promotion (shown in darker grey) was annotated in 44 cases overall (28.6%).

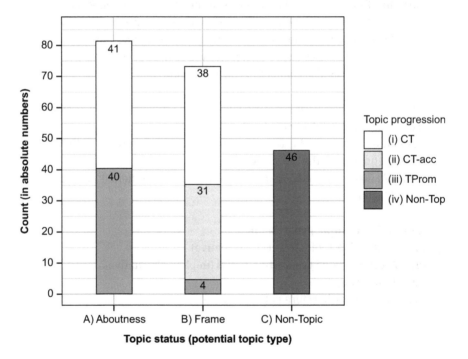

Figure 1: Annotation of Potential Topic Type and Topic Progression.

As predicted by Lahousse (2007) and in spite of a broader conception of implicit topics, accommodation of Contrastive Topics was exclusively annotated for potential frame-setting topics (temporal and local). Combined with explicit Contrastive Topics, we find that frame-setting adverbials that are formally isolated by post-initial *aber* predominantly constitute non-exhaustive alternatives (94.5% as compared to 5.5% Topic Promotion). Expressions denoting (sets of) entities, on the other hand, are split between progressions with (explicit) Contrastive Topics and Topic Promotion (50.7% and 49.3%, respectively). Since the latter is considered a common discourse strategy to 'properly' introduce discourse referents (*Let me tell you something about Paul. He is such a nice guy.*), it is to be expected that it should primarily occur with potential aboutness topics.

Given that, according to Breindl (2011), post-initial *aber* only isolates topical elements, the high frequency of non-topical constituents in the corpus data is most striking. Regardless of the notion of topicality one wants to adopt – sentence adverbials, focus particles and expressions of simultaneity fall outside of that. In section 3, we have seen examples discussed by Büring (2016) who shows with (28) that the negation particle *nicht* may also be CT-marked, i.e. highlighted as (part of) a non-exhaustive alternative by prosodic means. While the corpus data consist of newspaper articles and therefore do not provide prosodic information, none of the non-topical data can felicitously be read with a CT-intonation, i.e. hat contour. With this, instances with post-initial *aber* isolating non-topical constituents do not behave in the same way as the instances with potentially topical constituents – neither potential aboutness or frame topics, nor Contrastive Topics or Topic Promotion.

5 Discussion: Structural versus non-structural contrast

The results of the corpus study presented in the previous section show that the overall majority (77%) of constituents isolated by post-initial *aber* are potentially topical. The distinction between potential topic type (aboutness or frame), on the one hand, and type of topic progression ((accommodated) Contrastive Topics or Topic Promotion), on the other, reveals that both types of topic progression occur with both types of potential topics.

Both, expressions denoting (sets of) entities and frame-setting adverbials, can denote a non-exhaustive alternative to an overt, or in the case of frame-setters also covert, alternative in the first conjunct. The effect of such formally marked alternatives is the same for both types of constituents, cf. Krifka's (2008) notion of delimitation mentioned in section 3 or Büring's (2016) view that CT-marking is not restricted to a certain type of constituent. As discussed in section 2, this effect, i.e. the implicature of comparability involved with contrastive topics, is central for (information structurally defined) contrast, cf. 'formal contrast/opposition' (Sæbø 2003; Umbach 2005; Jasinskaja 2012) or 'contrastive comparison' (Breindl, Volodina, and Waßner 2014). Hence, the corpus examples in (27) and (28) above do not differ in that regard, i.e. they both provide points of comparison (of two payment methods in (27) and two seasons in (28)).

Moreover, both, potential aboutness and frame topics isolated by post-initial *aber*, can provide a re-introduced or 'promoted' topic. While this type of topic progression clearly predominates with aboutness rather than frame topics (40 as compared to 4 instances, respectively), I do not detect a conceptual difference between cases with promoted aboutness topics such as in (32) above and those with promoted frames as in (33) that go beyond the frame/aboutness-divide.

(33)   *Seit der Jahrtausendwende stagnierte der Umsatz der Branche, während er sich im Internet$_i$ alle fünf Jahre verdoppelte. [Dort$_i$]$_{FT}$ **aber** will der Riese Amazon den Markt für sich haben und verzichtet dafür auf einige kurzfristige Gewinne.*
'Since the turn of the millennial, the branch's turnover stagnated, while it doubled every five years on the internet$_i$. There CONN the giant Amazon wants to monopolize the market, dispensing with short-term profits.'
Z14/JAN.00454 Die Zeit (Online-Ausgabe), 23.01.2014, Bloß schnell raus

As we have seen in section 2, Breindl, Volodina, and Waßner (2014) distinguish contrast with *aber* that involves Contrastive Topics from what they call 'weak contrast' involving Topic Promotion. As I have argued above, however, the similarities become more apparent when keeping in mind the central aspect of contrast: alternatives. In the case of Contrastive Topics, the alternatives are part of the denotations; in the case of Topic Promotion, the alternatives lie on a more abstract – or rather: formal – level, displaying an alternative choice of topic. The common feature of the data where the prefield constituent formally isolated by post-initial *aber* is potentially topical is that this constituent is marked as an alternative topic, be it contrastive or promoted, aboutness or frame. With this, these cases can not only be subsumed under one information structurally defined notion of contrast, they also clearly dissociate from the data with isolated non-topical constituents that do not allow for either interpretation of alternatives.

Making up almost a quarter of the data, non-topical constituents isolated by post-initial *aber* are no peripheral matter. The question is what post-initial *aber* does in these cases if it does not mark alternatives on an information structural level. A closer (qualitative) look at these data provide interesting insights, with two kinds of constituents sticking out.[15]

The first group, which makes up 16 cases, contains sentence adverbials such as *tatsächlich* 'indeed/in reality', *vielleicht* 'maybe' or *wundersamerweise* 'astonishingly'. In all of these cases, the interpretation of contrast is that of Denial of Expectation, as in (25) discussed in section 3.2. As I have argued there, the violated expectation that "girl power" become an accessible form of feminism is encoded by further formal means, i.e. the modal verb *sollte* 'should have'. For Blühdorn (2008: 220), the interaction between connectives and linguistic devices encoding epistemic modality such as modal verbs, epistemic particles and verb modus (indicative vs. conjunctive) is related to an epistemic interpretation of the connection. And indeed, the other cases with formally isolated sentence adverbials contain such markers in the first conjunct, e.g. a shift from conjunctive *hätten gebraucht* 'would have needed' to the indicative *war* 'was' in (34):

(34) *„Wir hätten"*, *sagt sie*, *„einen neutralen Vermittler gebraucht. Je früher, desto besser." [Vielleicht]$_{NT}$ **aber** war das Projekt Piz Tschütta von Anfang an zum Scheitern verurteilt.*
'"What we would have needed", she says, "was a neutral mediator. The earlier, the better." Maybe CONN the project Piz Tschütta was doomed to fail from the beginning.'
Z14/FEB.00089 Die Zeit (Online-Ausgabe), 06.02.2014, Licht aus!

According to Blühdorn (2008), this indicates a sentence connection on the epistemic level (cf. Sweetser 1990), i.e. the connection of two epistemic states: something that might be or might have been and something that is or was. Since in our case, the connective is the contrastive *aber*, these two states are interpreted as non-compatible alternatives, i.e. an assumption or expectation and its violation. Interestingly, this also falls in line with Sæbø's (2003: 268) formulation that the alternatives may be "individuals, places, times, *worlds* [emphasis mine, RZ], or sets of sets of such entities" as mentioned above. My proposal would be that the shift from alternative individuals and frames to alternative worlds involves a shift to Denial of Expectation contrast.[16]

---

15 The non-topicality of the two cases that do not fall into either group is due to a focus particle (cf. focus restriction Molnár 1998): *nur zwei Drittel der Schüler* ('only two thirds of the students') and *so eisig-realistisch* (' so cold-heartedly realisitic'). How such cases fit into the picture painted here remains an open question for future research.
16 A suggestion for how to formalize this kind of contrast is given in Zieleke (2021), where I use the terminology 'generic contrast'.

The second group, which makes up 28 cases, contains expressions of comparison such as *noch weniger* 'even less' and the dominant *vor allem* 'above all', 16 instances. The latter in particular, which encodes an evaluation, prompts an interpretation as contrastive evaluation or Argumentative Contrast, as discussed for (26) in section 3.2 above. In (26), two (co-existing) features of vinyl are compared to each other in two conjuncts. *Vor allem aber* strongly advocates that the feature described in the second conjunct be evaluated as more relevant. Again, we find a connection to Sæbø's (2003) thoughts on the make-up of contrastive alternatives in that he also states that they can be "ordered along some scale" (2003: 268). Again, my proposal here is that expressions of such an ordering involve a shift from information structural to argumentative alternatives, leading to Argumentative Contrast.

The evaluative comparison of two co-existing aspects is also prevalent in cases with expressions of simultaneity isolated by post-initial *aber*, as e.g. *zugleich* 'at the same time' in (35):[17]

(35) *Betriebswirtschaftlich ist das heikel. Zwar spricht das Prädikat „mild" jene Zielgruppe an, die Wert auf „mild" legt. [Zugleich]$_{NT}$ **aber** schreckt es alle anderen ab.*
'Economically, this is precarious. Admittedly, the predicate "mild" attracts the target group. At the same time CONN all other potential customers are put off.'
Z14/MAR.00326 Die Zeit (Online-Ausgabe), 20.03.2014; „Mild"

Both observations are in line with Corminboeuf's (2014) discussion of alternative ways to mark contrastive relations in French. In particular, he analyzes morpho-syntactic means that distinguish between what Anscombre (2002, cited by Corminboeuf 2014) calls 'direct and indirect counter-argumentation' ("la contre-argumentation « directe » et la contre-argumentation « indirecte »", Corminboeuf 2014: 2370): opposing polarity, modality, and aspectuality in the conjuncts in the case of 'direct' contrast (2014: 2371–2372), and scalar markers such as the superlative or quantifiers in the case of 'indirect' contrast (2014: 2374). As the examples for 'direct' and 'indirect counter-argumentation' in (36) and (37) show, respectively (examples (13) and (15) in Corminboeuf 2014: 2370), these relations correspond to Denial of Expectation and Argumentative Contrast in our terminology.

---

17 An additional hint that isolated expressions of simultaneity invoke the same argumentative interpretation as expressions of comparison is *zwar* ('admittedly') in the first conjunct in (35), cf. Leuschner and van den Nest (2012) who discuss the construction *zwar . . . aber* as an indicator for Argumentative Contrast.

(36) *Les autruches sont des oiseaux, **mais/pourtant** elles ne volent pas.*
      'Ostriches are birds, but/yet they don't fly.'

(37) *Je ne prends pas de dessert : j'adore le sucré, **mais** ça fait grossir.*
      'I won't have dessert: I love sweets, but it's fattening.'

As this discussion has shown, the 23% of the data where post-initial *aber* formally isolates a non-topical constituent are no unaccountable exceptions to a construction otherwise marking topicality. Rather, we have to redefine the function of post-initial *aber*, on the one hand, and the formal features of different kinds of contrast, on the other. My proposal is as follows: Post-initial *aber* formally isolates the prefield constituent and marks it as an *alternative*. This matches well with both, the general concept of contrast and the overall (albeit abstracted) function of German post-initial adverb connectives. A possibility to consolidate the different approaches to topicality discussed in section 3 might be to use Krifka's (2008) term of delimitation which incorporates alternativeness: post-initial *aber* marks the prefield constituent as a delimitator, referring to aboutness-topics, frames, worlds or scales.

The formal features of these isolated constituents then make up different kinds of contrast. Constituents that have topic potential, i.e. expressions denoting (sets of) entities and frame-setting adverbials, provide information structural alternatives. I suggest to call this information structurally defined contrast that relies on a specific topic development *Structural Contrast*. Constituents that do not have topic potential, in particular focal elements, sentence adverbials, and expressions of comparison, provide alternatives on a different level. Accordingly, I suggest the term *Non-Structural Contrast*. As we have seen, further formal features such as the type of expression formally isolated and expressions of epistemic modality in the conjuncts in general then allow for a distinction between Denial of Expectation (by reference to alternative worlds) and Argumentative Contrast (by reference to an ordered scale). Which of these further formal means are crucial and how this can be integrated into a theory of contrast remains to be analyzed with bigger data sets.

6 Summary

In this article, I set out to investigate German post-initial *aber* and its potential to mark contrast via information structural means. In order to find out whether post-initial *aber* formally isolates topic alternatives, we had to refine a notion of topicality that can account for similarities between different constructions. Admitting both, expressions denoting (sets of) entities and frame-setting adverbials, to be considered as topical in Chafe's sense in that "the topic sets *a spatial, temporal, or individual framework* within which the main predication holds" (Chafe 1976: 50), allowed us to identify the similarities between them. The corpus data presented in section 4 showed that both types of potential topics correspond to information structural alternatives involving different kinds of topic development: Contrastive Topics with the alternatives as part of the denotations and Topic Promotion with the more abstract (discourse organizational) alternatives of topic choice.

This information structurally defined contrast that relies on a specific topic development, for which I suggested the term *Structural Contrast*, makes up 77% of the data with post-initial *aber*. In the other 23% of the data, the constituents formally isolated by post-initial *aber* are non-topical such as focal elements, sentence adverbials, and expressions of comparison. I suggested the term *Non-Structural Contrast*. As the discussion of the corpus data shows, however, this term should not imply that there are no relevant structural features – both sub-types of contrast, Denial of Expectation and Argumentative Contrast, display specific formal patterns involving a specific type of expression formally isolated by *aber* (indicating alternative worlds and alternatives ordered on a scale, respectively) and expressions of epistemic modality in the conjuncts. Rather, the alternatives evoked by contrast with post-initial *aber* do not lie on a structural level: in the case of Denial of Expectation, *aber* marks alternative epistemic states, whereas in the case of Argumentative Contrast it marks alternative evaluations of (co-existing) facts.

With its function to formally isolate the prefield constituent, German post-initial *aber* thus provides the possibility to distinguish different kinds of contrast via purely formal means. Future research will have to catalog these means and investigate their role in conjunctions with *aber* in other syntactic positions as well as their transferability to contrastive connections in other languages.

References

Anscombre, Jean-Claude & Oswald Ducrot. 1977. Deux mais en français? *Lingua* 43(1). 23–40.

Asher, Nicholas & Laure Vieu. 2005. Subordinating and coordinating discourse relations. *Lingua* 115(4). 591–610.

Blakemore, Diane. 1989. Denial and contrast: A relevance theoretic analysis of "but". *Linguistics and Philosophy* 12(1). 15–37.

Blühdorn, Hardarik. 2008. Epistemische Lesarten von Satzkonnektoren – Wie sie zustande kommen und wie man sie erkennt. In Inge Pohl (ed.), *Semantik und Pragmatik – Schnittstellen*, 217–251. Frankfurt am Main: Lang.

Blühdorn, Hardarik. 2017. Diskursmarker: Pragmatische Funktion und syntaktischer Status. In Hardarik Blühdorn, Arnulf Deppermann, Henrike Helmer & Thomas Spranz-Fogasy (eds.), *Diskursmarker im Deutschen: Reflexionen und Analysen*, 311–336. Göttingen: Verlag für Gesprächsforschung.

Breindl, Eva. 2011. 'Nach Rom freilich führen viele Wege': zur Interaktion von Informationsstruktur, Diskursstruktur und Prosodie bei der Besetzung der Nacherstposition. In Gisella Ferraresi (ed.), *Konnektoren im Deutschen und im Sprachvergleich: Beschreibung und grammatische Analyse*, 17–56. (Studien zur deutschen Grammatik 53). Tübingen: Narr.

Breindl, Eva, Anna Volodina & Ulrich Hermann Waßner. 2014. *Handbuch der deutschen Konnektoren 2. Semantik der deutschen Satzverknüpfer*. Berlin: Mouton de Gruyter.

Büring, Daniel. 1997. *The Meaning of Topic and Focus — The 59th Street Bridge Accent*. London: Routledge.

Büring, Daniel. 2016. (Contrastive) topic. In Caroline Féry & Shinichiro Ishihara (eds.), *The Oxford Handbook of Information Structure*, 64–85. Oxford: Oxford University Press.

Chafe, Wallace L. 1976. Givenness, contrastiveness, definiteness, subjects, topics and point of view. In Charles N. Li (ed.), *Subject and Topic*, 27–55. New York: Academic Press.

Corminboeuf, Gilles. 2014. L'identification des relations de discours implicites: Le cas de l'adversation. *SHS Web of Conferences* 8. 2367–2382.

Daneš, Frantlšek. 1970. Zur linguistischen Analyse der Textstruktur. *Folia Linguistica* 4(1–2). 72–78.

Fetzer, Anita. 2012. Textual coherence as a pragmatic phenomenon. In Keith Allan & Kasia M. Jaszczolt (eds.), *Cambridge Handbook of Pragmatics*, 447–467. Cambridge: Cambridge University Press.

Givón, Talmy. 1983. *Topic Continuity in Discourse*. Amsterdam/Philadelphia: Benjamins.

Imo, Wolfgang. 2017. Diskursmarker im gesprochenen und geschriebenen Deutsch. In Hardarik Blühdorn, Arnulf Deppermann, Henrike Helmer & Thomas Spranz-Fogasy (eds.), *Diskursmarker im Deutschen: Reflexionen und Analysen*, 49–72. Göttingen: Verlag für Gesprächsforschung.

Jacobs, Joachim. 2001. The dimensions of topic-comment. *Linguistics* 39(4). 641–681.

Jasinskaja, Katja. 2010. Corrective contrast in Russian, in contrast. *Oslo Studies in Language* 2(2). 433–466.

Jasinskaja, Katja. 2012. Correction by adversative and additive markers. *Lingua* 122(15). 1899–1918.

Jasinskaja, Katja & Henk Zeevat. 2008. Explaining additive, adversative and contrast marking in Russian and English. *Revue de Sémantique et Pragmatique* 24(1). 65–91.

Kiss, Katalin É. 2002. *The Syntax of Hungarian*. Cambridge: Cambridge University Press.

König, Ekkehard. 1991. Concessive relations as the dual of causal relations. In Dietmar Zaefferer (ed.), *Semantic Universals and Universal Semantics*, 190–209. Berlin/New York: Foris.

Krifka, Manfred. 2008. Basic notions of information structure. *Acta Linguistica Hungarica* 55(3–4). 243–276.

Lahousse, Karen. 2007. Implicit stage topics. A case study in French. *Discours. Revue de linguistique, psycholinguistique et informatique. A journal of linguistics, psycholinguistics and computational linguistics* 1. 1–23.

Lakoff, Robin. 1971. If's and but's about conjunction. In Charles J. Fillmore & D. Terence Langendoen (eds.), *Studies in Linguistic Semantics*, 3–114. New York: Irvington.

Lang, Ewald & Marcela Adamíková. 2007. The lexical content of connectors and its interplay with intonation. An interim balance on sentential connection in discourse. In Andreas Späth (ed.), *Interfaces and Interface Conditions*, 199–230. Berlin/Boston: De Gruyter.

Leuschner, Torsten & Daan Van den Nest. 2012. Die *zwar. . . aber*-Relation im Gegenwartsdeutschen: Funktionsweise–Variation–Grammatikalisierung. *Deutsche Sprache* 40(1). 2–31.

Malchukov, Andrej. 2004. Towards a semantic typology of adversative and contrast marking. *Journal of Semantics* 21(2). 177–198.

Miltsakaki, Eleni, Aravind Joshi, Rashmi Prasad & Bonnie Webber. 2004. Annotating discourse connectives and their arguments. In *Proceedings of the Workshop Frontiers in Corpus Annotation at HLT-NAACL, Boston, Massachusetts, USA, 2004*, 9–16. Cambridge: Association for Computational Linguistics. https://aclanthology.org/W04-2700.pdf

Molnár, Valéria. 1998. On the syntax, phonology, semantics and pragmatics of the so-called "contrastive topic" in Hungarian and German. *Acta Linguistica Hungarica* 45(1). 89–166.

Molnár, Valéria, Verner Egerland & Susanne Winkler. 2019. Exploring the architecture of topic at the interface of grammar and discourse. In Valéria Molnár, Verner Egerland & Susanne Winkler (eds.), *Architecture of Topic*, 1–43. Berlin/Boston: De Gruyter.

Riester, Arndt, Lisa Brunetti & Kordula De Kuthy. 2018. Annotation guidelines for questions under discussion and information structure. In Evangelia Adamou Katharina Haude & Martine Vanhove (eds.), *Information Structure in Lesser-described Languages: Studies in Prosody and Syntax*, 403–443. Amsterdam: Benjamins.

Roberts, Craige. 1998. Focus, the flow of information, and universal grammar. In Peter Culicover & Louise McNally (eds.), *The Limits of Syntax*, 109–160. Leiden: Brill.

Rudolph, Elisabeth. 2012. *Contrast*. Berlin: De Gruyter.

Sanders, Ted J. M., Wilbert Spooren & Leo G. M. Noordman. 1992. Toward a taxonomy of coherence relations. *Discourse Processes* 15(1). 1–35.

Sæbø, Kjell J. 2003. Presupposition and contrast: German *aber* as a topic particle. *Proceedings of Sinn und Bedeutung* 7. 257–271.

Sweetser, Eve. 1990. *From Etymology to Pragmatics: Metaphorical and Cultural Aspects of Semantic Structure*. Cambridge: Cambridge University Press.

Umbach, Carla. 2005. Contrast and information structure: A focus-based analysis of *but*. *Linguistics* 43(1). 207–232.

Winterstein, Grégoire. 2012. What *but*-sentences argue for: An argumentative analysis of *but*. *Lingua* 122(15). 1864–1885.

Zieleke, Regina. 2021. The incausality of 'dennoch' and 'trotzdem': Generic contrast. *Proceedings of Sinn und Bedeutung* 25. 924–938.

Clara Lombart

7 Definition of contrast in spoken and signed data: An overview

Abstract: Spoken and signed languages are governed by the same information-structure categories (Kimmelman and Pfau 2016, 2021). Among these, we find contrast, which directly influences the encoding of utterances, e.g., by being expressed by specific prosodic features or syntactic constructions. However, the expression of contrast is not systematic and has been debated in the literature (Zimmermann and Onéa 2011). Contrast has also been defined in various ways, sometimes as a subtype of focus or topic and sometimes as an independent information notion. In addition, several perspectives have been adopted, some related to information or discourse structures and others linked to the formal properties of contrast encoding. As a result, the linguistic phenomena that do and do not fall under the umbrella of contrast remain unclear. To better reflect the variety of phenomena covered by contrast, contrast can be regarded not as a unique discursive or pragmatic notion but as divided into several categories (or 'degrees') (Repp 2016). Different typologies have been proposed by various researchers. No consensus has been reached and some concepts are still being discussed, including exhaustivity, mirativity, and emphasis. In this paper, we claim that contrast can be classified into three types according to the categorisation proposed by Umbach (2004), Hartmann and Zimmermann (2009), Kimmelman (2014), and Navarrete-González (2019, 2021): discourse opposition, selection, and correction. We demonstrate how the categories of other typologies and debated notions are distributed in this three-type classification. We particularly address debates related to the expression of contrast (e.g., by focusing on its universality or the methodology adopted by the researchers) and its types of pragmatic and discursive meanings (such as restriction, expansion, or stance). Our approach is based on a literature review and observations of signed and spoken data. We argue that both modalities should be considered in the studies to fully understand the notion of contrast.

Acknowledgements: We acknowledge all the LSFB signers and French speakers. We also thank Laurence Meurant, Natasha Phillips, the reviewers, and the editors for their insightful comments and suggestions on earlier versions of this paper.

https://doi.org/10.1515/9783110986594-007

1 Introduction

Contrast has been the subject of various studies on spoken languages (SpLs) and signed languages (SLs) which adopt different perspectives. Some are related to the functions of contrast and the relations between discourse segments and follow a Discourse Structure (DS) perspective (e.g., Umbach 2004; Repp 2016). Others are associated with the specific types of pragmatic meanings and follow an Information Structure (IS) perspective (e.g., Halliday 1967; Lambrecht 1994), while still others define contrast from formal properties and the use of a specific linguistic marking.

According to the DS perspective, contrast refers to the opposition between (at least) two pieces of information: an utterance or part of it differs in one or more details from an activated propositional frame (Dooley and Levinsohn 2001). From this perspective, contrast can be defined as "the dependency relation between two or more contextually opposed alternatives in discourse" (Navarrete-González 2019: 20). It determines the semantic interpretation of an utterance, as it is correlated with specific truth conditions and conversational implicatures (Umbach 2004).

From an informational perspective, the understanding of an utterance is mediated through the linguistic and situational contexts, but also depends on pragmatic aspects, as claimed by Lambrecht (1994: 5): "[IS is the] component of sentence grammar in which propositions as conceptual representations of states of affairs are paired with lexical-grammatical structures in accordance with the mental states of interlocutors who use and interpret these structures as units of information in given discourse contexts". Since its first descriptions and definitions, IS has always been associated with the formal properties of the linguistic expressions at the syntactic (Rochemont 1986; Lambrecht 1994; Kiss 1998; Lillo-Martin and Quadros 2008; Wilbur 2012; Kimmelman 2014; Cruschina 2021), morphological, lexical (Hartmann and Zimmermann 2009; Crasborn and van der Kooij 2013; Brysbaert and Lahousse 2020), prosodic (Féry 2008; Crasborn and van der Kooij 2013; Kimmelman 2014; Di Cristo 2019), and gestural levels (Ferré 2014; Debreslioska and Gullberg 2020; Esteve-Gibert et al. 2021).

However, a recurrent problem in the literature is that there is no clear-cut boundary between the informational, discursive and formal perspectives and these are frequently conflated. For instance, prosodic variations demarcate contrastive elements, making them more perceptually salient e.g., by assigning them prominence (Terken 1991). However, contrast as a discursive or pragmatic notion is sometimes assimilated with prosodic notions of contrastive pitch, accent, or emphasis (see Chomsky 1971; Calhoun 2009; Dohen and Lœvenbruck 2009; Ferré 2014 for examples of this kind of mismatch). Similarly, information categories, such as contrast, can be defined based on the syntactic positions or structures they occupy (Halliday 1967; Kiss 1998). As a result, it is sometimes difficult to know whether what is being studied corresponds to contrast from a discursive, pragmatic or formal perspective (Kimmelman and Pfau 2016, 2021). Another issue is that contrast is generally associated with the notions of focus or topic, and these terms have also been used in a dual sense (sometimes by the same author) to refer to syntactic or phonological categories, pragmatic interpretations, or discursive aspects (Gundel and Fretheim 2006). This disparity has given rise to a multitude of definitions of contrast that are sometimes barely comparable, leading to an absence of consensus in the literature.

Furthermore, different approaches have been adopted in SpL and SL studies. Theories on IS and DS were elaborated for SpLs and then simply applied to SLs in the 2000s (Kimmelman and Pfau 2016). Previous research has emphasised that SpLs and SLs share similarities in the functioning of IS and DS. This means that information status or types of categories at the discursive or informational levels as well as the structural properties of their prosodic, syntactic, morphological, or lexical encoding are governed by analogous principles in both sets of languages (Wilbur 2012). However, the formal cues used to encode information have been claimed to be different since SpLs rely on voice, and SLs use manual (e.g., variations of sign duration) and non-manual cues (e.g., facial expressions) (Kimmelman and Pfau 2016). Interestingly, other studies dedicated only to SpLs have demonstrated that hand, eyebrow, head, and torso gestures can be used to perform the same functions as spoken cues, and that speech and gesture form an integrated system (e.g., Shattuck-Hufnagel and Ren 2018; Esteve-Gibert et al. 2021). As gestures and signs use the same manual and non-manual articulators and are adopted in similar contexts, such as when indicating information units, their comparison becomes relevant to identifying possible similarities between language modalities and aspects that belong to a language (type) (Gabarró-López and Meurant 2022). Özyürek (2021: 1) summarises this idea by stating that "[u]nderstanding how expressions not only in vocal but also in the visual modality contribute to our notions of language structure, use, processing, and its transmission (i.e., acquisition, evolution, emergence) in different languages and cultures should be a fundamental goal of language sciences". However, no study has yet been devoted to this type of investigation at the informational and discursive levels.

From this perspective, the purpose of this paper is to bring together research on SpLs and SLs and introduce a common theoretical framework that can serve as a basis for cross-modal comparisons. We aim to review the literature on contrast and clarify discussions and murky areas by presenting a typology of this information category. The classification presented in this study is not new in the field, but was formulated by Umbach (2004), Hartmann and Zimmermann (2009), Kimmelman

(2014), and Navarrete-González (2019, 2021). To date, no study has sought to link this categorisation with other proposals and frameworks to overcome the debates and find a common ground between various theories. With this aim in mind, we illustrate and justify our remarks with examples extracted not only from previous research, but also from a set of comparable corpora of a SL and a SpL: the LSFB Corpus (Meurant 2015), the corpus of French Belgian Sign Language (*Langue des Signes de Belgique francophone*), and the FRAPé Corpus (Meurant et al. under construction), a Belgian French corpus.

In line with the authors cited below, we consider the following types of contrast: discourse opposition (parallel contrast), selection (selective contrast), and correction (corrective contrast). These categories are defined in Section 3 along with their specific types of discursive and pragmatic meanings. Before that, Section 2 reviews the main arguments related to the discussions mentioned below in this introduction. Section 4 presents a discussion and conclusion.

2 Definition of contrast in studies on information and discourse structures

Whether in SpLs or SLs, contrast has been the subject of various discussions. Some concern the nature of contrast, which is sometimes conceived as a parameter of focus or topic and sometimes as an independent notion (Section 2.1). Others are related to the methodology used to conduct research on IS or DS (Section 2.2), and the possible universality of contrast (Section 2.3). Additional debates pertain to the binary or non-binary character of contrast (Section 2.4).

2.1 The notion of contrast in studies on information and discourse structures

Debates regarding the notion of contrast began in the 1970s. From this time, contrast has been regarded as a property of focus or topic, forming contrastive focus or topic. These information units/categories have been apprehended in opposition to information focus or topic. However, the mere existence of contrast has also been questioned from a conceptual point of view, because some scholars have claimed that no formal marker allows for a distinction between contrastive focus/topic and its non-contrastive counterpart (e.g., Bolinger 1961; Jackendoff 1972; Lambrecht 1994; Ladd 1996; Schlenker et al. 2016).

More specifically, contrast has mainly been associated with focus, and debates about the distinction between contrastive focus (sometimes named identificational focus or exhaustive focus) and information focus (also labelled plain focus, ordinary focus, presentational focus, non-exhaustive focus, completive focus, or question-answer focus) began with a controversy between Bolinger (1961) and Chomsky (1971). Bolinger (and then Jackendoff 1972; Selkirk 1984; Lambrecht 1994; Ladd 1996; Büring 2003; Samek-Lodovici 2005; Carnaval, Moraes, and Rilliard 2022) maintains that the prosody of information and contrastive foci is identical, i.e. that similar pitch accents are used to encode both information units/categories.

The potential differences in marking between the two notions can be explained by the fact that information and contrastive focus are usually located at different places in an utterance, which affects their prosodic realisations. A similar point of view can be found in Schlenker et al. (2016), who defend the unified point of view of focus in ASL (American Sign Language) and LSF (French Sign Language). These positions are based on the assumption that information and contrastive foci are formally the same and, consequently, identical at the pragmatic or discursive level.

Moreover, these unitary positions stand on the theory of alternatives (Rooth 1992; Schwarzschild 1999; Brunetti 2003; Krifka 2008; Matić and Wedgwood 2013). According to this view, focus is always contrastive because it triggers a set of alternatives (Rooth 1992), such as in (1). In this example, Signer B explains that when she was working in a clothing store, people used to call her 'the linen seller'. This became her nickname in LSFB.

(1)   Context – Signer A asks: Where does your nickname 'the linen seller' come from?
      Signer B/Glosses: *[WORK LINEN]*$_{Focus}$ *MADAM LINEN DEAF PT:PRO1 PT:PRO3*[1]
      Signer B/Translation: 'I **[worked in a clothing shop]**$_{Focus}$, so deaf people used to call me 'the linen seller'.'
      (LSFB Corpus, Session 7, Task 2)

'Work in a clothing shop' in (1) is the information focus of the utterance and implies a set of alternatives that includes all the possible substitutions, i.e, other reasons to have a nickname related to linen. The only difference stated in the literature between information and contrastive foci is that they involve different pragmatic and semantic exploitations of the set of alternatives. Indeed, information focus is

---

1 The gloss PT.PRO1 means that the sign is a personal pronoun. pt.pro1 is a personal pronoun of the first person ('*I*') and PT.PRO3 is a personal pronoun of the third person ('*they*').

characterised by an open set (i.e., alternatives are not identified in the context) and contrastive focus by a closed set (i.e., identified and delimited alternatives) (Krifka 2008).[2] This is exemplified in (2), where 'retired' is a contrastive focus and indicates that, contrary to the assumption made by Signer A, Signer B is no longer working. Two possible alternatives [working and being retired] are included (i.e., a closed set of alternatives). Conversely, in (1), the information focus implies that the set is open to all possible origins for the nickname.

(2)   Context – Signer A asks: Are you still working?
       Signer B/Glosses: *NO-MORE FINISH [**RETIRED**]*$_{Focus}$
       Signer B/Translation: 'No, I am [**retired**]$_{Focus}$ now.'
       (LSFB Corpus, Session 7, Task 2)

Chomsky (1971; and later, other scholars such as Chafe 1976; Rochemont 1986; Vallduví and Vilkuna 1998; Krahmer and Swerts 2001; Katz and Selkirk 2011) opposes this view by presenting arguments in favour of prosodic differences between information and contrastive foci in several SpLs such as English, French, Hungarian, Estonian, Finnish, Portuguese, Italian, Catalan, Russian, Hindi, and Mandarin Chinese. The main argument is that both types of focus are indicated by different types and degrees of prosodic prominence (i.e., by the absence or presence of a certain pitch accent). These cues are not related to the functioning of the prosodic structures, but to dissimilar grammatical representations in the syntactic structure/information structure interface. Similar observations have been made for ASL (Wilbur and Patschke 1998), HSL (Croatian Sign Language) (Milković and Radošević 2021), LSC (Catalan Sign Language) (Navarrete-González 2021), DGS (German Sign Language) (Herrmann 2015), NGT (Dutch Sign Language), and RSL (Russian Sign Language) (Kimmelman 2014). Analogous remarks have also been formulated for the syntactic or lexical differences between information and contrastive foci, both in SpLs (Kiss 1998; Zubizarreta 1998; Donati and Nespor 2003; Skopeteas and Fanselow 2010; Lahousse, Laenzlinger, and Soare 2014) and SLs (Lillo-Martin and Quadros 2008; Kimmelman 2014). Other arguments have been derived from cognitive psycholinguistics. For instance, Chen, Li, and Tang (2012) have shown, in an eye-tracking study, that contrastive and information foci are processed differently during reading in Chinese, and as a result, are not subject to the same linguistic principles.

---

2 It should be noted that the open set of alternatives is still "pragmatically delimited by the encyclopaedic or shared knowledge of the conversation participants, but what is crucial is that no alternatives are explicitly active or given in the context" (Cruschina 2021: 6).

Approaches that distinguish and those that do not distinguish between information and contrastive foci have led to different conclusions and have been equally criticised. Formal perspectives have been criticised for the fact that their arguments do not apply to some languages, such as English or German, where the marking of contrast is ambiguous (Molnár 2002). In addition, some researchers (Zimmermann 2008; Destruel and Velleman 2014) have claimed that, contrary to authors who support the unitary view state (Rooth 1992; Schwarzschild 1999; Brunetti 2003; Krifka 2008; Matić and Wedgwood 2013), the alternative perspective is compatible with the distinction between information and contrastive foci. For instance, according to Zimmermann (2008) and Destruel and Velleman (2014), focus exploits a set of alternatives, whereas contrast distinguishes a relevant set for its interpretation, leading to a distinction between information and contrastive foci. Conversely, semantic approaches are problematic in the sense that many languages, such as Hungarian or Finnish, have a specific contrast marking that differs from the one exploited for focus or topic (Navarrete-González 2021). The following section addresses these considerations.

2.2 The possible universality of contrast in studies related to discourse and information structures

The fields of DS and IS have also been characterised by debates concerning the status of contrast across languages in terms of functional, pragmatic, or formal aspects. For instance, IS has always been linked with the formal properties of the linguistic expression, and contrast has often only been defined from its linguistic expression in such theories. However, as pointed out in Section 1, it is not uncommon in the literature to confuse contrast with prosodic or syntactic notions, such as prominence or focalisation. This problem is compounded when the authors define contrast from a single and systematic marking. These ambiguities could be linked to the fact that contrast has been seen as part of an utterance that conveys information that the speaker/signer wishes to present as salient. S/he wants to draw the attention of the addressee by using different syntactic/prosodic strategies (Halliday 1967; Lambrecht 1994).

However, some studies (see Féry 2008; Zimmermann and Onea 2011 for a review) have demonstrated that there is no exclusive relationship between contrast and the formal markers that express it. These cues can also mark other linguistic components (Matić and Wedgwood 2013), e.g., syntactic structures in SLs (Wilbur 2000; Pfau and Quer 2010). Nevertheless, these considerations are set aside in research that tends to present contrast as unambiguously and uniquely encoded, with these findings being based on elicited or read material (see Section 2.3). From this perspective, Matić and Wedgwood (2013: 129) declare that contrast (which is assimilated to focus) is "an inherently problematic category, which has been used to draw together phenomena in the wrong way: as instances of a single underlying entity, as opposed to potentially independent entities that produce interestingly similar effects".

Other authors (e.g., Riester, Brunetti, and De Kuthy 2018) have tried to be more nuanced by saying that what has been misleading in past studies is the claim that languages have a specific syntactic position, accent, or lexical particle related to only one information unit, such as contrast. According to this view, information-structure categories, such as focus, topic, and contrast, seem to be universal at the functional and pragmatic levels, but not at the formal level (Riester, Brunetti, and De Kuthy 2018). These categories are included in all languages documented so far but are expressed through linguistic means specific to a (group of) language(s) (Vallduví and Vilkuna 1998; Gundel and Fretheim 2006; Zimmermann and Onea 2011; Repp 2016; Di Cristo 2019; Larrivée 2022). This indicates that contrast is a distinct category at the level of DS, attached to distinct types of pragmatic meanings but marked by specific cues depending on the language or context.

However, apart from the discussions about language universals (Evans and Levinson 2009), the assumption of the stability of information notions across languages is problematic. According to Matić and Wedgwood (2013), IS studies have mainly addressed abundantly described languages, and new evidence (in relation to parameterisation, introduction of additional informational-structural primitives, and reduction to a single common factor) related to lesser-known languages sometimes undermines previous conclusions (see also Section 2.3). Furthermore, many theories of contrast have been formulated for SpLs only, but their validity for SLs has not been questioned. For example, the prosodic marking of focus and contrast has been explained by Gussenhoven (2004) through the theory of Effort Code: information considered important for the speaker is produced with greater effort in articulation, which gives rise to greater precision and larger pitch movement. Kimmelman and Pfau (2021: 598) note the following regarding SLs:

> Various researchers have argued that the same biological motivation applies to prosodic marking in sign languages (. . .). While the notion of pitch does not apply, signers can also use greater effort to articulate signs which will lead to higher velocity, larger amplitude, clearer boundaries, etc., and this effort can be interpreted as relating to new and important information.

However, the theory of Effort Code does not seem to fully apply to all SLs. For example, Herrmann (2015) has shown that focused elements may be de-accentuated while the rest of the utterance is marked by prosodic cues in DGS. This type of encoding, which allows the focus to be identified, is not consistent with the Effort Code theory because focus is not expressed with greater effort. In other words, a theory formulated for one language or set of languages is not always relevant to another language or set of languages (Kimmelman and Pfau 2021). Considering SpLs and SLs thus allows us to test claims formulated in relation to contrast (this remark applies to all areas of linguistics), which are sometimes regarded as universal.

2.3 Methodology

In addition to the theoretical issues explained in the previous sections, other problems concern the methodology employed to study contrast in SpLs and SLs. Much research on IS or DS in SLs has been conducted on controlled materials, i.e., on elicitations or translations from a SpL to a SL, and not on spontaneous data. Furthermore, because most studies have been established on single-signer datasets and small data samples (Baker and van den Bogaerde 2012), interactional data are lacking. These gaps are summarised by Fenlon and Hochgesang (2022: 1): "Although linguists have devised methods to elicit judgments in systematic ways, we have, for a long time, been unable to take advantage of a large, machine-readable resource that could provide us with a viewpoint that does not rely on introspection and instead provides us with a more usage-based perspective."

Studies on IS or DS in SLs have also been limited to a few languages, and more data diversity is required. Research has mainly focused on Western SLs, but it seems relevant to take into account less-documented SLs to open new avenues for a more thorough definition of contrast and its functioning across languages (Kimmelman and Pfau 2021). Conversely, studies on contrast in SpLs have considered more diverse and unrelated languages (e.g., English, French, Hungarian, Estonian, Finnish, Portuguese, Italian, Catalan, Russian, Hindi, or Mandarin Chinese). Nevertheless, even for SpLs, many works have been established on controlled lab speech, and more specifically, reading-aloud materials (e.g., Wagner and Windmann 2016). In other words, whether in SpLs or SLs, studies that exploit spontaneous and less-guided data are scarce and needed, as authentic data allow for a more reliable account of the real linguistic encoding of contrast in natural contexts (Sandler 1999).

In summary, diversity in contrast expression in SpLs and SLs has not been sufficiently documented. Consequently, some principles of contrast marking may have been underestimated or overlooked because of the methodology. For example, laboratory speech is encoded by more identifiable patterns than spontaneous speech, which heavily relies on the context. Hence, some of the results presented in the previous sections may have been biased because they were task- or context-dependent, or they only reflected reading aloud or laboratory conditions. Other biases may be related to the conception of contrast as a binary notion, which is the subject of the following lines.

2.4 Contrast as a binary notion

As shown in 2.1 and 2.2, no consensus has been reached for the distinction between information and contrastive foci. This lack of agreement is further complicated by the fact that some authors have reduced the concept of information focus to contrastive focus (e.g., Rooth 1992), or vice versa (e.g., Schwarzschild 1999).

Two remarks concerning what we outlined in Sections 2.1–2.3 are required. First, when contrast has been considered in the approaches cited below, it has been defined as a property of focus or topic, with a different manifestation in each case. As contrast has often been attached to another information unit or category, it is sometimes difficult to understand what the results of a study refer to (e.g., to focus only, contrast only, or focus and contrast). To overcome this limitation, some authors (Vallduví and Vilkuna 1998; Molnár 2002; Kenesei 2006; Neeleman and Titov 2009; Navarrete-González 2019, 2021) have emphasised the independence of contrast from other information-structure categories. This assumption of independence is supported by formal observations regarding DS and IS since contrastive elements are characterised by specific markers.

Second, contrast has mostly been envisaged in a binary manner in the literature: as present [+ contrast] or absent [– contrast]. In recent years, this unified view has been challenged in studies that describe several types (or degrees) of contrast, from the perspective of both IS (Gussenhoven 2008; Hartmann and Zimmermann 2009; Cruschina 2021) and DS (Molnár 2002; Umbach 2004; Repp 2016). These types generally correspond to the degree of opposition with the alternatives (from the weakest opposition to the strongest) (Repp 2016). They are correlated with various types of pragmatic meanings, which give rise to different formal markers (Destruel and Velleman 2014), depending on the specificities of each language (Repp 2016). This allows the addressee to decode the context of the utterance, i.e., to understand its presuppositions and implicatures (Stavropoulou and Baltazani 2021). Moreover, higher degrees of contrast seem related to a greater possibility of encoding, both prosodically (Navarrete-González 2021) and syntactically (Cruschina 2021) in SpLs and SLs. However, this conception of contrast as consisting of subtypes remains scarce in the literature, even though it offers a better vision of contrast and the functioning of its marking.

Some contrast typologies have been proposed in the literature on IS or DS. None of them has reached a consensus, which reinforces our observations on the lack of comparability between studies. For instance, Molnár (2002) formulates a contrast hierarchy at the discourse level following three criteria: (i) 'highlighting', when an element stands out from the rest of an utterance (especially prosodically), (ii) 'dominant contrast', which refers to the generation of a set of alternatives (and consequently, the exclusion of other possibilities), and (iii) 'membership in a set', which is related to the explicit nature of the alternatives or their belonging to a limited group. Therefore, the concept of contrast is characterised, at the discourse level, by three dimensions related to (i) the exclusion of elements (all exclusion vs. some exclusion), (ii) the alternative set (open vs. closed), and (iii) the co-occurrence of contrast with theme (focus) or rheme (topic).

Similarly, Repp (2016) differentiates several types of contrast (in the sense of contrastive focus) by taking into account the following discourse relations established between the alternatives: (i) the type of set (open or closed), (ii) the explicit or implicit character of alternatives (which is related to their identifiability), and (iii) the presence or absence of exclusion. In addition, Destruel and Velleman (2014) identify different contrast categories based on their conflict with expectations about the world or metalinguistic expectations about the discourse. The first type of expectations consists of assertions or presuppositions that express beliefs about the world. The second one includes "beliefs about the direction in which the discourse is going, expressed, among other ways, by marking content as at-issue or not-at-issue" (Destruel and Velleman 2014: 199).

Another theory related to contrast degrees has been developed by Umbach (2004) for SpLs, and then applied by Navarrete-González (2019, 2021) to SLs. This theory is the perspective adopted in this chapter, and is described in the following sections.

3 Contrast degrees and their specific types of discursive or pragmatic meanings

Contrast degrees have been defined and identified from either functional or pragmatic aspects or from the observation of their formal properties at the prosodic, syntactic, or lexical level (Schwarzschild 1999). Both approaches differ in the way they examine the interface between the interpretation of information-structure categories (viz., semantic and pragmatic aspects) and their linguistic encoding (viz., formal elements). The perspective adopted by the authors differs depending on the weight assigned to one of these facets (Di Cristo 2019).

The typology presented in this paper is based on both discursive and semantic criteria, and includes discourse opposition (parallel contrast), selection (selective contrast), and correction (corrective contrast).[3] This classification has been elaborated by Umbach (2004) and Repp (2016) at the discourse level and then applied by Hartmann and Zimmermann (2009), Kimmelman (2014), and Navarrete-González (2019, 2021) at the informational level.

Following a widely held view in IS research, we consider that the interpretation of an utterance, and consequently the information-structure categories that comprise it, largely depends on context and discourse (Gundel 1999). From this perspective, information is added to the discourse following the assumptions of the speaker/signer and addressee. In other words, a speaker/signer adjusts his/her words to what s/he assumes to be the temporary state of mind of the addressee at the time of discourse (Chafe 1976). As this approach is based on discourse and pragmatics, it is possible to compare SpLs and SLs since they tend to rely on different strategies of encoding (Kimmelman and Pfau 2016). However, this approach is not disconnected from grammatical considerations because DS, IS, and formal considerations are interconnected. The aim is to provide a basis for the comparison between SpLs and SLs, which allows us to understand the notion of contrast in its entirety, and then to study the markers used in each language to encode it.

In the following sections, we define discourse opposition, selection, and correction, and we connect these notions with categories previously reported in the literature. These explanations are accompanied by a description of contrast meanings both at the IS and DS levels.

3.1 Discourse opposition

At the functional level, discourse opposition involves a contrast based on similarity plus dissimilarity (viz., comparability): the contrastive alternatives belong to the same set and are semantically comparable to each other (Navarrete-González 2021). Each element is characterised by a particular and independent meaning, but all components have a common integrator. This condition is the basis of the concept of alternative (Umbach 2004). For example, in (3), a LSFB signer explains the emergence of CrossFit as a discipline: an American trainer tried to combine different sports skills to create a new sport. Several aspects of CrossFit are listed in (3) as contrasts and the set of alternatives refers to skills and qualities. It only concerns sporting skills (e.g., speed), which is the common integrator, and does not include all human qualities.

---

3 These degrees are discrete categories, even if contrast can be conceptualised as a gradable notion. This is a prerequisite to understand how contrast markers function and what discourse conditions license them.

(3) Context – Signer A: Everything from A to Z?
Signer B/Glosses: *DEVELOP FS:Z UNTIL FS:A [ENERGY]$_{DO1}$ UNTIL [STRONG]$_{DO2}$*
PT:LBUOY [BOMB]$_{DO3}$ ALSO [BOMB FAST]$_{DO4}$ [SPEED]$_{DO5}$ 1 TIME LIST HAVE SAY
TITLE DEVELOP 10 TITLE 10 POINT[4]
Signer B/Translation: 'Yes everything, [STRENGTH]$_{DO1}$, [ENDURANCE]$_{DO2}$,
[POWER]$_{DO3}$, [EXPLOSIVENESS]$_{DO4}$, [SPEED]$_{DO5}$. Basically, there are ten points.'
(LSFB Corpus, Session 23, Task 15)

At the pragmatic level, discourse opposition consists of contrasting two (or more)
identically structured propositional frames that differ in two (or several) places
(Dooley and Levinsohn 2001). Utterance (4) exemplifies this in French: a contrast
is established between two elements of a picture encoded by similar grammatical
structures (*d'un côté/de l'autre côté*).

(4) *D'un côté t'as [UN CANARD]$_{DO1}$ et puis de l'autre côté t'as [UN LAPIN]$_{DO2}$.*
'On one side you've got [A DUCK]$_{DO1}$ and then, on the other side, you've got [A
RABBIT]$_{DO2}$.'
(FRAPé Corpus, Session 5, Task 9)

Discourse opposition may also appear in enumerations (Navarrete-González 2019),
as demonstrated in example (5), in which Speaker B lists all the colours that Speaker
A must use to draw a face. These different colours consist of distinct discourse oppositions.

(5) A: *J'dois prendre quelles couleurs ?*
'What colours should I use?'
B: *Tu dois prendre du [ROUGE]$_{DO1}$. Y'a plein de couleurs, tu dois prendre toutes*
les couleurs. Du [ROUGE]$_{DO1}$, du [NOIR]$_{DO2}$.
'You must use [RED]$_{DO1}$. There are lots of colours, you must take all the colours.
[RED]$_{DO1}$, [BLACK]$_{DO2}$.'
A: *Du noir.*
'Black.'
B: *Du [VERT]$_{DO3}$.*
'[GREEN]$_{DO3}$.'
A: *Du vert.*
'Green.'

---

4 The gloss FS means that the sign was spelt (in that case, the sign consisted of the letter Z or A). The
gloss PT:LBUOY means that the signer used a pointing to list different elements.

B: *Du [BLEU]$_{DO4}$.*
'[BLUE]$_{DO4}$.'
A: *Foncé ou clair ?*
'Dark or light?'
B: *Foncé.*
'Dark.'
A: *D'accord, du bleu foncé ou clair ?*
'Okay, dark or light blue?'
B: *Clair. Du [VIOLET]$_{DO5}$, de [L'ORANGE]$_{DO6}$ et du [JAUNE]$_{DO7}$.*
'Light. [PURPLE]$_{DO5}$, [ORANGE]$_{DO6}$ and [YELLOW]$_{DO7}$.'
(Frapé Corpus, Session 1, Task 16)

Discourse opposition has been apprehended as a form of contrastive focus or contrast in many studies on SpLs (Chomsky 1971; Rochemont 1986; Dik 1997; Zimmermann 2008; Hartmann and Zimmermann 2009; Zimmermann and Onea 2011; Ferré 2014; Stavropoulou and Baltazani 2021) and SLs (Wilbur and Patschke 1998; Navarrete-González 2019, 2021; Hartmann, Pfau, and Legeland 2021). These studies followed either the DS or IS perspective, so a consensus seems to have been reached between the two approaches.

However, other scholars have included discourse opposition in the category of information focus (Umbach 2004; Repp 2016; De Kuthy, Reiter, and Riester 2018; Vander Klok, Goad, and Wagner 2018) and it is particularly the case for studies that follow a discursive perspective. For instance, Umbach (2004) has claimed that when only regarding the notion of comparability, each focus is contrastive as it triggers a set of alternatives (see Section 2.1). Similarly, Repp (2016) has stated that discourse opposition does not involve a contrast between the alternatives, since both parts of the opposition have the same contribution to the QUD (Question Under Discussion).[5] Nevertheless, as Navarrete-González (2021) points out, we can find an opposition at the alternative level since an explicit contrast is present between the two discourse segments. This argument indicates, according to Navarrete-González (2021), that discourse opposition is a type of contrast and not a type of information focus.

To sum up, no consistency can be found regarding discourse opposition in the literature, which echoes what we argued above about the lack of comparability between studies. The same observations may be formulated for selections.

---

5 The QUD theory is based on the idea that a question, which is most of the time implicit, is answered or addressed in every sentence formulated by a speaker (Roberts 2012).

3.2 Selection

Selection consists of choosing an alternative from a list (Navarrete-González 2021). At the pragmatic level, this situation generally occurs when answering an alternative question (Dik 1997) (see the answer to "Dark or light (colour)?" in (5)). Another possibility is the completion of an utterance by the addressee to aid the speaker/ signer, who is hesitant or searching for words, as in (6). In this example, Speaker A describes categories from a set of images that show similar objects, viz., food. During his explanation, he cannot remember the pasta type represented on a sheet of paper, and Speaker B completes his sentence.

(6) A: *Tu as des pâtes dont j'oublie toujours la forme. . . qui sont beh qui sont enroulées comme ça.*
'You've got pasta that I always forget the shape of. . . that is hum that is rolled up like this.'
B: *[TORTELLINI]ₛₑₗ, peut-être?*
'[TORTELLINI]ₛₑₗ, perhaps?'
A: *Je pense, j'en ai aucune idée.*
'I think so, I have no idea.'
(FRAPé Corpus, Session 14, Task 17)

At the discourse level, selection implies a contrast due to similarity plus dissimilarity (see Section 3.1) and contrast due to exclusion. This second meaning necessarily produces exhaustivity as selection involves an exclusive choice made in favour of one member of a closed and directly accessible set of explicitly mentioned and contextually conditioned alternatives (Chafe 1976; Rooth 1992; Kiss 1998; Calhoun 2009; Wilbur 2012). Only one of these alternatives is considered acceptable, and the other possibilities are excluded to make the proposition true (Navarrete-González 2021). This can be seen in (7), where 'cake' in B implies the exclusion of another dessert ('ice cream') mentioned during the interaction.

(7) Context – Signer A: For dessert, we eat that big round cake I was telling you about earlier.
Signer B/Glosses: *PT:DET PREFER [CAKE]ₛₑₗ BUT ICE CREAM WAIT SLICE PALM-UP[6]*
Signer B/Translation: 'I prefer [CAKE]ₛₑₗ to ice cream.'
(LSFB Corpus, Session 6, Task 3)

---

6 The gloss PT:DET means that the signer used a pointing as a determiner.

Exhaustivity has been extensively discussed in the literature on contrast. In studies on both IS and DS, it has often been argued that contrast results from exhaustivity, especially by authors who oppose contrastive focus and information focus. According to this view, information focus cannot be characterised by the notion of exhaustivity, while contrastive focus can (Kiss 1998). Rather, information focus requires an open set of contextually conditioned alternatives, and may be the only true condition (e.g., in the answer to a question; Büring 2016) but does not necessarily have to be. Moreover, the alternatives do not need to be clearly stated in the case of information focus but may be inferred or presupposed (Lambrecht 1994).

However, some scholars, both from DS (e.g., Vallduví and Vilkuna 1998; Destruel and Velleman 2014) and IS (e.g., Brunetti 2003; Schlenker et al. 2016) perspectives have considered that defining contrast on the basis of exhaustivity is too absolute. Indeed, according to Vallduví and Vilkuna (1998), the effect of contrast is merely identificational, and exhaustivity should be regarded as a conversational implicature of this effect. Furthermore, exhaustivity concerns only two types of contrast: selection and correction (Navarrete-González 2021). Thus, several contrastive constructions are not exhaustive, such as discourse oppositions (see Section 3.1). Conversely, non-contrasting utterances may be exhaustive, e.g., while containing a cleft (Lahousse, Laenzlinger, and Soare 2014), as in (8). In this example, a speaker describes a drawing of a face that contains several shapes. The only alternative considered true and acceptable is 'triangles' and the other possibilities (i.e., other possible ear forms) are implicitly excluded but without any contrast (see also example (1)).

(8) *Alors, il lui reste ses oreilles. C'est [**des triangles**]$_{Focus}$ qui partent juste en dessous de ses yeux.*
'Then he has his ears. These are [**triangles**]$_{Focus}$ that start just below his eyes.'
(FRAPé Corpus, Session 1, Task 16)

In summary, exhaustivity creates confusion in the literature, as it has been conflated with contrast (Kiss 1998), information focus (Lillo-Martin and Quadros 2008; Schlenker et al. 2016), or one of their subtypes (Dik 1997; Krifka 2008; Cruschina 2021). What stands out from the preceding observations is that the presence of an exhaustive effect and its contrastive or non-contrastive interpretation depends on the context (Schlenker et al. 2016) and on the need or lack thereof, at a particular moment during a discourse, for an exclusive construction. Therefore, exhaustivity is a type of pragmatic meanings related to contrast, but it is not the only one and is not present in all circumstances. Defining contrast solely based on exhaustivity may limit the researcher's perspective and prevent him/her from considering all instances of contrast. Moreover, because exhaustivity refers to both selections and corrections, it is difficult to make it a particular type.

It is also worth noting that further nebulous areas in the literature concern the categorisation of selections in relation to other information units or categories. Selection has been sometimes considered a type of contrast or contrastive focus in SpLs (Dik 1997; Calhoun 2009; Hartmann and Zimmermann 2009; Zimmermann and Onea 2011) and SLs (Wilbur and Patschke 1998; Kimmelman 2014; Navarrete-González 2021) studies that have adopted an informational or discursive perspective. Contrast has also been confused with selection (Astésano et al. 2004), while in other papers (e.g. Krifka 2008), selection has not been conceptualised as a contrastive unit. Other debates have concerned the notion of correction, which is defined in the following section.

3.3 Correction

Correction has been analysed more than discourse opposition or selection and has always been related to contrast (or contrastive focus) in studies on SpLs (Dik 1997; Hartmann and Zimmermann 2009; Zimmermann and Onea 2011; Ferré 2014; Jiménez-Fernández 2015; Vander Klok, Goad, and Wagner 2018; Stavropou lou and Baltazani 2021) and SLs (Wilbur and Patschke 1998; Kimmelman 2014) that have adopted either an informational or discursive perspective. Contrast has also sometimes been confused with correction at the pragmatic or formal level (see van der Kooij, Crasborn, and Emmerik 2006; Skopeteas and Fanselow 2010; Katz and Selkirk 2011; Crasborn and van der Kooij 2013; Carnaval, Moraes, and Rilliard 2022 for examples of this kind of mismatch). This type of confusion is problematic because the term 'contrast' may refer to one notion or another (discourse opposition, selection, or correction) depending on the study, which reinforces the vagueness of this concept as well as the difficulty of comparing different research.

In this paper, correction is regarded as the highest degree of contrast. It is not a homogeneous category at the pragmatic level, as it includes two types of structure: rejection and replacement. In the first case, a speaker/signer contradicts a piece of information previously mentioned (Dik 1997; van der Kooij, Crasborn, and Emmerik 2006; Calhoun 2009; Wilbur 2012; Ferré 2014). For instance, in (9), two signers discuss means of transportation and their characteristics and do not agree with each other. One corrects the other, and there is an incompatibility and inconsistency between the corrective alternative and the preceding alternative at the discourse level. The antecedent is explicitly mentioned in (9), but it is worth noting that it may also be deictically identified (Bianchi and Bocci 2012).

(9) Context – Signer A: The hot-air balloon has no engine.
Signer B/Glosses: *PT:DET [HAVE ENGINE]*$_{CORR}$ *STEAM.VOLCANO*
Signer B/Translation: 'No, the hot-air balloon [HAS AN ENGINE]$_{CORR}$.'
(LSFB-Corpus, Session 37, Task 17)

The same observations can be formulated for remplacement. However, in this case, the alternative considered false is substituted with another one (Navarrete-González 2019, 2021). This use is illustrated in (10), where a speaker explains a path to another person.

(10) *Tu démarres, tu suis la route. Au carrefour tu tournes ni à gauche ni a droite, tu prends [LA PETITE RUE QUI PART DE TRAVERS]*$_{CORR}$.
'You start up, you follow the road. At the crossroads, you turn neither left nor right, you take [THE SMALL STREET THAT GOES OFF AT AN ANGLE]$_{CORR}$.'
(Frapé Corpus, Session 6, Task 8)

At the level of the utterance encoding, replacement may involve lexical or syntactic strategies to expand or restrict what has been stated before with *even*-phrases, *also*-phrases, or *only*-phrases (see example (11)) (Dik 1997; Calhoun 2009; Wilbur 2012; Herrmann 2015).

(11) Context – Signer: The objectives of dictation are to be able to write well during the exams.
Signer B/Glosses: *[ORTHOGRAPHY ONLY ORTHOGRAPHY]*$_{CORR}$
Signer B/Translation: 'It's [ORTHOGRAPHY, ONLY ORTHOGRAPHY]$_{CORR}$.'
(LSFB Corpus, Session 19, Task 15)

The distinction between rejection and replacement is not unanimously accepted in the literature because correction has sometimes been equated with rejection (with or without a distinction from replacement), or because other categories of correction are taken into account. For instance, Dik (1997) and Wilbur (2012) identify, at the level of DS, several types of contrastive focus in SpLs and SLs, including restriction, expansion, and replacement. Moreover, at the pragmatic level, Ferré (2014) differentiates self-corrections and other-corrections while Calhoun (2009: 13) separates corrections from adverbial foci (i.e., *only*- or *even*- structures) and 'other' (i.e., "is clearly [c]ontrastive, but does not fall into any of the above types, e.g., *it was so good that I had forgotten it was CHRISTMAS EVE*"). Other authors, such as Büring (2012), consider that *only-phrases* form a focus subtype (viz., 'associated focus'). As a final example, Gussenhoven (2008: 11–12) discerns corrections ("direct rejection of an alternative") from counter-presupposition ("involves a correction of information which the speaker detects in the hearer's discourse model"). In this paper, we include the subtypes listed above under the label of correction because they are characterised by the same pragmatic and discursive aspects as the prototypical usage of correction. What differs is the level of form, e.g., the use of a specific structure or marker, such as an *only*-phrase or a contrastive accent.

Moreover, at the pragmatic level, correction is related to: (i) similarity plus dissimilarity, (ii) exclusion, and (iii) violation of expectations. The first meaning is explained in Section 3.1 while exhaustivity is described in Section 3.2. It is, however, worth noting that exhaustivity is linked to two distinct meanings: (i) the one mentioned in Section 3.2, and (ii) the exclusion of the possibility that another item added to the contrastive element makes the proposition true. This second meaning can imply the restriction or expansion of the alternatives, which gives rise to the different types of rejection specified above.

Concerning the violation of expectations, contrast arises in reaction to the speaker/signer's assumptions about himself/herself, the addressee, the world, or the current discourse pattern. Indeed, the contrastive element includes an instruction to the addressee not to simply add a new piece of information to their knowledge state, but to delete an existing one (Vallduví 1992). This instruction may take the form of affirmation or denial, which triggers different formal markings. For instance, in a study of the body leans prosodically used in NGT along with corrections, van der Kooij, Crasborn, and Emmerik (2006) conclude that forward leans accompany an affirmative correction (12) while backward leans occur on a denial correction (13). The exceptions may be explained by articulatory constraints and adaptations to the body leans made by the addressee.

(12) Signer A: I don't think your brother is learning ASL.
Signer B: Yes, [**MY BROTHER IS LEARNING ASL**]$_{CORR}$ (forward lean).
(van der Kooij, Crasborn, and Emmerik 2006: 1605)[7]

(13) Signer A: Your neighbour sold his car.
Signer B: No, he [**DIDN'T SELL HIS CAR**]$_{CORR}$ (backward lean)
(van der Kooij, Crasborn, and Emmerik 2006: 1605)

In studies that adopt an IS perspective, correction is sometimes distinguished from mirative focus, defined as follows: "the proposition asserted is more unlikely or

---

7 These examples are about correction of polarity, where there are only two alternatives. It is worth noting that correction is not only possible in those cases, but also when referring to a proper set of alternatives (even though two alternatives are mainly involved in a specific context, such as in (9)–(13)).

unexpected with respect to the alternative propositions" (Cruschina 2021: 5). Like correction, mirative focus is characterised by an opposition between the expectations and what is asserted (DeLancey 1997). This is exemplified in (14).

(14) *Ci avevano detto che avremmo visto solo zebre e leoni e invece [una tigre]*_{Mirative focus} *abbiamo visto ieri allo zoo.*
They had told us that we would only see zebras and lions and instead we saw [a tiger]_{Mirative focus} yesterday at the zoo.'
(Cruschina 2021: 6)

According to Cruschina (2021), mirative focus differs from correction, because they are both defined by distinct types of alternatives. Alternatives are always explicit for correction because contrast involves, in that case, the presence of an antecedent. Otherwise, the corrective statement would be infelicitous, such as in "Who bought the newspaper? B: *JOHN bought it, not Paul" (Cruschina 2021: 12). Conversely, mirative focus does not necessarily imply that the alternatives are active or not given but can also be based on shared knowledge, interlocutors' belief systems, or common ground. These conceptual remarks are supported by empirical evidence since some studies have demonstrated formal differences in the marking of mirative focus, compared to the encoding of correction, at the prosodic (Bianchi, Bocci, and Cruschina 2016) or syntactic level (Cruschina 2021).

A similar notion to mirative focus in SL studies is emphatic focus (Lillo-Martin and Quadros 2008; Wilbur 2012; Kimmelman and Pfau 2016). Kimmelman (2014: 16) explains that "[t]his type of focus appears when the sentence describes something unexpected. In more formal terms, it is used when the alternative in focus is the least or the greatest element on some scale". The notion of emphatic focus is also found in the literature on SpLs, where it "may also serve to express a high degree or reinforce the degree of something" (Ferré 2014: 273), as in (15). In this example, a speaker indicates that the duration of one labour is particularly long according to his opinion.

(15) *Elle a accouché vers Noël, elle a mis [vingt heures]*_{Emphatic focus} *si tu veux*
She gave birth around Christmas, it took [twenty hours]_{Emphatic focus} you see
(Ferré 2014: 273)

In all cases, emphatic/mirative focus allows speakers or signers to evaluate what they are saying, their point of view, or their stance (e.g., being surprised by an unexpected piece of information). Thus, mirativity concerns types of pragmatic and discursive meanings that are superimposed on the informational ones, but are not related to IS and DS *per se*. It consists of an extra-interpretative dimension rather than a core feature of the definition of contrast (see Larrivée 2022 for a similar point of view). This suggestion is in line with theories of mirativity (Aikhenvald 2012), which describe a range of mirative meanings, including contrast (or 'counter-expectation'), but also other aspects, such as surprise or sudden discovery. These remarks allow us to explain the fluidity of the alternatives stated by Cruschina (2021) and the formal differences established between corrections and mirativity/emphasis in SpLs and SLs.

To sum up, correction is a single information-structure category at the discursive and pragmatic levels. However, depending on additional types of pragmatic meanings (e.g., expansion, restriction, affirmation, mirativity, or denial), the markers used by speakers and signers to encode this degree of contrast will differ. From a discursive perspective, these additional meanings do not identify several subtypes of correction because they are not specifically related to IS, but to the speaker/signer's stance or the use of a specific linguistic structure. This distinction is essential because it is not uncommon to notice that these notions are confused in the literature. However, it is only by distinguishing between contrast and other pragmatic aspects that we can fully understand the functioning and expression of contrast in SLs and SpLs.

4 Discussion and conclusion

This paper proposes an answer to the issue of the variety of definitions of contrast across theoretical frameworks and languages. This diversity may be attributed to several factors. First, scholars have often focused on a one-size-fits-all approach or taken into account additional types of pragmatic meanings (e.g., mirativity, expansion, restriction) or formal cues (e.g., syntactic or prosodic encoding). As stated throughout the article, this type of approach is problematic in that various notions belonging to different language levels are considered under the same label, making the comparison between studies difficult and muddying the literature on what constitutes contrast. These different perspectives also reinforce the gaps between SpLs and SLs, whereas taking both modalities into account allows for a better understanding of contrast and its functioning at the discursive and pragmatic levels.

Second, depending on the type of data under study (e.g., interactional data or reading-aloud materials), conclusions may differ between authors. Some conclusions drawn so far may be biased because they do not reflect the actual use of language but are based on elicitations or intuitions. More spontaneous interactional data are thus needed. The terminology used for contrast is also inconsistent across studies (Zimmermann and Onea 2011).

Furthermore, by abandoning the binary distinction between [+ contrast] and [-contrast] for a classification in favour of several degrees of contrast based on the pragmatic and discursive exploitation of the set of alternatives, we can bring together the different points of view stated in the literature on SpLs and SLs and on DS and IS. These degrees are inspired by Umbach (2004), Hartmann and Zimmermann (2009), Kimmelman (2014), and Navarrete-González (2019, 2021), and consist of discourse opposition, selection, and correction. These are related to different types of discursive and pragmatic meanings: (i) similarity plus dissimilarity, (ii) exclusion, and (iii) violation of the expectations. The concept of comparability (similarity plus dissimilarity) echoes the definition of contrast based on the notion of alternative (Rooth 1992; Kiss 1998). Similarly, contrast due to exclusion is related to exhaustivity. This paper has also identified two ways of approaching exhaustivity: (i) the exclusion of the possibility that something other than the contrastive element makes the proposition true, and (ii) the exclusion of the possibility that another item added to the contrastive element makes the proposition true. The first meaning is connected to selection, and the second is related to correction. We also have to keep in mind that, in the literature, contrast in general is sometimes only associated with exhaustivity, but we have demonstrated that (i) this is not the case for discourse opposition, and (ii) other types of pragmatic meanings, such as comparability and violation of the expectations, play an important role. Finally, the definition of contrast as the violation of expectations about the speaker/signer or the world is another perspective adopted in a few studies to apprehend contrast (Zimmermann 2008; Destruel and Velleman 2014), sometimes in relation to mirativity/unexpectedness (Bianchi, Bocci, and Cruschina 2016; Cruschina 2021). In the literature, contrast is strongly associated with correction, while discourse opposition and selection are less studied. Further analysis of all contrast types is essential to fully understand the functioning of contrast, as well as systematic comparisons between contrast degrees. Considering more than one contrast type allows for a better understanding of the range of meanings related to contrast and the markers used to encode it.

Another advantage of the typology described in this paper is that it is based on discursive and pragmatic aspects, as contrast degrees are defined by their discursive and pragmatic relationships with the properties of the set of alternatives. This approach avoids the often-bemoaned circularity of IS studies, i.e., the use of prosodic or syntactic markers to identify information units that are then described at the formal level (De Kuthy, Reiter, and Riester 2018). Because this theory can be applied to both SpLs and SLs, it offers the possibility of using a common theoretical framework across languages, making cross-linguistic comparisons easier.

Whether languages distinguish between the three degrees of contrast at the formal level remains to be determined. For example, Navarrete-González (2019, 2021) has shown that discourse opposition, selection, and correction are expressed by the same combination of markers in LSC, which differs only by the addition of non-manual cues in more contrasted contexts and in relation to other interpretations. Such a view is not widespread in the literature and some scholars like Hartmann and Zimmermann (2009) have observed no difference between these subtypes in Gùrùmtùm, the Chadic language they study. Research on other sets of languages is, therefore, required to address these debates. Nevertheless, such studies should be wary of the unifying or universalist view, since what is true for one language may not be true for another, as explained in Section 2.4. Comparisons between SpLs and SLs can also shed light on this issue.

Another question concerns the existence of contrast as a single information unit or category. Some authors have stated that contrast is a subtype of focus (viz., contrastive focus) and is opposed to information focus, while being characterised by different degrees (Zimmermann and Onea 2011; Cruschina 2021). Other scholars have demonstrated the independence of contrast at the informational (Kenesei 2006; Neeleman and Titov 2009; Navarrete-González 2019, 2021) or discursive levels (Vallduví and Vilkuna 1998; Molnár 2002). We cannot answer this question in this paper, but we would like to point out that a parallel analysis of the relationship between focus and contrast and between topic and contrast based on natural data would resolve this question. Additional ambiguity concerns the unity of the notion of contrast: Is contrast divided into different degrees, or is each degree an information-structure category on its own? Destruel and Velleman (2014) and Navarrete-González (2021) support the first view, while Umbach (2004) claims the second.

In conclusion, the contrast typology presented in this paper seems to be an interesting tool for bringing together views on contrast, its types of discursive or pragmatic meanings (i.e., similarity and dissimilarity, exclusion, and violation of expectations), and related notions such as emphasis, exhaustivity, and mirativity. This classification also offers a way of analysing the sensitivity of a particular language to the use of a specific type of contrast marking, both in SpLs and SLs.

Funding information

This research was funded by a F.R.S.- FNRS Research Fellow Grant (FC 38997).

References

Aikhenvald, Alexandra. 2012. The essence of mirativity. *Linguistic Typology* 16(3). 435–485. https://doi.org/10.1515/lity-2012-0017

Astésano, Corine, Cyrille Magne, Michel Morel, Annelise Coquillon, Robert Espesser, Mireille Besson & Anne Lacheret-Dujour. 2004. Marquage acoustique du focus contrastif non codé syntaxiquement en français. In Bernard Bel & Isabelle Marlien (eds.), *Actes des XXVᵉˢ Journées d'Étude sur la Parole (JEP 2004)*. https://www.afcp-parole.org/doc/Archives_JEP/2004_XXVe_JEP_Fes/actes/jep.htm

Baker, Aanne & Beppie van den Bogaerde. 2012. Communicative interaction. In Roland Pfau, Markus Steinbach & Bencie Woll (eds.), *Sign language. An International Handbook*, 489–512. Berlin/Boston: De Gruyter Mouton.

Bianchi, Valentina & Giuliano Bocci. 2012. Should I stay or should I go? Optional focus movement in Italian. In Christopher Piñon (ed.), *Empirical Issues in Syntax and Semantics* 9, 1–18. http://www.cssp.cnrs.fr/eiss9/

Bianchi, Valentina, Giuliano Bocci & Silvio Cruschina. 2016. Focus fronting, unexpectedness, and evaluative implicatures. *Semantics and Pragmatics* 9(3). 1–54. https://doi.org/10.3765/sp.9.3

Bolinger, Dwight. 1961. Contrastive accent and contrastive stress. *Language* 37(1). 83–96. https://doi.org/10.2307/411252

Brunetti, Lisa. 2003. Is there any difference between contrastive focus and information focus? In Matthias Weisgerber (ed.), *Proceedings of the Conference "sub7 – Sinn und Bedeutung"*, 53–69. Konstanz: Fachbereich Sprachwissenschaft der Universität Konstanz.

Brysbaert, Jorina & Karen Lahousse. 2020. Les marqueurs de contraste au contraire, par contre et en revanche en français parlé et écrit, formel et informel. *SHS Web of Conferences* 78. https://doi.org/10.1051/shsconf/20207801010

Büring, Daniel. 2003. On d-trees, beans, and b-accents. *Linguistics and Philosophy* 26(5). 511–545. https://doi.org/10.1023/A:1025887707652

Büring, Daniel. 2012. Focus and intonation. In Russell Gillain & Graff Delia (eds.), *Routledge Companion to Philosophy of Language*, 103–115. London: Routledge.

Büring, Daniel. 2016. (Contrastive) topic. In Caroline Féry & Shinichiro Ishihara (eds.), *The Oxford Handbook of Information Structure* 1, 64–85. Oxford: Oxford University Press.

Calhoun, Sasha. 2009. What makes a word contrastive? Prosodic, semantic and pragmatic perspectives. In Dagmar Barth-Weingarten, Nicole Dehé & Anne Wichmann (eds.), *Where Prosody Meets Pragmatics*, 53–77. Leiden: Brill.

Carnaval, Manuella, João Antônio de Moraes & Albert Rilliard. 2022. Focus types in Brazilian Portuguese: Multimodal production and perception. *DELTA: Documentação de Estudos Em Lingüística Teórica e Aplicada* 38(3). 1–34. https://doi.org/10.1590/1678-460x202258944

Chafe, Wallace. 1976. Givenness, contrastiveness, definiteness, subjects, topics, and point of view. In Charles Li (ed.), *Subject and Topic*, 25–55. New York: Academic Press.

Chen, Lijing, Xingshan Li & Yufang Yang. 2012. Focus, newness and their combination: Processing of information structure in discourse. *PLoS ONE* 7(8): e42533. https://doi.org/10.1371/journal.pone.0042533

Chomsky, Noam. 1971. Deep structure, surface structure, and semantic interpretation. In Danny Steinberg & Leon Jakobovits (eds.), *Studies on Semantics in Generative Grammar* 107, 62–119. Berlin/Boston: De Gruyter Mouton.

Crasborn, Onno & Els van der Kooij. 2013. The phonology of focus in sign language of the Netherlands. *Journal of Linguistics* 49(3). 515–565. https://doi.org/10.1017/S0022226713000054

Cruschina, Silvio. 2021. The greater the contrast, the greater the potential: On the effects of focus in syntax. *Glossa: A Journal of General Linguistics* 6(1). 1–30. https://doi.org/10.5334/gjgl.1100

De Kuthy, Kordula, Nils Reiter & Arndt Riester. 2018. QUD-based annotation of discourse structure and information structure: Tool and evaluation. In Nicoletta Calzolari, Khalid Choukri, Christopher Cieri, Thierry Declerck, Sara Goggi, Koiti Hasida, Hitoshi Isahara, Bente Maegaard, Joseph Mariani, Hélène Mazo, Asuncion Moreno, Jan Odijk, Stelios Piperidis, Takenobu Tokunaga (eds.), *Proceedings of the Eleventh International Conference on Language Resources and Evaluation (LREC 2018)*. https://aclanthology.org/L18-1304

Debreslioska, Sandra & Marianne Gullberg. 2020. The semantic content of gestures varies with definiteness, information status and clause structure. *Journal of Pragmatics* 168. 36–52. https://doi.org/10.1016/j.pragma.2020.06.005

Delancey, Scott. 1997. Mirativity: The grammatical marking of unexpected information. *Linguistic Typology* 1(1). 33–52. https://doi.org/10.1515/lity.1997.1.1.33

Destruel, Emilie & Leah Velleman. 2014. Refining contrast: Empirical evidence from the English it-cleft. In Christopher Piñon (ed.), *Empirical Issues in Syntax and Semantics* 10, 197–214. http://www.cssp.cnrs.fr/eiss10/index_en.html

Di Cristo, Albert. 2019. *Conditionnements de l'Information et Marquages Prosodiques dans les Langues Naturelles. Première Partie : La Structure Informationnelle et Ses Déterminants*. hal-02149640

Dik, Simon. 1997. *The Theory of Functional Grammar: The Structure of the Clause, Complex and Derived Constructions*. Berlin/Boston: De Gruyter Mouton.

Dohen, Marion & Hélène Lœvenbruck. 2009. Interaction of audition and vision for the perception of prosodic contrastive focus. *Language and Speech* 52(2–3). 177–206. https://doi.org/10.1177/0023830909103166

Donati, Caterina & Marina Nespor. 2003. From focus to syntax. *Lingua* 113(11). 1119–1142. https://doi.org/10.1016/S0024-3841(03)00015-9

Dooley, Robert & Stephen Levinsohn. 2001. *Analyzing Discourse: A Manual of Basic Concepts*. Dallas: SIL International.

Evans, Nicholas & Stephen Levinson. 2009. The myth of language universal: Language diversity and its importance for cognitive science. *Behavioral and Brain Sciences* 32(5). 429–448. https://doi.org/10.1017/S0140525X0999094X

Esteve-Gibert, Núria, Hélène Lœvenbruck, Marion Dohen & Mariapaola D'Imperio. 2021. Pre-schoolers use head gestures rather than prosodic cues to highlight important information in speech. *Developmental Science* 25(1). 1–12. https://doi.org/10.1111/desc.13154

Fenlon, Jordan & Diane Brentari. 2021. Prosody: Theoretical and experimental perspectives. In Josep Quer, Roland Pfau & Annika Herrmann (eds.), *Routledge Handbook of Theoretical and Experimental Sign Language Research*, 70–94. London: Routledge.

Fenlon, Jordan & Julie Hochgesang (eds.). 2022. *Signed Language Corpora*. Gallaudet: Gallaudet University Press.

Ferré, Gaëlle. 2014. A multimodal approach to markedness in spoken French. *Speech Communication* 57. 268–282. https://doi.org/10.1016/j.specom.2013.06.002

Féry, Caroline. 2008. Information structural notions and the fallacy of invariant correlates. *Acta Linguistica Hungarica* 55(3–4). 361–379. https://doi.org/10.1556/ALing.55.2008.3-4.10

Gabarró-López, Sílvia & Laurence Meurant. 2022. Contrasting signed and spoken languages: Towards a renewed perspective on language. *Languages in Contrast* 22(2). 169–194. https://doi.org/10.1075/lic.00024.gab

Gundel, Jeannette. 1999. On different kinds of focus. In Peter Bosh & Rob van der Sandt (eds.), *Focus. Linguistic, Cognitive and Computational Perspectives*, 293–305. Cambridge: Cambridge University Press.

Gundel, Jeanette & Thorstein Fretheim. 2006. Topic and focus. In Laurence Horn & Gregory Ward (eds.), *The Handbook of Pragmatics*, 175–196. Hoboken: Blackwell Publishing.

Gussenhoven, Carlos. 2004. *The Phonology of Tone and Intonation*. Cambridge: Cambridge University Press.

Gussenhoven, Carlos. 2008. Types of focus in English. In Chungmin Lee, Matthew Gordon & Daniel Büring (eds.), *Topic and Focus*, 83–100. (Studies in Linguistics and Philosophy 82). Dordrecht: Springer.

Halliday, Michael. 1967. *Intonation and Grammar in British English*. Berlin/Boston: De Gruyter Mouton.

Hartmann, Katharina, Roland Pfau & Iris Legeland. 2021. Asymmetry and contrast: Coordination in sign language of the Netherlands. *Glossa: A Journal of General Linguistics* 6(1). 1–33. https://doi.org/10.16995/glossa.5872

Hartmann, Katharina & Malte Zimmermann. 2009. Morphological focus marking in Gùrùntùm (West Chadic). *Lingua* 119(9). 1340–1365. https://doi.org/10.1016/j.lingua.2009.02.002

Herrmann, Annika. 2015. The marking of information structure in German Sign Language. *Lingua* 165(2). 277–297. https://doi.org/10.1016/j.lingua.2015.06.001

Jackendoff, Ray. 1972. *Semantic Interpretation in Generative Grammar*. Cambridge: MIT Press.

Jiménez-Fernández, Ángel. 2015. Towards a typology of focus: Subject position and microvariation at the discourse–syntax interface. *Ampersand* 2. 49–60. https://doi.org/10.1016/j.amper.2015.03.001

Katz, Jonah & Elisabeth Selkirk. 2011. Contrastive focus vs. discourse-new: Evidence from phonetic prominence in English. *Language* 87(4). 771–816. https://doi.org/10.1353/lan.2011.0076

Kenesei, István. 2006. Focus as identification. In Valéria Molnár & Susanne Winkler (eds.), *The Architecture of Focus*, 137–168. Berlin/Boston: De Gruyter Mouton.

Kimmelman, Vadim. 2014. *Information Structure in Russian Sign Language and Sign Language of the Netherlands*. Amsterdam: University of Amsterdam dissertation.

Kimmelman, Vadim & Roland Pfau. 2016. Information structure in sign languages. In Caroline Féry & Shinichiro Ishihara (eds.), *The Oxford Handbook of Information Structure*, 814–833. Oxford: Oxford University Press.

Kimmelman, Vadim & Roland Pfau. 2021. Information structure: Theoretical perspectives. In Josep Quer, Roland Pfau & Annika Herrmann (eds.), *The Routledge Handbook of Theoretical and Experimental Sign Language Research*, 591–613. London: Routledge.

Kiss, Katalin. 1998. Identificational focus versus information focus. *Language* 74(2). 245–273. https://doi.org/10.1353/lan.1998.0211

Krahmer, Emiel & Marc Swerts. 2001. On the alleged existence of contrastive accents. *Speech Communication* 34(4). 391–405. https://doi.org/10.1016/S0167-6393(00)00058-3

Krifka, Manfred. 2008. Basic notions of information structure. *Acta Linguistica Hungarica* 55(3–4). 243–276. https://doi.org/10.1556/ALing.55.2008.3-4.2

Ladd, Dwight. 1996. *Intonational Phonology*. Cambridge: Cambridge University Press.

Lahousse, Karen, Christopher Laenzlinger & Gabriela Soare. 2014. Contrast and intervention at the periphery. *Lingua* 143. 56–85. https://doi.org/10.1016/j.lingua.2014.01.003

Lambrecht, Knud. 1994. *Information Structure and Sentence Form. Topic, Focus, and the Mental Representations of Discourse Referents*. Cambridge: Cambridge University Press.

Larrivée, Pierre. 2022. The curious case of the rare focus movement in French. In Davide Garassino & Daniel Jacob (eds.), *When Data Challenges Theory: Unexpected and Paradoxical Evidence in Information Structure*, 183–202. Amsterdam: John Benjamins.

Lillo-Martin, Diane & Ronice Müller de Quadros. 2008. Focus constructions in American Sign Language and Língua de Sinais Brasileira. In Josep Quer (ed.), *Signs of the Time: Selected Papers from TISLR 2004*, 161–176. Seedorf: Signum.

Matić, Dejan & Daniel Wedgwood. 2013. The meanings of focus: The significance of an interpretation-based category in cross-linguistic analysis. *Journal of Linguistics* 49(1). 127–163. https://doi.org/10.1017/S0022226712000345

Meurant, Laurence. 2015. *Corpus LSFB. First digital open access corpus of movies and annotations of French Belgian Sign Language (LSFB)*. Namur: LSFB-Lab, University of Namur. http://www.corpus-lsfb.be

Meurant, Laurence, Alysson Lepeut, Sílvia Gabarró-López, Anna Tavier, Sébastien Vandenitte, Clara Lombart & Aurélie Sinte. Under construction. *Corpus de français parlé: Vers la construction d'un corpus comparable LSFB - Français de Belgique*.

Milković, Marina & Tomislav Radošević. 2021. Non-manual markers in Croatian Sign Language – a look at the current state. *Grazer Linguistische Studien* 93. 137–59. https://doi.org/10.25364/04.48:2021.93.5

Molnár, Valéria. 2002. Contrast – from a contrastive perspective. In Hilde Hasselgård, Stig Johansson, Bergljot Behrens & Catherine Fabricius-Hansen (eds.), *Information Structure in a Cross-Linguistic Perspective*, 147–161. Leiden: Brill.

Navarrete-González, Alexandra. 2019. The notion of focus and its relation to contrast in Catalan Sign Language (LSC). *Sensos-e* 6(1). 18–40. https://doi.org/10.34630/SENSOS-E.V6I1.2565

Navarrete-González, Alexandra. 2021. The expression of contrast in Catalan Sign Language (LSC). *Glossa: A Journal of General Linguistics* 6(1). 1–22. https://doi.org/10.5334/gjgl.1102

Neeleman, Ad & Elena Titov. 2009. Focus, contrast, and stress in Russian. *Linguistic Inquiry* 40(3). 514–524. https://doi.org/10.1162/ling.2009.40.3.514

Özyürek, Aslı. 2012. Gesture. In Roland Pfau, Markus Steinbach & Bencie Woll (eds.), *Sign Language. An International Handbook*, 626–646. Berlin/Boston: De Gruyter Mouton.

Özyürek, Aslı. 2021. Considering the nature of multimodal language from a crosslinguistic perspective. *Journal of Cognition* 4(1). 1–5. https://doi.org/10.5334/joc.165

Pfau, Roland & Josep Quer. 2010. Nonmanuals: Their grammatical and prosodic roles. In Diane Brentari (ed.), *Sign Languages*, 381–402. Cambridge: Cambridge University Press.

Repp, Sophie. 2016. Contrast: Dissecting an elusive information-structural notion and its role in grammar. In Caroline Féry & Ishishara Shinichiro (eds.), *The Oxford Handbook of Information Structure*, 270–289. Oxford: Oxford University Press.

Riester, Arndt, Lisa Brunetti & Kordula De Kuthy. 2018. Annotation guidelines for questions under discussion and information structure. In Evangelina Adamou, Katharina Haude & Martine Vanhove (eds.), *Information Structure in Lesser-described Languages: Studies in Prosody and Syntax*, 403–443. Amsterdam: John Benjamins.

Roberts, Craige. 2012. Information structure: Towards an integrated formal theory of pragmatics. *Semantics and Pragmatics* 5(6). 1–69. https://doi.org/10.3765/sp.5.6

Rochemont, Michael S. 1986. *Focus in Generative Grammar*. Amsterdam: John Benjamins.

Rooth, Mats. 1992. A theory of focus interpretation. *Natural Language Semantics* 1(1). 75–116. https://doi.org/10.1007/BF02342617

Sandler, Wendy. 1999. Prosody in two natural language modalities. *Language and Speech* 42(2–3). 127–142. https://doi.org/10.1177/00238309990420020101

Samek-Lodovici, Vieri. 2005. Prosody-syntax interaction in the expression of focus. *Natural Language and Linguistic Theory* 23(3). 687–755. https://doi.org/10.1007/s11049-004-2874-7

Schlenker, Philippe, Valentina Aristodemo, Ludovic Ducasse, Jonathan Lamberton & Mirko Santoro. 2016. The unity of focus: Evidence from sign language (ASL and LSF). *Linguistic Inquiry* 47(2). 363–381. https://doi.org/10.1162/LING_a_00215

Schwarzschild, Roger. 1999. Givenness, avoidF and other constraints on the placement of accent. *Natural Language Semantics* 7(2). 141–177. https://doi.org/10.1023/A:1008370902407

Selkirk, Elisabeth. 1984. *Phonology and Syntax: The Relation between Sound and Structure*. Cambridge: MIT Press.

Shattuck-Hufnagel, Stefanie & Ada Ren. 2018. The prosodic characteristics of non-referential co-speech gestures in a sample of academic-lecture-style speech. *Frontiers in Psychology* 9: 1–13. https://doi.org/10.3389/fpsyg.2018.01514

Skopeteas, Stravos & Gisbert Fanselow. 2010. Focus in Georgian and the expression of contrast. *Lingua* 120(6). 1370–1391. https://doi.org/10.1016/j.lingua.2008.10.012

Stavropoulou, Pepi & Mary Baltazani. 2021. The prosody of correction and contrast. *Journal of Pragmatics* 171. 76–100. https://doi.org/10.1016/j.pragma.2020.10.004

Terken, Jacques. 1991. Fundamental frequency and perceived prominence of accented syllables. *Journal of the Acoustical Society of America* 89(4). 1768–1776. https://doi.org/10.1121/1.401019

Umbach, Carla. 2004. On the notion of contrast in information structure and discourse structure. *Journal of Semantics* 21(2). 155–175. https://doi.org/10.1093/jos/21.2.155

Vallduví, Enric. 1992. *The Informational Component*. New York: Garland.

Vallduví, Enric & Maria Vilkuna. 1998. On rheme and kontrast. *The Limits of Syntax* 29. 79–108. https://doi.org/10.1163/9789004373167_005

van der Kooij, Els, Onno Crasborn & Wim Emmerik. 2006. Explaining prosodic body leans in sign language of the Netherlands: Pragmatics required. *Journal of Pragmatics* 38(10). 1598–1614. https://doi.org/10.1016/j.pragma.2005.07.006

Vander Klok, Jozina, Heather Goad & Michael Wagner. 2018. Prosodic focus in English vs. French: A scope account. *Glossa: A Journal of General Linguistics* 3(1), 1–47. https://doi.org/10.5334/gjgl.172

Wagner, Petra & Andreas Windmann. 2016. Re-enacted and spontaneous conversational prosody: How different? In Jonathan Barnes, Alejna Brugos, Stefanie Shattuck-Hufnagel & Nannette Veilleux (eds.), *Proceedings of the International Conference on Speech Prosody* 8, 518–522. https://doi.org/10.21437/SpeechProsody.2016-106

Wilbur, Ronnie. 2000. Phonological and prosodic layering of nonmanuals in American Sign Language. In Karen Emmorey (ed.), *The Signs of Language Revisited: An Anthology to Honor Ursula Bellugi and Edward Klima*, 215–244. Mahwah: Lawrence Erlbaum.

Wilbur, Ronnie. 2012. Information structure. In Roland Pfau, Markus Steinbach & Bencie Woll (eds.), *Sign Language: An International Handbook*, 462–489. Berlin/Boston: De Gruyter Mouton.

Wilbur, Ronnie & Cynthia Patschke. 1998. Body leans and the marking of contrast in American Sign Language. *Journal of Pragmatics* 30(3). 275–303. https://doi.org/10.1016/S0378-2166(98)00003-4

Zimmermann, Malte. 2008. Contrastive focus and emphasis. *Acta Linguistica Hungarica* 55(3–4). 347–360. https://doi.org/10.1556/ALing.55.2008.3-4.9

Zimmermann, Malte & Edgar Onea. 2011. Focus marking and focus interpretation. *Lingua* 121(11). 1651–1670. https://doi.org/10.1016/j.lingua.2011.06.002

Zubizarreta, Maria. 1998. *Prosody, Focus, and Word Order*. Cambridge: MIT Press.

Part III: **Analyzing contrast using the Question Under Discussion model**

Lisa Brunetti

8 Contrast in a QUD-based information-structure model

Abstract: In this paper I look at contrast within the model of information-structure annotation proposed by Riester, Brunetti, and De Kuthy (2018), Riester (2019), Brunetti, De Kuthy, and Riester (2021), which is based on the notion of "Question under Discussion" or QUD (Roberts [1996] 2012, among many others). The model assumes that every utterance in a discourse is preceded by an implicit question, and proposes four principles that constrain the formulation of such questions. One principle, "Parallelism", accounts for two or more utterances answering the same QUD. Such a discourse configuration provides the ground for contrast (Umbach 2004, 2005; Repp 2016); specifically, what is called "Simple" Parallelism accounts for occurrences of contrastive focus, while "Complex" Parallelism is relevant when two alternative sets are evoked, namely with contrastive topics. I assume that contrast is accounted for in terms of contrastive discourse relations and make the working hypothesis that contrastive relations always co-occur with Parallelism. Partially following Repp (2016), I assume four contrastive relations, specifically: SIMILAR, OPPOSE, CORR(RECTION) and CONCESSION; and describe what contextual and semantic restrictions make these relations different. By analyzing naturalistic data from spoken and written interviews in Italian and French, whose utterances were annotated for their QUDs and information structure and for their contrastive relations, I show how the differences among these relations can be partially accounted for in terms of their QUD structure. I also look at the interplay between contrastive relations and Simple and Complex Parallelism. I eventually show and discuss cases where contrastive relations and Parallelism do not co-occur. This mostly happens when a CONCESSION relation holds between the discourse segments.

1 Introduction

Contrast is a much studied and yet still elusive notion in both information-structure and discourse studies. In this paper, I try to shed more light on this phenomenon by looking at occurrences of contrastive focus and topic in naturalistic data of

Acknowledgements: I wish to thank the two anonymous reviewers for their insightful comments, which helped me to clarify the ideas presented in this paper and to sharpen my claims. I also thank for their questions and comments the audience of the 'International Workshop on the Expression of Contrast and the Annotation of IS in Corpora', held at KU Leuven on November 18–19, 2021.

https://doi.org/10.1515/9783110986594-008

two Romance languages, French and Italian, and by analyzing them through the lenses of the model of information-structure annotation proposed by Riester, Brunetti, and De Kuthy (2018), Riester (2019), Brunetti, De Kuthy, and Riester (2021). This model's assumption (from now on, RBK's model) is that sentence information structure and discourse structure are strictly interdependent, and that discourse structure is obtained by formulating, for each utterance of a text, its "Question under Discussion" or QUD (van Kuppevelt 1995; Roberts 2012; Ginzburg 1996; Onea 2016; among many others), namely a (generally) implicit question that each utterance is meant to answer. The notion of Question under Discussion is by now well established in information-structure studies and there is a vast literature that proposes different models (see Velleman and Beaver 2016 for a review). While these models can be extremely sophisticated, they sometimes lack clear, applicable criteria to formulate QUDs, and are therefore less effective when naturalistic data are studied. One advantage of RBK's model is precisely that it provides specific, applicable principles to formulate QUDs. These principles are mainly based on the reconstruction of the utterance's given content, and have the advantage of not relying on linguistic form, namely they can be applied to languages whose representation of information-structure is not well understood yet.

RBK's model is based on four principles, which will be presented in Section 2. One of them, called "Parallelism", accounts for cases in which two or more utterances answer the same QUD. My starting point is that such a discourse configuration is the natural locus of contrast (Umbach 2005; Repp 2016).

My notion of contrast takes roots in the Alternative Semantics framework (Rooth 1985, 1992; Büring 1997). Alternative Semantics take focus and topic to be alternative-set evoking phenomena. I assume, following part of the literature (see Neeleman and Vermeulen 2013 and references quoted in there) that contrast needs, but does not reduce itself to, the presence of alternative sets. I argue that alternatives may get instantiated in the discourse by utterances that precede or follow the utterance that evokes them. In that case, following RBK's model, a QUD is formulated that is answered by the utterances that form the alternative set, namely the principle of Parallelism mentioned above applies. When such a discourse configuration arises, a contrastive discourse relation holds between the two (or more) utterances. My working hypothesis is that the inverse is also true: whenever a contrastive relation holds between two utterances, the discourse structure is one accounted for by the principle of Parallelism.

Given the importance, for the purposes of this paper, of RBK's model of QUD and information-structure annotation, in the next section I will briefly summarize how the model works (for a detailed description, see Riester, Brunetti, and De Kuthy 2018, Riester 2019, Brunetti, De Kuthy, and Riester 2021). In Section 3 I will then give a more detailed account of the notion of contrast that I assume. I will try, along the lines of Umbach (2004, 2005) and Repp (2016), to define contrast by combining an Alternative-Semantics-based definition with a definition in terms of discourse relations. I will also present the contrastive discourse relations that I assume, namely SIMILAR, OPPOSE, CORR(ECTION) (cf. Repp 2016) and CONCESSION (Umbach 2004; Webber et al. 2019), and define them with the help of the QUD structure that can be reconstructed when such relations occur. In Section 4 I will apply my analysis to naturalistic data from French and Italian oral and written interviews, and look at the interplay between contrastive relations and QUD structure, and in particular at the co-occurrence of contrastive relations and Parallelism. In Section 5 I will discuss cases of contrast without Parallelism. In Section 6 I will draw some conclusions.

2 A QUD- and IS-annotation model

As mentioned in the Introduction, the model I'm adopting is based on the assumption that a (generally implicit) question precedes each utterance of a discourse. The goal of the model is to provide criteria to formulate such a question and through it, to derive the information structure (from now on, IS) of each utterance.

Riester and colleagues assume an Alternative Semantics' (Rooth 1985, 1992; Büring 1997) framework for focus and topic, which I briefly resume below. Rooth (1992) proposes that a sentence containing a focus feature – represented in English by an accent – such as *[Mary]$_F$ likes Sue* has an ordinary semantic value plus an additional "focus semantic value" that corresponds to a set of propositions of the type *x likes Sue*, where the value of the variable in each proposition is one of the possible alternatives to the focus in the relevant context. Following Rooth's path, Büring (1997) proposes an alternative-based account for topic marking in German and English. A topic – again represented by an accent in these languages – evokes a set of alternatives, but in this case, they are alternative *questions*. For instance, in Büring's example in (1), the topic feature (marked by a topic accent on *female*) evokes a set of the type: *What did the x pop stars wear?*.

(1)   A: *What did the pop stars wear?*
      B: *[The female]$_T$ pop stars wore caftans.*
      (Büring 1997: 69)

Since a question can be defined as a set of propositions corresponding to its potential answers (Hamblin 1973), it turns out that *two* sets of alternatives are at stake, as illustrated in (2), from Büring (1997), where the sets are represented by curly brackets.

(2) *{{the female pop stars wore caftans, the female pop stars wore dresses, the female pop stars wore overalls,...},*
     {the male pop stars wore caftans, the male pop stars wore dresses, the male pop stars wore overalls,...},
     {the female or male pop stars wore caftans, the female or male pop stars wore dresses, the female or male pop stars wore overalls,...},
     {the Italian pop stars wore caftans, the Italian pop stars wore dresses, the Italian pop stars wore overalls,...},...}
     (Büring 1997: 68)

The difference between the focus and the topic variables lies on their effects on discourse and can be accounted for by appealing to the notion of Question under Discussion: the value of the focus variable provides an answer to the current QUD, while the topic variable does not (Roberts 2012; Büring 2003). In order to understand whether an alternative set is a focus or a topic one, it is therefore crucial to know what the QUD structure is.

Within RBK's model, QUDs are formulated according to four principles, three of which are given in (3), from Brunetti, De Kuthy, and Riester (2021). These principles basically state that a QUD must have a congruent answer (corresponding to the target utterance) and that it must contain all and only its answer's given content:

(3) i.   Q-A-Congruence: A QUD must be answerable by the assertion that it immediately dominates.
     ii. Maximize-Q-Anaphoricity: the QUD should be formulated using all the given semantic content of its answer.
     iii. Q-Givenness: An implicit QUD can only consist of given content.
     (Brunetti, De Kuthy, and Riester 2021: 17)

The formulation of the QUD is therefore a way to reconstruct the target utterance's given content (the background), while the focus is the new piece of information that answers the QUD. For instance, in (4), given the local linguistic context represented by A_1, the only given content of A_2 is *she*. The utterance's QUD must therefore only contain a reference to the speaker's mother (in addition to the wh-phrase and to anything that may be necessary to formulate a grammatical question). Consequently, *was born in a town on the other side of the world* is labeled as focus and *she* as background. Following Rooth's (1992) conventions, the annotation only marks the focus by means of F-indexed square brackets, while the background is what is left outside the focus within the "focus domain" (the sum of focus and its background), marked by brackets and a squiggle sign ~.[1]

(4) A_1 *While studying here, my father met my mother.*
    Q_2 What about Obama's mother?
    > A_2 [She [was born in a town on the other side of the world.]$_F$]~
    (Brunetti, De Kuthy, and Riester 2021: 18)

Through the formulation of QUDs, a discourse structure is derived in RBK's model, under the form of a tree whose terminal nodes are the answers to the QUDs (the actual utterances of the text). See Riester (2019) for a detailed explanation of how the QUD-tree is built. What is sufficient to know for the purposes of this paper is that, in the QUD-annotated examples that will follow, the symbols >, >>, >>>, etc. indicate the level of embedding of questions and answers in the discourse tree.

2.1 The principle of Parallelism

The fourth principle for the formulation of QUDs, Parallelism, is what mostly interests us for the present purposes, since it is strongly related to contrast (cf. Umbach 2005). The principle is given in (5), from Brunetti, De Kuthy, and Riester (2021), and accounts for pairs or lists of utterances – generally coordinated ones – that answer the same QUD:

(5) Parallelism: A QUD that is directly answered by two or more answers is formulated on the basis of the semantic content that is shared by the answers.
    (Brunetti, De Kuthy, and Riester 2021: 18)

The principle overrides Q-Givenness, in that the QUD can be made of *new* content if that content is shared by all the utterances that answer the QUD. Example (6) is taken from a French spoken sociolinguistic interview (CFPP2000 corpus, Branca-Rosoff et al. 2009). The speaker is answering a question from the interviewer about what districts of Paris she likes. By convention, implicit QUDs are given in italics.[2]

---

1 For the sake of simplicity, in the examples that follow the information-structure annotation will only be given on the utterances that are relevant for the discussion.
2 Some of the pauses, fillers, repetitions, interruptions, etc. that are present in the transcription of the CFPP2000 corpus have been removed for the sake of clarity.

(6) A_{23} *alors euh j'aime beaucoup euh tout c'qui est euh: aux environs de bah*
     j'aime beaucoup le septième euh où qu'ce soit
     'so ehm I love very much all that is close to. . . well I love the 7th district
     very much, no matter where'

   Q_{24} Where specifically, within the 7th district?

   >$A_{24'}$ *[que ça   soit [vers   la Tour-Maubourg]$_F$]~*
     'be it towards the Tour-Maubourg'

   >$A_{24''}$ *[que ce   soit [ici]$_F$]~*
     'be it here'

   (French, CFPP2000, 7ème)

This is an example of Simple Parallelism. The segments $A_{24'}$ and $A_{24''}$ share some semantic content (represented by the almost identical parts *que ça soit* and *que ce soit*) and differ with respect to the answer they give to Q_{24}: the principle in (5) therefore applies.

Example (7), from the same corpus, is an instance of Complex Parallelism. Spk1 is the interviewer (a linguist) and Spk2 is the interviewee, a person living in the 13th district of Paris.

(7) > Q_1 Spk1:   *comment est-c'que euh toi ou tes parents vous êtes arrivés*
     dans l'quartier (. . .)
     'how did you or your parents arrive in the district (. . .)?'

   > > $Q_{1.1}$ How did you arrive in the district?

   > > > $A_{1.1}$ Spk2:   *alors, donc [[moi]$_{CT}$ j'suis arrivé à Paris [j'étais tout petit]$_F$]~ (. . .)*
     'so, as for myself, I arrived in Paris as a little child'

   > > $Q_{1.2}$ How did your parents arrive in the district?

   > > > $A_{1.2}$ *et [[mes parents]$_{CT}$ sont venus à Paris [pour le boulot]$_F$]~*
     'and my parents came to Paris for work'

   (French, CFPP2000, 13ème)

In this example, the QUD is not implicit but is explicitly uttered by the interviewer.[3] The characteristic of Complex Parallelism is that the question is only partially answered by each utterance ($A_{1.1}$ and $A_{1.2}$); each utterance however fully answers a subordinate QUD ($Q_{1.1}$ and $Q_{1.2}$). This is basically the QUD analysis that Büring (2003,

---

3 QUDs can be questions that are actually produced by a speaker. Unlike implilcit questions, which follow the principles in (3), overt questions can be made of new content. Also, they are not necessarily answered by the utterance that follows; if not, an implicit QUD has to be formulated after the explicit one.

following Roberts 2012) gives to contrastive topics in English and German: a super-ordinate question is followed by sub-questions whose answers are partial answers to the super-question. Such a QUD structure not only identifies the focus variable but also the topic variable, which is indexed with CT (for Contrastive Topic) in (7).

The difference between Simple and Complex Parallelism is basically that, with the former, the topic is fixed and the only evoked alternative set is the one introduced by the focus, while with Complex Parallelism, the topic varies too. For the same discourse structures, Umbach (2005) talks about "simple contrast" and "double contrast". Indeed, the discourse structures where Parallelism applies represent what is required at the discourse level in order to have contrast: discourse segments that share some content and differ in some respects. This point is discussed in more details in the next section, where I present my assumptions about the notion of contrast.

3 What is contrast?

Contrast can be viewed as one of the possible "pragmatic uses" (Krifka 2008: 250) of focus or topic alternatives. Focus or topic alternatives satisfy what Repp (2016) calls an intuitive definition of contrast – one that may be found in dictionaries – namely that contrast refers to "differences between similar things" (Repp 2016: 270): the alternatives evoked by focus or topic share their content (similarity), except for the value given to the variable(s) (dissimilarity). Nevertheless, such a definition is not sufficient. In order to have contrast, the relationship between the alternatives must be subject to certain contextual or semantic constraints. Differences in these constraints give rise to different types of contrast (Krifka 2007; Cruschina 2021). For Rooth (1992), contrast arises in situations where the context provides a phrase/sentence whose semantic value corresponds to one of the alternatives evoked by the focus or the topic. Other scholars have pointed out that the alternatives should be clearly identifiable, others that they should be limited in number, others that they should be both (see Molnár 2022 for a survey). Neeleman and Vermeulen (2013) argue that the meaning of contrastive focus encodes at least one false alternative.[4] For contrastive topic, they propose that the additional interpretive effect of contrast is that the speaker is unwilling to utter (at least) one alternative.[5] Following Umbach (2004) and Repp (2016), I argue that a way to identify the defining prop-

---

4 In fact, they discuss *corrective* focus. See more on correction and how it differs from other types of contrasts in Section 3.1.
5 See more on this in Section 4.3.

erties of contrast (or better, of different types of contrast) is to look at this notion from a discourse perspective, namely to look at contrastive discourse (or rhetorical, or coherence) relations. I will focus on this line of studies in the next sub-section. I will argue that contrastive relations can be partially defined and differentiated by taking into account the QUD structure that is reconstructed for the contrasting segments and their preceding context.

3.1 Contrast as a discourse relation

Discourse relations (Hobbs 1985; Mann and Thompson 1988; Asher and Lascarides 2003; Webber et al. 2019, among many others) are interpretative relations between utterances of a text: they give the function of an utterance with respect to the preceding utterance(s). For instance, an utterance can express the cause, the result, or the goal of what is described in the preceding utterance(s); it can elaborate on or explain what is said in the preceding utterance(s), etc. Discourse relations are often marked by discourse markers or by subordinating/coordinating conjunctions, such as 'therefore', 'however', 'in order to, 'but', 'yet', 'because'.

Among discourse relations, scholars have identified contrastive ones. Various classifications of contrastive relations have been proposed, and analyses differ with respect to the number of such relations and their exact definition (as well as their names), so that different aspects related to contrast are highlighted. I will not go through the proposals here but refer to Repp (2016) for a summary. Despite the variety of proposals, as Repp observes, "the basic ingredient to the CONTRAST relation in all theories is that there must be similarities as well as dissimilarities between two discourse segments." (Repp 2016: 277). In other words, we are back to the property (similarity plus dissimilarity) of focus and topic alternatives, which is the premise for contrast (cf. Neeleman and Vermeulen 2013). That means that the informational and the discourse view on contrast are compatible and in fact complementary: the discourse segments that are in a contrastive relation make the alternative set (or a subset of it) explicit. In other words, a contrastive relation between two (or more) discourse segments satisfies Rooth's requirement for contrast, namely that one or more alternatives be explicitly provided by the context. In addition, each relation specifies the different contextual and interpretative constraints among discourse segments. According to Cuenca, Postolea, and Visconti (2019: 6), "two discourse segments (S1 and S2) are in contrast when their meanings *conflict* [emphasis mine] either at the semantic or the pragmatic level. In the latter case, the opposition is established between inferences, not contents per se". I borrow from Repp (2016) the classification of contrastive discourse relations into SIMILAR, OPPOSE, and CORR(ection), and I add a CONCESSION relation. The type of "conflict" subsumed by each of these relations is described in the rest of this section through the QUD structure that can be reconstructed in each case, following RBK's principles.

Let us start with the SIMILAR relation. Repp defines SIMILAR as a relation where propositions can both be true in the evaluation world, and both "make the same kind of contribution to the current question under discussion" (Repp 2016: 8). An English constructed example from Repp (2016: 8) is given in (8):

(8) *John was mowing the lawn. Pete was pruning the roses.*
    (Repp 2016: 8)

Within RBK's framework, (8) may have the following QUD (and IS) structure.[6] The two utterances, like Repp says, answer the same QUD, but do it here indirectly through the sub-questions $Q_{1.1}$ and $Q_{1.2}$; in other words, this is a case of Complex Parallelism.

(9) Q_1 What were John and Pete doing?
    > $Q_{1.1}$ What was John doing?
    > > $A_{1.1}$ *[[John]$_{CT}$ was [mowing the lawn]$_F$]~.*
    > $Q_{1.2}$ What was Pete doing?
    > > $A_{1.2}$ *[[Pete]$_{CT}$ was [pruning the roses]$_F$]~.*

SIMILAR is what Cuenca, Postolea, and Visconti (2019) call a "weak contrast". Indeed, the only requirement for the contrasting segments is to (directly or indirectly) answer the same QUD. In other words, what is needed in order to have a SIMILAR relation is just a Parallelism configuration.

The OPPOSE relation is, like SIMILAR, one where both propositions are true in the evaluation world. Repp distinguishes OPPOSE from SIMILAR in that the former is such that the two utterances make *opposing* contributions to the current QUD. For instance in (10), the presence of *but* signals "that the first conjunct serves as an argument for some background assumption whereas the second conjunct serves as an argument against it", where "the background assumption might have been that John and Pete would mow the lawn together." The sentence "tells us that this expectation is violated" (Repp 2016: 8).

---

6 Since no context (under the form of a preceding utterance) is given, this is just the QUD structure that seems more plausible given the meaning of the sentences in (8).

(10) *John was mowing the lawn but Pete was pruning the roses.*
(Repp 2016: 8)

(11) Q_1 Were John and Pete mowing the lawn?
   > $Q_{1.1}$ What was John doing?
   > > $A_{1.1}$ *[[John]$_{CT}$ [was mowing the lawn]$_F$]~*
   > $Q_{1.2}$ What was Pete doing?
   > > $A_{1.2}$ *but [[Pete]$_{CT}$ [was pruning the roses]$_F$]~*.

I propose, making Repp's definition more precise, that two utterances in an OPPOSE relation represent propositions of opposite polarity, each *partially* answering a preceding QUD that asks for confirmation of some background assumption. In other words, a Complex Parallelism configuration is at stake, where the super-question is a polar one. In the QUD structure in (11), the polar question Q_1 asks whether the background assumption that both John and Pete were mowing the lawn is true. Q_1 is indirectly answered through the answers to the two sub-questions $Q_{1.1}$ and $Q_{1.2}$, which partly confirm and partly disconfirm the truth of such assumption.

In this example the proposition of opposite polarity (*Pete was not mowing the lawn*) is inferred from $A_{1.2}$ and triggered by *but*. Cases like this are not uncommon in naturalistic data, as we will see in Section 4. The constructed English example in (12a) is however more transparent, since the two segments explicitly contain two predicates of opposite polarity.[7] Its QUD structure is given in (12b).

(12) a. *John mowed the lawn, but Pete did not.*
   b. Q_1 Did John and Pete mow the lawn?
     > $Q_{1.1}$ Did John mow the lawn?
     > > $A_{1.1}$ *[[John]$_{CT}$ [mowed]$_F$ the lawn]~*
     > $Q_{1.2}$ Did Pete mow the lawn?
     > > $A_{1.2}$ *but [[Pete]$_{CT}$ [did not]$_F$ ~~mow the lawn~~]~*.

The relation CORR(RECTION) is the only one expressing an "exclusive" contrast in Cuenca, Postolea, and Visconti's (2019) terms. That means that the two utterances are not compatible, namely one is negated to assert the other. In terms of QUD-structure, the contrasting utterance replaces an answer to a QUD that has been given before in the discourse, for instance by another participant in the conversation, or an implicit answer that contains some knowledge that is taken for granted by the

---

7 Since the verb is the same, ellipsis applies to its second occurrence.

speakers, given their world knowledge, as we will see in the French and Italian data presented in Section 4. Consider my constructed examples in (13).

(13) a. Spk 1: *John pruned the roses.*
    b'. Spk 2: *John did not prune the roses,*
               he mowed the lawn.
    b". Spk 2: *Pete pruned the roses,*
               not John.

A QUD structure for (13a–b') follows Simple Parallelism and both assertions answer a QUD about the tasks that John performed in the garden, as illustrated in (14).

(14) Q_1 What did John do in the garden?
    > $A_{1'}$ Spk 1: *John pruned the roses.*
    > Q_2 Did John prune the roses?
    > > A_2 Spk 2: *[John [did not]$_F$ prune the roses]~,*
    > $A_{1''}$ *[he [mowed the lawn]$_F$]~*

The contrasting utterances are A_1' and A_1'' , which both answer Q_1. The proposition expressed by A_1' is believed to be true by some participant in the conversation (Spk1) but not by the one who utters A_1'' (Spk2). The assertion in A_2 is uttered in order to reject A_1', which is then replaced by the correct answer ($A_{1''}$). In (13a–b"), the order is different: the speaker first replaces A_1' with A_1'' and then explicitly rejects A_1', as shown in (15).

(15) Q_1 Who pruned the roses?
    > $A_{1'}$ Spk 1: *[[John]$_F$ pruned the roses]~.*
    > $A_{1''}$ Spk 2: *[[Pete]$_F$ pruned the roses]~,*
    > Q_2 Did John prune the roses?
    >> A_2 *[[not]$_F$ John]~.*

Note that the QUD and sub-QUDs with CORR are not polar questions. This is due to the difference between OPPOSE and CORR in terms of their function in discourse. With OPPOSE, the speaker partially agrees on and partially denies the truth of some background assumption that is still under discussion, represented by the polar QUD (cf. Farkas and Bruce 2010). With CORR, the speaker's assertion substitutes the addresee's one, or one that is assumed by the addressee to be true, as a correct answer to the QUD.

    I finally add a CONCESSION relation to Repp's classification, namely a relation where one conjunct goes against the expectations triggered by the other, in that it contradicts the default inference from the other conjunct (Umbach 2004). In Webber et al.'s (2019) Penn Discours TreeBank annotation guidelines, "Concession is meant to be used when a causal relation expected on the basis of one argument is cancelled or denied by the situation described in the other" (Webber et al. 2019: 23). Example (16) from Repp (2016: 277) shows a typical concessive marker in English, the subordinating conjunction *although*.

(16)　*Although Miller is a good politician, Smith was chosen for the task.*
　　　(Repp 2016: 277)

The QUD and IS structure of (16) are the following:

(17)　Q_1　　Who was chosen for the task?
　　　$> Q_2$　　Despite what?
　　　$>> A_2$　*[Although [Miller is a good politician]$_F$]~*,
　　　$> A_1$　*[[Smith]$_F$ was chosen for the task]~* .

In this example, no Parallelism configuration applies to the contrasting segments. As we will see in Section 5.1, CONCESSION may indeed (though not always) occur in contexts that do not fit Parallelism's requirements, that is, where the two discourse segments do not both answer the same QUD.[8] Unlike OPPOSE, the alternatives do not have to make predications of opposite polarity, because the "conflict" does not arise from that, but from the incompatibility of one alternative and the inference triggered by the other. Unlike CORR, all alternative propositions are true in the evaluation world, though one triggers the inference that the other *should* be false.

　　Summarizing, contrast requires the presence of focus or topic alternatives. It also demands that such alternatives be instantiated by actual utterances in the discourse, so that a contrastive relation can be established between them. The type of contrastive relation depends on particular contextual and semantic restrictions, which can be identified thanks to the QUD-structure associated with the contrasting pairs. SIMILAR and OPPOSE differ from each other in that with SIMILAR, the utterances provide different answers to the QUD (directly or indirectly) but they are not restricted in any particular way, while OPPOSE requires that the contrasting utterances make predications of opposite polarity, and that each of them partially contributes to answer a polar QUD. Hence, OPPOSE is only compatible with Complex Parallelism. With CORR, both utterances answer the same QUD but one is rejected

---

8 On the relationship between CONCESSION and QUD-structure, see also Hesse, Klabunde, and Benz, this volume, though their definition of CONCESSION seems more restricted than mine.

as false, while the other substitutes it as the correct answer. Finally, CONCESSION has the additional requirement that one alternative goes against the expectations triggered by the other.

In the following section, I will test on naturalistic data of French and Italian the above proposals concerning the interplay between the QUD-structure and the different discourse relations, and see to what extent contrastive discourse segments follow the principle of Parallelism from RBK's QUD-model.

4 Contrastive focus and topic in QUD-annotated naturalistic data

The data I have analyzed in this study consisted of short excerpts from three spoken French interviews and two Italian written interviews, for a total of about 2630 words for French and 1770 for Italian. The French excerpts were part of the following corpora: two interviews of the CFPP2000 corpus (Branca-Rosoff et al. 2009), namely one to a person living in the 13th district of Paris (*13ème*) and one living in the 7th district (*7ème*); and an interview with a French writer, from the Rhapsodie corpus (Lacheret, Kahane, and Pietrandrea 2019). The two Italian texts were taken from two blog interviews, one to the writer of a novel (*Senza etichette*),[9] and one to the author of a blog and an e-book on bilingualism (*Bilingue per gioco*).[10]

The texts were divided into discourse segments, for a total of about 430 segments, and each segment was annotated for QUDs and IS, according to RBK's model.[11] The distribution of words and segments is given in Table 1. An annotation was also realized of the four contrastive relations discussed above: SIMILAR, OPPOSE, CORR and CONCESSION. Table 1 also shows the number of contrasts and their distribution with respect to these relations.[12]

---

9 http://www.deaplanetalibri.it/blog/intervista-allautrice-di-senza-etichette-m-verdiana-rigoglioso
10 https://www.lacasanellaprateria.com/bilingue-per-gioco-intervista-a-letizia/
11 Following Riester, Brunetti, and De Kuthy (2018), discourse segments were constituted by (full or elliptical) independent sentences. Coordinating sentences were also divided into separate segments. Also, following Brunetti, De Kuthy, and Riester (2021), appositive relative clauses, adjunct clauses, and even non-clausal adjuncts could be considered as separated segments, depending on their information-structural status.
12 The annotation of contrastive relations was done by the author with the help of Ting He and Serin Lahcene, whom I thank here. The QUD annotation of the Italian blog interviews was done by both the author and Marta Berardi (see De Kuthy, Brunetti, and Berardi 2019 for inter-annotator agreement). The French QUD annotation was done by the author.

Table 1: Distribution of words, segments, and contrasts in the QUD-annotated texts.

	Words	Segments	Contrastive relations				TOTAL contrasts
			Similar	Oppose	Correction	Concession	
CFPP2000 (*13ème*)	1250	105	13	6	0	9	26
CFPP2000 (*7ème*)	1040	99	16	7	2	8	32
Rhapsodie	340	31	3	2	3	1	9
Total French	**2630**	**235**	**32**	**15**	**5**	**18**	**67**
Blog *S.E.*	702	84	18	0	0	3	20
Blog *Bil. per gioco*	1070	110	14	4	6	6	34
Total Italian	**1772**	**194**	**32**	**4**	**6**	**9**	**54**
TOTAL	**4402**	**429**	**64**	**19**	**11**	**27**	**121**

As shown in Table 1, SIMILAR was the most frequent relation. That is expected since the only restriction among the alternatives is for them (or part of them) to be instantiated by discourse segments that answer the same QUD. CORR was the least frequent relation, and this is expected too, since this relation is used to deny the truth of a proposition, so it can only be found in an exchange, unless the speaker/writer contradicts some implicit general assumption. Such a property reduces the contexts of occurrence of this relation. OPPOSE and CONCESSION were also more frequent than SIMILAR, because they must satisfy additional constraints: with OPPOSE, the contrasting segments must represent predications of opposite polarity, while in the case of CONCESSION, one utterance must deny the expectation of the other.

I will now discuss various examples and see to what extent and in what way contrastive relations occur with Simple and Complex Parallelism in my data.

4.1 Contrastive relations with Simple Parallelism

Example (6), repeated below, is a clear case of Simple Parallelism and the two discourse segments are in a SIMILAR relation. Indeed, they provide two possible answers to the question *Where specifically, within the 7th district?*

(6) A_{23} *alors euh j'aime beaucoup euh tout c'qui est euh: aux environs de bah j'aime beaucoup le septième euh où qu'ce soit*
       'so ehm I love very much all that is close to. . . well I love the 7th district very much, no matter where'

    Q_{24} Where specifically, within the 7th district?

   >$A_{24'}$ *[que ça soit [vers   la Tour-Maubourg]$_F$]~*
       'be it towards the Tour-Maubourg'

$>A_{24''}$ *[que ce   soit [ici]$_F$]~*
     'be it here'
(French, CFPP2000, 7ème)

As we noticed earlier, the shared content is (almost) syntactically identical. That helps to identify the two alternatives. No other marking is present, which is typical of a SIMILAR relation in my data.

No examples of OPPOSE were found with Simple Parallelism. Indeed, as I said above, the definition of an OPPOSE relation requires the presence of two sets of alternatives, hence Complex Parallelism.

A CORR relation with Simple Parallelism is illustrated in (18), which is taken from a spoken interview of a journalist with a French writer, Françoise Giroud.

(18) $> Q_2$ What about your father?
   $> > A_{2'}$ Spk1:   *votre père était riche*
                'your father was rich'
   $> > Q_3$ Was he 'rich'?
   $> > > A_3$ Spk 2: *[riche [c'est un grand mot]$_F$]~*
                'rich is a big word'
   $> > A_{2''}$ *mais enfin disons qu'[il [appartenait à cette bourgeoisie euh*
                qui n'a pas de problèmes d'argent]$_F$]~
                'but well let's say that he belonged to that bourgeoisie ehm
                who does not have money problems'
   (French, Rhapsodie)

The writer corrects the journalist who says that her father was rich, by explaining that 'rich' is not the right word to define her father's financial situation; she specifies that her father rather 'belonged to that bourgeoisie that did not have money problems'. We can interpret the speaker's comment in A_3 as a way to deny the interviewer's statement ('Your father was rich'). $A_{2''}$ answers the same QUD about the father as $A_{2'}$.

The example just seen is one where CORR occurs between two explicit utterances, which are uttered by two different speakers. This is however not common in my data. In my data CORR mostly occurs between an explicit utterance and an implicit one, corresponding to some background assumption whose truth the speaker explicitly denies. Consider (19), from the same French interview. The writer is here talking about her poor childhood. We can assume that *ce qui est dur* 'what is hard' and *ce qui est horrible* 'what is horrible' are in this context meant to be synonymous (the speaker is simply varying her language for stylistic reasons, in order not to repeat the same adjective twice).

(19) $> A_7$ *c'est une expérience ça que je n'ai jamais oubliée*
            'That is an experience I've never forgotten'
     $> Q_8$ What is hard, in this experience?
     $\gg A_8'$ ~~[What is hard is [to be poor]$_F$]~~~.
     $>> Q_9$ Is it hard to be poor?
     $>>> A_9$ *[ce qui est dur [(. . .) ce n'est vraiment pas]$_F$ d'être pauvre (. . .)]*~
            'What is hard (. . .), it is not really to be poor'
     $>> A_8''$ *[ce qui est horrible [c'est de se dire je n'en sortirai jamais]$_F$]*~
            'What is horrible, it is to tell oneself: "I'll never get out of it"'
(French, Rhapsodie)

The speaker is correcting the easily inferable statement that being poor is a hard experience. The CORR relation is between that implicit statement ('It is hard to be poor', added to the QUD structure as A_8') and the explicit one in A_8'' ('It is hard to tell oneself "I'll never get out of it"').[13] The implicit statement is easily reconstructed thanks to the explicit denial of its truth ('What is hard is not to be poor', in A_9). With A_9, the speaker wants to deny that A_8' is the correct answer to Q_8, so that she can then replace it with a different answer (A_8''). Since the implicit positive statement (A_8') and the statement that replaces it (A_8'') are both answers to the same QUD (Q_8), they are parallel in the QUD structure.

Consider finally a CONCESSION relation with Simple Parallelism. An Italian example is (20). The CONCESSION relation is here lexically marked by *anche se* 'even if'.

(20) $> Q_{10}$ What about your linguistic background?
     $>> A_{10'}$ *[Io (per fare un esempio) [parlo fluentemente inglese]$_F$]*~,
            'As an example, I speak English fluently'
            (. . .)
     $>> A_{10''}$ *[[sono senz'altro bilingue]$_F$]*~
            'I am defintely bilingual'
     $>> A_{10'''}$ *nel senso che [[ho pieno controllo di due codici linguistici]$_F$]*~,
            'in the sense that I have full control over two linguistic codes'
     $>> A_{10''''}$ *anche se [[non sono bilingue precoce]$_F$]*~.
            'even though I am not an early bilingual'
(Italian, blog interview, *Bilingue per gioco*)

---

13 The reconstructed linguistic content is struck through in the example, and it is written in English.

The speaker is arguing that having full master of two languages and therefore being bilingual does not necessarily mean to have acquired both languages early in life; on the contrary, and against what one might expect, someone who speaks fluently two languages may not be an early bilingual. In order to provide an example, the speaker says that she speaks English fluently though she did not acquire it early in life. The contrasting utterances are the last two in the example: the first one (*ho pieno controllo di due codici linguistici* 'I have full control over two linguistic codes') triggers the inference contradicted by the second (*non sono bilingue precoce* 'I am not an early bilingual').[14]

4.2 Contrastive relations with Complex Parallelism

Complex Parallelism is less frequent than Simple Parallelism with all relations except OPPOSE (9 examples out of 64 with SIMILAR, 3 out of 27 with CONCESSION, not attested with CORR). Let us discuss the less common relations first.

An example with SIMILAR is (7), repeated below:

(7) > Q_1 Spk1:   *comment est-c'que euh toi ou tes parents vous êtes arrivés dans l'quartier (. . .)*
                        'how did you or your parents arrive in the district (. . .)?'
     > > $Q_{1.1}$ How did you arrive in the district?
     > > > $A_{1.1}$ Spk2: *alors, donc [[moi]$_{CT}$ j'suis arrivé à Paris [j'étais tout petit]$_F$]~ (. . .)*
                        'so, as for myself, I arrived in Paris as a little child'
     > > $Q_{1.2}$ How did your parents arrive in the district?
     > > > $A_{1.2}$ *et [[mes parents]$_{CT}$ sont venus à Paris [pour le boulot]$_F$]~*
                        'and my parents came to Paris for work'
(French, CFPP2000, 13ème)

The two utterances are two partial answers to the (here, explicit) superordinate question 'How did you or your parents arrive in the district?'. The presence of the clitic left dislocated strong pronoun *moi* 'me' in $A_{1.1}$ helps to recognize it as one of the two topic alternatives (*moi* vs *mes parents*) (for the relation between clitic left dislocation and CT in French, see for example Barnes 1985; Lambrecht 1994; Riou and Hemforth 2015; see also Section 4.3). Syntactic identity (*j'suis arrivé à Paris* 'I

---

14 Notice that in this example, there are four utterances that answer the same QUD Q_{10}: the first two are in a SIMILAR relation, the last two are in a CONCESSION relation.

came to Paris' / *mes parents sont venus à Paris* 'my parents came to Paris') helps to identify the shared content between the two alternative propositions. Note that this example could not be a case of OPPOSE relation, as shown by the fact that the QUD is not a polar question: the QUD is about the circumstances which brought the speaker and his family to Paris, and not about whether certain specific circumstances did bring (or not) him or his parents to Paris.

CONCESSION too is present with Complex Parallelism. An example is (21), where the same speaker as in (7) talks about his apartment.

(21) A_{48} *surtout que pour des immeubles de l'OPAC on a la chance de pas être sur l'périph*
'above all, as social housing, we are lucky that we are not on the beltway'

Q_{49} Where are buildings of social housing?

$> Q_{49.1}$ Where are many of them?

$> > A_{49.1}$ *[parce que [beaucoup d'immeubles (. . .) des HLM]$_{CT}$ sont quand même [en périphérie]$_{F}$]~*
'because many buildings of social housing are actually in the suburbs'

$> Q_{49.2}$ Where is yours?

$> > A_{49.2}$ *et [[nous]$_{CT}$ on est euh quand même [dans l'centre du treizième]$_{F}$]~*
'and *we* are actually in the center of the 13th district'

(French, CFPP2000, 13ème)

The fact that the building where the speaker and his family live is within Paris (*dans le centre du treizième* 'in the center of the 13th district (of Paris)') is unexpected, knowing that most buildings of social housing are in the periphery. The second alternative denies the expectation triggered by the first one. The clitic left dislocation of the strong pronoun *nous* in the second conjunct (*nous, on est. . .*) identifies the second topic alternative: *nous* means 'the building of social housing where we live', and it contrasts with *beaucoup d'immeubles des HLM* 'many builings of social housing'. The adverb *quand meme* 'actually' marks the CONCESSION relation.

No examples of CORR were found with Complex Parallelism. That can be explained by the fact that what is corrected is generally the value of one variable, not two: either an entity is substituted, for which a predication holds ('Mary won, not Pete'), or the substitution concerns what is predicated of an entity ('Mary did *not* take the bike, she went by train').

Finally, as I said, OPPOSE only occurs with Complex Parallelism. An example is given in (22). The speaker (again, the same speaker of (7) and (21)) is explaining that he did not have a hard time to find an apartment of social housing, because the apartments with a suitable price for him – namely those of an intermediate price – were the most easy to find.

(22) $>> Q_{42}$ Is the waiting time long to get an apartment of social housing?
  $>>> Q_{42.1}$ What is the waiting time to get really affordable social housing?
  $>>>> A_{42.1}$ *c'est-à-dire que [[les HLM vraiment pas chers là]$_{CT}$ [y a des queues et une attente incroyable]$_F$]~*
    'That is, for really cheap social housing, there are never-ending lines and an incredibly long waiting time'
  $>>> Q_{42.2}$ What is the waiting time to get intermediate cost social housing?
  $>>>> A_{42.2}$ *[[dans la gamme intermédiaire]$_{CT}$ comme ici [on a un petit peu plus de chance euh d'aboutir]$_F$]~*
    'in the intermediate (price) range (for apartments of social housing), like here, we have a little more chance to succeed'
  (French, CFPP2000, 13ème)

We consider contrast as OPPOSE here because 'to have more chance to succeed' is interpreted as meaning that the waiting line was not long, contrary to what happens with cheaper apartments. In other words, a predication of opposite polarity is inferred.

In most of the examples of OPPOSE from my dataset, the focus value is represented by the predicate, and the topic value by the entity of which the predication holds. In two cases from an Italian blog the reverse occurs: the predicate is the CT and the entity which it predicates about is the focus, as shown in (23):

(23) A_{41} *Un rischio c'è,*
      'There is a risk'
      (. . .)
  $> Q_{43}$ What is this risk?
  $>> Q_{43.1}$ Is this risk to focus on what?
  $>>> A_{43.1}$ *[Quello [[di focalizzarsi troppo]$_{CT}$ [sulle lingue]$_F$]~*
      'to focus too much on languages'
  $>> Q_{43.2}$ Is this risk not to focus on what?
  $>>> A_{43.2}$ *e [[perdere di vista]$_{CT}$ [il bambino]$_F$]~,*
      'and to lose sight of the child'
  (Italian, blog interview, *Bilingue per gioco*)

This is an excerpt of the *Bilingue per gioco* blog interview. The speaker is saying that teaching a second language to ones's child is risky in one respect, namely that one may focus too much on the goal (the child's learning a second language) and lose sight of the child's needs. *Perdere di vista il bambino* 'to lose sight of the child' can be paraphrased as "not to focus (enough) on the child", namely it can be considered as a proposition predicating the opposite of $A_{43.1}$. Since the predicate 'to focus on' is contained in the sub-QUDs (but with different polarity in each sub-QUD), it is the contrastive topic. Each sub-QUD asks about the entity that holds of the predicate, so 'languages' and 'the child' are the foci.

Finally, the French example below illustrates what Umbach (2005) calls "crossed alternatives": "In each of the conjuncts there has to be a focus in the theme part, i.e. a contrastive topic, and a focus in the rheme part. Complexity arises from the fact that the alternatives need not be parallel, i.e. both relating to either a contrastive topic or a rheme focus. They may also be "crossed", one of them relating to a contrastive topic and the other one to a rheme focus" (Umbach 2005: 10).

(24) Q_5 What about your grandfather?

    > Q_6 Spk1:   *il vivait avec vous ou enfin avec tes parents?*
                         'Did he live with you or, I mean, with your parents?'

   > > A_6 Spk2:   *non non non non*
                         'no no no no'

   > > Q_7 Did your whole family come to Paris?

  > > > $Q_{7.1}$ Where did your grandparents go?

  > > > > $A_{7.1}$ *[[mes grands-parents]$_{CT}$ [(. . .) sont restés dans l'sud]$_F$]~*
                       'my grandparents (..) stayed in the South'

  > > > $Q_{7.2}$ Who came to Paris?

  > > > > $A_{7.2}$ *[c'est [juste mes parents]$_F$ qui sont montés]~*
                       'it's just my parents who came (to Paris)'

(French, CFPP2000, 13ème)

$A_{7.1}$ and $A_{7.2}$ are parallel in the QUD tree and each partially answers Q_7; what is different with respect to previous examples of OPPOSE is that the sub-questions they answer ask for the value of different focus variables: $Q_{7.1}$ asks about the place where a certain member of the family (the grandparents, which is the fixed topic) went to live; $Q_{7.2}$ asks about which member of the family went to live to a certain place, that is Paris (the fixed topic). The cleft construction in $A_{7''}$ confirms that $Q_{7.2}$ is formulated correctly, since a clefted constituent in French typically corresponds to the focus.

4.3 Contrastive marking and implicit alternatives

I have argued in Section 3 that the realization as discourse segments of (some of) the alternative propositions evoked by focus or topic is essential to have contrast, which corresponds to a contrastive relation between such segments. We have also seen in Section 4.1 that for many instances of CORR, this requirement must be revised in that what the context provides is not the alternative utterance, but a statement that denies the truth of the alternative utterance.

In other examples from my French and Italian naturalistic data, which I am presenting in this section, contrast is inferred from a specific syntactic construction, and no explicit alternative needs to be present in the discourse.[15] Some examples of this type concern the relation CORR. In Italian, a focus fronting and a cleft construction can both have a corrective function (see Brunetti 2009; De Cesare 2017; Cruschina 2021); in French, only cleft constructions do (see De Cesare 2017; Cruschina 2021). Consider the Italian example in (25).

(25) Q_{13} Spk1: *Una definizione del termine "bilingue"?*
                     'A definition of the term 'bilingual'?'
      $> Q_{14}$ What is the problem with a definition of the term 'bilingual'?
      $> > A_{14'}$ Spk2: [~~Il problema è che~~ [Ce ne sono tante]$_F$]~
                     '~~(The problem is that)~~ there are many of them'
      $> > A_{14''}$ [[Questo]$_F$ è il problema]~,
                     'That is the problem'
      ~~$> > A_{14'''}$~~   ~~[The problem is [to find a definition of 'bilingual']$_F$]~~~
      (Italian, blog interview, *Bilingue per gioco*)

The interviewer asks the interviewee to give a definition of the term 'bilingual'. The interviewee does not answer the question directly, but first comments on the question by saying that (the problem with answering this question is that) there are (too) many definitions of such a term. The speaker provides two answers to Q_{14}, which are in a SIMILAR relation with each other. The second utterance, however, is a fronted focus construction, which also corrects the inference that the problem to answer the question is to find a definition of the term (what the question is about). What the speaker wants to say is that, paradoxically, the problem is the opposite, namely that one has to choose among too many existing definitions. An implicit conjunct is therefore reconstructed as in $A_{14'''}$, and interpreted as being in a CORR relation with $A_{14''}$.[16]

---

15 According to Bianchi, Bocci, and Cruschina (2015) and Cruschina (2021), this inference is a conventional implicature (in the sense of Potts 2005).
16 I do not exclude that the fronted focus may be mirative (instead of corrective): the utterance would deny the expectation that the problem to answer the question is to find a definition of the term 'bilingual'. Since in Italian focus fronting can be used for both mirativity and correction (Cruschina 2021), I leave the issue open here.

The QUD structure in (25) follows Simple Parallelism's requirements. Other examples where contrast is triggered by a linguistic construction follow Complex Parallelism and correspond to the phenomenon discussed by Büring (1997) under the name of "purely implicational" topic, on data from English and German. In Büring's data illustrating this phenomenon, topic alternatives are triggered by a particular accent, but no alternative proposition is explicitly given in the discourse (cf. also Neeleman and Vermeulen 2013). The effect is that an inference is made, which is taken to be a conversational implicature (Grice 1975) by Lambrecht (1994), Büring (2003), and others; the inference is either that the same predicate does *not* hold for the implicit topic (strong implicature), or that the speaker does not know whether it holds or not (weak implicature).[17]

The contrastive marking in my French and Italian data can be fronting of a constituent; the presence of such a fronted constituent makes the utterance not appropriate as an answer to the preceding QUD (cf. Westera 2019). Consider the two examples (26) and (27), one in French and one in Italian.

(26) Q_{36} Spk1: *pour toi ça a été rapide pas rapide à ton avis ça?*
'For you was it fast, not fast, in your opinion?'

> A_{36} Spk2: *bah j'pense que par rapport à beaucoup d'gens ça a été un peu rapide*
'well, I think that with respect to most people that was rather fast'

> Q_{37} How fast?

> > A_{37} *ça nous a pris deux ans j'pense à peu près*
'it took us about two years, I think, more or less'

(French, CFPP2000, 13ème)

(27)   Spk2: *E la mamma non madrelingua (. . .) può utilizzare questi stessi strumenti per far sì che la seconda lingua entri a far parte della vita dei bambini in modo molto ludico e leggero*
'The non native-speaking mother (. . .) can use the very same instruments to make the second language become part of the children's life in a very playful and light manner'

> Q_{29} Spk1: *Funziona?*
'Does it work?'

---

17 Hara (2006), who analyzes how this interpretive effect is triggered by the Japanese particle *wa*, takes it to be a *conventional* implicature.

> > A_{29} Spk2: *Le mamme, sia madrelingua che non, se ne dicono entusiaste*
> > 'The mothers, both native and non-native speakers, say they
> > are enthusiastic about it'

(Italian, blog interview, *Bilingue per gioco*)

In both examples, the utterance that triggers the contrasting inference is the one that is supposed to answer an explicit polar question (Q_{36} in (26) and Q_{29} in (27)). However, the speaker does not just answer 'yes' or a 'no', but provides additional information; as a consequence, the utterance is interpreted as answering an implicit sub-question.

Consider (26) first. The additional information provided by A_{36} is represented by a fronted prepositional phrase, *par rapport à beaucoup de gens* 'with respect to many people', which restricts the domain of application of the predicate. It is the presence of such additional expression – which is interpreted as a CT – that makes the hearer infer that there might be an alternative such that, with respect to some other criterion (in other words, with a different CT), the process of finding a flat cannot be considered as fast. For instance, the duration of the search might not be viewed as fast generally speaking, or according to the speaker's expectations, or with respect to other criteria, as suggested in the (struck through) reconstructed segment and its sub-question in (26').[18]

(26') Q_{36} Was it fast?
> $Q_{36.1}$ Was it fast, with respect to (what happened to) many
>   people?
> > $A_{36.1}$ Spk2:   *bah j'pense que [[par rapport à beaucoup d'gens]$_{CT}$ ça [a*
>   *été un peu rapide]$_F$]~*
>   'well, I think that with respect to most people that was
>   rather fast'
> ~~$Q_{36.2}$~~   ~~Was it fast, with respect to criterion x? . . .~~
> > ~~$A_{36.2}$~~   ~~[[With respect to criterion x]$_{CT}$ it [was not fast]$_F$]~~~

(French, CFPP2000, 13ème)

As the QUD annotation shows, $A_{36.1}$ answers the sub-question $Q_{36.1}$, parallel to $Q_{36.2}$; the latter contains a different restriction for the predicate to hold and is answered

---

18 The fact that different inferences may be triggered makes it plausible that the inference is indeed a cancellable, conversational implicature. Another factor in favor of such an analysis is that A_{37} implies that $Q_{37.2}$ and $A_{37.2}$ are not present, since A_{38} is a continuation of $A_{37.1}$.

by the implicature triggered by $A_{36.1}$.[19] Given such an implicature, the contrastive relation here seems to be an OPPOSE one. A CONCESSION relation however is also plausible, if one accepts the following paraphrase: "Despite the fact that, compared to many people, the search was fast, with respect to criterion x, it was long".

The contrastive effect of a fronted element observed in (26) has already been discussed for French by Prévost (2003), who comments as follows about a similar sentence: "*À Drain, on y est bien* 'At Drain, we feel good' (Internet, touristic site), meaning: At Drain and not elsewhere (or at any event, not as good!)." (Prévost 2003: 70).[20] Another means, in French, of evoking the presence of a CT, namely of a secondary open variable (not predicted by the current QUD) is clitic left dislocation, as in (28), from Garassino and Jacob (2018):

(28) a. *Monsieur le Président, (. . .) il faut rendre honneur à la présidence française, il faut rendre honneur au président Chirac, qui a été au charbon, qui a combattu et qui a vaincu sur sa vision de l'Europe*
'Mr. President (. . .) we should honor the French Presidency, we should honor President Chirac. He was at the coalface, he fought and conquered for his vision of Europe'

b. *parce que, lui il   a   une vision*
because   he 3SG.NOM have.PRS.3SG a   vision
'because he does have a vision'

(Garassino and Jacob 2018: 9)

The dislocated *lui* 'he' (*lui il a une vision*) triggers an OPPOSE relation with an implicit discourse segment of the type: "the other politicians do *not* (have a vision)".

Consider now the Italian example in (27), repeated below as (27'). The speaker answers the question 'Does it [her method to grow bilingual children, *ndr*] work?', which can be interpreted as 'Would you say that the method works?', since the question is addressed to her.

(27') > Q_{29} Spk1: *Funziona?*
'Does it work?'
➤➤ ~~$Q_{29.1}$~~   ~~What do you say?~~

---

19 If no implicature is understood by the hearer, then, following Brunetti, De Kuthy, and Riester (2021), *par rapport à beaucoup de gens* is interpreted as an *IS-peripheral* adjunct, namely an independent discourse segment that answers a sub-QUD of the QUD that is answered by the rest of the sentence.

20 My translation from French. Original : "*À Drain, on y est bien* (Internet, site touristique), sous-entendu: À Drain et pas ailleurs (ou en tout cas, on n'est pas aussi bien !)."

> > > A~~29.1~~   [[As for myself]~~CT~~, [I don't say anything]~~F~~].
> > Q₂₉.₂   What do the mothers say?
> > > A₂₉.₂   Spk2:   *[[Le mamme, sia madrelingua che non]*CT *[se ne dicono*
                *entusiaste]*F*]]~.*
                'The mothers, both native and non-native speakers, say
                they are enthusiastic about it'
(Italian, blog interview, *Bilingue per gioco*)

By attributing the affirmative answer to a third person, specifically the main users of her method – the mothers – the speaker uses a rhetorical strategy that allows her to make a positive comment on her own method without sounding immodest. The rhetorical strategy exploits the OPPOSE relation that can be inferred between the speaker's own opinion and the mothers' opinion. The most probable implicature is that the speaker does not provide an opinion of her own on the method (or that her opinion is not important). We can paraphrase what the speaker means as follows: "*I won't say anything, but the mothers (who have more authority to judge the method than I do, since it is made for them), say that it works*".[21]

5 Mismatch between Parallelism and contrast

The analysis of naturalistic data that I have conducted on French and Italian interviews was also meant to check whether contrast is always found in a discourse configuration that fits Parallelism requirements. Since SIMILAR is defined as occurring when two segments answer the same QUD, by definition SIMILAR occurs with Parallelism. What about the other contrastive relations? We have seen above that a contrastive relation can hold between an explicit and an implicit utterance, which is inferred from the linguistic form of the explicit one: in such cases, Parallelism is preserved only if the implicit utterance is included in the QUD structure: either another answer is added to the same QUD (cf. the example with CORR in (25)), or a sub-QUD and its answer are added (cf. (26) and (27)). As for CONCESSION, we already noticed in Section 3.1 that it may not satisfy Parallelism's requirements. That is confirmed by naturalistic data, as I am going to show in Section 5.1. In Section 5.2, I will then present two examples of non-concessive contrast that do not follow Parallelism.

---

21 The relation cannot be CONCESSION, since neither the paraphrase "Despite the fact that the mothers are enthusiastic about it, I won't give my opinion" nor "Despite the fact that I won't give my opinion, the mothers are enthusiastic about it" seem to correspond to the speaker's intended meaning.

5.1 Absence of Parallelism with concession

In more than half cases of CONCESSION, Parallelism does not apply. Recall that Parallelism requires that two (or more) segments be at the same level in the QUD-tree and answer the same QUD (see exx. (6) and (7)). Typically, such segments are syntactically coordinated (cf. Umbach 2005), which means that syntactic coordination and discourse coordination (in the sense of Asher and Vieu 2005) coincide. CONCESSION, however, may hold between a matrix clause and a subordinate clause. Therefore, neither syntactic nor discourse coordination seem to be necessary for a CONCESSION relation to occur.[22]

Let us consider some examples from the dataset. A case of syntactic and discourse subordination is the Italian example in (29). Following Brunetti, De Kuthy, and Riester (2021), the subordinate clause – which is nested inside the matrix clause but independent at a discourse level – is represented by dividing the matrix clause into two parts (A_{25}... and ...A_{25}). The same index number and the three dots signal that A_{25}... and ...A_{25} form one single discourse segment.[23]

(29)   *La mamma (. . .) parla la propria lingua ai figli*
                   'The mother (. . .) speaks her own language to her children'
   $>>Q_{25}$ What do children often do (concerning their mother's language)?
   $>>>A_{25}$...   *(. . .) molto spesso [i bambini*
                   '(. . .) very often the children'
   $>>>Q_{26}$ Despite what?
   $>>>>A_{26}$ *pur [[capendola perfettamente]$_F$]~*
                   'though understanding it perfectly'
   $>>>...A_{25}$ *[non parlano attivamente]$_F$ la sua lingua]~*
                   'very often the children, even if they understand it perfectly, do not proactively speak her language'
   (Italian, blog interview, *Bilingue per gioco*)

The subordinate clause in A_{26} is introduced by the conjunction *pur* 'even if', explicitly marking CONCESSION: the expectation driven from A_{26} is that the children, who perfectly understand the language, also speak it, while this is denied by the following assertion. The verb in A_{26} has a non-finite form (gerundive) and the clause is nested inside the matrix clause. Following Brunetti, De Kuthy, and

---

22 See Brunetti, De Kuthy, and Riester (2021) for a discussion on the interplay between syntax and discourse.
23 See Brunetti, De Kuthy, and Riester (2021, Section 4.4) for a discussion on this annotation choice.

Riester (2021), I interpret this clause as an IS-peripheral discourse segment,[24] namely as a segment that does not contribute to answer the matrix's QUD, but answers its own QUD, subordinated to the matrix's QUD (see Q_{26}). As a consequence, A_{25} and A_{26} are in a configuration that does not fit the requirements of the Parallelism's principle.

A_{26} is a parenthetical, non-finite, subordinated clause and is therefore easily interpreted as discourse-subordinated with respect to the matrix clause (and not answering the same QUD). However, discourse subordination (absence of Parallelism) can also occur when two segments are coordinated, as in (30).

(30)   >A_{30} *et on a pu déménager parce qu'on a eu l'opportunité d'l'OPAC*
                      'and we could move because we had the opportunity of social housing'

     > Q_{31} Why did you need that opportunity?

     > > Q_{32} You needed because you started to look for what?

     > > > $A_{32'}$ *parce que sinon [on avait commencé à chercher [à louer ou à acheter]$_F$]~*
                      'because we had started to look for a place to rent or to buy'

     > > > Q_{33} What about that search?

     > > > > A_{33} *et c'est vrai qu'[[c'était un petit peu hors budget quoi]$_F$]~*
                      'and it's true that it was a little bit above our budget'

     > > > $A_{32''}$ *[on avait commencé à lorgner [du côté de la banlieue]$_F$]~*
                      'we had started to look (for an apartment) in the suburbs'

     > > > Q_{34} What about this search?

     > > > > A_{34} *mais [[en y étant pas tout à fait convaincus d'vouloir y aller]$_F$]~*
                      'but not being totally willing to go there'
     (French, CFPP2000, 13ème)

This example shows two pairs of segments, both in a CONCESSION relation, which are both syntactically coordinated by a conjunction (*et* 'and' between $A_{32'}$ and A_{33}, and *mais* 'but' between $A_{32''}$ and A_{34}). The first pair is in a CONCESSION relation because $A_{32'}$ ('we had started to look for a place to rent or to buy') triggers the inference that the speaker could afford to rent or buy an apartment, while the second conjunct denies it by saying that the prices were outside the speaker's reach. The second pair is in a CONCESSION relation because $A_{32''}$ ('we had started to look for apartments in the suburbs') triggers the inference that the speaker liked the idea of living in the suburbs, while this is denied by the second conjunct. The QUD analysis for each

---

24 See also footnote 19.

pair is such that the second conjunct is discourse-subordinated to the first (it is at a lower level in the QUD-tree): indeed, A_{33} and A_{34} are clearly side-comments that do not answer the question in Q_{32}. Despite syntactic coordination, Parallelism does not hold.[25]

Consider finally (31). The interviewer is closing her blog interview by asking the interviewee, who is the author of an e-book on bilingualism, why one should buy her book.

(31) Q_{57} Spk1 : *Concludendo, perché comprare* In che lingua giochiamo?
                         'Concluding, why should one buy *In che lingua giochiamo*?'
                         (. . .)
    > A_{57} Spk2 : *[Perché [abbiamo a disposizione tantissime risorse ,]$_F$]~*
                         'Because we have plenty of resources at our disposal'
    > Q_{58} Despite that, what happens?
    > > A_{58} *ma [[nemmeno ce ne rendiamo conto]$_F$]~*
                         'but we don't even notice them'
    (Italian, blog interview, *Bilingue per gioco*)

A CONCESSION relation holds between A_{57} and A_{58}: since there are plenty of resources (to raise a bilingual child), one would expect that they are visible to everybody; on the contrary, we do not see them, and therefore don't use them. The QUD is explicit and is made by the interviewer. In order for this question to have an appropriate answer, A_{58} must be included in the answer: one should buy the book because it is not easy to realize how many resources there are at our disposal. Note that an answer made of A_{57} alone would not make sense in this context: "We must buy the book because we have many resources". Therefore, A_{58} cannot be an independent answer to the question, but must be part of A_{57}, the answer to Q_{57}; at the same time, it answers a subordinated QUD, Q_{58}. The absence of Parallelism is therefore evident in this example.

5.2 Absence of Parallelism in other contexts

The dataset finally also contains some non-concessive contrasts where a QUD-structure that obeys Parallelism cannot be reconstructed. The reason for the failure to

---

25 Notice, however, that in the second pair, the verb of the second conjunct (A_{34}) takes gerundive mode, and non-finiteness is a typical feature of subordination.

reconstruct Parallelism may just be that the preceding QUD structure does not allow for it. An example is (32), where two crossing contrastive relations are present:

(32) $> Q_{16.1}$ What about this neighborhood, on one side?

  $> > A_{16.1}$ *(. . .) [[d'un côté]$_{CT}$ j'suis dans un quartier [très calme (. . .)]$_F$]~*
  '(. . .) on one side I'm in a very quiet neighborhood (. . .)'

  $> Q_{16.2}$ What about this neighborhood, on the other side?

  $> > A_{16.2}$ *et pourtant [[~~de l'autre coté~~]$_{CT}$ ~~je suis dans un quartier où~~ [on profite de tous les commerces de proximité]$_F$]~*
  'and yet ~~[on the other side]~~ we benefit of all local shops'

  $> > Q_{17}$ What about the presence of local shops?

  $> > > Q_{17.1}$ Are there local shops in certain (quiet) neighborhoods?

  $> > > > A_{17.1}$ *alors que [[dans certains quartiers]$_{CT}$ [y'en a pas]$_F$]~*
  'while in certain neighborhoods there aren't any'

(French, CFPP2000, 7ème)

$A_{16.2}$ is a contrasting alternative of $A_{16.1}$: a CONCESSION relation holds between the two segments, explicitly marked by *pourtant* 'yet': the district is calm, yet it is full of local shops. So far, Parallelism is observed.[26] However, $A_{17.1}$ is, in its turn, in an OPPOSE relation with $A_{16.2}$ (cf. the adversative conjunction *alors que* 'while'): the speaker is saying that in her district they benefit of local shops, while in other districts that is not the case (there are no local shops). The clitic left dislocated prepositional phrase *dans certains quartiers* 'in certain districts' explicitly marks a CT.[27] This demands a QUD structure with a super-question Q_{17} and a sub-question $Q_{17.1}$; however, no parallel sub-question $Q_{17.2}$ follows. The presence of the contrasting pair $A_{16.1}$ and $A_{16.2}$ blocks the possibility for $A_{16.2}$ (which clearly also contrasts with $A_{17.1}$) to answer a parallel sub-question $Q_{17.2}$.

Finally, a couple of examples were found in the data where contrast seems to occur between entities inside propositions rather than between propositions. In such cases, the discourse segments in which the entities are mentioned do not need to be in a Parallelism configuration. Consider (33):

---

26 Though we must assume an elided 'on the other side' in $A_{16.2}$, given the presence of 'on one side' in $A_{16.1}$.
27 What the speaker actually means is perhaps 'in certain other *quiet* neighborhoods.

(33) > Q$_7$ What did they do in Paris?
>> A$_{7'}$ *et puis en fait [ils ont [profité euh d'l'opportunité d'cet appartement]$_F$]~*
            'and then, in fact, they took the opportunity of this apartment'
(. . .)
>> A$_{7''}$ *et puis après [ils ont [acheté leur propre appartement (. . .)]$_F$]~*
            'and then later they bought their own apartment'
>> A$_{7'''}$ *et donc [[ont libéré l'appartement de mes grands-parents]$_F$]~*
            'and so they freed my grandparents' apartment'
>> Q$_{11}$ What happened in that apartment?

>>> A$_{11}$ *[dans lequel [moi-même je me suis installé]$_F$]~ (. . .)*
            'where I moved myself (. . .)'
(French, CFPP2000, 13ème)

The whole chunk of discourse is about an apartment in Paris that the speaker's grandfather bought, where his parents lived, and in which the speaker went living after his parents moved. The use of the reflexive/intensifier *leur propre* 'their own' in A$_{7''}$ indicates that the speaker wants to contrast his grandparents' apartment with his parents' apartment. The assertions in which the two apartments are mentioned (A$_{7'}$ and A$_{7''}$) are indeed in a Simple Parallelism configuration, and the VPs are parallel foci; however, contrast seems to concern the two apartments, not the two predicates expressed by the VPs. An even clearer case is A$_{11}$, where the speaker uses the reflexive/intensifier *moi-même* 'myself'[28] in order to contrast himself with his parents and with his grand-parents, concerning the relationship that they had with the apartment: his grand-parents bought it, his parents went living in it, the speaker went living in it afterwards. Yet, the segment containing *moi-même* is an appositive relative clause that answers a sub-QUD with respect to the QUD of the matrix clause; therefore, a Parallelism configuration does not hold between A$_{7'''}$ and A$_{11}$.

6 Conclusions

In this paper I have argued that contrast demands that (some or all of) the alternatives evoked by focus or topic be explicitly expressed in the discourse by means of discourse segments; by consequence, the discourse configurations that follow Parallelism in Riester, Brunetti and De Kuthy's (2018) model, where more than one dis-

---

28 For the intensifying function of these reflexives, see e.g. Koenig and Siemund (2005).

course segment answers the same QUD, are potential loci of contrast. Different constraints between the discourse segments in a Parallelism configuration determine the different contrastive relations that may hold between them. I have shown that such constraints can be partially spelled out in QUD-structure terms. The analysis of naturalistic data from French and Italian presented in this paper, which were annotated for their QUD- and IS-structure and for their contrastive relations, has allowed me to confirm and clarify the relationship between the QUD structure and various contrastive relations.

The relation called SIMILAR, following Repp (2016), only requires that the discourse segments answer the same QUD, namely that they occur in a configuration that follows Parallelism. Other relations have additional requirements. I've argued that OPPOSE demands that the alternatives make predications of opposite polarity, which is shown by the fact that the QUD they answer is a polar one. Furthermore, OPPOSE is only compatible with Complex Parallelism. CORR(RECTION) demands two alternatives that both answer the same QUD but one is rejected as not true, while the other replaces it. No cases of Complex Parallelism were found with CORR in my data. Indeed, correction with Complex Parallelism would mean that two focus values, holding of two different topics, are both replaced by a different value, which presumably is a rare situation. We have also seen that CORR generally holds between an explicit and an implicit alternative, the latter corresponding to some general assumption whose truth the speaker explicitly denies. Finally, CONCESSION requires that one alternative triggers an inference that is denied by the other (Webber et al. 2019). The two alternatives may or may not answer the same QUD.

I have also discussed cases where a particular syntactic construction, such as fronting, clefting or clitic left dislocation, signals that the utterance is in a contrastive relation (CORR in the case of focus marking, OPPOSE or CONCESSION with topic marking) with an implicit alternative. In such cases, Parallelism is only respected if we assume that the inferred contrasting alternative is part of the QUD structure.

My data have shown that CONCESSION, which is a relation that may hold between a matrix clause and a subordinate clause, may occur in a discourse configuration that does not follow Parallelism. Syntactic subordination is a potential marking for discourse subordination in my data, and the same is true for syntactic coordination: in about two thirds of my examples, syntactic subordination is associated with discourse subordination and syntactic coordination with discourse coordination. However, it is the formulation of the QUD structure that eventually reveals whether the relation between segments in a CONCESSION relation is a coordinating or a subordinating one.

In few examples of my dataset, Parallelism is absent when a non-concessive contrast is present. I have illustrated this by means of two examples: in one, the first segment already forms a contrasting pair with a preceding segment and cannot therefore also be in a Parallelism configuration with the second segment; in the other example, contrast seems to occur among entities, not propositions, without a corresponding parallel structure at the discourse level.

My data have eventually shed some light on the linguistic marking of contrast in French and Italian. Lexical marking helps identifying contrasting relations: both OPPOSE and CONCESSION can be signaled by an adversative conjunction (*ma, mais* 'but'), but CONCESSION also has specific markers such as *pourtant* 'yet' in French, or subordinating conjunctions like *pur, anche se* 'even if' in Italian, or other markers of subordination such as a non-finite verb (French). Simple and Complex Parallelism can also be syntactically marked, and in that case, as discussed above, a contrastive relation holds between an explicit and an implicit discourse segment: CORR with Simple Parallelism, marked by fronting or clefting, and OPPOSE or CONCESSION with Complex Parallelism, marked by fronting or clitic left dislocation.

References

Arregi, Karlos. 2003. Clitic left dislocation is contrastive topicalization. *University of Pennsylvania Working Papers in Linguistics* 9(1). 31–44.

Asher, Nicolas & Alex Lascarides. 2003. *Logics of Conversation*. Cambridge: Cambridge University Press.

Asher, Nicholas & Laure Vieu. 2005. Subordinating and coordinating discourse relations. *Lingua* 115. 591–610.

Barnes, Betsy K. 1985. *The Pragmatics of Left Detachment in Spoken Standard French*. Amsterdam: Benjamins.

Bianchi, Valentina, Giuliano Bocci & Silvio Cruschina. 2015. Focus fronting and its implicatures. In Enoch O. Aboh, Jeannette Schaeffer & Petra Sleeman (eds.), *Romance Languages and Linguistic Theory 2013: Selected papers from 'Going Romance' Amsterdam 2013*, 1–20. Amsterdam: Benjamins.

Branca-Rosoff, Sonia, Serge Fleury, Florence Lefeuvre & Mat Pires. 2009. Discours sur la ville. Corpus de Français Parlé Parisien des années 2000 (CFPP2000). Technical report. https://ed268.univ-paris3.fr/CFPP2000/

Brunetti, Lisa. 2009. Discourse functions of fronted foci in Italian and Spanish. In Andreas Dufter & Daniel Jacob (eds.), *Focus and Background in Romance Languages*, 43–82. Amsterdam: Benjamins.

Brunetti, Lisa, Kordula De Kuthy & Arndt Riester. 2021. The information-structural status of adjuncts: A QUD-based approach. *Discours* 28. https://doi.org/10.4000/discours.11454

Büring, Daniel. 1997. *The Meaning of Topic and Focus — The 59th Street Bridge Accent*. London: Routledge.

Büring, Daniel. 2003. On d-trees, beans, and b-accents. *Linguistics and Philosophy* 26(5). 511–545.

Cruschina, Silvio. 2021. The greater the contrast, the greater the potential: On the effects of focus in syntax. *Glossa: A Journal of General Linguistics* 6(1). 1–30.

Cuenca, Maria Josep, Sorina Postolea & Jacqueline Visconti. 2019. Contrastive markers in contrast. *Discours* 25. https://doi.org/10.4000/discours.10326

De Cesare, Anna-Maria. 2017. Cleft constructions. In Elisabeth Stark & Andreas Dufter (eds.), *Manual of Romance Morphosyntax and Syntax*, 536–568. (Manuals of Romance Linguistics 17). Berlin/New York: De Gruyter Mouton.

De Kuthy, Kordula, Lisa Brunetti & Marta Berardi. 2019. Annotating information structure in Italian: Characteristics and cross-linguistic applicability of a QUD-based approach. In Annemarie Friedrich, Deniz Zeyrek & Jet Hoek (eds.), *Proceedings of the 13th Linguistic Annotation Workshop, Florence, Italy, August 2019*, 113–123. Cambridge: Association for Computational Linguistics.

Farkas, Donca F. & Kim B. Bruce. 2010. On reacting to assertions and polar questions. *Journal of Semantics* 27(1). 81–118.

König, Ekkehard & Peter Siemund. 2005. Intensifiers and reflexives. In Martin Haspelmath, Matthew S. Dryer, David Gil & Bernard Comrie (eds.), *The World Atlas of Language Structures*, 194–197. Oxford: Oxford University Press.

Krifka, Manfred. 2008. Basic notions of information structure. *Acta Linguistica Hungarica* 55(3–4). 243–276.

Ginzburg, Jonathan. 2012. *The Interactive Stance. Meaning for Conversation.* Oxford: Oxford University Press.

Grice, Herbert Paul. 1975. Logic and conversation. In Peter Cole & Jerry L. Morgan (eds.), *Syntax and Semantics 3: Speech Acts*, 41–58. New York: Academic Press.

Jackendoff, Ray. 1972. *Semantic Interpretation in Generative Grammar*. Cambridge: MIT Press.

Hara, Yurie. 2006. Implicature unsuspendable: Japanese contrastive wa. In Pascal Denis, Eric McCready, Alexis Palmer & Biran Reese (eds.), *Proceedings of the 2004 Texas Linguistics Society Conference, Somerville, MA, 2004*, 35–45. http://www.lingref.com/cpp/tls/2004/index.html

Hamblin, Charles L. 1973. Questions in Montague English. *Foundations of Language* 10. 41–53.

Hobbs, Jerry. 1985. *On the Coherence and Structure of Discourse* [technical report no. CSLI-85-37]. 1–36. Stanford: Center for the Study of Language and Information at Stanford University.

Lacheret, Anne, Sylvain Kahane & Paola Pietrandrea (eds.). 2019. *Rhapsodie: A Prosodic Syntactic Treebank of Spoken French*. Amsterdam/Philadelphia: Benjamins.

Lambrecht, Knud. 1994. *Information Structure and Sentence Form: Topic, Focus and the Mental Representations of Discourse Référents*. Cambridge: Cambridge University Press.

Mann, William C. & Sandra A. Thompson. 1988. Rhetorical structure theory: Toward a functional theory of text organization. *Text* 8(3). 243–281.

Molnár, Valéria. 2002. Contrast – from a contrastive perspective. In Hilde Hasselgård, Stig Johansson, Bergljot Behrens & Cathrine Fabricius-Hansen (eds.), *Information Structure in a Crosslinguistic Perspective*, 147–161. Amsterdam: Rodopi.

Myhill, John & Zhiqun Xing. 1996. Towards an operational definition of discourse contrast. *Studies in Language* 20. 303–360.

Neeleman, Ad & Reiko Vermeulen. 2012. The syntactic expression of information structure. In Ad Neeleman & Reiko Vermeulen (eds.), *The Syntax of Topic, Focus, and Contrast: An Interface-based Approach*, 1–38. Berlin/New York: Mouton de Gruyter.

Onea, Edgar. 2016. *Potential Questions at the Semantics-Pragmatics Interface*. Leiden: Brill.

Repp, Sophie. 2016. Contrast: Dissecting an elusive information-structural notion and its role in grammar. In Caroline Féry & Shinichiro Ishihara (eds.), *The Oxford Handbook of Information Structure*, 270–289. Oxford: Oxford University Press.

Riester, Arndt. 2019. Constructing QUD trees. In Malte Zimmermann, Klaus von Heusinger & Edgar Onea (eds.), *Questions in Discourse. Vol. 2: Pragmatics*, 163–192. Leiden: Brill.

Riester, Arndt, Lisa Brunetti & Kordula De Kuthy. 2018. Annotation guidelines for questions under discussion and information structure. In Evangelia Adamou Katharina Haude & Martine Vanhove (eds.), *Information Structure in Lesser-described Languages: Studies in Prosody and Syntax*, 403–443. Amsterdam: Benjamins.

Riou, Étienne & Barbara Hemforth. 2015. Dislocation clitique de l'objet à gauche en français écrit. *Discours* 16. https://doi.org/10.4000/discours.9037

Roberts, Craige. 2012 [1996]. Information structure: Towards an integrated formal theory of pragmatics. *Semantics and Pragmatics* 5(6). 1–69.

Rooth, Mats. 1985. *Association with Focus*. Amherst: University of Massachusetts at Amherst dissertation.

Rooth, Mats. 1992. A theory of focus interpretation. *Natural Language Semantics* 1(1). 75–116.

Umbach, Carla. 2004. On the notion of contrast in information structure and discourse structure. *Journal of Semantics* 21(2). 155–175.

Umbach, Carla. 2005. Contrast and information structure: A focus-based analysis of *but*. *Linguistics* 43(1). 207–232.

Van Kuppevelt, Jan. 1995. Discourse structure, topicality and questioning. *Journal of Linguistics* 31(1). 109–147.

Velleman, Leah & David Beaver. 2016. Question-based models of information structure. In Caroline Féry & Shinichiro Ishihara (eds.), *The Oxford Handbook of Information Structure*, 86–107. Oxford: Oxford University Press.

Webber, Bonnie, Rashmi Prasad, Alan Lee & Joshi Aravind. 2019. *The Penn Discourse Treebank 3.0 Annotation Manual*. Philadelphia: University of Pennsylvania. https://catalog.ldc.upenn.edu/docs/LDC2019T05/PDTB3-Annotation-Manual.pdf

Westera, Matthijs. 2019. Rise-fall-rise as a marker of secondary QUDs. In Daniel Gutzmann & Katharina Turgay (eds.), *Secondary Content*, 376–404. Leiden: Brill.

Christoph Hesse, Ralf Klabunde, and Anton Benz

9 Contrast, concession, and QUD-trees

Abstract: This paper presents an analysis of Contrast and Concession in the QUDGen corpus, a corpus annotated with Question-under-Discussion (QUD) tree representations of discourse structure a la Riester et al. (2018). Contrasts and Concessions in the corpus were identified based on 24 discourse markers (e.g., *but* and *although*). Contrast is the emphasis of dissimilarity between discourse units (e.g., *John is tall, but Bill is short*). Concession is a relation between discourse units, where one unit is presented as unexpected with respect to the other unit (e.g., *Although it is raining, we're going for a walk*). We use these corpus examples to test the theoretical assumption that Contrast and Concession differ in the internal structure of the discourse relation: Contrast is assumed to contrast two equally important discourse units; in Concession, the concession is secondary to the non-concessive unit. In QUD discourse trees, Contrast should thus have coordinating internal QUD structure (e.g., *How tall is John? How tall is Bill?*); Concession should have subordinating QUD strcuture, where the concessive part's QUD is a sub-QUD to the non-concessive part (e.g., *What are we doing?* asking for *going for a walk* as a sub-QUD to *What is the weather like?*). Results show the majority of Contrasts and Concessions in the corpus conform with the hypothesised coordinating/subordinating QUD structure divide. However, we also find counterexamples of Contrasts with subordinating QUD structure and Concessions with coordinating QUD structure, which we discuss in more detail.

1 Introduction

This paper presents a corpus study testing the hypothesis that Contrast (e.g., *John is tall, but Bill is short*) is a coordinating rhetorical relation while Concession (e.g., *Although it is raining, we're going for a walk*) is a subordinating rhetorical relation. The corpus is our own, which has annotation of discourse structure using QUD trees (cf. Riester et al., 2018).

Ackowledgements: We thank our annotators Jeniffer Callou, Mariya Hristova, Hathiya Muzni, Dorothea MacPhail, and Johanna Wrede for their work. The research conducted in this paper and the associated project is funded by the Deutsche Forschungsgemeinschaft (DFG) [KL 1109/7-1; BE 4348/5-1].

https://doi.org/10.1515/9783110986594-009

In Rhetorical Structure Theory (RST, Mann & Thompson, 1988; König, 1983), Contrast is assumed to be a multi-nucleus relation, where the contrasting discourse units are of equal importance. Concession is assumed to be a nucleus-satellite relation, where the concessive unit is a satellite—a unit of secondary importance—to the non-concessive nucleus. The nucleus-satellite distinction signifies the relative weight of importance which a discourse unit can have within a rhetorical relation. The nucleus is a unit of primary importance, the satellite a unit of secondary importance, relative to some nucleus. Rhetorical relations can be distinguished using the nucleus-satellite distinction: There are (i) rhetorical relations where all discourse units are nuclei (e.g., in Narration, a series of events is a linear order of event nuclei). (ii) There are rhetorical relations where one discourse unit is a nucleus and the other its satellite (e.g., in Elaboration, the elaboration is the satellite to the unit it is elaborating on).

We chose a QUD approach (Klein & von Stutterheim, 1987; van Kuppevelt, 1995, 1996; Roberts, 1996, 2012) to the hypothesis of coordination/subordination in Contrast and Concession because the RST approach does not allow us to investigate assumptions about the internal structure of the rhetorical relations Contrast and Concession. RST analyses particular examples of Contrast as Contrast *because* the contrasting units are identified as nuclei. Similarly for Concession, RST identifies particular examples as Concession *because* the contrasting units are identified as nucleus and satellite. A QUD approach does not make this *a priori* assumption. The guidelines by Riester et al. are not specifically tailored towards modeling rhetorical relations in general nor Contrast or Concession in particular. Our extensions do not affect the annotation of Contrast or Concession, and are similarly to Riester et al. not tailored towards Contrast and Concession. In the present paper we thus test whether annotated QUD structures match assumptions about relational structure. Multi-nucleus relations should have coordinating QUD structure, nucleus-satellite relations should have subordinating QUD structure. The QUD approach allows us to investigate relational structure independent of relation identification.

There are established QUD analyses of semantic-opposition Contrast (Büring, 2003; Jasinskaja & Zeevat, 2008) and denial-of-expectation Concession (Brunetti et al., 2021), but the guidelines we used for annotating our corpus (Riester et al., 2018, with our own extensions for non-at-issue content and discourse goals) were not specifically tailored towards modeling Contrast and Concession. In Contrast the two sub-QUDs of contrastive topics mirror one another. In Concession, the satellite answers a dedicated sub-QUD.

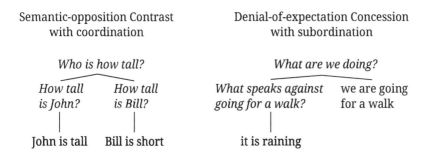

This paper discusses examples of Contrast and Concession from our corpus in order to asses whether the general-purpose QUD annotation guidelines used match analyses established in the literature (Büring, 2003; Brunetti et al., 2021). Namely, we are interested in whether the general purpose guidelines lead to Contrasts having coordinating QUD structure and Concessions having subordinating QUD structure.

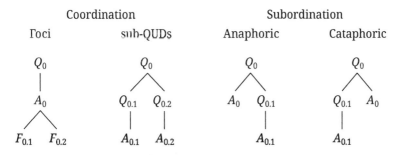

Büring (2003) analyses semantic-opposition Contrast with contrastive foci and contrastive topics as a coordinated QUD structure (mirroring RST analysis that Contrast is a multi-nucleus relation). Brunetti et al. (2021) analyses Concession as a subordinating QUD structure, where the concessive part has a dedicated QUD which is subordinated to the QUD of the non-concessive part (mirroring RST analysis that Concession is a nucleus-satellite relation).

We identify examples of semantic-opposition Contrast and Concession in the corpus through Contrast discourse markers (e.g., German *sondern*, English *but*) and Concession discourse markers (e.g., German *obwohl*, English *although*). This lexical approach to identification has multiple consequences: (i) It means we only look at explicitly marked Contrasts and Concessions and exclude implicit Contrasts and Concessions. This disconnects identification of semantic-opposition Contrasts and Concessions from theoretical assumptions about relations' internal structure, a disconnect necessary for testing assumptions about their structure. (ii) Some of these markers are unambiguous markers (e.g., German *sondern*, English *but*, only marks Contrast; German *sonst*, English *else*, *otherwise*, only marks Concession) while other markers are ambiguous and can be used with both Contrast and Concession (e.g., German *aber*, meaning *but*, is ambiguous as is English *but*). So we tally corpus examples distinguishing these classes of markers. (iii) We are able to tally how many Contrasts have coordinating QUD structure and how many Concessions have subordinating QUD structure.

The results of this corpus analysis show that about 90% of Contrasts have coordinating QUD structure and about 90% of Concessions have subordinating QUD structure. Closer examination of all corpus examples of those 10% of Contrasts and Concessions not conforming to the theoretically expected QUD structure reveals factors relevant to proper Contrast/Concession analysis neither covered by the general-purpose guidelines used by us, Riester et al. (2018), or the analyses by Büring (2003) or Brunetti et al. (2021). (i) Modeling the given-new distinction in QUD discourse structures is done by restricting topics through introduction of subordinate QUDs. This can lead to apparent subordinating Contrasts where the given-new distinction takes precedence over considerations necessary for Contrast. (ii) Expectations necessary for denial of expectations are not modeled into QUD trees because they have no explicit correspondence in the annotated text, but these expectations are needed in the analysis. (iii) Hypotheticals and counterfactuals can lead to apparent coordinating Concessions. Similar to expectations, hypotheticals and counterfactuals rely on implicit information not represented in QUD trees because they have no explicit correspondence in the annotated text.

We will approach the question of Contrast and Concession's internal relational structure by first looking at the theoretical background and then going into corpus analysis. In the theoretical background, we will define the terms semantic-opposition Contrast and denial-of-expectation Concession, and introduce Question under Discussion (QUD), QUD approaches to Contrast (Büring, 2003; Jasinskaja & Zeevat, 2008; Jasinskaja, 2012) and Concession (Brunetti et al., 2021). Before we go into corpus analysis, we will give a brief overview of the QUD annotation guidelines by Riester et al. (2018) and our own guidelines, an extension of Riester et al. (2018), followed by an overview of the corpus. The results of our corpus analysis will be discussed in two parts: (a) Corpus cases of Contrast and Concession conforming with theoretically expected QUD structures. (b) Corpus cases of Contrast and Concession *not* conforming with the theorized QUD structures. The exceptional cases in (b) will be discussed in more detail, highlighting the aspects missing in current QUD analyses.

2 Theoretical background

2.1 Contrast

There are many definitions of Contrast in the literature. For our purposes, the important assumption in definitions of Contrast is that Contrast is a multi-nucleus discourse relation (König, 1983; Mann & Thompson, 1988; Asher & Lascarides, 1998), i.e. that the contrasted discourse constituents stand in a coordinated discourse structure to one another. The definition of Contrast by Asher & Lascarides (2003); Asher & Vieu (2005) is a very general definition which captures the basic intuition.

> **Definition of Contrast (Asher & Lascarides, 2003)**
> Contrast is the emphasis of dissimilarity between discourse units whose content is "opposite" in some respect, and is typically marked by the connective *but*.

Asher & Lascarides' (2003) definition of contrast applies to cases of semantic opposition as in (1), where there are two contrasting topics, *John* and *Bill*, and two contrasting foci, the antonyms *tall* and *short*:

(1) John is tall, but Bill is short. (Lakoff, 1971) *semantic opposition*

Besides antonymic contrasts such as in (1), some researchers such as Lakoff (1971), Malchukov (2004), and Jasinskaja & Zeevat (2008) recognise other types of Contrast:

(2) a. This ring is beautiful, but expensive. *counter-argument*
        (Jasinskaja & Zeevat, 2008)
     b. John started to run, but fell.   *prevention/cancellation*
        (Malchukov, 2004)

(2a) has two contrasting foci *beautiful* and *expensive*, both of which relate to the shared topic *ring*. Also, *beautiful* and *expensive* are not antonyms like *tall* and *short* in (1), but are in semantic opposition in the sense that ring aesthetics and price are two aspects of evaluating the quality of a ring. (2b) has two contrasting foci, two events, a *starting-to-run* event and a *falling* event. Running and falling are not antonyms, but they are in semantic opposition in the sense that one prevents the other. In this work we adopt a definition of semantic-opposition Contrast which includes the cases in (1) and (2).

A common test for contrastiveness is accessibility for anaphoric reference due to an obligatory shared topic. In (2a), for instance, both *beautiful* and *expensive* refer to the ring. In (2b), we could have an anaphoric pronoun in the *but*-clause, *John started to run, but he fell*, which would refer back to *John*. Sometimes the term Contrast is restricted to cases where we have both alternating focus constituents and contrasting topics as in (1), but for the present paper we do include cases with alternating focus constituents and common topic under the term Contrast.

Our main focus in this paper is on the coordination between the two clauses: *p, but q*. Because of this coordination it is commonly assumed that Contrast is a multi-nucleus discourse relation (König, 1983; Mann & Thompson, 1988; Keller, 1995; Zeevat, 2011). In example (1), we are contrasting John and Bill's height, applying the same standard to both of them for deciding if their actual height warrants the attributions *tall* or *short*. This semantic opposition is a pairwise contrast (two contrastive topics, two contrastive foci). In (2a), we are contrasting two criteria of evaluating the ring: its aesthetics versus its price (two contrastive foci of the the common topic "ring"). In (2b), we are contrasting two events or state of affair: a running event and a falling event. In each case, the two contrasting things are weighed against each other with each thing being equally important, which gives rise to the intuition they are coordinated nucleus-nucleus discourse units rather than subordinated nucleus-satellite constructions.

Although it is common in the literature to discuss short examples of Contrast such as those in (1) and (2), it is important to note that the contrasting discourse units can also be multiple propositions relating to the same topic, chunks of text, paragraphs, and larger units. Definitions of Contrast are deliberately vague in this respect. For our corpus analysis, we limit ourselves to single-sentence contrasts and contrastive parallel sentences, but exclude contrasts on larger discourse levels in order to keep categorisation and analysis tractable. We also limit ourselves to contrasts with explicit discourse markers, and thus exclude implicit contrasts.

There are also differences in the literature with respect to the terms Contrast and Concession: (i) In discussing Concession, the term "contrast" is often used to describe the relation between the implicit assumption being denied and the explicit proposition giving rise to the implicit assumption. In this paper, we use the term "Contrast" exclusively for semantic-opposition-type nucleus-nucleus rhetorical relations. "Contrast" is also the term used in RST for semantic-opposition Contrast. (ii) Some researchers such as Lakoff (1971) call denial-of-expectation-type relations Contrast (e.g., *John is tall, but he's no good at basketball*), while others such as Crevels (2000) classify them as Concession. For the purposes of this paper, we take the question whether the relation is nucleus-nucleus or nucleus-satellite to be of primary importance. At the same time, all of our corpus examples of denial of expectation are clearly nucleus-satellite relations (with either anaphoric or cataphoric QUD embedding). We therefore classify all denial-of-expectation corpus examples as Concessions. We thus refrain from using the term "Contrast" there, and instead only use "Contrast" to mean a semantic-opposition coordinating nucleus-nucleus discourse relation.

2.2 Concession

Concession is a discourse relation closely related to Contrast. The assumption is that while Contrast contrasts two propositions of equal rhetorical importance, i.e. that Contrast is a nucleus-nucleus rhetorical relations, Concession is a nucleus-satellite rhetorical relation, where the concessive proposition is of secondary importance to the nucleus proposition. Here we give a definition in our own words, but similar definitions can be found in the literature (cf. Mann & Thompson, 1988; König, 1983):

> **Definition of Concession**
> Concession is a discourse relation between two propositions. One of the two is presented as unexpected (contraexpectation, mirativity) with respect to the other (*We are going for a walk* is unexpected given *It is raining*). The unexpected proposition is then called the concession and is the satellite to the non-concessive nucleus. Markers include *although, even (though), yet, nevertheless,* and certain senses of *but* and *while*.

The important assumption in definitions of Concession for the present paper is that the concessive element stands in a nucleus-satellite discourse relation to its antecedent, where the Concession is the satellite and the antecedent is the nucleus (König, 1983; Mann & Thompson, 1988; Zeevat, 2011). Contrary to Contrast, Concession is thus assumed to have a subordinating discourse structure. Important for us in the present paper is whether a denial of expectation leads to a subordinating or coordinating relationship between the contrasting elements. In this paper we want to probe the assumed analogy between rhetorical structure and contrasthood or concessionhood. To this end we use established QUD annotation guidelines (Riester et al., 2018), which—importantly—, unlike Rhetorical Structure Theory (RST), are not specifically designed for annotation of Contrast and Concession, but which feature coordinating QUD/focus structures and subordinating QUD structures. We identify Contrasts and Concessions based on 24 discourse markers and look at whether semantic-opposition Contrasts have coordinating QUD structure and whether denial-of-expectation Concessions have subordinating QUD structure.

Views differ on how denial of expectation is computed: whether *although p, q* implicates a presupposition *if p, then normally ¬q'* (Haspelmath & König, 1998;

König & Siemund, 2000) or whether *although p, q* raises a scalar implicature, where *p* and alternative *p*'s form a set of alternatives and *q* eliminates alternatives (Bennet, 1982; Lycan, 1991).

We will not go into a discussion of the merits of the individual approaches to denial-of-expectation computation, but we draw the reader's attention to this to show that much research effort has been spent on solidifying the assumption that denial of expectation requires more elaborate pragmatic machinery than "simple" Contrast. In the present paper we test this assumption of a fundamental difference between Contrast and Concession by looking at the discourse structure in Contrast and Concession, specifically whether it is coordinating (Contrast-like) or subordinating (Concession-like).

It is also important to point out that Concession markers can have language-specific semantics. For instance, the relation between the two concessively contrasting elements can be causal or additive (Jasinskaja, 2010) but need not be (Pander Maat, 1998). It can also take the form of a corrective Elaboration (Jasinskaja, 2013). German *doch* (roughly English *yet, however, although*) is such a special marker which raises a presupposition which the constituent marked by *doch* denies. Certain discourse markers are also typical markers of Concession (e.g., *although* in English). Some markers are dedicated Contrast and Concession markers while other markers can mark both. For the purposes of our corpus analysis, we therefore tallied Contrast and Concession uses of common German discourse markers. Like English *although*, some of these German markers turn out to be Concession or Contrast markers. Other German markers turn out to be ambiguous, i.e. can be used to mark both Contrast and Concession.

Similar to how definitions of Contrasts allow for the contrasting discourse units to be more complex than propositions, Crevels (2000) recognises four levels of Concession, i.e. a concessive relation between discourse units at four different discourse levels illustrated by the examples in (3).

(3) a. Although it is raining, we're going for a walk.   *content concession*
   b. He's not at home, although his car is parked in front *epistemic concession*
      of the house.
   c. Even though I am calling a bit late, what are your *speech act concession*
      plans this evening?
   d. I speak and write Serbian, Albanian, Turkish and *text level (revision)*
      Dutch, but I cannot express my true feelings in any
      other language than Romani. Although, now that I
      come to think of it, I have done it many times.

On Crevels' (2000) view, the size of discourse units p and q which stand in a concessive *although p, q* relationship to one another increases as follows: content < epistemic < speech act < text.[1] We give Crevels' examples in (3) in order to illustrate that Concession can happen on different levels of syntactic complexity. Similar views are found in Rhetorical Structure Theory (RST), for instance, which distinguishes different classes of discourse relations (semantic, pragmatic, textual, cf. Stede et al., 2017).

2.3 Question under Discussion

In order to investigate the theoretical claim that one of the differences between Contrast and Concession is that Contrast is a multi-nucleus relation with coordinating discourse structure and Concession is a nucleus-satellite relation with subordinating structure, we use texts from the QUDGen corpus annotated for discourse structure using Question under Discussion (Amaral et al., 2007; Roberts et al., 2009; Simons et al., 2010; Beaver et al., 2017):

Definition of Question under Discussion (QUD)
Question under Discussion is the "main point" or central discourse topic phrased as an interrogative to which the discourse serves as an answer.

QUD-based approaches (Klein & Von Stutterheim, 1987; van Kuppevelt, 1995, 1996; Roberts, 1996, 2012) assume that discourse should be analysed as complex answers to implicit or explicit questions (the QUD) – an assumption which goes at least as far back as Carlson (1983). The QUD is meant as a formulation of informational demands of the intended addressee of the discourse. On this view, complex discourse consists of a sequence of information units which incrementally and cumulatively address the central discourse topic. Therefore, individual informational discourse units are in and of themselves seen as answers to implicit questions which partially answer the discourse QUD. Since the answers to these partial QUDs add up to answer the overall discourse QUD, QUD-based theories take partial QUDs to be subordinated to the overall discourse QUD in tree-like hierarchical structures. This allows information to percolate from answers to these sub-QUDs upwards in the tree to aggregate as an answer to the overall discourse QUD.

---

1 We use Crevels' terminology here verbatim. However, it is, of course, noteworthy that Crevels' use of the term "epistemic" here might be debatable. The term "epistemic" refers to beliefs, which are implicit. Crevels seems to be identifying explicit discourse units as beliefs. At the same time, what the parked car means is an epistemic question.

QUD trees model discourse coherence as a hierarchy of QUDs and sub-QUDs, where sub-QUDs speak to the same topic as their super-QUDs. In QUD-terms, discourse is coherent when individual pieces of information answer QUDs which relate to the same overarching discourse topic. Depending on where QUDs are located within trees in terms of depth, they contain discourse topics or assertive topics (cf. Stalnaker, 1978): discourse topic when they are higher in the tree, assertive topics when they are lower, i.e. on the level of individual assertions. Focus constituents are answers to QUDs (Rooth, 1985, 1992; Krifka & Musan, 2012). We can also conceptualise QUDs as introducing unfilled discourse variables whose value is provided by focus constituents in their answers.[2] Question under Discussion is now firmly established as an explanatory concept in the theory of information structure.

Three QUD-approaches are of particular interest to us here: (i) Büring's (2003) approach to contrastive topics and contrastive focus, (ii) QUD-trees a la Riester and colleagues (2018, 2019) as a model of discourse structure, and (iii) Jasinskaja's QUD approach to Contrast of the semantic-opposition kind (Jasinskaja & Zeevat, 2008; Jasinskaja, 2012).

2.3.1 QUD approach to contrast by Büring

Büring (1997, 2003) uses QUD-tree structures as a model of contrastive topic and contrastive focus. For illustration consider example (1), repeated here as (1a), which features both contrastive topics and contrastive focus:

(1) a. John is tall, but Bill is short.

The Contrast in example (1) is twofold: (i) The two topics *John* and *Bill* of the two propositions contrast with one another, and (ii) the two foci *tall* and *short* contrast with one another. According to QUD-based theories, topics are part of QUDs, in this case, *John* and *Bill*. Analogously, the two foci *tall* and *short* are answers to QUDs. *Tall* answers the QUD *How tall is John?*, and *short* answers the QUD *How tall is Bill?* However, we also need a QUD which elicits the set of persons whose height we are inquiring about. We thus need to nest the two QUDs *How tall is John?* and *How tall is Bill?* under a QUD *Who is how tall?* so that because of subordination in this tree structure the *who*-part of the discourse QUD is answered before the *how*-part. *Tall* and *short* are antonyms. John and Bill's height is measured; there is some

---

2 This is somewhat reminiscent of the focus-presupposition distinction and the notion of open presupposition in Prince (1992).

arbitrary height below which using the term *short* is appropriate and above which the term *tall* is appropriate. The Contrast in (1) thus allows an antonymic reading and a scalar reading.

Representing a QUD tree as a tree graph with QUDs and answers as nodes and edges showing dependency is common practice (see 1b). Riester et al. (2018) offer an alternative representation (see 1b) using indentation for subordination, which we will employ in this paper for space-saving reasons in long corpus examples. In the indentation style, QUDs and answers are represented as individual lines. Line indentation and QUD/answer indexing shows dependency (e.g., $A_{0.2}$ is the answer to QUD $Q_{0.2}$, and $Q_{0.1}$ and $Q_{0.2}$ are sub-QUDs to Q_0).

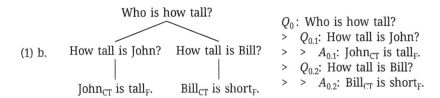

(1) b.

Q_0 : Who is how tall?
\> $Q_{0.1}$: How tall is John?
\> \> $A_{0.1}$: John$_{CT}$ is tall$_F$.
\> $Q_{0.2}$: How tall is Bill?
\> \> $A_{0.2}$: Bill$_{CT}$ is short$_F$.

Since many of the corpus examples we give in this paper are rather long, we will mostly opt for the indentation mode of QUD trees.

2.3.2 QUD approach to contrast by Jasinskaja

Recall that in the QUD tree of example (1) according to Büring (2003) the topics *John* and *Bill*, which are part of the sub-QUDs *How tall is John?* and *How tall is Bill?*, are targeted in the super-QUD *Who is how tall?* The super-QUD is a two-fold QUD, two-fold because it contains two wh-questions: *Who are we talking about?* and *How tall are they?* Jasinskaja & Zeevat (2008) and Jasinskaja (2012) combine this idea of a two-fold QUD with Umbach's (2004) proposal that Contrast marks a CONFIRM-DENY discourse relation. The result is a special double-question: one a wh-question, the other a binary "whether something is the case" question. Applied to example (1), repeated here,

(1) John is tall, but Bill is short. (Lakoff, 1971)

Jasinskaja and colleagues would argue there are two questions being answered: *Whether x is tall?* and *How tall is x?* The foci *tall* and *short* answer the *How tall is x?* question, where we fill in *John* and *Bill* for and receive a height *tall* and *short*, respectively. With respect to the whether-question, *John is tall* confirms that John's height is great enough—relative to some threshold—to qualify as tall. Analogously, *Bill is short* denies that—relative to the same height threshold—Bill's height justifies the use of *tall*. Whether the terms *tall* and *short* are appropriate depends on how tall *John* and *Bill* are. So the *how-* and *whether*-question are answered together. The important insight that Jasinskaja & Zeevat (2008) and Jasinskaja (2012) take on from Umbach is that Contrast comes from John and Bill's height being measured against the same threshold.

Jasinskaja et al.'s approach models Contrast with semantic opposition, however in the car and motorcycle reviews in our QUDGen corpus we find many more non-semantic opposition cases of Contrast. In semantic-opposition cases of Contrast the standard of comparison is often a measurement scale, e.g., in (1) the standard of comparison is physical height. Based on our corpus we can say that in non-semantic-opposition cases of Contrast, the standard of comparison takes on an argumentative nature. In the next section we describe our approach to annotating QUD trees in the QUDGen corpus.

2.3.3 QUD approach to concession by Brunetti

Brunetti et al. (2021) point out that when QUD trees are used in modeling Concession relations, and the concessive satellite is subordinated to the non-concessive nucleus, there are two possible QUD structures of subordination: The sub-QUD of the concessive satellite can be (i) cataphoric or (ii) anaphoric. The concessive satellite in (4a) and (4b) recieves its own sub-QUD Q_2. Q_1 in (4a) and (4b) is super-ordinated to both the nucleus answer and the concession. Hence, the satellite's QUD is a sub-QUD to the nucleus' QUD, thereby signifying in tree structure that the satellite is subordinate to the nucleus. However, depending on the linear order of nucleus and satellite, the Concession's sub-QUD can be anaphoric or cataphoric.

When the satellite comes before the nucleus (S-N), the Concession's sub-QUD, Q_2, is a cataphoric sub-QUD as in (4a):

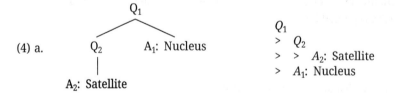

(4) a.

When the satellite comes after the nucleus (N-S), the Concession's sub-QUD, Q_2, is an anaphoric sub-QUD as in (4b):

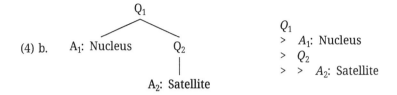

(4) b.

In this paper, we want to test whether the concessive part has its own QUD, and examine exceptional cases. We are interested in Concessions which have a subordinating rhetorical relation (either anaphoric with nucleus-satellite order or cataphoric with satellite-nucleus order) but which do not have subordinating QUD structure. In our corpus analysis we count both anaphoric N-S and cataphoric S-N Concessions as subordinating QUD structure without distinguishing them. Instead, our focus in this paper is on discussing corpus examples from our QUDGen corpus which feature Concessions which apparently have coordinated rather than subordinated QUD structure. In discussing these exceptional cases we highlight how other factors influence QUD structure with respect to coordinating versus subordinating structures, in particular, two factors: (i) the given-new distinction and (ii) the representation of background knowledge and expectations in QUD tree structure.

The given-new distinction drives subordination such that new information answers a sub-QUD to the super-QUD of given information. Although given-new leads to subordinating QUD structure, it can interfere with nucleus-satellite relational subordination in interesting ways, which we will discuss in Section 4.

2.3.4 QUD-trees a la Riester

Riester and colleagues (2018) use QUD trees as a model of focus structure. On their view, the given/new distinction in information structures drives QUD formulation: Given information is part of QUDs; new information, on the other hand, forms focus constituents in answers to QUDs (cf. Büring, 2008). In hierarchical QUD trees information which is new, focused information in sub-QUDs can perculate upwards in the tree as given information in super-QUDs higher up in the tree. QUDs speaking to more general argumentative points are higher in the tree, while less general ones are lower in the tree. This makes sense since we want concrete discourse arguments to derive from more general ones, all of which collectively speak towards the central discourse topic. We can see abstraction[3] at work in the QUD tree we gave for example (1): the two sub-QUDs *How tall is John?* and *How tall is Bill?* presuppose

---

[3] We take "abstraction" to be the inverse of topic restriction.

that we know that we are inquiring about John and Bill's height. Their super-QUD *Who is how tall?* is thus more general and more abstract than the two sub-QUDs because the *who*-part of the QUD has not been answered yet. In the sub-QUDs *How tall is John?* and *How tall is Bill?* the *who*-part of the super-QUD has been answered and is thus given information.

Riester et al. (2018) propose a number of constraints on QUD annotation on the basis of focus structure, i.e. analysing discourse structure in terms of given information and new information:

– QUDs must be answerable by the proposition(s) that they immediately dominate.
– QUDs make reference to the immediate preceding discourse, i.e. they consist of given/salient material.
– Therefore, QUDs must be located as high in the QUD tree as possible.[4]

The following example from the QUDGen corpus shows abstraction, the given/new distinction, and the constraints by Riester et al. (2018) at work in argumentative QUDs:

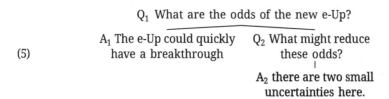

(5)

Q_1 What are the odds of the new e-Up?

A_1 The e-Up could quickly have a breakthrough

Q_2 What might reduce these odds?

A_2 there are two small uncertainties here.

In RST terms we might argue that A_2 is an Elaboration on A_1. The QUD approach shows that A_1 and A_2 answer a common topic: the car's chances of success. In the RST analysis it would be ambiguous what we are elaborating on: the *breakthrough* or the car in general. Answer A_1 introduces the car's potential breakthrough and also limits the probability of this breakthrough with the modal *could*. A_1 feeds into Q_2 (in the sense of van Kuppevelt, 1995) as Q_2 extends on the *odds*-topic introduced in Q_1 or, to put it differently, by following up on the limitation introduced by A_1: The fact that we are talking about the odds of a breakthrough needs to be established as given information before we can ask what reduces these odds. Therefore, Q_2 is more concrete than Q_1, but because Q_2 extends on the topic of Q_1, Q_2 must necessarily be subordinate to Q_1.

Oftentimes Contrast and Concession relations rely on background knowledge or expectations. However, background knowledge and expectations are often not made explicit in texts but are pragmatically inferred. QUD tree annotation, on the

---

4 This is not a principle in Riester et al. (2018) but it follows from them.

other hand, is commonly used for annotation of discourse structure. However, this poses the fundamental question if and how information such as background information and expectations should be modeled in QUD trees when they have no overt corollary in the given text. Proposing that they should be part of QUD trees would open up a host of new issues as to what QUD trees are actually meant to model (discourse structure, rhetorical relations, pragmatic inference such as presuppositions and implicature derivation, to name a few). In this paper, our aim is not to settle the debate what should be incorporated into QUD trees or not. Instead, we focus on highlighting natural language corpus examples of Contrast and Concession which contradict current QUD approaches with respect to coordinating and subordinating tree structure, and we discuss what specific factors might be causing them to contradict current theory. Before we get to corpus examples, we will introduce the QUDGen corpus, QUD annotation guidelines, and criteria for identifying Contrast and Concession examples.

3 The QUDGen corpus and QUD annotation

The corpus analysis of Contrast and Concession we discuss in this paper uses our own corpus, the QUDGen corpus (Hesse et al., 2022), which contains 30 car and motorcycle reviews annotated with QUD trees according to annotation guidelines by Riester et al. (2019) and our own extensions. Individual texts come from the German newspapers FAZ (Frankfurter Allgemeine Zeitung) and Welt, and are, on average, about 720 words in length. The corpus is available here: github.com/christoph-hesse/question-under-discussion. Each text was annotated at least twice. Final QUD structures were negotiated as a compromise between annotators.

We extended on the annotation guidelines by Riester and colleagues by combining top-down (starting from annotations of larger text units through subdividing to smaller units) and bottom-up (starting from focus structure) annotation. The approach by Riester and colleagues focuses on annotating congruent QUDs which reflect a text's focus structure (Kuthy et al., 2018; Riester et al., 2018; Riester, 2019). Top-down annotation, on the other hand, is focused on annotating discourse QUDs which reflect speaker goals and discourse goals (Onea, 2019; Roberts, 1996, 2012). Since speakers and discourse goals tend to be very broad while focus structure is highly detailed and constrained by syntax, the main challenge during annotation was bridging the gap between the top-down and bottom-up view. Bridging was achieved through QUDs in the tree structures which reflect argument structure under the assumption that coherent discourse structures information in order to achieve broad discourse goals (cf. Klein & von Stutterheim, 1987; van Kuppevelt, 1995; Roberts, 1996; Ginzburg, 1996; von Stutterheim, 1997).

Important for the present paper is that annotation was led by a thorough analysis of focus structure, as laid out in Riester et al. (2018). Semantic-opposition Contrast and Concession *did not* receive special annotation *because* they were identified as Contrast and Concession, but because their coordinating or subordinating QUD structure arose from focus structure and the rules of QUD formulation laid out by Riester and colleagues. Since these annotation guidelines were not specifically tailored to the analysis of semantic-opposition Contrast and Concession, what we are testing with the corpus analysis in the present paper is whether Contrast will have the expected coordinating QUD/focus structure, and whether Concession will have the expected subordinating QUD structure. In our discussion of corpus examples we will specifically focus on counterexamples to theoretical expectations because we think they highlight (i) the role of the topic restriction inherent in subordinating QUDs for modeling the distinction between given and new information, and (ii) if and where expectations necessary for denial-of-expectation Concessions should be incorporated into QUD trees.

Inter-annotator agreement of focus constituents and topic constituents (i.e. referential expressions within the background[5]) show that annotations do not differ significantly from other annotations of information structures found in the literature. Table 1 gives the inter-annotator agreement concerning focus structure and topic structure in the QUDGen corpus using two metrics: Fleiss' κ and Krippendorf's α.

Table 1: Inter-annotator agreement on focus structure and topic structure in the QUDGen corpus.

	κ	α
Focus	0.40	0.70
Topic	0.30	0.65

Note that coefficients of topic structure do not reflect different topic types. For comparison with other annotation studies on information structure, it is important to point out that syntactic complexity of single sentences greatly affects the coef-

---

5 Texts in the QUDGen corpus commonly features backgrounds which only contain topical referential expressions. So for the purposes of this paper, we use the terms "topic" and "background" interchangeable.

ficients. For example, De Kuthy et al. (2015) annotated focus structure in German question-answer pairs from the CREG-1032 learner corpus and the QUIS corpus, both of which elicited question-answer pairs in a controlled manner. Both the CREG corpus and the QUIS corpus feature significantly lower syntactic complexity of individual sentences than our QUDGen corpus (κ = 0.75 for focus in CREG, and κ = 0.87 in QUIS). In the annotation study by Ritz et al. (2008) κ values for both focus and topic annotations are given. The data in Ritz et al. (2008) are question-answer pairs, two dialogues, and texts from the Potsdam Commentary Corpus (PCC) with the texts from the PCC being syntactically more complex than the question-answer pairs and dialogues. The κ values for topic and focus structures in question-answer pairs are 0.75 and 0.51, respectively, 0.51 and 0.44 in dialogues, and 0.44 and 0.19 in the PCC texts.

For the purposes of corpus analysis, we use a list of 24 German discourse markers which are known to mark semantic-opposition Contrast and denial-of-expectation Concession to identify Contrast and Concession examples lexically (see Table 2). We use the semantic-opposition-based definition of Contrast by Asher & Lascarides (2003): Contrast is the emphasis of dissimilarity between discourse units whose content is "opposite" in some respect. We also make the assumption that contrastive topics relate to the same super-topic. For instance, in *The front seats are excellent, but if you have to sit in the back, the little leg room typical for this class is disappointing* (taken from the corpus), the two contrastive topics, front seats and back seats, relate to the same super-topic of car seats. For the corpus analysis, we define Concession as a discourse relation between two propositions. One of the two is presented as unexpected with respect to the other. We recognise two degrees of unexpectedness: denial of expectation and implication of something unexpected. Similar to Contrasts, the contrastive topics in Concessions must relate to the same super-topic. The distinction between Contrast and Concession is made based on unexpectedness being involved or not (or lexically based on discourse markers, when they are unambiguous Contrast/ Concession markers). Apart from Concession, there are other discourse-structural causes for subordinating QUD structure: (i) Syntactically subordinating clauses receive their own sub-QUD due to topic restriction (e.g., *Jane talked to Mary who she trusts*). (ii) Evaluative statements modifying assertions receive sub-QUDs (e.g., The new engine comes with a much appreciated 400 horsepowers). We begin our corpus analysis with a general overview of Contrast and Concession uses in the next section.

Table 2: Number of corpus occurrences of 24 different German contrast and concession markers.

Marker	Contr.	Conc.	Marker	Contr.	Conc.
aber (but)	41	25	jedoch (however, although)	4	–
doch (still, after all, yet)	19	8	stattdessen (instead, rather)	4	–
allerdings (however, although)	8	2	im Gegensatz zu (contrary to)	3	–
dennoch (nevertheless)	5	3	dann aber/doch (yet again)	2	–
immerhin (at least, even)	6	1	eher (rather)	2	–
trotzdem (however)	4	2	trotz (despite)	2	–
statt (instead)	3	1	zwar/aber/(je)doch (yet)	2	–
wobei (however, whereat)	1	3	einerseits/andererseits	1	–
obwohl (although)	1	2	(on the one hand/other hand)		
sondern (but)	14	–	im Unterschied dazu (contrary to)	1	–
dagegen (against, however)	9	–	indes (however, meanwhile)	1	–
(doch) während (yet, while)	7	–	sonst (else, otherwise)	–	1
dafür (instead)	6	–			
				146(75%)	48(25%)

4 Contrast and concession in the corpus

One possible avenue towards a unified QUD-view of Contrast and Concession would be to assume the following hypothesis:

Contrasts have coordinating QUD tree structures,
Concessions subordinating QUD tree structure.

It is common in the literature on Contrast and Concession to identify examples through their discourse markers. At the same time, it is a well-known fact that some discourse markers such as English *but* can be markers of both Contrast and Concession. Therefore, a first step in our corpus analysis was to look at a variety of German Contrast and Concession markers and to see which of them are unambiguous markers of Contrast and Concession, and which can be used in both. In the end we looked at 24 discourse markers (not counting stacked markers because they are combinations of the 24 markers[6]) listed in Table 2. In total we found 146 lexically marked occurrences of Contrast in the corpus, and 48 occurrences of Concession. Contrasts are identified as discourse units in semantic opposition to one another and relating to a shared topic. Concessions are iden-

---

6 Since there was only a handful of these stacked markers, we excluded them for the purposes of this paper.

tified as one discourse unit raising expectations which the concessive discourse unit denies/contradicts. When unambiguous Contrast and Concession markers are used, we also rely on the markers to identify the example in question. Some discourse markers among the 24 appeared quite often (e.g., *aber*, 'but', appeared 41 times in Contrasts and 25 times in Concessions), while others only appeared once (e.g., *sonst*, 'else', 'otherwise'). We found most markers are ambiguous (77%, 150/194). English *but*, a well-known marker of both Contrast and Concession, has two German equivalents *aber* and *sondern*. Interestingly, *sondern* appears 14 times in our corpus and always as a marker of Contrast. *Aber*, on the other hand, is an ambiguous marker of both Contrast (41 times in the corpus) and Concession (25 times). Table 3 lists the ambiguous markers *aber* through *obwohl* 'although' in descending frequency. The markers thereafter are unambiguous, at least in our corpus.

Let's look at the ambiguous markers next. About two thirds of the time, ambiguous markers are used in Contrasts, one third of the time in Concessions.

Table 3: Contrast:concession ratio among ambiguous markers.

Marker	Contrast	Concession	Binomial (all %)		
			Prob	Lower	Upper
aber	41(62%)	25(38%)	62	49.3	73.8
doch	19(70%)	8(30%)	70	49.8	86.3
allerdings	8(80%)	2(20%)	80	44.4	97.5
dennoch	5(63%)	3(37%)	63	24.5	91.5
immerhin	6(86%)	1(14%)	86	42.1	99.6
trotzdem	4(67%)	2(33%)	67	22.3	95.7
statt	3(75%)	1(25%)	75	19.4	99.4
wobei	1(25%)	3(75%)	25	00.6	80.6
obwohl	1(33%)	2(67%)	33	00.8	90.6
	88(65%)	47(35%)			

Table 3 shows the ratio of the ambiguous markers being used in Contrast versus Concession. Overall, we see 88 Contrast uses versus 47 Concession uses, about a 2:1 ratio. Given enough corpus occurrences, we can use a binomial test (H_0: Ratio is the same for all lexical items; result: H_0 cannot be rejected) to estimate lower and upper 95% confidence intervals on the Contrast:Concession ratio on a per-marker basis (the success probability estimated by the binomial test is the percentage of Contrast uses per marker). For *aber* with 41:25, the confidence interval falls between

49.3% and 73.8% Contrast uses of *aber*. For *doch*,[7] *allerdings, dennoch, immerhin,* and *trotzdem* we find similar confidence intervals. Of course, the lower the token count the less reliable confidence estimates will be. Nevertheless, per-marker Contrast:Concession ratios follow the overall ratio of 2:1. Recall that with all markers, ambiguous and unambiguous, the ratio between Contrast:Concession was 146:48 (about 3:1). The Contrast:Concession ratio for ambiguous marker thus goes in the same direction as the overall ratio with unambiguous markers included. We conclude that (i) ambiguous Contrast/Concession markers are truly ambiguous, (ii) that the 2:1 ratio in ambiguous marker use is due to there being three times as many Contrasts (146) as Concessions (48) in the corpus. So it does not seem like ambiguous markers have a tendency either way.

Table 4: Breakdown of Contrast & Concession relations by QUD structure: coordination (parallel foci or QUDs) or subordination.

Marker	Contrast		Concession	
	Coord	Subord	Coord	Subord
aber	41	–	–	25
doch	17(90%)	2(10%)	3(37%)	5(63%)
allerdings	6(75%)	2(25%)	–	2
dennoch	4(80%)	1(20%)	–	3
immerhin	5(83%)	1(37%)	–	1
trotzdem	2(50%)	2(50%)	–	2
statt	3	–	–	1
wobei	1	–	–	3
obwohl	1	–	1(50%)	1(50%)
	80(91%)	8(9%)	4(9%)	43(91%)

Given our hypothesis, QUD structure should help distinguish Contrast and Concession uses of the ambiguous discourse markers. For instance, the hypothesis would predict that when *aber* occurs in a coordinated QUD sub-tree, in a discourse constituent parallel to another constituent, then this should be a Contrast. On the other, when *aber* occurs in a discourse constituent whose QUD is subordinate to another QUD in a local sub-tree, then the hypothesis would predict this to be a Concession

---

7 *Doch* also has uses which are neither marking Contrast nor Concession, e.g., *Das Bild ist doch gut geworden* (That picture *doch* turned out well), where *doch* expresses strong positive valuation. Corpus example (17) below allows for this non-contrastive/non-concessive reading of *doch*, but we do not think it is the most salient reading.

use of *aber*. Table 4 shows the breakdown of coordinating QUD structures and subordinating QUD structures for Contrast and Concession uses of all ambiguous markers.

We count semantic-opposition cases of Contrast with coordinated focus constituents and add them together with the count of coordinated sub-QUDs. Similarly for subordination, we add up the counts of anaphoric and cataphoric subordination. The following overview summarises all possible coordinating and subordinating QUD structures relevant to our analysis.

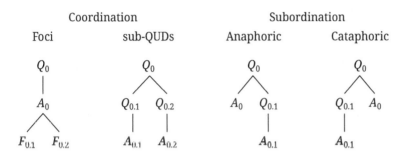

Coordination		Subordination	
Foci	sub-QUDs	Anaphoric	Cataphoric

In Table 4, a clear trend emerges: 91% (80/88) of Contrasts have coordinating focus/ QUD structure, and 91% (43/47) of Concessions have anaphorically/cataphorically subordinating QUD structures. The hypothesis seems to be on the right track. In the next three sections, we take a closer look at individual corpus examples which support the hypothesis (Section 4.1), and in particular, those 12 corpus examples which go against the hypothesis (Sections 4.2 and 4.3).

Given the length of some of the corpus examples, we simplify the indentation style used by Riester et al. (2018) even further: An answer to a QUD is not indented but displayed on the same level as its respective QUD. QUDs and answers are not indexed unless needed; hierarchy is signified primarily through indentation.

QUD tree   Riester et al.   Present paper

Q_0 Q_0 Q
$Q_{0.1}$ $Q_{0.2}$ $>$ $Q_{0.1}$ $>$ Q
$A_{0.1}$ $A_{0.2}$ $>$ $>$ $A_{0.1}$ $>$ A
                           $>$ $Q_{0.2}$ $>$ Q
                           $>$ $>$ $A_{0.2}$ $>$ A

4.1 Coordinating contrasts and subordinating concessions

In the previous section, we saw that 90% of Contrast uses of the ambiguous discourse markers *aber* through *obwohl* have, as the hypothesis predicts, coordinating QUD structure and 91% of Concession uses have, as the hypothesis predicts, subordinating QUD structure. Contrasts are primarily discussing pros and cons of vehicles and vehicle parts, and design decisions, e.g., opting for a stronger engine, but cutting costs by offering fewer drive assistant functionality, or banking on nostalgia rather than actual improvements. They fit the definition of semantic-opposition Contrast. Take the following example:

(6)   **Q$_1$:**   *How are the front seats?*
      A$_1$:   The front seats are excellent,
      Q$_2$:   *How are the back seats?*
      A$_2$:   but if you have to sit in the back, the little leg room typical for this class is disappointing.

Comfortable front seats are in contrast to uncomfortable back seats. Comfort expressed by the adjective *excellent* is the opposite of the discomfort expressed by *disappointing little leg room*, two contrastive foci. We also have two contrasting topics: the front seats versus the back seats. Both contrasting topics speak to one common super-topic: how comfortable the seats are. This is a Contrast rather than a Concession because there is no unexpectedness involved. The 91% of semantic-opposition Contrasts in the corpus have coordinated QUD structures as coordination of argumentative units, i.e. complex parallelism in the sense of (Brunetti et al., 2021, cf. Section 2.3.3).

The 91% of Concessions in the corpus, which have subordinating QUD structure, present (a) alternative evaluations, e.g., liking or disliking certain interior design choices, and (b) presenting evaluations in light of technical or regulatory limitations, e.g., size limits or emission limits, or that electric cars are required by law to have artificial engine sounds. In Crevels' (2000) terms, most of the subordinating Concessions operate on the content, epistemic, and text level.

Example (7) features a Concession with anaphoric subordination structure, i.e. the super-QUD *How is it in the case of the Versys?* is answered before the anaphoric sub-QUD *What is the driving experince like?* is answered.

(7) **Q:** *What is Kawasaki not known for?*
    A: Kawasaki is not known for tranquil "retro."
  > **Q:** *What is Kawasaki known for then?*
  > **A:** Rather, they like to go all out.
  > > **Q:** *How is it in the case of the Versys?*
  > > **A:** Fortunately, in the case of the Versys, without being excessively loud.
  > > > **Q:** *What is the driving experience like?*
  > > > **A:** <u>But</u> (Ger.: 'aber') you cannot help but put the pedal to the metal
  > > > > **Q:** *What is the result of driving fast?*
  > > > > **A:** so that the cockpit's off-the-shelf incline indicator shows values past 40 degrees.

While the Concession receives its own dedicated sub-QUD, it relates to a super-topic shared with the non-concessive part: Kawasaki is known for producing high-performance motorcycles. This is a Concession rather than a Contrast because of the unexpectedness involved: High engine performance is traditionally associated with the engine being loud. The quiet engine of the Versys thus raises the expectation that it would not be high performance. But this inference would be a mistake because the reason the engine is quieter is not that it was not high performance but that it is an electric rather than a combustion engine. Thus, the expectation raised by the quiet engine sound is denied: denial-of-expectation Concession.

In Section 2.3.3 we pointed out that Concessions can also have cataphoric subordination structure, where the sub-QUD of the satellite concession is answered before the super-QUD of the nucleus non-concession. In the QUDGen corpus, we find that 92% (40 of 43) of Concessions have anaphoric subordination QUD structure (see Table 5). We count both anaphorically and cataphorically embedding Concessions as cases of Concession in-line with the theory. In Section 4.2, we discuss corpus examples where QUD structure in Contrasts disagrees with theoretically predicted structure. In Section 4.3, we discuss corpus examples where Concessions apparently do not embed the concessive part in QUD structure.

Even though about 90% of the data support the hypothesis, the remaining 10% of data pose a challenge to the hypothesis and warrant a closer look. In the following two sections we will look at each of the subordinating Contrasts and coordinating Concessions that pose a challenge for the hypothesis.

Table 5: Breakdown of Concession relations by QUD structure: coordination (parallel foci or QUDs) or anaphoric or cataphoric subordination.

	Coord	Subord	
		Anaphoric	Cataphoric
Concession	4	40 of 43	3 of 43

4.2 Subordinating contrasts

If our working hypothesis is correct, we would expect all Contrasts to have coordinating QUD structures, i.e. (a) two foci coordinated as answers to a single QUD or (b) two sub-QUDs coordinated under a common super-QUD. The following corpus examples of subordinating Contrast go against this hypothesis. Let us discuss in more detail why they have subordinating QUD structure rather than coordinating structure. We identify three types of potential causes which make the examples in this and the next section exceptional cases: They involve hypotheticals, counterfactuals or at least a contra-expectation, or some form of explicit or implicit topic restriction.

In this section, we consider all corpus examples of semantic Contrast with sub-ordinating structure. The Contrast marker is underlined; contrastive elements are indicated using dashed underlines. The first example in (8) shows a Contrast embedded under the epistemic verb *think*:

(8)   **Q:**   *What would one think given the engine sound?*
       A: When you start the 2-liter four-cylinder gasoline engine of the Volvo S60 T4, you would think
   >   **Q:**   *What would one think given the engine sound?*
   >   **A:**   that Volvo was still (Ger.: 'doch') offering the S60 as a diesel
   >   >   **Q:**   *Why would you think it's still a diesel engine?*
   >   >   **A:**   because the turbo direct-injection engine is not quiet by a long shot.

The semantic-opposition Contrast in (8) is between what is and what is not: the Volvo has a gasoline engine and not a diesel engine. Example (8) features the verb *think*, which introduces a sub-QUD *What would one think given the engine sound?* Since our annotation guidelines are close to Riester (2019), we too tried to have leaf-node QUDs model focus structure. Special verbs such as *denken* (E.: 'think'), which for syntactic grammaticality require a *that*-clause, by virtue of their syntax, will dictate that the *that*-clause in focus structure will be subordinated to the matrix clause containing the verb *think*. We can see a good example of this in (8) where this makes it so that the *that*-clause is the clause which contains the contrastive discourse marker *doch* (E.: 'still'). The *because*-clause gives an Explanation why sound is the central point of comparison in the Contrast. The Contrast thus features subordinating QUD structure due to the verb *think* and not due to a nucleus-satellite relationship between the contrasting discourse units. This is a special case of topic restriction.

Example (9) shows a semantic-opposition Contrast between too much and too little acceleration.

(9) **Q:** *What was the acceleration of the previous model like?*
    A: We criticized the Niu moped's abrasive acceleration.
   > **Q:** *How is the acceleration different in the current model?*
   > **A:** China hear our pleading: the NGT accelerates <u>softly, almost shyly</u> at the intersection.
   > > **Q:** *How is the change in acceleration evaluated?*
   > > **A:** Excuse us, <u>but</u> (Ger.: *doch*) <u>that is a little too much restraint</u>.

The authors' wish for improved acceleration in example (9) is not shared by readers. In the previous review, the authors critiqued the abrasive acceleration. In this new model, acceleration is not abrasive anymore, but, in the authors opinion, the pendulum swung to much in the other direction. Notice that since the authors are aware that this is their personal wish, not shared by the readers, the authors have to make this private objective public by stating it explicitly before the *doch*-clause can mark the Contrast. Since the *doch*-part contains an evaluation, the QUD is *How is the change in acceleration evaluated?*, and this evaluation must be subordinate to the statement about a change in acceleration. This is another case of topic restriction: We first need to establish that there was a change in acceleration before the evaluation can reference it as given information. Notice that this makes it so that the contrastive *doch*-clause is new information, as we would expect from focus structure.

Example (10) contrasts what speaks for or against the Akropovic exhaust: it adds a certain charm but is also expensive.

(10) **Q$_1$:** *What is the most attractive extra?*
    A$_1$: The bike will <u>unfold its true charm</u> only with the
   > **Q$_{1.1}$:** *Where is the Akropovic exhaust installed?*
   > **A$_{1.1}$:** scrambler-like higher set [Akrapovic exhaust] <u>on</u> the right side of the vehicle,
    A$_1$: Akrapovic exhaust (position in German original)
   > **Q$_{1.2}$:** *How much does the Akropovic exhaust cost?*
   > **A$_{1.2}$:** which, <u>however</u> (Ger.: 'allerdings'), <u>costs an additional 1,300 euros</u>.

Example (10) is a case of semantic opposition similar to (2a) *The ring is beautiful, but expensive.* The exhaust makes the motorcycle more beautiful (gives it more charm), but it is very expensive. In example (9) we saw how evaluations, when they come after technical specifications, will be subordinate in the QUD structure. Notice that in (10) it is the other way around: we start with an evaluation (*will unfold its true charm*) and follow up with two technical specifications (where the exhaust is located, and how much it costs). At the same time it does not seem like this is a Concession because what is the expectation being denied here? That this exhaust is a must-have? That the exhaust would be an attractive purchase exactly because it is expensive (sort of as a show-off)? None of these seem appropriate. Notice that in the original German syntax, the topic referent *Akrapovic exhaust* is a focus constituent to the super QUD *What is the most attractive extra?* The *allerdings*-clause, on the other hand, is subordinated because of topic restriction: the clause specifies the price of the *Akrapovic exhaust*. Similar to (8) and (9), topic restriction and the given-new distinction take precedence over considerations of Contrast.

Example (11) features a semantic opposition Contrast between what is displayed on the digital monitor and what is not: it shows a tachometer but not other data of the onboard computer. The metonymy in the first sentence allows the *however*-clause to be an Elaboration what is not displayed: tachometer both stands for what is displayed on the digital monitor as well as for the monitor itself.

(11) Q: *What is there to say about the tachometer (on the handlebar)?*
   A: The asymmetrically mounted circular [digital] tachometer is clearly readable.
   > Q: *What is there to say about the onboard computer (which outputs speed to the tachometer)?*
   > A: The well-accessorized onboard computer, however (Ger.: 'allerdings'), does not reveal its secrets while driving, no matter how much you pay extra;
   > > Q: *What would that require?*
   > > A: that would require controlling [the onboard computer] from the handlebar,
   > > > Q: *How can you control the onboard computer from the handlebar?*
   > > > A: which is not possible.

In (11) the contrastive discourse marker *allerdings* (E.: 'however') occurs as part of a contra-Evaluation: if more data of the onboard computer could be displayed, the author's evaluation of the vehicle would be more positive. As we have seen before, Evaluation leads to subordination in QUD structure. The Contrast is between what is and what is not: One would like to have some sort of display for the onboard computer on the handlebar, but there is none. Notice that the sub-QUDs *What would that require?* and *How can you control the onboard computer from the handlebar?* in their answers have the two contrasting elements in them. What leads to the subordinating structure is the fact that the authors chose to wrap this Contrast into another evaluative statement about the option of a computer display not even being available as an extra.

Example (12) shows a semantic-opposition Contrast between what kind of turning circle you would expect the Bentley limousine to have without four-wheel drive, given its length, and its actual turning circle being much smaller. The text does not explicitly mention the limousine's length and that it could be problematic for the turning circle, but this assumption is salient given that Bentley limousines are generally known for being big.

(12) **Q:** *What should the Flying Spur's turning circle be able to do?*
      A: In order for the turning circle to <u>still</u> (Ger.: 'dennoch') conform to road conditions
      > **Q:** *What does the Flying Spur get in order for the turning circle to still conform to road conditions?*
      > **A:** the [Bentley] Flying Spur gets a four-wheel drive.

Notice that although the Contrast is between expectation and reality, there is a special twist how the engineers at Bentley managed to reduce the turning circle, the option to toggle the four-wheel. Since the discourse relation of the *four-wheel drive* statement is the reason why the turning circle is much smaller than expected, the Reason relation forces a subordinating QUD structure. The Reason relation is a type of topic restriction: the reason takes its antecedent as given information.

Example (13) features another example of topic restriction leading to an apparent subordinating Contrast. The Contrast in (13) is a case of semantic opposition between the minimum and maximum effective range. QUD subordination occurs because of the Explanation relation which explains why the maximum range is much higher than the minimum range.

(13) **Q:**   *What is the battery capacity?*
    A: According to Harley, the 15.5 kWh lithium-ion battery
  >   **Q_1:**   *What battery range is possible cross-country?*
  >   **A_1:**   provides a range of <u>roughly 150 kilometers</u> in cross-country use (lit.: "mixed use");
  >   **Q_2:**   *What battery range is possible in cities?*
  >   **A_2:**   in cities,
  > >   **Q:**   *What is beneficial to the battery while driving in cities?*
  > >   **A:**   where stop-and-go allows for lots of recuperation,
  > > >   **Q:**   *What range is possible because of recuperation?*
  > > >   **A:**   <u>even</u> (Ger.: 'immerhin') <u>roughly 230 [kilometers]</u>.

The effective range of electric vehicles depends on many factors, among them driving speed and conditions. Example (13) gives an estimate of the effective range by giving a minimum and a maximum range. The topic restriction occurs when, similar to example (12), a Reason relation is added to the statement of the maximum range. The Reason relation explains, from an engineering perspective, why stop-and-go in cities allows to intermittently recharge the battery. Since the Reason relation takes *in cities* as given information, the statement of the maximum range ends up being subordinated although the Contrast is between minimum and maximum effective range.

The semantic opposition Contrast in example (14) is between what would drive up the price (elaborate manufacturing process) and whether the price is as high as one would expect. (14) is similar to (2a) *The ring is beautiful, but expensive*: 'Manufactoring is complicated (and this should drive up the price), but a reasonable price is achievable.'

(14) **Q_1:**   *How does the design Al-c-Cf (of the aluminum model compared to the carbon-fiber model)?*
    A_1:   The aluminum model almost looks exactly like the carbon-fiver model,
    Q_2:   *What is the manufacturing process Al-c-Cf like?*
    A_2:   despite <u>the manufacturing process being more complicated</u>, as BMC emphasizes, because of all the steps involved and the limitations in possible shapes. Still, all of this does not make finesse impossible: the lower bar of the bike frame is one piece.
  >   (expectation raised by *despite*-clause: manufacturing cost drives up prices)
  >   **Q:**   *What is the price Al-c-Cf despite more complicated manufacturing?*
  >   **A:**   <u>Nonetheless</u> (Ger.: 'trotzdem'), <u>prices are achievable</u>, if you can even say that in this price range.

Example (14) has an apparent subordinating Contrast because of topic restriction. Similar to (10), price statements are given dedicated sub-QUDs on the assumption that what is being priced here is given information at that point. Topic restriction interferes in this way despite the complication that this example also involves a denial of expectation: The complexity and manufacturing costs of aluminum and carbon-fibre frames are compared, and of course, higher manufacturing cost affects the total price of the vehicle, but notice that the reason of embedding the *trotzdem*-clause remains topic restriction, not denial of expectation.

(15) is another example of an explanation leading to a subordinating QUD.

(15) **Q₁:** *What is missing from the three-wheeler?*
    A₁: No, we don't mean the left back-wheel. We're missing the handbrake on the handlebar next to the acceleration.
    >   **Q:** *What do two-wheel drivers expect? (Explicit expectation)*
    >   **A:** Who's used to two-wheelers, wants to pull the handbrake, *but* grasps at nothing.
    Q₂: *What alternative brake is there?*
    A₂: Instead, there's a foot-pedal.
    >   **Q:** *How is the lack of an alternative to the brake-pedal evaluated?*
    >   **A:** Still (Ger.: 'trotzdem'), we would have liked an additional handbrake.

What causes the Contrast in example (15) to have subordinating rather than coordinating QUD structure is a counter-evaluation: People who are used to motorcycles would expect a hand-brake but there is none for the three-wheel vehicle in (15). Elsewhere in the text it is explained that the manufacturer deliberately avoided giving the vehicle motorcycle characteristics so that drivers with a regular car license could drive it. The Contrast is between what is and what is not: if this three-wheel vehicle drove like a motorcycle you would expect there to be a hand-brake yet there is none. The *two-wheel-driver*-explanation, however, is given in a sub-QUD structure, where that sub-QUD is the expectation in the counterfactual. So the embedding of the explanation causes apparent subordinating Contrast.

Table 6 summarises the factors we identified as causes of subordinating QUD structure in Contrasts. In 6 of the 8 examples, topic restriction of some sort causes subordinating QUD structure; in the other 2 examples we find counterfactuals. In the next section we look at coordinating Concession examples in the corpus.

Table 6: Potential factors causing Contrasts to have subordinating rather than coordinating QUD structure.

Ex	Marker	Factors	
		Evaluation	Topic restriction
8	doch	–	yes
9	doch	–	yes
10	allerdings	–	yes
11	allerdings	yes	–
12	dennoch	–	yes
13	immerhin	–	yes
14	trotzdem	–	yes
15	trotzdem	yes	–

4.3 Coordinating concessions

Given our working hypothesis, we would expect all Concessions to have subordinating QUD structure, i.e. the concessive discourse constituent should be the answer to a sub-QUD, subordinated under another super-QUD for the non-concessive part. However, the following four corpus examples of coordinating Concessions go against this hypothesis. Let us look at them in more detail to find out why they deviate from the expected subordinating structure.

(16) **Q:** *What did Renault decide?*
       A: When Renault decided to discontinue the cute Modus and replace it with the Captur, this was not risky.
   > **Q:** *How good was this decision?*
   > **A:** The SUV-hype was foreseeable and <u>although</u> (Ger.: 'obwohl') there are still customers shedding tears for the Modus, the success [of the Captur] is underniable.

The Concession in (16) is that although there are still customers who prefer the previous model of the Captur, the Modus, the Captur will likely have market success. The Concession is between the *although*-clause and the matrix clause (the success of the Captur is undeniable). However, annotation shows the Concession coordinated in focus structure with the undeniable success, contrary to the expected subordination. Our annotation guidelines dictate syntactically subordinate clauses should receive dedicated sub-QUDs. It seems annotators deviated from the guidelines here.

One could imagine adding the missing sub-QUD *What could limit the success of the Captur?* With this sub-QUD the Concession would have the expected subordinating QUD structure, in-line with theory.

(17) **Q:** *What changes were made to the vehicle?*
> **Q₁:** *How noticeable are the changes?*
> **A₁:** Most passers-by will hardly be able to tell the difference between the pre- and the post-Facelift model,
> **Q₂:** *How can you tell the post-Facelift model from the RX?*
> **A₂:** <u>after all</u> (Ger.: 'doch'), most find it hard to identify the RX as such.

Example (17) talks about a Lexus which was overhauled, hence the name Facelift. The Concession in (17) is an elaboration why people are unlikely to be able to tell the difference between the pre-Facelift model and the post-Facelift model. As a discourse relation, we would expect an Elaboration to be subordinated the same way we would expect a Concession to be subordinated. The reason why the Concession is not subordinated in (17) seems to be due to the sub-QUDs *How noticeable are the changes?* and *How can you tell the post-Facelift model from the RX?* addressing related yet different aspects: The answer to *How noticeable are the changes?* suggests that the changes between the pre- and post-Facelift model are so small that they are hardly noticeable, and the text elaborates on how little was changed elsewhere. The answer to *How (well) can you tell the post-Facelift model from the RX?*, on the other hand, is concessive because it gives yet another reason why the difference between pre- and post-Facelift is unlikely to be noticed: the Lexus RX sold so few units that most people would not recognise it anyway. One might question whether (17) is a case of denial-of-expectation Concession. However, in order to be able to judge the difference between the pre- and post-facelift model, people would have to be familiar with the pre-model. One could argue that this is the expectation being denied here. Notice that at the same time, we have two reasons for the changes to not be noticeable: small technical changes and little brand recognition because of low sales. Yet, since both factors add up (low brand recognition reduces the already low noticeability even further), the *doch*-clause is concessive without being subordinated. Importantly, (17) involves a hypothetical: If, hypothetically, the RX had more brand recognition, the differences between pre- and post-Facelift would still be too small to be noticeable. Structurally, since the *doch*-clause elaborates on Q₁, Elaboration would call for Q₂ to be subordinated to Q₁, which would give the subordinate QUD structure expected for a Concession.

(18) **Q:** *What is the history of the Mitsubishi ASX?*
    A: Already nine years ago, Mitsubishi had a good nose with the ASX
  > **Q_1:** *What did Mitsubishi have a nose for?*
  > **A_1:** which market segment would explode in the future.
  > > **Q:** *What evidence is there for the predicted market success?*
  > > **A:** More than 1.36 million units of the compact Japanese SUV sold since then.
  > **Q_2:** *What are the future prospects of the ASX?*
  > **A_2:** <u>However</u> (Ger.: 'doch'), by now there is plenty of competition on the road.

(18) involves a hypothetical about future prospects. Since expectations about future prospects are, by definition, purely speculative, their concessive denial is different from denial of expectations based on factual or past evidence ("phenomenal" Concession). Example (17) weighs the likelihood of success by contrasting sales numbers with the Concession that there is growing competition. Similar to (17) the measurement scale of sales numbers as a measure of success allows for the Concession to be coordinated. Like (17), the sales figures and the growing competition are presented as focused, new information, information which is distinct from one another. Yet, even though it is presented as separate pieces of information, world knowledge tells us that every customer who buys from competitors is a lost Mitsubishi customer. So world knowledge tells us the two pieces of information are connected. Our annotation guidelines require that the *which*-clause explaining what Mitsubishi had a good nose for has to have a sub-QUD (*nose* is the head noun of the sub-clause). Nevertheless A and A_1 are the *p* that the *doch*-clause *q* concedes to (*p* however *q*). This is the subordinating QUD structure we would expect in Concessions: Q_2 is subordinate to the Q-and-Q_1 compound. The *which*-clause having its own sub-QUD only makes (18) seem like a coordinated structure. We thus would characterise (18) as a case of QUD-structural ambiguity because of the annotation requirement rather than a counterexample to the subordination expected in a Concession.

(19) **Q:** *What kind of engine does the motorcycle have?*
  > **Q_1:** *What did Piaggio do with the engine?*
  > **A_1:** Piaggio comprehensively overhauled the 278-cubic-meter one-cylinder engine
  > **Q_2:** *What is the engine called (now)?*
  > **A_2:** which is now called 300 hpe.
  > > **Q:** *What does the abbreviation stand for?*

> > **A:** The abbreviation stands for high performance engine,
> > > **Q:** *What does the abbreviation suggest?*
> > > **A:** which sounds impressive but also a little cocky
> > > > **Q:** *Why does the abbreviation sound cocky?*
> > > > **A:** considering its max power of 17.5 kW / 23.8 horsepowers and the fact that motorcycles nowadays have 200 horsepowers.
> **Q₃:** *How powerful is the engine compared to previous Vespas?*
> **A₃:** <u>Still</u> (Ger.: 'doch'), this Vespa is indeed the most powerful Vespa of all time, which the Italians proudly point out.

The Concession in the *doch*-clause of example (19) needs to be viewed in light of the Contrast marked by *but* ('but'). The *but*-Contrast talks about the misleading name of the engine, an abbreviation which stands for high performance, and contrasts it with factual information about the engine's actual performance being sub-par compared to competitors. The Concession then follows-up by introducing a different angle, namely that Piaggio's statement was "high performance" not compared to competitors but to other mopeds by Piaggio—a type of implicit topic restriction relative to the expectation that "fastest" means compared to all mopeds, not just Vespas. The Concession introduces this shift in comparison class as new information, and so, like we have seen, focus structure takes precedence over relational structure, leading to coordination instead of the expected subordination.

Notice how the Concession (although p, q) in (19) can be reanalysed as: Although it has low horse-powers, it is a high performance engine in the sense that it is the most powerful Vespa engine. Under this analysis, the horse-power-statement would be cataphorically subordinated to the most-powerful-Vespa statement, where the Concession would have the expected subordinating QUD structure rather than the coordinating structure annotated in (19). The QUD structure in (19) is not conforming to the expected subordinating Concession structure because the horsepower-statement is embedded under the explanation of the abbreviation. As we have seen before, the annotation guidelines prioritize subordination for Elaboration and Explanation, but not necessarily for Concession.

We have seen how examples (16) through (19) can be reanalysed or how annotations could be refined to put them in-line with the theoretically expected subordinating Concession structure. Because of this we do not regard them as true counterexamples, which means we only count the Contrast examples in (8) through (15) as counterexamples because of the factors laid out in Table 6.

5 Conclusion

This paper presented a corpus study where 30 German car and motorcycle reviews were annotated for Question under Discussion according to guidelines by Riester et al. (2018) building on previous work (cf. Roberts, 1996, 2012; Onea, 2013, 2016, 2019). The corpus study focuses on Contrast and Concession. The literature on Contrast and Concession suggests that Contrast is a multi-nucleus discourse relation while Concession is a nucleus-satellite discourse relation (König, 1983, 1986; Mann & Thompson, 1988). In this paper we investigated whether the nucleus-nucleus/nucleus-satellite distinction between Contrast and Concession translates to coordinating versus subordinating structures in QUD trees.

Contrasts and Concessions where identified by 24 German discourse markers. The analysis looked how many Contrasts have coordinating QUD/focus structure, and how many Concessions have subordinating QUD structure. About 90% of Contrasts in the corpus have coordinating QUD structure suggesting multi-nucleus structure. And about 90% of Concessions in the corpus have subordinating QUD structure suggesting nucleus-satellite structure. The apparent mismatches in the remaining 10% are cases where implicit assumptions are negated, but these implicit assumptions are not represented as branches in the QUD trees. Or they are cases where counterfactuals, hypotheticals or speculation are involved. If implicit assumptions were represented in the trees, the 10% of Contrasts and Concessions would fall in line with the theoretic assumption that Contrast has coordinated structure and Concession subordinated structure. In the exceptional cases, focus structure and relational structure do not match, since they follow different rules. Future research, thus, should investigate how assumptions should be represented in QUD trees or in QUD approaches to discourse structure, in general.

Resources

The QUDGen corpus is available here: github.com/christoph-hesse/question-under-discussion. Contrasts and Concessions examined in this paper are listed in the subfolder ContrastConcession.

References

Amaral, Patricia, Craige Roberts & E. Allyn Smith. 2007. Review of The Logic of Conventional Implicatures by Chris Potts. *Linguistics & Philosophy* 30. 707–749.

Asher, Nicholas & Alex Lascarides. 1998. Questions in dialogue. *Linguistics and Philosophy* 21. 237–309.

Asher, Nicholas & Alex Lascarides. 2003. *Logics of conversation*. Cambridge University Press.

Asher, Nicholas & Laure Vieu. 2005. Subordinating and coordinating discourse relations. *Lingua* 115. 591–610.

Beaver, David, Craige Roberts, Mandy Simons & Judith Tonhauser. 2017. Questions under discussion: Where information structure meets projective content. *Annual Review of Linguistics* 3. 265–284.

Bennet, Jonathan. 1982. Even if. *Linguistics and Philosophy* 5. 403–418. Brunetti, Lisa, Kordula De Kuthy & Arndt Riester. 2021. The information-structural status of adjuncts: A question-under-discussion-based approach. *Discours* 28.

Büring, Daniel. 1997. *The meaning of topic and focus: The 59ᵗʰ Street Bridge Accent*. London, UK: Routledge.

Büring, Daniel. 2003. On d-trees, beans, and b-accents. *Linguistics & Philosophy* 26. 511–545.

Büring, Daniel. 2008. What's new (and what's given) in the theory of focus? In *Proceedings of the 34th annual meeting of the berkeley linguistics society*, 403–424. BLS.

Carlson, Lauri. 1983. *Dialogue games: An approach to discourse analysis*. Dordrecht: Reidel.

Crevels, Mily. 2000. Concessives on different semantic levels: A typological perspective. In Elizabeth Couper-Kuhlen & Bernd Kortmann (eds.), *Topics in linguistics: Cause condition-concession-contrast; cognitive and discourse perspectives*, 313–339. Mouton de Gruyter.

De Kuthy, Kordula, Ramon Ziai & Detmar Meurers. 2015. Learning what the crowd can do: A case study on focus annotation. *Proceedings of the 6th Conference on Quantitative Investigations in Theoretical Linguistics* doi: 10.15496/publikation-8631.

Haspelmath, Martin & Ekkehard König. 1998. Concessive conditionals in the languages of europe. In Johan van der Auwera (ed.), *Adverbial constructions in the languages of europe*, 563–640. Mouton de Gruyter.

Hesse, Christoph, Maurice Langner, Ralf Klabunde & Anton Benz. 2022. Testing focus and non-at-issue frameworks with a question-under-discussion-annotated corpus. In *Proceedings of the language resources and evaluation conference*, 5212–5219. Marseille, France: European Language Resources Association. https://aclanthology.org/2022.lrec-1.559.

Jasinskaja, Katja. 2010. Corrective contrast in russian, in contrast. *Oslo Studies in Language* 2. 433–466.

Jasinskaja, Katja. 2012. Correction by adversative and additive markers. *Lingua* 122(15). 1899–1918. doi:https://doi.org/10.1016/j.lingua.2012.08.015. https://www.sciencedirect.com/science/article/pii/S0024384112001738. SI: Additivity and Adversativity.

Jasinskaja, Katja. 2013. Corrective elaboration. *Lingua* 132. 51–66.

Jasinskaja, Katja & Henk Zeevat. 2008. Explaining additive, adversative, and contrast marking in russian and english. *Revue de Sémantique et Pragmatique* 24. 65–91.

Keller, Rudi. 1995. The epistemic weil. In Dieter Stein & Susan Wright (eds.), *Subjectivity and subjectivisation: linguistic perspectives*, 16–30. Cambridge University Press.

Klein, Wolfgang & Christiane von Stutterheim. 1987. Quaestio und referentielle Bewegung in Erzählungen. *Linguistische Berichte* 109. 163–183.

König, Ekkehard. 1983. Polysemie, Polaritätskontexte und *überhaupt*. In Harald Weydt et al. (ed.), *Partikeln und Interaktion*, 160–171. Tübingen: Niemeyer.

König, Ekkehard. 1986. Conditionals, concessive conditionals and concessives: Areas of contrast, overlap and neutralization. *On conditionals* 229246.

König, Ekkehard & Peter Siemund. 2000. Causal and concessive clauses: Formal and semantic relations. In Elizabeth Couper-Kuhlem & Bernd Kortmann (eds.), *Cause-condition-concession-contrast, cognitive and discourse perspectives*, 341–360. Mouton de Gruyter.

Krifka, Manfred & Renate Musan. 2012. *The expression of information structure, volume 5 of the expression of cognitive categories*. Berlin/Boston: De Gruyter Mouton.

van Kuppevelt, Jan. 1995. Discourse structure, topicality, and questioning. *Journal of Linguistics* 31. 109–147.

van Kuppevelt, Jan. 1996. Inferring from topics: Scalar implicatures as topic-dependent inferences. *Linguistics and Philosophy* 19. 393–443.

Kuthy, Kordula De, Nils Reiter & Arndt Riester. 2018. QUD-based annotation of discourse structure and information structure: Tool and evaluation. In *Proceedings of the 11th Language Resources and Evaluation Conference (LREC)*.

Lakoff, Robin. 1971. If's, and's and but's about conjunction. In Charles J. Fillmore & D. Terence Langendoen (eds.), *Studies in linguistic semantics*, 114–149. New York: Holt, Rinehart and Winston.

Lycan, William G. 1991. Even and even if. *Linguistics and Philosophy* 14. 115–150.

Malchukov, Andrej L. 2004. Towards a semantic typology of adversative and contrast marking. *Journal of Semantics* 21. 177–198.

Mann, William C. & Sandra A. Thompson. 1988. Rhetorical structure theory: Toward a functional theory of text organization. *Text* 8. 243–281.

Onea, Edgar. 2013. *Potential questions in discourse and grammar*. Göttingen: ms, University of Göttingen.

Onea, Edgar. 2016. *Potential questions at the semantics-pragmatics interface*, vol. 33 Current Research in the Semantics/Pragmatics Interface. Leiden: Brill.

Onea, Edgar. 2019. Underneath rhetorical relations: the case of result. In Malte Zimmermann, Klaus von Heusinger & Edgar Onea (eds.), *Questions in discourse*, Leiden, The Netherlands: Brill.

Pander Maat, Henk. 1998. Two kinds of concessives and their inferential complexity. In A. Knott, J. Oberlander, J. Moore & T. Sanders (eds.), *Levels of representation in discourse. working notes of the international workshop on text representation,*, 45–54. Edinburgh, UK.

Prince, Ellen F. 1992. The ZPG letter: Subjects, definiteness, and information-status. In Sandra A. Thompson & William C. Mann (eds.), *Discourse description: Diverse analyses of a fundraising text*, 295–325. Amsterdam/Philadelphia: John Benjamins.

Riester, Arndt. 2019. Constructing QUD trees. In Malte Zimmermann, Klaus von Heusinger & Edgar Onea (eds.), *Questions in discourse: Pragmatics*, vol. 2, 403–443. Leiden: Brill.

Riester, Arndt, Lisa Brunetti & Kordula De Kuthy. 2018. Annotation guidelines for questions under discussion and information structure. In Evangelia Adamou, Katharina Haude & Martine Vanhove (eds.), *Information Structure in Lesser-Described Languages: Studies in Prosody and Syntax*, 403–443. Amsterdam: Benjamins.

Roberts, Craige. 1996. Information structure in discourse: Toward an integrated formal theory of pragmatics. In Jar Hak Yoon & Andreas Kathol (eds.), *Osu working papers in linguistics*, vol. 49, 91–136. Ohio: The Ohio State University, Department of Linguistics.

Roberts, Craige. 2012. Information structure in discourse: towards an integrated formal theory of pragmatics. *Semantics and Pragmatics* 5. 1–69.

Roberts, Craige, Mandy Simons, David Beaver & Judith Tonhauser. 2009. Presupposition, conventional implicature, and beyond: A uniform account of projection. In *Proceedings of the workshop on new directions in the theory of presupposition, esslli 2009*.

Rooth, Mats. 1985. *Association with focus*: University of Massachusetts Ph.d. dissertation.

Rooth, Mats. 1992. A theory of focus interpretation. *Natural Language Semantics* 1. 75–116.

Simons, Mandy, Judith Tonhauser, David Beaver & Craige Roberts. 2010. What projects and why. *Semantics and Linguistic Theory* 20. 309–327.

Stalnaker, Robert. 1978. Assertion. In Peter Cole (ed.), *Syntax ans semantics 9: Pragmatics*, 315–332. Academic Press.

Stede, Manfred, Maite Taboada & Debopam Das. 2017. Annotation guidelines for rhetorical structure. *University of Potsdam and Simon Fraser University*.

Zeevat, Henk. 2011. Rhetorical relations. In Claudia Maienborn, Klaus Von Heusinger & Paul Portner (eds.), *Semantics: An international handbook of natural language and meaning*, 946–970. Walter de Gruyter.

Subject index

https://doi.org/10.1515/9783110986594-010